S0-EIB-941

ABE 5801

MUIRHEAD LIBRARY OF PHILOSOPHY

An admirable statement of the aims of the Library of Philosophy was provided by the first editor, the late Professor J. H. Muirhead, in his description of the original programme printed in Erdmann's *History of Philosophy* under the date 1890. This was slightly modified in subsequent volumes to take the form of the following statement:

'The Muirhead Library of Philosophy was designed as a contribution to the History of Modern Philosophy under the heads: first of Different Schools of Thought—Sensationalist, Realist, Idealist, Intuitivist; secondly of different Subjects—Psychology, Ethics, Aesthetics, Political Philosophy, Theology. While much had been done in England in tracing the course of evolution in nature, history, economics, morals and religion, little had been done in tracing the development of thought on these subjects. Yet 'the evolution of opinion is part of the whole evolution'.

'By the co-operation of different writers in carrying out this plan it was hoped that a thoroughness and completeness of treatment, otherwise unattainable, might be secured. It was believed also that from writers mainly British and American fuller consideration of English Philosophy than it had hitherto received might be looked for. In the earlier series of books containing, anomg others, Bosanquet's *History of Aesthetic*, Pfleiderer's *Rational Theology since Kant*, Albee's *History of English Utilitarianism*, Bonar's *Philosophy and Political Economy*, Brett's *History of Psychology*, Ritchie's *Natural Rights*, these objects were to a large extent effected.

'In the meantime original work of a high order was being produced both in England and America by such writers as Bradley, Stout, Bertrand Russell, Baldwin, Urban, Montague, and others, and a new interest in foreign works, German, French and Italian, which had either become classical or were attracting public attention, had developed. The scope of the Library thus became extended into something more international, and it is entering on the fifth decade of its existence in the hope that it may contribute to that mutual understanding between countries which is so pressing a need of the present time.'

The need which Professor Muirhead stressed is no less pressing today, and few will deny that philosophy has much to do with enabling us to meet it, although no one, least of all Muirhead himself, would regard that as the sole, or even the main, object of philosophy. As Professor Muirhead continues to lend the distinction of his name to the Library of Philosophy it seemed not inappropriate to allow him to recall us to these aims in his own words. The emphasis on the history of thought also seemed to me very timely; and the number of important works promised for the Library in the very near future augur well for the continued fulfilment, in this and other ways, of the expectations of the original editor.

H. D. LEWIS

MUIRHEAD LIBRARY OF PHILOSOPHY

General Editor: H. D. Lewis
Professor of History and Philosophy of Religion in the University of London

Action by SIR MALCOLM KNOX
The Analysis of Mind by BERTRAND RUSSELL
Belief by H. H. PRICE
Brett's History of Psychology edited by R. S. PETERS
Clarity is Not Enough by H. D. LEWIS
Coleridge as a Philosopher by J. H. MUIRHEAD
The Commonplace Book of G. E. Moore edited by C. LEWY
Contemporary American Philosophy edited by C. P. ADAMS and W. P. MONTAGUE
Contemporary British Philosophy first and second Series edited by J. H. MUIRHEAD
Contemporary British Philosophy third Series edited by H. D. LEWIS
Contemporary Indian Philosophy edited by RADHAKRISHNAN and J. H. MUIRHEAD 2nd edition
Contemporary Philosophy in Australia edited by ROBERT BROWN and C. D. ROLLINS
The Discipline of the Cave by J. N. FINDLAY
Doctrine and Argument in Indian Philosophy by NINIAN SMART
Ethics and Christianity by KEITH WARD
Essays in Analysis by ALICE AMBROSE
Ethics by NICOLAI HARTMANN translated by STANTON COIT 3 vols
The Foundations of Metaphysics in Science by ERROL E. HARRIS
Freedom and History by H. D. LEWIS
The Good Will: A Study in the Coherence Theory of Goodness by H. J. PATON
Hegel: A Re-examination by J. N. FINDLAY
Hegel's Science of Logic tranlsated by W. H. JOHNSTON and L. G. STRUTHERS 2 vols
History of Aesthetic by B. BOSANQUET 2nd edition
History of English Utilitariansism by E. ALBEE
History of Psychology by G. S. BRETT edited by R. S. PETERS abridged one volume edition 2nd edition
Human Knowledge by BERTRAND RUSSELL
A Hundred Years of British Philosophy by RUDOLF METZ translated by J. N. HARVEY, T. E. JESSOP, HENRY STURT
Ideas: A General Introduction to Pure Phenomenology by EDMUND HUSSERL translated by W. R. BOYCE GIBSON
Identity and Reality by EMILE MEYERSON
Imagination by E. J. FURLONG

𝔐uirbead 𝔏ibrary of 𝔓bilosopby

EDITED BY H. D. LEWIS

CONTEMPORARY AMERICAN PHILOSOPHY

CONTEMPORARY AMERICAN PHILOSOPHY

SECOND SERIES

Edited by JOHN E. SMITH
Yale University, USA

LONDON · GEORGE ALLEN & UNWIN LTD
NEW YORK · HUMANITIES PRESS INC.

PRINTED IN GREAT BRITAIN
in 11 on 12pt Imprint
BY
W & J MACKAY & CO LTD, CHATHAM

CONTENTS

INTRODUCTION

American philosophy, like God, has been declared dead by some, non-existent by others, and bogged down in academic irrelevance by still others. The fact is, as the following essays show, all three opinions are either false or in need of radical revision. If one identifies philosophy exclusively with one particular school or style of thought and denies the name to all other positions, a country like America, embracing, as it does, a plurality of philosophical outlooks, is likely to be thought of as having no philosophy at all. If, however, one sees philosophy as tending inevitably to more than one point of view and one manner of thinking, and if one regards the critical dialogue between different views as belonging to the nature of philosophy itself, America must be seen as philosophically rich and fertile.

In one important respect, it must be admitted, critics of philosophy in America have been right; the development and teaching of philosophy almost exclusively within the walls of colleges and universities has resulted in thinking which is often directed, not to the perplexing issues of existence but to what other philosophers have written or said. Santayana issued a warning years ago in which he said that the academy would kill philosophy in America. I cannot agree that this has happened, but only a fool would ignore the danger hinted at in his sombre remark. Philosophy confined to classrooms, textbooks and professors breeds a pedantic spirit. Happily, as the essays in this volume demonstrate, no such spirit prevails; philosophy is conceived by the contributors as neither insulated nor isolated from the facts and concrete situations that go to make up the world—scientific, political, psychological, speculative, ethical, religious and social. While these essays do not represent any single point of view, all of the contributors are united in their belief that philosophical thinking makes a difference to human life in thought *and* action. Nor is the 'making a difference' to be construed in some narrow, utilitarian sense that is supposed to spell expediency. It means instead that man cannot hope to realize himself in the world and live at peace with his neighbours without some *clear understanding* both of his own nature and the nature of the universe in which he finds himself. And in order to achieve that understanding, he must attempt to resolve difficult questions of a theoretical sort such as the possibility of human freedom in a scientifically conceived world, the impact of language on our view of reality, the rational foundations of our moral judgements and of our religious beliefs, the meaning of tragedy and the rationale of democracy, the role of philosophy in self-knowledge and the bearing of technology on our ideals and purposes.

The aim behind the present volume is to present a cross-section of the philosophical thinking that has been taking place on the American scene. No one could claim to offer, in a volume of this size, adequate representation of every standpoint—such is the complexity and variety of outlook involved. Major strands of thinking are represented and a reader willing to make the effort will find himself rewarded with some understanding of the American philosophical situation after the middle of the century.

I do not intend to make the almost inevitable mistake of summarizing the contents of the essays here collected. Each writer is eminently capable of communicating his own message without the help of paraphrase. A few general comments are in order, however, that may serve to outline the philosophical scene that emerges from these essays. To begin with, the contributors are remarkably free of self-consciousness about philosophy itself. Instead of reflexive accounts about what philosophy is, whether it is still possible, how to pursue it, and indeed the many preliminary questions that have all but exhausted modern philosophers, the authors are concerned to discuss the issues they raise head-on and without apology. Second, it is important to notice the underlying interest in the impact of science on philosophical issues and immediate human concerns. The growth of the social sciences, the vast expenditure of energy in America on scientific research plus the omnipresence of the technological results make it impossible for American philosophers to ignore the topic. Third, the problems of moral philosophy have been of continuing importance to American thinkers, and it would be an error to suppose that the dominant place given to second-order questions about the language of ethics has driven out the consideration of moral values themselves. Finally, there is a growing sense that a theory of man, of the human self, must stand high on the philosophical agenda and that in the decades ahead the most urgent problem will be man's capacity for making an accurate and a just estimate of himself.

John E. Smith

New Haven, 1969

BIOGRAPHICAL NOTES

BRAND BLANSHARD was born in Fredericksburg, Ohio, on August 27, 1892. He received his A.B. from the University of Michigan in 1914, his A.M. from Columbia in 1918, a B.Sc. from Oxford in 1920 and the Ph.D. from Harvard in 1921. During his long and distinguished career Blanshard was the recipient of many honorary degrees, among which are Litt.D., Swarthmore, 1947; L. H. D. Bucknell, 1954, Colby, 1956, Trinity, 1957, and LL.D. from Oberlin in 1956 and the University of St Andrews in 1959. Blanshard was a Rhodes scholar from 1913 to 1915. He began his teaching career at the University of Michigan in 1921 and taught subsequently at Swarthmore College, Columbia University, until 1945, when he became Professor of Philosophy at Yale. He became Sterling Professor in 1956 and served as Chairman of the Department 1959–61. Blanshard was Gifford Lecturer in 1952–3, and has been President both of the American Philosophical Association and of the American Theological Society. Blanshard is the author of *The Nature of Thought*, 2 vols, 1940; *Reason and Goodness*, 1960; *Reason and Analysis*, 1962; in addition he has edited philosophical works with others and has written many articles in philosophical journals.

JOHN HERMAN RANDALL, JR, was born in Grand Rapids, Michigan on February 14, 1899. He received his A.B. in 1918, his A.M. 1919 and his Ph.D. in 1922, all from Columbia University. He was awarded the honorary degree of Litt.D. from Ohio Wesleyan University in 1961. He began his teaching career at Columbia, where he became professor in 1935 and in 1951 was named the F. J. E. Woodbridge Professor of Philosophy. He is a Fellow of the American Academy of Arts and Sciences and a member of the Renaissance Society of America, in which he served as President from 1953 to 1957. He is the author of *The Problem of Group Responsibility*, 1922; *The Making of the Modern Mind*, 1926; *Our Changing Civilization*, 1929; *The Role of Knowledge in Western Religion*, 1958; *Nature and Historical Experience*, 1958; *Aristotle*, 1960; *The Career of Philosophy*, 2 Vols, 1962–5; *How Philosophy Uses its Past*, 1963. In addition, Randall has written numerous articles and contributed to many co-operative volumes.

PAUL WEISS was born in New York City on May 19, 1901. He attended the College of the City of New York, where he received a B.S.S. degree 1927; he received the A.M. in 1928 and the Ph.D. in 1929, both from Harvard. In 1960 he was awarded the L.H.D. degree by Grinnell College. Weiss began his teaching career at Harvard and Radcliffe in 1930. Between that time and his coming to Yale in 1946 he taught at Bryn

Mawr College. In 1962 he was appointed Sterling Professor of Philosophy at Yale. He has held many distinguished lectureships and was the founder of the Metaphysical Society of America and has been President of the American Philosophical Association. In addition to editing, with Charles Hartshorne, the *Collected Papers of Charles S. Peirce*, he is the author of many volumes, among which are: *Reality*, 1938; *Nature and Man*, 1947; *Man's Freedom*, 1950; *Modes of Being*, 1958; *Our Public Life*, 1959; *Nine Basic Arts*, 1961; *History: Written and Lived*, 1962; *The God We Seek*, 1965, and *Philosophy in Process*.

WILLIAM K. FRANKENA was born in Manhattan, Montana, on June 21, 1908. He received his A.B. at Calvin College in 1930, his A.M. at the University of Michigan in 1931, and his Ph.D. at Harvard in 1937. He began his academic career at the University of Michigan in 1937 and was appointed professor in 1947. He has been a visiting professor at Harvard, Columbia, and the University of Tokyo. Frankena was Guggenheim Fellow in the year 1948–9. He has contributed essays to *The Philosophy of G. E. Moore*, 1942; *Philosophical Analysis*, 1950; *Language, Thought, and Culture*, 1958; *Religion and the State University*, 1958; *Essays in Moral Philosophy*, 1958.

F. S. C. NORTHROP was born in Janesville, Wisconsin, November 27, 1893. He received his A.B. from Beloit College in 1915; his A.M. from Yale in 1919 and his Ph.D. in 1924 from Harvard. He holds an honorary LL.D. from the University of Hawaii. He began his teaching career at Yale in 1923, becoming Professor of Philosophy in 1932, and was named Sterling Professor of Philosophy and Law in 1947. During his tenure at Yale he was Master of Silliman College. Northrop has been visiting professor at the Universities of Iowa, Michigan, Virginia, Hawaii, and the National University of Mexico. In 1949 he was awarded the Order of Aztec Eagle by the Government of Mexico. He is a Fellow of the American Academy of Arts and Sciences and he has served as President of the American Philosophical Association. In addition to numerous articles, his works are: *Science and First Principles*, 1931; *The Meeting of East and West*, 1946; *The Logic of the Sciences and the Humanities*, 1947; *The Taming of the Nations*, 1952, which was awarded the Freedom House award; *European Union and United States Foreign Policy*, 1954; *The Complexity of Legal and Ethical Theory*, 1959; *Philosophical Anthropology and Practical Politics*, 1959; *Man, Nature and God*, 1962.

RODERICK M. CHISHOLM was born in 1916. He graduated from Brown University and received his Ph.D. from Harvard University. He served in the United States Army from 1942 to 1946, and has been Barnes Foundation Professor of Philosophy at the University of Pennsylvania and at the Barnes Foundation of Merion, Pennsylvania. He is Professor of Philosophy and Romeo Elton Professor of Natural Theology at Brown University. He was Fulbright Professor at Karl-Franzens-Universität in Graz, Austria, in 1959-60. He delivered the Nellie Wallace Lectures in philosophy at Oxford University in 1967, and the Carus Lectures at the Pacific Division of the American Philosophical Association in 1967. He was President of the Eastern Division of the American Philosophical Association in 1968. He is the author of *Perceiving—A Philosophical Study*, 1957; *Realism and the Background of Phenomenology*, 1960, and he has contributed numerous articles to philosophical journals.

SIDNEY HOOK was born in New York City on December 20, 1902, and attended the College of the City of New York, where he obtained a B.S. degree in 1923. In 1926 he received an A.M. and in 1927 a Ph.D. both from Columbia. He began his academic career as a lecturer at Columbia in 1927 and as Instructor in Philosophy at Washington Square College, New York University, in the same year. He has been professor at New York University since 1939. Hook was a Fellow of the Center for Advanced Studies in the Behavioral Sciences at Stanford, in 1961 and the organizer of the Conference on Method in Philosophy and Science. He was elected President of the Eastern Division of the American Philosophical Association in 1959. He is the author of: *Education for Modern Man*, 1946; *Heresy, Yes—Conspiracy, No*, 1953; *The Ambiguous Legacy: Marx and the Marxists*, 1955; *Common Sense and the Fifth Amendment*, 1957; *Political Power and Personal Freedom*, 1959; *The Quest for Being*, 1961; *The Paradoxes of Freedom*, 1962; *World Communism: A Documentary History*, 1963. In addition he has written numerous articles and contributed to co-operative volumes.

JOHN WILD was born in Chicago on April 10, 1902. He received the Ph.B. from the University of Chicago in 1923, the A.M. in 1925 and the Ph.D. in 1926, both from Harvard. He holds an honorary L.H.D. from Ripon College. He began his teaching career as an instructor at the University of Michigan in 1926 and went, in the next year, to Harvard, becoming Professor of Philosophy in 1946. In 1961 he became Professor of Philosophy and Chairman of the Department at Northwestern University. From 1963 until 1969 he was Professor of Philosophy at Yale University. He has been a visiting professor at the Universities of Chicago, Hawaii, and Washington. In 1953 he was Powell Lecturer at the University of Indiana. He served as President of the Eastern Division of the American Philosophical Association in 1960. He is currently Professor of Philosophy at the University of Florida. He is the author of: *George Berkeley*, 1936; *Plato's Theory of Man*, 1946; *Introduction to Realistic Philosophy*, 1948; *Plato's Modern Enemies and the Theory of Natural Law*, 1953; *The Challenge of Existentialism*, 1955; *Existence and the World of Freedom*, 1967; *The Radical Empiricism of William James*, 1969.

CHARLES HARTSHORNE was born in Kittanning, Pennsylvania, on June 5, 1897. He studied for two years at Haverford College, but received his A.B. from Harvard in 1921. He received an A.M. in 1922 and the Ph.D. in 1923, both from Harvard. After two years of post-doctoral study abroad he returned to Harvard, where he began his teaching career as an assistant to A. N. Whitehead. In 1928 he joined the Faculty at the University of Chicago, becoming Professor of Philosophy in 1949. From 1955 until 1962, he was Professor of Philosophy at Emory University in Georgia, and since 1962 he has been Professor of Philosophy at the University of Texas. Hartshorne was Terry Lecturer at Yale in 1947 and Fulbright Lecturer at the Universities of Melbourne and Kyoto. In 1948 he served as President of the Western Division of the American Philosophical Association. In addition to scores of articles, including original contributions to ornithology, he has written: *The Philosophy and Psychology of Sensation*, 1934; *Beyond Humanism*, 1937; *Man's Vision of God*, 1941; *The Divine Relativity*, 1948; *Reality as Social Process*, 1953; *Philosophers Speak of God* (with William Reese), 1953; *The Logic of Perfection*, 1962; *Anselm's Discovery*, 1965; *A Natural Theology for Our Time*, 1967; *Creative Synthesis and Philosophic Method*, 1970.

DANIEL DAY WILLIAMS was born in Denver, Colorado, on September 12, 1910. He received his A.B. from the University of Denver in 1931, his A.M. from the University of Chicago in 1933, a B.D. from the Chicago Theological Seminary in 1934, and a Ph.D. from Columbia in 1940. He is an ordained minister of the Congregational Church. He was Professor of Theology in the Federated Theological Faculty of the University of Chicago before going to the Union Theological Seminary in 1954, where he is Roosevelt Professor of Systematic Theology. He was a member of the Congregational delegation to the Faith and Order Conference in Lund, Sweden, in 1952. He is the author of: *The Andover Liberals*, 1941; *God's Grace and Man's Hope*, 1949; *What Present-Day Theologians are Thinking*, 1952; *The Minister and the Care of Souls*, 1961; *The Spirit and the Forms of Love*, 1968. In addition he has contributed articles on philosophy and theology to many co-operative volumes.

PETER A. BERTOCCI was born in Elena, Italy, on May 13, 1910. He received his A.B. degree in 1931 from Boston University, his A.M. from Harvard in 1932 and his Ph.D. from Boston University in 1935. His teaching career began in 1935 at Bates College, where he taught until 1944, when he was appointed Professor of Philosophy at Boston University. In 1953 he was appointed Borden Parker Bowne Professor. He has been visiting professor at Harvard, at the University of Vermont and at San José. In 1950 he was a Fulbright Research Scholar in Italy and in 1960 he filled the same post in India. He has published many articles and contributed to various reference works. He has written the following books: *The Empirical Argument for God in Late British Thought*, 1938; *The Human Venture in Sex, Love, and Marriage*, 1949; *Introduction to the Philosophy of Religion*, 1951; *Free Will, Responsibility, and Grace*, 1957; *Religion as Creative Insecurity*, 1958; *Why Believe in God?* 1963; *Personality and the Good: Phychological and Ethical Perspectives* (with Richard M. Millard), 1963; *Sex, Love, and the Person*, 1967.

RICHARD J. BERNSTEIN was born in New York, May 14, 1932. He received his A.B. from the University of Chicago in 1951, his B.S. from Columbia University in 1953 and his Ph.D. from Yale University in 1958. He has taught at Yale University and Haverford College, and has also been a visiting professor at the Hebrew University, Jerusalem. At present he is Chairman of the Philosophy Department at Haverford College and editor of *The Review of Metaphysics*. His works include *John Dewey: On Experience, Nature and Freedom*; *John Dewey*; and *Perspectives on Peirce*. He has written an introduction to a new edition of William James's *Essays on Radical Empiricism* and *A Pluralistic Universe* which will appear in 1970. His book *Praxis and Action* will also be published in 1970.

RICHARD M. RORTY was born in New York City on October 4, 1931. He was graduated from the University of Chicago and received his Ph.D. from Yale University. He taught at Yale and at Wellesley College, going in 1961 to Princeton, where he is now Associate Professor. He has contributed essays to collections and to philosophical journals and is the editor of *The Linguistic Turn: Recent Essays in Philosophical Method*, 1967.

JOHN E. SMITH was born in Brooklyn, New York, on May 27, 1921. He received his A.B. from Columbia in 1942, his B.D. from Union Theological Seminary (N.Y.) in 1945 and his Ph.D. from Columbia in 1948. In 1964 he was awarded an honorary LL.D. from the University of Notre-Dame. He began his teaching career in 1945 as an Instructor in Philosophy and Religion at Vassar College. In 1946 he went to Barnard College and Columbia, where he remained until 1952, when he was appointed at Yale. He became Professor of Philosophy at Yale in 1959. He was a Gates Lecturer at Grinnell in 1965, Dudleian Lecturer at Harvard in 1960, Suarez Lecturer at Fordham in 1963, and Aquinas Lecturer at Marquette in 1967. He was President of the American Theological Society in 1968. He is the author of: *Royce's Social Infinite*,

1950; *Value Convictions and Higher Education*, 1958; *Reason and God*, 1961; *The Spirit of American Philosophy*, 1963; *Religion and Empiricism*, 1967; *Experience and God*, 1968; *Themes in American Philosophy: Purpose, Experience and Community*, 1970. He is general editor of the Yale Edition of the Works of Jonathan Edwards, having edited Vol. II, *Religious Affections*.

ERROL E. HARRIS was born in South Africa and educated at Rhodes University College and later at Magdalen College, Oxford. His degrees include an M.A., B.Litt. (Oxon), and a D.Litt. (Rand). In 1949 he was appointed Hugh le May Research Fellow at Rhodes University, and since then has become Bollingen Research Fellow (1960–3), Ford Foundation Research Fellow in International Affairs (1964–5), National Science Foundation Research Fellow (1968) and Terry Lecturer at Yale University (1957). He has been Professor of Philosophy at the University of the Witwatersrand in Johannesburg, Roy Roberts Professor in the University of Kansas and Acting Head of the Department of Logic and Metaphysics at Edinburgh University, and he is now Professor of Philosophy at Northwestern University, Evanston, Illinois. His writings are:

The Survival of Political Man, 1950; *Revelation Through Reason*, 1958,
Nature, Mind and Modern Science, 1954,
The Foundations of Metaphysics in Science, 1965,
Annihilation and Utopia, 1966,
Fundamentals of Philosophy, 1969.

THE LIMITS OF NATURALISM

BRAND BLANSHARD

I. THE ISSUE

The purpose of this paper is to consider whether science, as currently conceived, is adequate to the study of the mind.

The claim of natural science to cover the whole field of knowledge has been stated often and confidently. Bertrand Russell has remarked that what is knowledge is science, and what is not science is not knowledge. This is a very large claim, but even doubters are commonly reluctant, in view of the imposing success of science, to suggest any limits to its advance. Its standing in the eyes of learned and laymen alike has never been higher. In physics, in biology, in astronomy, in medicine, it has achieved one impressive breakthrough after another, with resulting advances in technology that have transformed our way of life. Since I am going to venture presently on some questions about its adequacy, let me say at once that I think these achievements of science should be met with unqualified gratitude and admiration. If one compares the progress made in the past century in natural science with that made in other intellectual disciplines—in humanistic scholarship, for example, or history or theology—the achievement of science seems unique. It is the most impressive intellectual fact of our age.

Nevertheless thoughtful humanists have begun to raise questions about the current pretensions of science. Is it truly justified in claiming all knowledge as its province? Is it really qualified to take over the domain of the historian, the moralist and the critic? Jacques Barzun[1] and Joseph Wood Krutch,[2] Douglas Bush[3] and Floyd Matson[4] have offered sharp strictures on these claims. They have protested that to carry over the methods of physical science into the study of man and his works is to beg some very important questions about human nature. These men, who are all humanists, hold that science, as now conceived, is unqualified in principle to deal with the set of activities with which humanists are concerned, and that any attempt to deal with them in a purely scientific way

[1] *Science the Glorious Entertainment*   [2] *The Measure of Man*
[3] *Engaged and Disengaged.*   [4] *The Broken Image.*

is bound either to bypass them or to distort them. In this not very popular view I think the humanists are right, and I shall devote this paper to the attempt to say why I think so.

If the issue is to be argued profitably, we must know at the outset what 'the humanities' and 'scientific method' are to mean.

By a humanistic study I shall mean in what follows an attempt to understand or appraise any conscious and purposeful human activity. History and biography are obvious examples of such study. So is the study of literature in all its forms—fiction, drama, poetry, and the rest; indeed, it is doubly so, for it involves studying not only the creative activities of the writer but also the activities of the creatures of his imagination. Studies of the religions and cultures of mankind would also be humanities, though not so far as they are mere transcriptions of fact, for a mere transcription of fact is not an attempt either to understand or to appraise. Studies of art, morality, humour, music and sport are likewise humanities. Philosophy and science hold ambiguous positions. Both are purposive activities of the human spirit, and the study of them as such would therefore rank among the humanities. But these activities themselves, so far as they are concerned with the structure of the physical world, would not be humanistic, for while they are attempts to understand, they are not attempts to understand human activity.

Next, when it is claimed that science can provide us with such understanding, what is meant by 'science'? No one would claim that science has achieved such understanding already. But many would say that if it has not, this is a failure in fact rather than in principle; there is nothing in human conduct that falls beyond the scope of scientific method, ideally employed. It is important, then, to see what such ideal employment requires. I call in aid here the words of some respected exponents of scientific method. In a list of 'criteria of the scientific method', Herbert Feigl puts in the first place 'intersubjective testability', remarking: 'This is only a more adequate formulation of what is generally meant by the "objectivity" of science.' It is 'the requirement that the knowledge claims of science be in principle capable of test (confirmation or disconfirmation, at least indirectly and to some degree) on the part of any person equipped with intelligence and the technical devices of observation and experimentation. The term *intersubjective* stresses the social nature of the scientific enterprise.'[1] This requirement is further explained by Gustav Bergmann and Kenneth Spence as

[1] *Readings in the Philosophy of Science*, ed. Feigl and Brodbeck, 11.

follows: Such terms as 'sensation', 'consciousness', and 'image' are not necessarily meaningless, but 'it is the methodological ideal of the sciences of behaviour to use such mentalistic terms only after they have been introduced by (*operational*) *definitions from a physicalistic meaning basis*'. These terms are properly used only when 'every statement which contains such terms can be tested by the *scientist's* observations (unquantified) and measurements (quantified) of physical objects'. All such terms, when used by scientists, 'should be behaviouristically defined'.[1]

This preliminary comment on terms sharpens the issue. The question before us now is: Can conscious and purposive human activity be dealt with by a scientific method in which mind is conceived in terms of physical behaviour and whose statements are tested by the common observation of such behaviour? There are naturalists, indeed, who would not accept this 'reductionist' view of scientific method, who would hold that mental activity is distinct from physical, even though all control of behaviour is exerted from the bodily side. We shall deal with this softer naturalism in the concluding part of this paper. But first regarding the more extreme form.

I begin on a note that is perhaps querulous. It is distressingly difficult to get from the harder naturalists a simple, straightforward statement of what they mean. Take the statements we have just been quoting. We are told that 'it is the methodological ideal of the sciences of behaviour to use such mentalistic terms only after they have been introduced by (operational) definitions from a physical-istic meaning basis'. What does this ponderous pronouncement mean? If a 'definition from a physicalistic meaning basis' is a state-ment that consciousness is physical, why not say so? On the other hand, if consciousness is not physical, not capable of being publicly observed, then to define it, in the interest of scientific convenience, as really being so is to begin with a manifest untruth which will vitiate everything that is later said about the conscious realm. It is as if these philosophers had an obscure sense that if their theory were put quite simply it would lack plausibility, and were trying to shield it unawares by a cover of thick magisterial prose.

Philosophers of science who are also humanists often write as if, for them, there were really no problem here at all. Thus Mr Feigl who is a distinguished example of both types, writes an article con-tending that every kind of knowledge that a reasonable humanist

---

[1] *Ibid.*, 104–5; italics in text.

can ask is provided for him by science. At the same time he says
that if knowledge is to be scientific it must be 'intersubjectively
testable' through observation or experiment. But take this at face
value and the science he is offering the humanist is one from which
the entire range of humanistic experience is excluded at the outset.
Suppose Professor Lowes wants to study what went on in Coleridge's mind in writing *Kubla Khan*, or what goes on in your mind
when you read it. Mr Feigl would agree, I think, that one cannot
observe by the naked eye or any conceivable instrument either
Coleridge's consciousness or yours, and it follows that the study of
this sort of object is off bounds for science. Mr Feigl lists twelve
of the most important criticisms of science offered by the humanist,
but for some reason this fundamental objection is not discussed.
And surely it *is* fundamental. The scientist says to the humanist,
'You have nothing whatever to fear from me; every legitimate field
of study is still left open to you by science as I conceive it,' and
then adds by implication: 'Of course the world of feelings and
purposes and memories and imagination and reflection in which you
live is for science non-existent or inaccessible.' On which my comment would be: Science cannot have it both ways. If it is what the
scientist here says it is, then the humanist world *is* off limits. If he
is to include that world in his study, then his science cannot be
confined to observable behaviour; its province and its methods
must be radically reconceived.

Scientists have naturally been uneasy about such wholesale ex-
clusions from their province. They are sure that if mental facts are
facts at all science can deal with them. But if it is to deal with them
they must be intersubjectively observable and confirmable, and that
means that they must be movements in space. This is the conviction that lies behind the long series of behaviourisms of the past
half-century. Three of them seem to me particularly revealing of
scientific struggle and frustration in dealing with mental facts.

II. THE EARLIER BEHAVIOURISM

Of these my favourite is the first. There was nothing mealy-mouthed
about John Watson. He hesitated for a time over whether his
behaviourism should be merely a method of study, with the existence of mental facts left doubtful, or whether he should deny
them altogether. But he came to see that for a behaviourist to admit
such facts was to admit the incompetence of his science in its own

special field, and he therefore decided 'either to give up psychology or else make it a natural science'.[1] If the behaviourist disregarded consciousness, he held, it was for the same reason that the chemist disregarded alchemy and the astronomer astrology, namely that he wished no longer to deal in fictions. 'If behaviourism is ever to stand for anything (even a distinct method) it must make a clean break with the whole concept of consciousness.' For this concept, like that of the soul, is a relic of medieval superstition. 'The behaviourist cannot find consciousness in the test-tube of his science. He finds no evidence anywhere for a stream of consciousness, not even for one so convincing as that described by William James.'[2] Science has moved beyond it. It must be dismissed like the other myths that survive from the childhood of the race.

Did this mean that Watson waved aside the whole humanist range of experience? Would he deny that there was any such thing as what Shakespeare meant by 'imagination' when he said that 'imagination bodies forth the forms of things unknown'? Would he deny what Hood meant by memory when he said, 'I remember, I remember the house where I was born'? Would he exclude what the Prayer Book means when it speaks of 'envy, hatred, and malice, and all uncharitableness'? Would he say that Carlyle was using words without meaning when he remarked that 'literature is the thought of thinking souls'? The answer to all these questions is Yes. Of course, nothing is clearer than that the persons who said these things were talking about conscious experiences, and it is hard to believe that Watson, when out of his white coat and his laboratory, would find any difficulty in following them. Yet his view of science required him to say that these words meant nothing. If such terms are to be retained by science, they must be equipped with a new set of meanings. Thus we may still use the word 'memory' if we mean by it 'the resumption of a habit after a period of no practice'; 'emotion' will refer to certain massive responses in the autonomic nervous system; and the philosopher will at last realize that 'thinking is merely talking, but talking with concealed musculature'. Images remained a puzzle to Watson; he did not know what in the nervous system to reduce them to, and being deficient in imagery, he hardly knew what he had to reduce. He was thus able, as some critic has noted, to elevate a personal defect into an ontological unreality.

<hr>

[1] *Behaviorism*, 6.
[2] J. B. Watson and W. McDougall, *The Battle of Behaviorism*, 26.

I do not intend to enter here upon an appraisal of Watson's behaviourism. I did that in some detail and with no effect some thirty years ago.[1] Two remarks must suffice. First, it is obvious that no humanist could be a Watsonian behaviourist, or such a behaviourist a humanist, except by virtue of a gargantuan muddle. What goes on in the mind of anyone who thinks he is both, it is hard to say; he is probably misreading behaviourism as meaning only that brain and consciousness are intimately connected causally. But this is not at all what the theory means; indeed, it is a denial of behaviourism, for it holds that cause and effect are distinct, and the distinctness of consciousness from the physical is just what Watson will not accept. Secondly, though many psychologists still call themselves behaviourists, few would admit that they are Watsonians. Even when they are reductionists, their reduction is more elaborate and sophisticated, less naïve and less interesting. With Watson you knew where you were. For courageous, dogmatic, forthright, Philistine obtuseness, he stands out like a monument on a plain.

III. PHYSICALISM

Our second type of behaviourism is the physicalism of the logical empiricists. Its motives were in part similar to Watson's. It wanted to make psychology a natural science, and this could not be done so long as entities were given entrance that were neither observable nor measurable by the methods of the other sciences. But the logical empiricists had a wider ambition than Watson. They had a programme for the unification of all the sciences and for the reduction of all other ways of knowing, philosophy for example, to the position of handmaids of science. The instrument by which both ends were to be effected was a new theory of meaning, formulated by Moritz Schlick. This laid it down that the meaning of any factual statement was its mode of verification. Make any statement of fact you wish, for example that it is snowing. Then ask yourself what would serve to assure you of its truth. You would presumably answer in this case, 'Going to the window and seeing snowflakes falling', or 'Going out and feeling them on head and hands'. Very well, Schlick would say, the meaning of your statement, 'It is snowing', is that if you went to the window or outdoors you would perceive falling snow. The statement has a meaning because it is verifiable, and the way of verifying supplies that meaning. But

[1] *The Nature of Thought*, I, Ch. 9.

suppose there is no way of verifying it. Then there is no meaning in it either. Kant said that an unknowable exists which is not in time. Is there any observation by which you could assure yourself that this statement is true? None. Then it is neither true nor false; it is meaningless; it says nothing. According to the logical empiricists, most of the statements of traditional metaphysics were of this kind, and the verifiability theory of meaning was the tool on which they relied for exposing such pseudo-knowledge.

Many persons who had been frustrated and repelled in their attempts to penetrate Teutonic metaphysics greeted this demand for clarity with acclaim. At first sight it seemed remarkably simple and compelling. But soon doubts developed. What about statements regarding the remote past or future? We cannot verify them; are they therefore meaningless? What about statements regarding photons and electrons, which are unobservable, or regarding tables and chairs at times when nobody observes them? Above all, what about other minds? Historians and biographers are largely concerned with what goes on in other minds, but they obviously cannot observe these as they can the movements of other bodies. No statements they make about other people's thoughts or feelings are verifiable in their own perception, and therefore if the test is rigorously applied they must all be set down as meaningless.

Note that the physicalists did not deny that these thoughts and feelings existed, for to deny their existence would be as meaningless as to affirm it. What they did was to introduce the notion of multiple languages, and then raise the question whether a sentence in the mental language was translatable into a sentence of the physical language, which was accepted as a meaningful question. It was the physical language that was fundamental, not that of psychology or the social sciences, for if 'mental' terms were introduced they could always be translated into the physical language, while the reverse process was not generally possible. If a man is said to be 'angry' or 'in pain', for example, there will always be some statement about the occurrence of a process in his body that will also be true. In accordance with the logic accepted by these theorists, two propositions will be technically equivalent to each other if both are always true or false together. By an inference of a very curious kind they seem to have passed from the plausible assertion that the mental and physical sentences are in this technical sense equivalent to the totally different and quite implausible assertion that the mental sentence can be translated into the physical one without change of content, in short that they say the same thing. If that is so, when I use the sentence 'You are in pain', my sentence can be translated without loss of meaning into 'You are now holding your head and grimacing'. Indeed, this is the only sort of meaning that a scientist may entertain. As Professor Feigl put it, 'to ascribe to our fellow men consciousness *in addition* to overt behaviour with discoverable physiological processes implies a transcendence, an introduction of unverifiable elements';[1] and such transcendence must be avoided if one is to avert the ultimate ignominy of talking metaphysics. Professor Ayer, writing about the same time, said that 'each of us must define the experience of others in terms of what he can at least in principle observe'. 'I must define other people in terms of their empirical manifestations—that is, in terms of the behaviour of their bodies, and ultimately in terms of sense contents.'[2]

It is curious how little awareness these positivists betrayed of what their doctrine implied for the humanities. Almost all of them had come into philosophy from science; they were evangelists of science; if their doctrine was destructive of speculative philosophy, they took that as good riddance; and in the implications of the doctrine for the study of literature and history they took little or no interest. These implications, however, were essentially the same as those of Watson's behaviourism. What, for example, would a physicalist make of Boswell? The biographer could indeed observe his subject's puffing and blowing, his sitting at his desk and his walking abroad, his avoidance of cracks in the pavement and his collecting of orange peel; and these, of course, have their interest. But the instant Boswell went beyond these bodily acts into Johnson's ideas and arguments, his feelings about Scots and Whigs, his fear of death, his affection for his Tetty, his wit and humour, his rages and his depressions, he was literally talking nonsense. But take all this away and what is left of Boswell's account? Virtually nothing at all, since then even Johnson's bodily oddities would have lost most of their significance for us. It is interesting to reflect that at the very time when the physicalists were propounding their doctrine Collingwood was writing a famous essay to show that the subject-matter of history was self-conscious and purposive activity.[3] On positivist premises any attempt to discuss activity of this kind must be meaningless, and hence, so far as Collingwood is right, the

[1] *Philosophy of Science*, I, 4 (1936).
[2] *Language, Truth and Logic*, 1st edn, 202, 203.
[3] *The Idea of History*, 308 ff. (1935).

historian is disinherited of his kingdom. To venture again at random, what would a physicalist make of James's *Varieties of Religious Experience*? Two generations of readers have found in it vivid descriptions of the experience of mystics, of divided selves and their unification, of conversion, of religious morbidity and healthy-mindedness. About these things James, as a scientific psychologist, presumably had no right to speak at all, and he was indulging in something like metaphysics when he did so.

We may be reminded that it is one thing to deny that someone else is conscious and another to deny the meaningfulness of saying that he is. But in a question of such practical importance as this the distinction is a quibble. Presumably one's action should accord with one's belief, and if one's belief is that to ascribe pain to a man with a broken leg is nonsense, one should act accordingly. There is clearly no reason to relieve a pain that one does not believe to exist. It may be said, again, that the implications we have just noted, even if all are accepted and put together, do not constitute a logical refutation of physicalism. This is true. It remains a logical possibility that one's friends are all automata, bodies to which no thought or feeling is to be ascribed, which have no memory or recognition of the person who greets them, and are as free from fear or pain as an IBM computer. This view was accepted by some of the seventeenth-century Cartesians regarding dogs and cats and led to irresponsible treatment of these animals. But that theory rested on a medieval theology which held that in the creation of animals, immortal souls had been denied them. This the positivists would rightly decry as mythology. At the same time they accepted a theory which made it illegitimate not only to ascribe pain to animals but also to ascribe it to their fellow human beings. I am not, of course, attacking anyone's character. Many of these writers I knew, and found them invariably kindly, thoughtful and sensitive persons who would not wish to hurt an earthworm. They would not dream of practising their theory, and those of them who are still living have all, I think, given it up. But physicalism remains an instructive episode in human thought. It shows that when one tries to make a philosophy out of the logic and method of natural science, without taking due heed of the rest of human experience, one is likely to wind up in absurdity. The positivists no doubt regarded such philosophers as the Cairds, A. E. Taylor and Bosanquet as victims of metaphysical superstition, but can one imagine any of these humane and civilized minds committing itself to anything as

incoherent with general human experience and as barbaric in its
larger implications, as physicalism was?

IV. THE BEHAVIOURISM OF SKINNER

It may be well to look at one other attempt to deal with human
experience in accordance with the demands of physical science, and
one which, unlike the other two, is flourishing today. Professor B.
F. Skinner, like Watson, denies the distinct existence of sensation
and thought, feeling and purpose. His chief difference from Watson
is this: that whereas Watson was much concerned to identify the
processes in the nervous system in terms of which sensation, thought
and emotion were now to be defined, Skinner bypasses this endeavour as being, at the present stage of science, unprofitable. We know
comparatively little about the chemistry and physics of brain cells
and of the conduction of nervous impulses through them, and the
growth of such recondite knowledge is likely to be slow. But the
study of behaviour, which is the proper business of psychology,
need not wait upon such knowledge, for we may study the connection of stimulus and response independently of it. We can vary
indefinitely the situations in which the organism is placed and note
how the response varies with each change. We may expose a pigeon
to a black, a white, and a red disc, of which it can get food only by
pecking the white one, and observe how many mis-pecks it makes
before learning to peck at the white disc only. Here we are studying the connection between observable stimuli and observable responses without any regard to the changes that may go on in the
pigeon's nervous system. That is the way we should study human
behaviour.

Suppose one replies to Skinner: Surely it is what happens
between the stimulus and the response, the part you are leaving out,
that is psychologically of most interest to us. Present those discs to
a man and he may do any one of a hundred things because he has
the power, which the pigeon has not, of taking thought. He can
consider, deliberate, entertain purposes, plan, and hence respond,
in a way you cannot foresee. Skinner would reply in three steps.
First, if you mean by such terms as 'deliberating' and 'planning' a
set of conscious processes distinct from what goes on in the body,
they are fictions; there are no such events.[1] Secondly, since they
are fictions, they cannot affect the responses that actually occur, and

[1] *Science and Human Behavior*, 30.

hence are of no value in explaining those responses. Thirdly, though they do not exist, the physical changes that we ought to mean by these names do exist and do make a difference, but it is a difference that it is needless at present to take into account. Suppose you have a series of events A, B, C, and that A is the sufficient cause of B, and B of C. Then if you know that A occurs, you know that C will occur, and you can connect A and C by a perfectly reliable causal law in which B does not figure at all. B here stands for events internal to the organism, the 'intervening variables' as the psychologists call them, between the observable stimuli and the observable responses. We have no doubt that Cs, forms of behaviour exhibited by the organism, issue from Bs, changes within the organism, and we have no doubt that the Bs are all ultimately due to changes occurring outside the organism. The two extremes are physical events that are within the present range of our observation. Most of the intervening variables are not. What is proposed is that, without denying the existence of these variables, we proceed to establish connections directly between the several forms of A— A^1, A^2, A^3—and the several forms of C—C^1, C^2, C^3. We shall then have a set of causal laws whose components are as truly observable as anything in physics.

Now there is no objection to seeking such linkages, and the method has been applied with success, particularly to lower animals. But certain comments should be made about what is distinctive in it. (1) It denies the existence of consciousness as flatly as Watson did. The classical works on psychology are full of discussions of sensation, imagery, emotion, the association of ideas, and the processes of thought. Professor Skinner tries hard to eliminate such misleading terms from his writing. The result is that for a humanist it makes curiously difficult reading. It is as if someone had taken a chapter of Proust or Henry James and attempted to rewrite it entirely in terms of the movements of muscle and limb on the part of the characters, with no mention of anything that went on in their minds. That thoughts and emotions do commonly express themselves in such motions seems clear enough, but an account of them exclusively in terms of these motions gives the impression of elaborate indirection or evasion, a continuous, gratuitous missing of the point.

(2) The fact that one can link directly the stimulus and the response, without mention of the intermediate links, does not imply that those links are absent. They are there and performing their

function, whether we take note of them or not. Would Professor
Skinner agree? Yes, if by these intermediate links we mean changes
in the nervous system; No, if they mean thoughts, choices or
purposes. When we say, for example, that what a man says is 'disorganized because his *ideas* are confused', or that he pauses because
he is trying to make up his mind, 'it is obvious that the mind and
the ideas, together with their special characteristics, are being
invented on the spot to provide spurious explanations'.[1] If Professor
Skinner omits talk about intervening *mental* variables, it is because
they never do intervene. His 'purpose' to sit down at his desk and
write makes no difference to what he does; he never 'chooses' to
write one sentence rather than another because its 'meaning' is
relevant to his 'end'; indeed, he never chooses to do anything if
that means that his 'choice' appoints what he does. You can never
explain an action, even in part, by saying that the man who did it
'intended' or 'preferred' or 'decided' or 'wished' or 'thought he
ought' to do it.

What are we to say of these programmes to make of psychology
a science like physics or chemistry? We must be clear what they are
proposing to us. Sometimes this is represented not as a denial of
consciousness but as a study of its physical aspects and connections. If mind is stimulated into action by physical events, expresses
itself in physical events, and is intimately and manifoldly connected
with events in the nervous system, is it not possible to confine oneself to the study of these events? The strict answer is No. How is
one to choose, for example, which events in the nervous system to
study except by noting which are correlated with mental events?
And then one is *not* confining oneself to physical events only.
Behaviourists have frequently put their position as if they were not
concerned with ontology but only with method. Professor Skinner
writes: 'The objection to inner states is not that they do not exist
but that they are not relevant in a functional analysis.'[2] This sounds
as if desires and purposes in the traditional sense were admitted to
exist, but were being ignored because they fell outside the scientific
province. But such language is misleading. If these psychologists
were asked whether science, as they conceive it, is adequate to the
study of mind, they would undoubtedly say Yes, and add that
science is the best means we have of dealing with any facts. If
mental events are ignored, then, it is not for methodological reasons
only. Science ignores mental facts, because these 'facts' are not

[1] *Ibid.*, 30.   [2] *Ibid.*, 35.

genuine facts. The words that seem to refer to them refer to physical facts or else to nothing. To talk about a non-physical purpose or intention is for Watson like talking astrology; for the physicalists, it is talking metaphysics; for Skinner it is a surrender to the 'fictional'; for Ryle it is the superstition of a 'ghost in the machine'.

V. THE FAILURE OF BEHAVIOURISM

To me there is something grotesque in a solemn argument about whether consciousness, the pains and pleasures, fears and desires that we commonly mean by these words exist. If a person insists that all he means by a toothache, for example, is a movement of some kind in his nervous system, he must be no doubt allowed the last word, for he is in a privileged position to know. But then so are the rest of us about our own meanings. I remember vividly an evening at Swarthmore when G. E. Moore was holding a conference hour for undergraduates. Only one student turned up that night, and he was a student in physics. The conversation began with his remarking that by his sensation of blue he meant a physical change in his optical nerve. Moore explained that he could understand this if what was meant was that such a change occasioned the sensation, but 'surely you don't mean', he went on, 'that the movement of particles in the nerves *is* your sensation of blue?' 'Yes,' the student insisted, that was exactly what he did mean, and he held to it despite Moore's expostulation. The veins began to stand out on Moore's forehead. He must have been through this countless times, and he apparently felt that a man who could believe that sort of thing could believe anything. The weariness and futility of the discussion overcame him, and he fell obstinately silent. After a time I led him away.

Argument about the point is not, however, necessarily futile. It did, after all, persuade the physicalists to change their view. But the arguments that are likely to be effective here are not technical; it is indeed the technical people, who approach the problem from an ideal language or from a preconceived notion of what is required by science, who seem most confused, and who most need to be brought back to common sense again. It is curiously easy to be mistaken about one's own meaning, and I can only think that behaviourists are the victims of this kind of confusion. There are many ways of showing this, though nearly all of them are variations of one general argument—that behaviourists cannot conform their intellectual practice to their reported meaning, that is, they cannot hold it consistently.

1. Consider the behaviourist who has a headache and takes aspirin. What he means by his 'headache' is, if he belongs to one school, a set of motions among the molecules that form the cells in his brain, or if he belongs to another, the grimaces or claspings of the head that an observer might behold. Since these *are* the headache, it must be these that he finds objectionable. But it is absurd to say that a set of motions in his head that he could not distinguish from a thousand others are objectionable; it would never occur to him to find them so except as they are associated with the conscious pain. In denying the pain, therefore, he is denying the only feature that makes the situation objectionable. Suppose, again, that he identifies the pain with the grimaces and outward movements. Then all he would have to do to banish the pain would be to stop these movements and behave in normal fashion. But he knows perfectly well that this is not enough; that is why he falls back on aspirin. In short, his action implies a disbelief in his own theory.

2. The characters he assigns to physical events are different from and incompatible with those he assigns to mental events. Physical changes are ultimately motions, and it is commonly assumed that what moves has mass, is governed by gravitational law, and moves in a certain direction with a certain velocity. But it would be nonsense to say that a pain or a memory has mass, gravity, direction or velocity. Again, we speak of a pain as sharp or dull, intense or mild, excruciating or easy to bear, and such terms are meaningless as applied to motions. Professor Skinner, when confronted with this consideration, agrees that 'a *motion* is not likely to be dull or excruciating. But *things* are. Indeed, these two adjectives are applied to pain just because they apply to the things which cause pain. A dull pain is the sort of pain caused by a dull object, as a sharp pain is caused by a sharp object. The term "excruciating" is taken from the practice of crucifixion.'[1] But (*a*) Dull toothaches or headaches are not normally caused by dull objects, or sharp ones by sharp objects. (*b*) Even when the term 'sharp' is used both of a physical thing and of a pain, it is used in wholly different senses. The sharpness or dullness of a thing is a matter of its shape; a pain has no

[1] B. Blanshard and B. F. Skinner, 'The Problem of Consciousness: A Debate', *Philosophy and Phenomenological Research*, Vol. XXVII, No. 3, March 1967, 329.

shape. (c) When Professor Skinner says that we call a pain sharp because the physical thing that causes it is sharp, he seems to admit the difference between the conscious process and its physical cause. He may say that he means here the cause outside the body, and that the sensation is a change within the body and presumably in the brain. But then he arrives at the same paradox as before, since a molecular thing or movement can no more be identified with a sensation than a molar thing or movement.

3. The implausibility of identifying the conscious event with a change in the brain may be seen in another way. When we refer to a conscious experience we may be perfectly clear what we mean, though if asked what brain change we were referring to we should not have the faintest notion how to answer. Plato could discuss with precision the varieties of pleasure, and Aristotle the varieties of inference, without knowing that these psychical processes were connected with the brain at all. Even when we do learn that these processes are causally correlated with changes in the brain, we may not know which brain changes are involved. We made a distinction a moment ago between the sharpness of a tool and the sharpness of a pain; the making of that distinction was a mental act which we can now recall. What exactly is the brain process that in our new way of thought we are supposed to be recalling? Not even Adrian or Penfield would attempt to specify the correlate of that act in the brain. Now, if we can specify clearly the mental act that we mean while quite unable to specify the physical change we are supposed to mean, to say that the two meanings reduce to one is most implausible.[1]

4. Even when we do know approximately what physical change is correlated with a given psychical change, there may be an extreme qualitative difference on one side which, so far as we know, corresponds to nothing on the other side. We know that when an impulse from the eye reaches a point in the back of the brain a sensation of colour normally arises, and that when an impulse from the ear reaches a point at the side of the brain a sensation of sound normally arises. No two experiences differ from each other more

[1] Cf. the following from Lord Brain: '. . . As regards the physical events occurring in the nervous system we have at present only the most elementary knowledge of them at comparatively simple levels of organization, and none at all of the ultimate physical basis of thinking, willing and remembering.' J. R. Smythies (ed.), *Brain and Mind*, 54.

completely than one of sound and one of colour. But the nervous impulses that are the correlates of these sensations seem to be the same in structure and movement. As Lord Adrian says, 'the surprising thing is that a disturbance of this kind in one part of a sheet of nerve cells [the cortex] should make us see a light, and that the same kind of disturbance in another part should make us hear a sound'.[1] If the sensations are entirely different while the nervous changes, so far as we know, are entirely alike, what we mean by the sensations must be distinct from what we mean by the physical changes.

5. The attempt at identification cannot get under way without the implicit admission of its untruth. You want to know, for example, what brain change is now to be identified with 'a sensation of colour' and what with 'a sensation of sound'. The test whether you have found the cerebral equivalent of a sensation of colour is whether, when you alter or remove that cerebral process, the sensation is affected. On that ground you eliminate everything in the brain but a small area in the occipital lobe as the basis of the colour sensation, and everything but a small area in the temporal lobe as the basis of the sound sensation. But the assumption of this procedure is that you have definite knowledge of the colour and sound sensations *before* you know what their physical correlations are. It is only because you have definite antecedent knowledge of these sensations that you can hunt for their correlates, or check your hypotheses as to what these are. If all you meant by sensation was its physical correlate, the search could not begin, for you would have no means of recognizing which of a million physical processes filled the bill. It is only if sensation and physical process are distinct that you ever reach the terminus of the search, a terminus which, once reached, is then incoherently identified with the starting-point.

6. The language used by behaviourists, despite their efforts to avoid compromising terms, continually betrays their position. Psychologists used to say that a response was confirmed or 'stamped in' if it was pleasurable, and inhibited or discouraged if it was disagreeable. But 'pleasurable' and 'disagreeable' clearly refer to qualities of conscious experience, and Professor Skinner reminds us that science therefore does not use such terms or any equivalents for them.[2] What we should say instead, for example, is that the

---

[1] *Body, Mind, and Death*, ed. A. Flew, 234.
[2] *Science and Human Behavior*, 81.

response of eating is 'reinforced' by one sort of food and 'extinguished' by another; these words are innocent of mentalist connotations. But he finds it impracticable to keep to this rule. He writes: '. . . Though we have been reinforced with an excellent meal in a new restaurant, a bad meal may reduce our patronage to zero', and again, on the next page, that in extinguishing a response, 'the currently preferred technique is punishment'.[1] Now, when we refer to an 'excellent' meal, is there no connotation of pleasantness? When we refer to a 'bad' meal or to punishment, is there no connotation of disagreeableness? Would an 'excellent' meal reinforce our tendency to repeat it if it were *not* pleasant? Would punishment be punishment if it were *not* disagreeable? It seems clear here that Professor Skinner, despite his gallant efforts to free his usage from the mentalistic blight, is not only reintroducing it but relying on it to make reinforcement and extinction intelligible.

However desperately the behaviourist tries to exclude these connotations of consciousness, they keep pouring in through the cracks of every wall he builds to keep them out. Strictly speaking, we should never say of Jones that he ran because he was afraid or because he wanted to catch a train, for these words attribute to him unobservable states with which science has nothing to do. But suppose Jones *says*, 'I am scared half to death' or 'I am frantic to catch that train'. It is perfectly legitimate to take such an 'observation report' into account because it is itself an observable part of Jones's behaviour. But is it? No doubt an external observer can hear a succession of sounds emitted by Jones's body, but is the emission of these sounds all we mean by Jones's *saying* something? Clearly not. The point has been made by Professor E. M. Adams in an article in which a large variety of these unnoticed but illicit usages by behaviourists are catalogued and analysed. 'In what sense', he asks, 'is "said" a pure observation term? Is it meaningful to ask, Does what he *said* make sense? Is what he *said* consistent? Can you put what he *said* differently? Can you translate what he *said* into French? Does he literally mean what he *said*? Is what he *said* supported by evidence? Was he justified in saying what he did? Is what he *said* true?'[2] These questions are clearly in order if 'say' is used as we all do in fact use it. But they are both irrelevant and unanswerable if the term is used strictly as an 'observation term'. A

[1] *Ibid.*, 70, 71.
[2] 'Mind and the Language of Psychology', in *Ratio*, Vol. IX, No. 2, Dec. 1967, 127.

mere series of heard sounds could not be 'justified' or 'supported by evidence' or 'said differently' or 'translated into French'; such expressions assume that the speaker was using the sounds to convey conscious meanings and that the hearer can apprehend those meanings. They must be used in this way by the behaviourist also if they are to do the work he asks of them. But he cannot in consistency use them so, since, for him, to apprehend the meanings of another mind would be to leap out of the physical world into forbidden territory. In short, he finds it impracticable to conform to his own requirements even in the use of so simple a word as 'say'.

7. These requirements he believes to be imposed on him by science, and in the interest of science, as he conceives it, he is quite ready to part company with common sense. But in other places he clings to common sense in a manner that places him in clear conflict with science. When Professor Skinner talks about stimuli he does not ordinarily mean the impact of micro-waves on nerve ends; he means observable things or changes such as coloured discs or the sounds of a voice or the impact of a hard object. Since these are observable, they are assumed to be physical. But would a physicist of sophistication take them to be physical, just as presented? Would he accept the colour of a disc as something spread out in physical space over the surface of the disc? Would he take the sounds that are heard, as distinct from waves in air, to be physical existents? Having explained to us that a football consists of millions of micro-particles in motion, would he add that this aggregate is *hard*? Most philosophers since Locke have held that the 'secondary qualities' belong in consciousness, not in the physical world, and reflective physicists have thought likewise. There is no doubt that we experience them, and they must, therefore, have lodgement in some recognized realm of being. But Professor Skinner has no room for them in any realm of being. If he puts them in physical space, as he seems inclined to do, he loses the much-coveted support of natural science. He cannot put them in consciousness, for there is no consciousness to put them in. Nor would he identify them, as Watson tried to do, with nervous changes in the body; to hunt for a sound in the nervous system he would consider absurd. In our conscious experience of nature these qualities are almost everywhere, but in the world of the behaviourist they are without a home.

8. Consider but one more paradox, which, if possible, is more striking still. In the round terms of traditional philosophy, the intrinsic values of life were often said to be truth, beauty and goodness. Whether we accept this thesis or not, the old terms are still of importance and in constant use. What meaning can the behaviourist attach to them? Take first the meaning of 'truth'. What is true is a proposition, a belief or an assertion, but these are not observable entities unless identified with movements of the lips or with other bodily movements. But it is meaningless to say that *movements* are true or false. There is nothing more true or false about any movement in the universe than any other. And since there are no events in the behaviourist universe except the motions of matter, it has no room for truth either.

Again, what would the term 'beauty' stand for in such a world? Is it a scientifically observable property? Hume imagines a geometer gloating over the beauty of one of his figures, say a five-pointed star. He proceeds to indicate its properties to an observer—the uniform structure of its five triangles, the equal length of their sides and of their bases, and so on. His companion then asks him to point out the quality of beauty that he has been speaking of. Could he do it? Hume rightly answers that it would be impossible, that beauty is not something that can be observed like a line or a shape. Still less is it something that could belong in a wholly physical world. Strictly speaking there is no beauty apart from the enjoyment of it, and the enjoyment of it is a form of consciousness. In a behaviourist world, a necessary condition of beauty would thus be lacking.

What about moral goodness? Moralists have commonly held that this depends either on the motive of an act or on the intrinsic values of its consequences. Sceptics regarding these positions have argued that 'good' and all other value terms are the expressions of emotions or attitudes in the minds of those who use them. No one of these theories of goodness could be restated in behaviourist terms without eviscerating them of their meaning. In short, the world of the behaviourist is one in which neither truth, beauty nor goodness, as traditionally understood, can consistently be given a place.

I have argued the case at wearisome length because behaviourism is not a historic curiosity merely, as by this time it ought to be, but is very much alive. Indeed, with the help of the Ford Foundation, the Carnegie Corporation and the Federal Government, Professor Skinner has recently produced a book on *The Technology*

of Teaching which offers a programme for making education entirely
a matter of physical conditioning. Such a work, with such support,
lends some colour to Count Keyserling's acid comment that behaviourism is the natural psychology of a people without inner life.
Furthermore, the movement has received encouragement, strangely
enough, from that traditional seat of the humanities, Oxford, in
Professor Ryle's brilliant and wayward book, *The Concept of Mind*.
I have not dealt with that book, partly because its account of the
mind is not, like our three American behaviourisms, an attempt
from within the circle of science to draw psychology back into the
fold, partly because it has been so effectively dealt with in its own
country. I have in mind particularly Professor C. A. Campbell's
essay, *Ryle on the Intellect*, in which the difficulty, even for a skillful
dialectician, of holding consistently to the behaviourist thesis, is
convincingly shown.[1]

VI. THE IDENTITY HYPOTHESIS

But materialism dies a lingering death. In recent years a number of
philosophers have been exploring whether the identity of mind and
matter cannot be rehabilitated, and to that end they have been
examining anew the notion of identity. The word 'is', they point
out, is ambiguous. There is the 'is' of definition and the 'is' of
composition. The 'is' of definition means a logical identity, as when
we say that a square is an equilateral rectangle. Here the identity
is such that neither side would be conceivable in the absence of the
other. We also use an 'is' of composition, as when we say that a
cloud is a mass of droplets in suspension, or that lightning is a
motion of electric charges.[2]

Here there is no identity of concept between subject and predicate, for either could be conceived without the other. Most holders
of the identity hypothesis are reluctant to say that consciousness
and bodily change are the same in the logical sense. They have
given up the view, which never was plausible, that the distinction
between mind and matter is a merely linguistic affair, and that when
a man says he has a toothache he is referring in a different language
to precisely what he means when he speaks of an injury to his dental
nerve, or to grimaces and gestures that would be observable from

[1] See his *In Defence of Freedom*, 243–75.
[2] U. T. Place, 'Consciousness is Just Brain Processes', in *Body, Mind, and Death*, ed. A. Flew, 278.

without. It is only too obvious that the one language is not translatable into the other. If the identity hypothesis does claim identity in the extreme or logical sense, then the arguments already adduced against behaviourism are in order again.

But in spite of the sophistication of the identity philosophers, some of them are advancing a theory that is hard to distinguish in principle from extreme behaviourist reductionism, apparently denying, for example, that there is any such thing as sensation, as distinct from bodily response. Thus Professor J. J. C. Smart imagines a group of congenitally blind men in the company of normal men who are sorting wools of different colours into piles. These piles are arranged in a series in which each pile is barely discriminable from its neighbours. The blind man knows that a tomato is called red, and lemons yellow, and he knows that when wool from a certain pile is dropped into a bowl of tomatoes the sighted people around him find it especially hard to pick it out, and when the wool from a certain other pile is dropped into a bowl of lemons it, too, becomes hard to pick out. The blind men thus coordinates the colour words for the various piles with the colour words used for objects he knows otherwise, such as tomatoes, lemons, and lettuce. Would the blind men use colour words in the same way that we do? Professor Smart replies that they would, and that 'the objective criteria for the redness of an object are exactly the same with them as with us. These objective criteria are the discriminatory responses of normal percipients. As against the common view that colour words are meaningless to the congenitally blind I would rather say, therefore, that the congenitally blind can understand the meaning of colour words every bit as well as sighted people can.[1]' He concludes: 'The idea that a congenitally blind man cannot understand colour words is connected, I suspect, with a pre-Wittgensteinian view of meaning not as "use" but as a mental experience which evokes and is evoked by a word.'

Here I am hopelessly pre-Wittgensteinian. To say that a blind man who learned to imitate the physical and verbal responses of normal men 'can understand the meanings of colour words every bit as well as sighted people can' implies that there is nothing in the colour discrimination of even normal men beyond their physical responses. The example surely gains such plausibility as it has

[1] In an article 'Colours' in *Philosophy*, Vol. XXXVI, No. 137, Apr.–July 1961, 141. I have abbreviated the illustration in a way that I hope does not obscure the principle.

through confusing two quite different kinds of discrimination. When the normal man discriminates red from yellow. he is distinguishing the content of two conscious sensory experiences. When the blind man responds 'correctly' with 'red' to one pile of wool in a series and 'yellow' to another, these vocal responses are not discriminations between colours at all. To say that they are is to return to Watson and Skinner with their attempt at literal conceptual identification of two things—a conscious experience and a physical response, which are as different in kind as any two things in the world. Does the normal man have no advantage over the blind man? Obviously he has. In what does it here consist? In this, that he can see or experience or be aware of colours, that he can imagine them, and distinguish them consciously. The blind man, having never experienced them, has not the slightest idea what these phrases mean to the man with sight.

Most defenders of the identity theory, however, are not reductionists of this type. They would prefer the other kind of identity, that of composition. The best analogy of the sense in which consciousness is brain process is to be found, in the opinion of Mr Place, in the statement that lightning is the motion of electric charges. The meaning of 'a flash of lightning is occurring' is clearly different from 'a motion of electric charges is occurring', as is evidenced by their being verified in totally different ways. Yet plain man and scientist alike are content to say that the lightning *is* the motion of electric charges. Why? Because the motions observed by the scientist 'provide an immediate explanation of the observations made by the man in the street. Thus we conclude that lightning is nothing more than a motion of electric charges, because we know that a motion of electric charges through the atmosphere, such as occurs when lightning is reported, gives rise to the sort of visual stimulation which would lead an observer to report a flash of lightning.'[1] If it is permissible to use 'is' in this case, there is no reason why we should not use it also in the case of consciousness and brain process. Suppose a scientist feels an acute pain. He is no more thinking of the motions in his nervous system than in seeing a flash of lightning he is thinking about the movements of electric charges. But he can perfectly well say, in the same sense of 'is', that the pain *is* the motion of particles in his brain.

I may have missed some link in the argument, but I must confess that I can see nothing in it that tends to show even the second type

[1] *Op. cit.*, 283.

of identity, let alone the first. The seen flash, which is a conscious event, does not *consist* of the motion of charges in the atmosphere; the two are entirely different and temporally distinct events. If we follow the analogy through, we shall have to deny that the conscious pain either *is* or *consists* of the change in the nerve; the most we can say is that the two events are connected. What sort of connection is this? Mr Place has suggested the answer when in discussing the lightning case he says that the motion of electric charges 'provides the immediate explanation' of the visible flash. And what does 'explanation' mean? It means what scientific explanation generally means—explanation through causal law. But such explanation, far from supporting the identity hypothesis, is incompatible with it. For if the nervous events and the pain are connected as cause and effect, their identity is out of the question. They are *two* events, not one.

VII. SOFT MATERIALISM

The attempt to establish identity appears to end, then, with a notion of consciousness not as identical with events in the nervous system but as their result or effect. We are thus carried on to epiphenomenalism. This, I suspect, is the position really implicit in the thought of most physiologists and psychophysicists of the day, whether they have heard the name or not. They would certainly not swallow the notion that consciousness does not exist, nor would they be prepared to equate it with physical motions, which amounts to the same thing. If they were to set out their position, it would probably run as follows: Sensations, emotions, recollections, judgments, acts of reasoning, desires, purposes, choices, are mental events, to which physical attributes like volume, mass and motion plainly do not belong. But there is the best of reasons to believe that, though not physical events themselves, they are always causally dependent on physical events, whose location in the cortex we are able to specify more and more definitely.

Does causation run in the opposite direction also, that is, from mind to brain? If causation means only correlation, we should be justified in saying Yes; we could say, as common sense does unhesitatingly, that if the dentist's injuring the nerve end causes the pain, it is also true that the patient's resolution to bear the pain stoically makes him sit still and restrain his outcry. But I do not think that most physiologists or psychologists really accept the cor-

44 CONTEMPORARY AMERICAN PHILOSOPHY

relation theory. Though they would say without hesitation that the injury to the nerve produces the pain, they would hesitate, long and probably in the end decline, to say that the resolution caused anything to happen in the body. As at least would-be natural scientists, they would say that physical events must have physical causes. Speaking strictly, therefore, a mental resolution or decision can never so much as divert the course of a nervous impulse as it passes across a synapse. What really produces the bodily change is not the mental event but the physical counterpart of that mental event, which is, of course, always present and available as the true cause. In this way we confine causal agency to events in the natural order and resist unwanted intrusions from a supernatural order, whether psychical or superstitious.

And if we deny causal efficacy to the psychical events, we may as well take the further step of denying them agency even in their own realm. Suppose we find our thoughts to have been following a line of 'free association' and passing idly from the blue sky to the blue Danube and thence to the St Louis blues. Has one associate given rise to another? In appearance Yes, in reality No. What has actually occurred is that the cortical basis of the first thought has given rise to the cortical basis of the second, and that of the second to that of the third. The succession of ideas is thus explained without yielding the claim of the physical order to be the exclusive source of all events, mental as well as physical. The theory is sometimes diagrammed as follows:

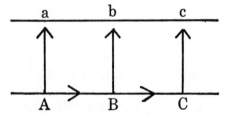

There is a series of cortical events, A, B, C, with a series of corresponding psychical events, a, b, c. The order of executive causality runs horizontally from A to B to C, and also upward from A to a, from B to b, and from C to c. But it does not run horizontally from a to b to c, nor downward from these to anything in the physical succession.

Stated thus in the abstract, the theory is neat and plausible, and as defended by such persuasive writers as T. H. Huxley and

Santayana, it is more plausible still. C. D. Broad has said of it: 'Unless there be reason to believe that minds can survive the death of their bodies, I should consider that some form of epiphenomenalism was the most reasonable view to take of the nature of mind and its relation to the body.'[1] It is not strictly a naturalist theory if that means one that remains within the limits of physical science, since it admits that consciousness is not physical in composition or attributes. But it is naturalistic in the sense that matter is regarded as the only agency in nature, the sole determinant of events, and the basis of all causal explanation. It seems to be the most plausible of those theories that by any stretch of the term can be called naturalistic. I suspect that many men of science accept it for this reason without giving much thought to its implications regarding human nature and practice. We shall do well, therefore, before commenting on its validity, to draw out some of these implications, so that if we are inclined to accept it we shall at least know to what we are committing ourselves.

The view implies that no volitions, purposes or desires ever influence behaviour. When one sits down at a desk in order to write a letter, one's intention makes no difference to one's sitting down or writing. No decision made by Eisenhower in Europe, or Mac Arthur in Korea or Westmoreland in Vietnam made the slightest difference in the conduct of their various wars. The purpose of Albert Schweitzer to serve the African needy had nothing causally to do with his going to Africa, any more than the purpose of Hitler to liquidate the Jews had any effects in the way of death or misery. Schweitzer did not do right, nor Hitler wrong; nor has anyone ever done anything good or bad, if that means that what he did issued out of his choice. The desire of a youth for an education never leads him to go to college, or his desire for a girl to propose to her, or his desire to win a race to enter a contest or to run faster. Again, our *thoughts* make no difference to what we do or say. There is nothing in Russell's fifty volumes that was written because he had one conviction rather than another. When a debater argues a case, his interest in proving that case never makes any difference to the words or sentences he uses. No student sitting for an examination will ever write a better paper because he thinks more clearly or recalls more completely the relevant facts. Shakespeare's conception of Lear or Cordelia had no influence on what he wrote in the play, nor did Coleridge's imagination make him set down or delete

[1] *Mind and Its Place in Nature*, 476.

anything in *The Ancient Mariner*. Euclid's seeing that the angles of a triangle must equal two right angles, Aristotle's seeing that a Barbara syllogism is valid, had no effect on what they taught. Again, feeling and sensation are without influence on conduct. The pain of getting burnt has no part in leading the child to avoid the fire. No one ever stops his car at a cross-road because he sees a red light rather than a green one. No one ever swears because he is angry, or sends a Valentine out of affection, or pays a debt from a sense of duty, or bundles up from fear of a cold. Again, no thought or purpose ever accounts for any mental event that comes after it. No one ever accepts a conclusion because he sees that the evidence demands it, or, for that matter, because he wants to believe it; rationalization in the Freudian sense is as impossible as it is to be rational, if that means being guided by what one takes to be the demands of reason. Nor does any idea ever give rise to another through resemblance or relevance or association. Beethoven never added one bar to another because of what aesthetic requirements demanded or seemed to demand. Consciousness, in short, is an impotent observer from the sidelines in the conduct of life.

What, then, is the real executive agent in biography and history? It is the body. It was Russell's durable and efficient body that wrote that row of volumes, with never an assist from his thought. The body is the only saint or sinner, for motives have nothing to do with what it does. There once was a body that, unprompted by its mind, made the set of marks on paper called *King Lear*, and another that rose to its feet and gave Churchillian speeches, while the consciousness of each of these bodies, like the fly that rode the elephant, no doubt took a pathetic satisfaction in its own performance. Of course, the brain of a man is an unimaginably complex apparatus, composed of billions of cells, each of which has countless components. Still the components are all physical, and the natural scientist believes that the laws governing their behaviour are in the end exclusively those of physics and chemistry.

VIII. THE FAILURE OF EPIPHENOMENALISM

Does our budget of paradoxes disprove the theory? No, I think not. It involves a prodigious change in our view of human nature, and, I think, a high degree of improbability, but not a decisive disproof. It is hard to set clear limits to what an apparatus as complex as the human body can do without purposive guidance. Fortunately we do not have to rely on probability only There are other considerations that seem to me to defeat the theory decisively.

First there is a consideration drawn from the nature of inference. I have several times made this point in print, and have been fortified by finding that the fire it drew seemed to leave it intact. Epiphenomenalists commonly hold that the laws of science are empirical laws, and therefore without logical necessity. In explaining why brain state B should follow brain state A, one cannot resort to any necessity linking the character or the content of these states. Nor can one resort to such necessity in explaining why the conscious state b follows the conscious state a, since in the realm of consciousness nothing exerts causal constraint on anything else. Now, I think this is false and can be shown to be so. Take any case of valid inference, 'Either the death of President Kennedy was the work of a group, or Oswald was the assassin. But no group was involved. Therefore Oswald was the assassin.' The inference here is a psychological succession, ending with the thought of the conclusion. Why did this terminal thought pop into mind instead of any one of a thousand others? The natural answer is that a moment before we had laid hold in thought of the premises, and that we went on to the thought of the conclusion because it was entailed by these premises. I think that this natural answer is correct, though it is not the whole of the answer. And it is quite inconsistent with epiphenomenalism, since it implies that one conscious event determines through its content or character (or more precisely through the logical relation of its content to another content) the emergence of a later event.

Let us move cautiously here. Implication and inference are, of course, not to be confused; implication is a timeless relation between characters; inference is a succession of events in time. What I am maintaining is that the timeless relation of implication which links the contents of the successive events plays a part in explaining why the inference took the course it did. Again, I am not maintaining that this relation of implication is the sole condition of the conscious passage, for there are many other conditions, such as an interest in knowing, being in normal health, perhaps having had a cup of coffee and not being at the moment distracted. But if one asks oneself why, with these premises in mind, one leaped to this conclusion rather than to the thought of cherry trees in May, one surely cannot disregard the fact that it is the conclusion required by the premises we just had in mind.

Indeed, we must note that the kind of explanation we are offering is doubly inconsistent with the epiphenomenalist account. That account holds, first, that the character of event *a* makes no difference to the occurrence of event *b*. But we can see in retrospect that unless an event having the character of *a*, that is, of being an apprehension of these premises, had occurred, there is no reason whatever to believe that the event *b* would have occurred. We can only believe, therefore, that the character of *a* did make a difference. Secondly, our explanation involves a *type of causation* of which epiphenomenalism knows nothing. We ordinarily think of the cause as preceding the effect. The entailment of the conclusion by the premises is neither before nor after the conclusion, because it is timeless. But since it does clearly contribute to the course of the inference, we must concede that causal influence is not confined to antecedents in time. Some critics, thinking this incredible, have insisted that the emergence in thought of the conclusion is rather due to a particular psychological event, the event of seeing that the premises entail the conclusion. This is both inconsistent with epiphenomenalism and logically circular. For what we have to explain is the emergence of the conclusion in the thinker's consciousness, and when he has seen that the conclusion is entailed, that conclusion is, of course, already before him. The critic is thus explaining the emergence by assuming that it has already occurred. What we must say, strange as it is from the naturalist point of view, is that it is not the thought of the entailment that contributes to the emergence of the conclusion, but the actual entailment itself. A. E. Taylor once wrote, in language alien to present ways of speech, of 'the initiative of the eternal'. That, to be sure, is metaphysics. It is none the worse for that. Indeed, I would suggest that when empirical and natural science reaches the level of human thinking it must either incorporate metaphysics or go bankrupt.

A theory that allows no influence of thought on behaviour has another consequence, which to some will be more disturbing. It is self-contradictory, in the sense in which it is self-contradictory to deny the Cartesian *cogito*; the thesis is inconsistent with its own enunciation and defence. When one states the thesis, it is with the intention of reporting one's belief to others; we assume that this intention will affect what we say, and without that assumption we should not have been so foolish as to entertain the intention at all. Again, we assume that it is possible, when considering whether a thesis is true, to order our thought about it with reference to our purpose, inhibiting ourselves from wandering off into irrelevance, dwelling specially on matters of greater importance, and moving on to a conclusion appointed by the weight of the evidence. If this process were not possible, there would be no point in thinking at all. Eminent present-day philosophers of science, following Santayana, whether knowingly or not, describe what happens in a course of thinking as follows. 'The dark engine of nature', as Santayana calls the process in the brain, grinds along a track of purely physical causality. There is presumed to be no such thing as purpose or relevance or evidence or necessity among the neurones of the cortex. Nevertheless, these churnings of the dark engine have a surprising way of pushing up into consciousness at the end conclusions that have every appearance of having been reached by the consideration of, and constraint by, relevant evidence. Since the working of the machine has been unguided by the purpose of the thinker, this happy ending is, relatively to that purpose, a piece of pure luck. Surely if our naturalistic psychologists really believed this about their own thinking, they would lack the heart to launch themselves on the process. If this process takes its course unaffected by considerations of relevance, and if the seen weight of evidence can make no difference to one's acceptance of a thesis, why think? Similarly, if the argument, transmitted to another mind, can make no difference to his conclusions, why try to communicate? The constant conduct of the naturalist in presenting and defending his theory is inconsistent with the truth of that theory.

Consider, thirdly, the moral aspect of this sort of naturalism. A moral choice commonly involves the contemplation of two or more courses of action and the election of one as the right one. There is much difference of opinion as to what makes a course right, but we do not need at the moment to raise that thorny question. Most of us would probably agree that there is some course of action that would be the right one to take, and that we should find and do it if we can. We should probably agree, further, that if we see or believe a course to be right, we ought to take it, and that in taking it because we do see or believe it to be right lies the highest form of moral goodness, even if not the only one, as Kant supposed. Now, the interesting thing is that for the kind of naturalism before us there is no such thing as a good action in this sense. No one ever chooses anything because he sees that he ought to, for one psychical event never causes another. No choosing or deciding to act in a certain way ever causes us to behave in that way, since that would be an action of the mental on the physical. Moral goodness in this sense ceases to be.

Indeed, the ethical consequences go far beyond this. On the theory, how could we even be egoists? The egoist is the man who habitually chooses his own good in preference to that of others. But to act with reference to one's own good once more assumes the possibility of the mental controlling the physical. Again, there can be no moral responsibility, since if nothing one's body does springs out of one's own volition, how could one be held accountable for it? Rewards and punishments would be pointless. They could not be justified retributively for the reason just given; they could not be justified as encouragement or deterrence, since that assumes that the anticipation of results may affect behaviour.

It seems fair to say that if no one ever acts as he does because he sees, or thinks he sees, one action to be better than another, ethics is being ruled off the board. It is true, however, that this type of naturalism has one advantage over behaviourism. It can recognize intrinsic values, even though it has no place for the pursuit of them. Pleasure and affection, knowledge and the experience of beauty, lie in consciousness, and for this sort of naturalism consciousness at least exists. On the other hand, for a consistent behaviourist there are no values, since there is no place for them in this universe. When Mr Rogers objected to Mr Skinner that science could decide questions of means but not of ends, Mr Skinner replied: 'Whether we like it or not, survival is the ultimate criterion.'[1] This reduction of value to fact, reminiscent of Herbert Spencer, is the inevitable behaviourist reply. It is perhaps enough to point out regarding it (1) that in some cases (extreme agony and helplessness, for example) survival is an evil not a good, and (2) that survival may have various forms, in which some are obviously better than others. In neither case could survival be the ultimate test.

There is one other consideration that should be mentioned if we are to see in perspective the attempt of natural scientists to deal with the mind. It is the extraordinary oscillation in their thought as to the meaning of 'physical'. In the usage of Professor Skinner, the term seems to mean what it does for common sense; physical objects are such things as tables, chairs, and one's body, which are all on a common footing in public space; and their shapes and sizes, weights and colours, belong to them in their own right. This thought of the body as a solid independent thing has also been

---

[1] *Cumulative Record,* 34.

standard among epiphenomenalists. Huxley, who invented the name, took this view for granted until he read Hume. From then on he was in trouble. Hume's thesis about the sensible order seemed irrefutable, namely that everything we immediately experience belongs in the realm of consciousness. But if you combine this with the common-sense view of the body, as Huxley tried to do, you end in a never-never land in which the universe has all but vanished. First you hold that the body, the solid observable thing, has a mind connected with it which is a useless by-product or shadow. You then find that this body, which is basic to mind, is itself a set of characters and relations all of which belong within consciousness. Hence the body, the basic reality for Huxley the biologist, becomes for Huxley the philosopher the fragment of a shadow.

Now, it is notorious, natural, and probably right that scientists should not concern themselves much with philosophy. In the common-sense view of the body they feel themselves, as Professor Skinner does, to be secure and with their feet on the ground. But this common-sense body, is of course, very far from that of the physicist, whose views of matter are taken by other scientists, at least in their professional moments, as authoritative. And if these others did think of the body as the physicist does, the mind-body problem would be transformed for them. It is instructive to see what has happened in the thought of that wonderful old man, Lord Russell. In his youth he was the leader of the extreme realists, holding that every quality of physical things, including one's own body, existed independently of its being experienced. In his last important work, *Human Knowledge: Its Scope and Limits*, he comes round to the view that everything we immediately experience lies in the realm of consciousness. The body is not now a solid object among others in public space, but a boiling mass of unobserved and unobservable particles in a space of their own. And the mind is not a set of shadowy processes, but the whole 'choir of heaven and furniture of earth' that forms one's experienced world.

Russell the ancient sage is nearer the truth, I think, than Russell the bright young man. And if so, the place of consciousness in the scientific scheme of things is transformed. For consciousness is then no longer a tenuous shadow whose very existence is doubtful, but our base and starting point, the region of greatest certainty, while the realm of the physical becomes a twilight zone of inference, of hypotheses about the invisible and impalpable, of flights of meta-physical speculation. Matter has become, says Russell with a dash of his pleasant hyperbole, 'a wave of probability undulating in nothingness'. No one knows much about it; Bohr's model of the atom was outdated a decade or two later. Meanwhile both the values and the certainties of life, which lie in the sphere of consciousness, are much the same as they were thousands of years ago.

IX. CONSCIOUSNESS NOT EXPENDABLE

It is time scientists ceased to downgrade consciousness, without which they would have no starting-point and no verification for their theories, and, of course, no theories either. Is there not something grotesque in the sight of psychologists, literally the scientists of the mind, denying that they have any distinct subject-matter, and insisting that even in this denial they are only talking? Why do they sacrifice their own discipline in this manner? Primarily because of a misplaced notion of rigour. Because thoughts and feelings are not public and measurable, they are not quite respectable as objects of study. If the inner life were accepted on its own terms as permeated by purpose, oriented toward values and striving to realize them, the purity of strictly natural science would be contaminated. True research and the hope for significant advance lie in turning away from teleology towards purpose-free physical science. And all this in spite of the fact that the one first-rate contribution to psychology in this century, that of Freud, sprang from a precisely opposite assumption.

If we may hope for the time when physical scientists will no longer down-grade the mind, we may perhaps also hope for the day when psychologists will cease to apologize for their minds. When they write an article or an argument, they are surely aware that their purpose has determined the course of their thought, and this knowledge is more certain than any theory that would make their thought the mirror or by-product of a hypothetical and purposeless process in their brains. When they find themselves acting for the good or the hurt of another, they may be more certain that they are acting for some purpose—even if they may be mistaken as to what it is—than they are of any theory of the conservation of energy or matter (assuming these still to be distinct) that would veto this kind of action. In holding to the existence and efficacy of consciousness they are not being naïve or rash; the rashness belongs rather to those who would deny the obvious in the interest of a speculative theory. A generation ago G. E. Moore, in his 'Defence of Common

Sense', brought the metaphysicians up short by asking them whether they were more certain that time and space were unreal than that they were writing a sentence on paper spread out in space before them and taking a minute or two to do it. Have we not a similar right to ask the metaphysicians of science whether they are really more certain that the energy in the physical universe remains in exact balance than that they have sometimes decided successfully to stand up or sit down. Such questions tend to put our 'certainties' in a better order of priority.

I am not, of course, opposing metaphysics; far from it. But I follow Hume in thinking that human nature is the best launching-pad for metaphysics, and that we should not, in the interest of ulterior conclusions, distort the facts about it at the outset. And those facts are not what scientific naturalism would have us think they are. In human nature as we know it at first hand, our thinking, feeling, and acting are suffused with purpose; our reasoning at its best is under controls of which empirical science knows nothing; our processes of creation in art and literature are, so to speak, Aristotelian processes, not Newtonian, in which that which is coming to be somehow determines the course of its own fulfilment; actions may be genuinely obligatory, and our sense of this may bring them about. These processes cannot be understood, or even properly studied, by a science whose model is physics.

In short, as was suggested at the beginning, science is at a cross-roads. Either it should reconceive its programme so that it can deal with the facts of mind, or, admitting that these facts fall beyond its province, it should cheer the birth of a more humane and sensitive discipline that can deal with them as they are.

TOWARDS A FUNCTIONAL
NATURALISM

J. H. RANDALL, JR

In 1934 I was asked to write a brief piece giving a kind of philosophical self-portrait, modelled on the series of *Die Philosophie in
Selbstdarstellung*, published in Germany during the 1920s, which
had already awakened emulation in two volumes of *Contemporary
British Philosophers* and two volumes of *Contemporary American
Philosophers*. The new volume was to pick up the odds and ends,
and to be entitled *Philosophy Today and Tomorrow*. I was presumably to serve as an odd rather than as an end, and to belong to
tomorrow rather than to today, as I was a young man of thirty-five
who had published some historical work, but as yet very little in
the way of philosophical analysis. Since in those days it was still
necessary to come to terms with Dialectical Materialism, I entitled
the piece 'Historical Naturalism'. I have continued to hold that
Nature and History are the two themes that are major concerns of
an inquiring philosophical mind, and the position I there set forth
I should not seriously quarrel with today.

But though that article states fairly well, I still judge, the position I had arrived at in 1934, in the last thirty years I have, I hope,
learned something more. That something more has not superseded
the earlier framework of 'naturalism' and (dare I use the term?)
'historicism'. It has rather developed within that framework, and
has, I hope enriched it. It was, as I now look back, in the 1930s that
I arrived at certain central ideas in several fields that I have since
been exploring, following out their ramifications and implications.

Hence it may be appropriate for one who first called himself a
'historical naturalist' to recount how he came to that position and
what he has managed to do with it.

Thus in a course in metaphysics in 1939 and 1940 I put Aristotle's
notion of *ousia* together with Dewey's notion of 'the situation', and,
with the assistance of the terminology of my teacher, F. J. E.
Woodbridge, came out with the idea of Substance as a co-operation
of processes—a notion I have since been trying to push into all the

branches of the Theory of Nature. A little earlier, in a course in the Theory of History, I started with American objective relativism in general, and Woodbridge's, as found in his *Purpose of History*, in particular, and pushed them into a full analysis of historical method and knowledge.

It was during the early thirties also that my ideas on religion began to assume a more settled form. The previous decade they had been predominantly negative and anti-theistic. But in an article in the *Christian Century* on 'The Order of Splendor' I began to take a more positive attitude towards the religious dimension of the Divine in the universe, to view religious 'knowledge' as symbolic rather than literal, and the functions of religion as not primarily noetic. These views crystallized in a section in *Preface to Philosophy* (1946), 'The Meaning of Religion for Man', written during the war. They were extended and deepened through a number of seminars given jointly with Paul Tillich during the forties, until his retirement from Union Theological Seminary. The fruits of this discussion with Tillich appeared in a piece, 'Naturalistic Humanism', in a volume *Patterns of Faith in America Today* (1957), and in my Mead-Swing lectures at Oberlin, *The Role of Knowledge in Western Religion* (1958).

These central ideas, that took controlling form in my mind during the late thirties, are, I judge, the source of whatever originality my more recent philosophical analyses may display. My concern with the history of philosophy, if in point of fact it was born simultaneously with my interest in philosophical analysis, and if both took form in a freshman course with John J. Coss at Columbia in 1915–16, was at least developed earlier, through the practical demands of teaching.

This brief chronological sketch has been offered to make clear that what I wrote in 1934, thirty-four years ago, still seems to hold: 'The author is aware of no intellectual crisis in his life, no loss of faith, no new gospel eagerly embraced. This means, he supposes, that the prejudices with which he started are still with him.' There has since been a steady and, I hope, fruitful development, which has brought what seem to be deeper and more illuminating insights. But there has been no radical reorientation.

Perhaps the greatest changes have been in my attitude toward religion. I entered college taking for granted the liberal Christianity my father believed in and preached, without what is today called a strong emotional commitment. As a freshman I was rather critical of the naturalism I encountered in my teachers, especially John J. Coss, and later Woodbridge and Wendell T. Bush. I was and still am greatly interested in religion—without such an interest, I have come to doubt whether any philosophizing can be other than truncated. But religion has never meant to me personally the fruits of an unquestioned faith. It has meant rather a fascinating set of problems, man's attempt to grapple both practically and intellectually with the nature of the world within which human life has its setting. I found in my teachers an equal interest, combined with a naturalistic interpretation of religion. Coss and Woodbridge were graduates of Union Theological Seminary; Bush was passionately concerned with the public aspects of religion, its ritual and art; John Erskine was addicted equally to expounding Santayana to all his classes, and to attendance at St Mary the Virgin's. Insensibly I absorbed this naturalistic attitude, until my initial objections seemed foolish.

The summer after my freshman year, I wrote a long study of Schleiermacher. His religious naturalism, which makes religious beliefs symbols of emotional attitudes—of 'the religious consciousness'—rather than of cognitive ideas, has undoubtedly had a lasting effect on my attitude; Santayana has always seemed to me to be in the same tradition. As a graduate student, I was introduced by Arthur Cushman McGiffert to the fascinating story of Christian thought, which has ever since been a central concern. From 1918 to his death in 1932, Felix Adler taught me many things: the ethical interpretation of the religious tradition; the concern with 'Godhead'; the great gulf between man as he inescapably is, as an empirical being, and man as he might be, as a member of the 'ethical manifold'; the ethical limitations of the teachings of Jesus.

After passing through a negative and anti-theistic phase, which culminated in my signing of the original Humanist Manifesto in 1932, I changed about 1935 to a more positive attitude towards the Divine as a feature of the natural world. I became less interested in merely denying theistic beliefs, and more concerned with reinterpreting them in naturalistic terms, while co-operating in practice with those who hold them. This led to the attempt to work out more precisely the non-cognitive functions of religious beliefs, and is signalized in the wartime study, 'The Meaning of Religion for Man', dating from the beginning of my close association with Paul Tillich, and in the last chapter of *The Role of Knowledge in Western Religion* (1958), embodying the fruits of that association. Perhaps the present state of my attitude is best expressed in the statement on 'Naturalistic Humanism'.

As a result of the influence of both Felix Adler, with his broad horizons, and of my father, with his passionate internationalism, I early came to feel as far too restricted not merely any single Christian tradition but the Christian tradition as a whole. This meant no swallowing up of differences that are essential in a single universal religion, but rather a religious pluralism, in which many religions not only complement each other, but can, hopefully, co-operate creatively with one another. Such a view is obviously bound up with a symbolic interpretation of specific and conflicting religious beliefs, something more familiar in other religions than in the too exclusive Christian tradition. I am convinced every religiously sensitive man should join as many different religious organizations as he can find time and energy for. After growing up with my father in a liberal Baptist church, I went with him to the Community Church of New York. I have long been a member of the Ethical Culture Society, and of the Congregational Church of Peacham, Vermont. I am a member of the Wider Quaker Fellowship. In the only non-Christian culture—outside of New York City—in which I have travelled, the Muslim, I have been much impressed by the Quaker-like simplicity of Islam. The problems of the relationships between the great world religions today are central, and have become primary in my concern with religion.

I

My first philosophic ideas were undoubtedly absorbed from my father. I can hardly remember when I did not with my mother attend church to hear him preach. But though it was my father who had prepared me to welcome it, it was in my college teachers that I found philosophic inspiration. The teachers at Columbia during my student days, 1915–22, were surely a distinguished band. I cannot recall one who was mediocre, or who did not at some time strike fire.

The student was doubtless none too ready to yield up his mind to those who taught him. It would perhaps be better to leave that behind, and to go on to the latest philosophical fashion—like the citizens of ancient Athens, to be eager to hear some new thing. The student, grown older—much older—cannot do this thing. To go on—yes—for these teachers all pointed forward. They none of them wished to create disciples, they all directed one on further. But to go back—or to branch off at a sharp tangent—or to take a different road—that would be to commit an act of disloyalty. It would be even worse. It would be to compromise one's own integrity—the integrity of that intellectual personality these men first revealed to him these many years ago.

The student has doubtless travelled far from the teachings that inspired him in that early morning of life. He has gone on, and never felt in the least constrained by those teachings. For they were in essence not a restriction but an emancipation: they proclaimed an open not a closed world. He has doubtless said more, but he cannot deny what his teachers said. He cannot break with their wisdom. He cannot but remain loyal.

In my freshman year I encountered two courses in philosophy. One was an introduction to philosophy, conducted by John J. Coss, a young and energetic graduate of Wabash College and of Union Seminary, just recently back from several years of study in Germany. He had been caught by Dewey's vision of applying intelligence to social affairs, and he preached a gospel of social control. But we studied Paulsen's *Introduction to Philosophy*, even then an old-fashioned but excellent textbook of late nineteenth-century idealism, admirably suited to serve as the foil for Dewey's ideas, but in itself opening up all the traditional philosophical problems. I was fascinated at the disclosure of this new intellectual world. On the whole, I tended to side with Paulsen against Coss and Dewey: the German then seemed the richer in ideas. But most of all, in this course I made the acquaintance of John Coss. Coss had a genius for singling out young students of promise, and then looking after all their interests with paternal care. He must have thought he saw possibilities in me, for he became a fast friend. He was the friend of everyone in the Department, but he had the gift of making each one feel that his regard for you was something special. His affection and his loyalty went out equally to others in that class of 1919, but I am certain that this side of Heaven I shall never find a truer guide, mentor, and friend.

My other course in philosophy as a freshman was actually a course in Lessing, Schiller, and Goethe, conducted by F. J. W. Heuser, ostensibly a philosophically-minded teacher of German literature, but also a master of the thought of the *Aufklärung* (he also taught a course in Schopenhauer and Nietzsche). I learned of the philosophical currents of the *Aufklärung*, and was duly fascinated. Here, too, was philosophy, now in a historical context, where the problems could all be seen in their genesis, and their import.

By the end of my freshman year I knew I wanted to study for honours in philosophy. At that time a philosophy sequence followed up the required freshman introductory course in the sophomore year with Dean Woodbridge's course in the history of philosophy. Woodbridge believed in beginning with the Greeks—you could go on from there anywhere, as Western philosophy has. He arranged the curriculum accordingly. Students normally went on with Dewey, as I did myself in my junior year. For Columbia's best philosophers even then taught undergraduates, as they have continued to do. From Dean Woodbridge I anticipated much. For I had met him at a fraternity initiation. He spoke, and he won my soul, both by what he said and by the way he said it. He was a master of the spoken word, a born speaker, artless master of all the arts of speech. He spoke on friendship, and, taking as his text the *Lysis*, gave one of his inimitable analyses and paraphrases of that superb dialogue. So the budding sophomore expected much of Dean Woodbridge.

He was not disappointed. Indeed, the month was not over, and Plato well begun, before he knew what he had to do with his life. It was not a decision taken: there was no thought of choice. He had to study philosophy, and such philosophy as Dean Woodbridge not so much taught as was. There is no problem about how to enlist future college teachers. It is irrelevant to aptitude tests and all that. All that is needed is a great intellectual personality. And if a college cannot furnish that, there is no use trying to recruit future ones. It had far better shut up shop. Fortunately, no college is so poor as not to possess a few. With them, the spark flashes, the soul takes fire, and the recruit is won.

I do not mean that as a sophomore I decided to make the teaching of philosophy a career. There was then no thought of teaching. It was merely that I had to study philosophy. When, as a second-year graduate student, Coss offered me the chance to teach, I was genuinely surprised. That I might teach philosophy had literally never occurred to me. The idea came as a novelty, but it was welcomed. In fact, I drifted insensibly into college teaching, with never a conscious decision or resolve.

That Woodbridge has been my great philosophical inspiration, that he has been the chief factor in my philosophical development, will come as a surprise to nobody. I have never attempted to conceal the obvious obligation; I have rather boasted of it. He has been my great teacher, along with Aristotle. He taught me how to understand the Greeks—with able assistance from Bush as to Plato. He taught me how to understand the history of philosophy. He taught me what Metaphysics is—and is not—and why it is important. He taught me the meaning of a philosophical naturalism. He gave my thought its fundamental realistic caste—a functional realism, like that of Plato and Aristotle—again with assistance from Bush. His essays still seem to me models of philosophical discourse. Perhaps above all he taught me to understand and appreciate Aristotle. For all his admiration for Plato's poetry, he was himself an incorrigible Aristotelian. And of all past teachers I have found Aristotle most stimulating and suggestive—the Aristotle I began by seeing through Woodbridge's eyes.

And yet my own philosophizing is judged, I believe, and probably rightly, to be a pushing of certain aspects—the more metaphysical and realistic aspects—of John Dewey's. It is Dewey's conception of the function of philosophizing as criticism I have been operating with. It is certain of Dewey's key ideas—like 'the situation', 'generic traits of experience', and 'transaction'—that I have pushed in my own attempts at philosophic analysis. Irwin Edman was kind enough to dedicate his last book to me as a 'Deweyan and Aristotelian'. Why do I not emphasize Dewey as my most influential teacher? Can all this be explained?

Yes, I think it can. As a junior I took Dewey's course in social and political philosophy. Coss had prepared me for Dewey, and I think I understood him. But that course was not central to my interest at the time. And it hardly revealed Dewey's controlling metaphysical ideas. The next year Dewey left for China, and was away during the entire course of my graduate study. I was not a personal student of Dewey's, nor did I ever enjoy with him a seminar, in which he was at his best as a teacher. My acquaintance with Dewey's thought has come mainly from his writings, above all, from *Experience and Nature*, which I studied carefully with a class when it came out. Of course, I have had innumerable chances to talk those writings over with him, and to receive much illumination. My experience with them has always been that after painfully working out a problem for myself I have then found that he had reached my solution beforehand. But never by my path. And it has always taken quite an effort to follow his own course in reaching our common truth. I fear I have never been able to think like Dewey. I should like to believe I think like Woodbridge.

Actually, Dewey and Woodbridge were very close together philosophically, in all but their very different languages. I long ago gave up trying to explain to students the precise difference. Woodbridge uses the language of the philosophies of being, Dewey that of the philosophies of experience—usually of Hegelian experience, not British. This confuses students today, who have forgotten the Hegelian tongue. I find the former language, that of being, more congenial myself, but I hope I can understand both. It is largely the same philosophy, but it is good to have more than one language in which to express it, lest we become entangled in our own terminology and mistake our words for things. Bush had a gift for expounding this common philosophy in still other tongues, with Jamesian metaphors.

And Aristotle? He uses Woodbridge's language of being—rather, Woodbridge used his—but the Aristotelianism of Aristotle is what Dewey, perhaps through Hegel, has singled out and pushed. He disentangles it from the Platonism remaining in Aristotle himself, and puts it in a still wider context in experience. Dewey can thus be said to be, in what I hope is an intelligible sense, 'more Aristotelian' than Aristotle himself. He has travelled further than Aristotle did away from Platonism towards the experienced world, from which Plato was prone to abstract, So Woodbridge, Dewey, and Aristotle seem to me, in what strikes me as significant and important in their thought to be actually very close together. They are all, in our present-day labels, functional realists and objective relativists, contextualists. The thought of each can be made to illuminate that of the other two. And in my own attempts at philosophical analysis, at metaphysical analysis, I should say, following Woodbridge, I have endeavoured, since the 1930s, to effect something of that mutual illumination.

II

For some ten years of early teaching my writing was largely on various projects in the history of thought, of which the chief was *The Making of the Modern Mind* (1926), written as a textbook for freshmen in the Contemporary Civilization course at Columbia. My own philosophical analysis emerged later, and more slowly. For some time I resisted the general atmosphere of philosophic naturalism, and especially the name, which seemed to me then confusing.

With the continuing help of Bush and his sensible indifference to names, and finally with the careful study of Dewey's *Experience and Nature*, I was at last won over. I had not heard these Carus lectures delivered at Union Seminary: in 1922 I was away on my honeymoon. They came to me with a great impact. Here was one piece of philosophic writing, I flattered myself, that I could understand every word of, and agree with completely. My reaction was like that of Justice Holmes: it seemed to me, this is the way the world goes. That volume has always been for me Dewey's masterpiece. It seemed not to contradict but to supplement Woodbridge's systematic statement in his *Realm of Mind*. And it freed Aristotle's functional realism and contextualism from all the constricting elements of Platonism in Aristotle himself. Here was an 'experimental' and a 'functional' naturalism I could wholeheartedly endorse.

Gradually there began to take form in my mind a philosophic enterprise. To start from Dewey's functional naturalism, to rephrase it with something of Woodbridge's emphasis on structure and his realism, and to state it in terms of the functionalism, the objective relativism, and contextualism and the operationalism and behaviourism, of Aristotle—that was a philosophic vision and programme that made sense to me. It held the great promise of shaping a keen analytical and critical tool. In some sense, though I hope I have been guided by the nature of the subject-matter to which I have tried to apply it, like religion, that vision and that programme have dominated everything I have tried to do in philosophy since.

With my natural leaning toward an historical approach, I set out with a course on 'The Emergence of Contemporary Philosophic Naturalism'. I started with James Mill, the British tradition at its nadir, and went on to John Stuart Mill's honest reconstruction of his father's assumptions into a radical empiricism and an experimental naturalism. I then took the idealists, T. H. Green and F. H. Bradley, showing how Green's strong Kantian structuralism, his dissolving of all 'feeling' into 'thought', provoked a reaction in Bradley—as in his contemporary Dewey—to an equally strong emphasis on 'feeling' and immediate experience. I showed how Bradley in the end reached a position that is in all but name a functional naturalism. From there I went to the realists of the next generation. I analysed the emergent evolution of Lloyd Morgan and Samuel Alexander, and led up to Whitehead, whose successive works were coming out during the period I was actively carrying on this course. Whitehead's many ideas I have found very suggestive, though his system is an obvious *tour de force*. I was thus able to exhibit naturalism as the product of two waves of criticism: first, of the idealistic criticism of the empiricists and their structureless world, and then of the scientific criticism brought by the realists, directed against the idealists, and putting structure in the wider context of experience in its non-reflective aspects. Naturalism thus emerged as a more critical and a more scientific statement of the total subject-matter of idealistic metaphysics.

In the middle thirties I resolved to go at the matter more directly. I began to give a course in Aristotle's writings, emphasizing those that fit in with my programme, and best bring out his functionalism, his behaviourism, and his contextualism. Starting with the *De anima*, where I laid stress on the concluding five chapters of Book III, the active side of behaviour, we have gone on to the *Physics* and the *De generatione et corruptione*, finishing usually with Books Zeta, Eta, and Theta of the *Metaphysics*. I have thus taken Aristotle as the very inventor of a functional 'naturalism'. I have always found this a most exciting course, and feel that I have a thorough grasp on at least these aspects of Aristotle's thought: in discussion it seems to me luminously transparent. The repeated readings of the Greek text have led to conclusions incorporated in my book on Aristotle. In rounding out that volume, I had occasion to study other Aristotelian writings I had not paid much attention to: the *De coelo*, the *Rhetoric*, and the minor biological writings. In them all I have found a wealth of suggestive ideas, and the development of a consistent viewpoint.

By the late thirties I felt I was ready to tackle directly a more systematic and analytical treatment of the two philosophical themes that interested—and still interest—me the most, History and Nature. I began to work up courses dealing with their problems directly, drawing on a wide variety of other positions as points of reference and often as foils, but eschewing any temptation at historical treatment. To the first course I gave the characteristically Woodbridgean title 'The Theory of History'. By this I mean a critical examination of the historical aspect of existence, and of the concepts by means of which men may find it intelligible. For the second I might have used Woodbridge's title, 'The Theory of Nature'. For I employ 'nature' as synonymous with all there is, as the inclusive, all-embracing concept, corresponding to 'being' for the Greeks or to 'reality' for the objective idealist. But, provoked by prevailing prejudices, I preferred to follow Woodbridge himself again, and to employ unashamedly the title, 'Metaphysics, Analytical and Empirical'.

The Theory of History, which I first taught in 1938, I thus take as itself a branch of metaphysics, dealing with both the temporal aspect of existence and with our knowledge of that temporal aspect —both with history as *Geschichte, was geschieht*, and as *Historia*, investigation—both with what has occurred in the past, and with our knowledge of that past. Finding the idealistic discussions of historical knowledge, in the Germans and the Italians of the last two generations, and in Collingwood, too alien to my own views to be profitable, I tried to follow the Americans, like Woodbridge, Morris R. Cohen, and Maurice Mandlebaum, in their realistic conception of historical knowledge. But I also adopted the objective relativism of Woodbridge's *Purpose of History*, which had impressed me greatly when it came out in 1916. In the Theory of History I found two major problems: how the present can understand and explain the past, and how the past, so understood, can illuminate and help us understand the present. On the first question, I largely followed Woodbridge, and, when it appeared in 1938, the relevant section of Dewey's *Logic*, which as usual seemed to have anticipated my conclusions. Perhaps the most novel idea to which my analysis led me was the notion of the 'focus' of a history, in terms of which it is selected, which I tried to locate in problems faced—Cassirer's *Aufgabe*. On the second problem, I tried to reconstruct the genetic method into a defensible form, in the spirit of Dewey, against the criticisms of Woodbridge, Cohen, and Sidney Hook. I found myself led into a pluralistic and institutional social philosophy. I also endeavoured to make precise the notion of historical determinism as a 'limiting' or setting of boundaries, and to find a place within those limits for the obvious fact of historical decision. The upshot is not too far from where the pluralistic Germans like Karl Mannheim and Karl Popper have come out, but is clearly reached by a rather different path.

At the meeting of the American Philosophical Association in Middletown in 1938 I set forth some of these views in a symposium with Arthur O. Lovejoy. I tried again to make my position clearer in Bulletin 6 of the Social Science Research Council. There, the erratic ideas of Charles Beard, I am afraid, tended to obscure what seemed to me my own clarity. Some of the fruits of my analysis I presented in a Trumbull lecture at Yale, on 'History and the Social Sciences', printed in the memorial volume for Morris Cohen,

Freedom and Reason (1951). I extended my horizons to speculative philosophies of history—Vico, Herder, Condorcet, Hegel, and Marx—in a course at the New York Society for Ethical Culture on the philosophy of history. In preparing the section on the Theory of History for my *Nature and Historical Experience*, I rewrote these papers and added others dealing with material from the latter part of my course. But I still hope to write a full-scale book on the Theory of History.

The Metaphysics I approached more circumspectly. In 1938–9 I gave a course in 'The Metaphysical Implications of Language', as I wanted to come to terms with contemporary nominalistic approaches. But in this I found myself involved in all the historical problems of metaphysics, and it led me far beyond language to deal with them even sketchily. Having thus learned that I could not approach metaphysics in restricted fashion, in the fall of 1940 I offered a course in the subject itself. I thus began my attempt to make Dewey and Aristotle illuminate each other, with assistance from Woodbridge. To acquaint students with the latter's thought —he had died the previous May—I took his metaphysical essays in *Nature and Mind* as texts and points of departure. I brought out his conception of structure, and then, by introducing the distinction between potentiality or powers and actuality or operations, I was led to the further distinction between functional and formal structure, and so to Woodbridge's own contrast between 'behaviour' and 'structure'—what I call 'formal structure'. With these tools, I analysed Aristotle's Substance, identifying it with Dewey's Situation, as a co-operation of powers or of processes, and tried to explore the relations involved. That led in turn to the analysis of various philosophical types of 'situation': the perceiving situation, the linguistic situation, the mental situation, the psychological situation in general, the artistic situation, the aesthetic situation, the moral situation, the religious situation, all in terms of an objective relativism and contextualism, and of a functional, behaviouristic psychology. By the time I left for a sabbatical in February, I could flatter myself that I had worked out a set of distinctions capable of handling in fresh terms many of the standing metaphysical problems, including those of perception, of determinism, and of human freedom—to say nothing of discovering just where Hume went wrong on causation.

Some of this material was written up in papers and published in *Nature and Historical Experience*. The paper on 'An Empirical,

Naturalistic, and Behaviouristic Account of Signs, Signification, Universals, and Symbols' grew out of a seminar on language with Arthur F. Bentley in 1940, in which Irwin Edman and Ernest Nagel also took part. It omits an analysis of language and communication. This part of my course, on 'The Art of Language and the Linguistic Situation: a Naturalistic Analysis', was published separately in the *Journal of Philosophy* in 1963.

III

When asked as to my central interests in philosophy, I have in the past usually replied that, aside from the history of philosophy, they are focused on metaphysics, lumping together my two concerns with the Theory of History and the Theory of Nature. But for me metaphysics includes also a metaphysical analysis of all the major cultural activities of man, not only science and the pursuit of knowledge, but also art, the moral life and religion as well. By a 'metaphysical analysis' I mean an analysis of the fundamental traits of an an activity, of the concepts in terms of which it may be understood, of its relation to other human activities, and of its implications for the character of the world in which it is carried on by human beings in co-operation with the environment of nature. I mean a seeing it in perspective, as it were, and in the context of the rest of the experienced world, instead of dealing with it in the isolation appropriate to a technical analysis in its own terms. And while I have been sharpening my tools of analysis I have become more and more interested in applying them to these cultural activities. My growing concern with the analysis of religion, which I set out by commenting upon, is only one case in point. Two such activities in which I am much concerned, but have as yet hardly attempted to analyse systematically, are art and the moral life.

In the chapter on 'Quality, Qualification, and the Aesthetic Transaction', I found myself led from a consideration of the metaphysical status of Quality—which, I tentatively conclude, can be viewed as derivative—to the analysis of the process of qualification in the aesthetic transaction, and in the prior artistic transaction. What is there briefly sketched has seemed to me suggestive, and I want to go on to a fuller analysis of these two transactions or situations. The distinction between the artistic and the aesthetic experience is one that was driven home in one of Dewey's most suggestive courses, which he unfortunately never wrote up, 'Varieties of Philosophic Experience'.

I want to follow this up, because I by no means relegate a consideration of art to the appendix. Rather, with Aristotle and Dewey, I regard art as a fundamental—indeed, as the most inclusive—metaphysical category, under which all the rest can be subsumed. Hence a clear analysis of the artistic situation when it is also functioning aesthetically—the way I should try to make sense out of the messy modern notion of 'fine art'—ought to throw much light on the metaphysical implications of art in general.

Over the years I have, of course, written much on various themes connected with the moral life. The inspiration of Felix Adler and John Dewey has been controlling, and I have tried to combine the two: Adler's insights into moral experience, and his attempted formulation of an ethical ideal, and Dewey's more Aristotelian objective relativism, and his analysis of moral criticism. In 1954 I wrote a paper on 'The Wrong and the Bad', inspired by a tiredness at the arguments between Oxford and Cambridge over the respective claims of the Right and the Good. My most recent attempt at combining Adler and Dewey was my Felix Adler Memorial Lecture, 'The Ethical Challenge of a Pluralistic Society' (1959).

But I have never been called upon to teach a systematic course in ethics. My approaches have been largely from the background of my pluralistic social philosophy. I have not as yet attempted a careful analysis of the moral situation by means of the tools of my metaphysical distinctions. Such an analysis I have at times been led close to. Thus it is clear that personality is not a starting-point, but rather the outcome of a process of personalization—I find myself returning to my father's older conception of 'the culture of personality'. And the same holds for moral character; it is not a matter of prior motive, but rather an achievement. An act, in these terms, would be right, not if its motives are right alone, and not even if its objective consequences are good, alone. An act is right only if it contributes to a process of moralization of the ethical performer, only if it heightens his sensitivity to moral values, and to the needs of personal relationships, and deepens his awareness of his true self and his controlling values, in relation to his obligations to others. This is a theme that needs further exploration.

IV

The self-portrait that will have emerged from these pages is of a man inspired by his teachers who continued along the path they pointed out to him. It might be said that he has never been able to free himself from their constricting hands, that he has continued to work upon problems central in their day, but left behind by the advance of the main body of the philosophical profession towards newer problems and towards a greater appreciation for technical virtuosity in the employment of some of the latest gadgets of analysis. But it might equally well be said that his teachers emancipated him from the assumptions controlling philosophical thought during the period of 'modern philosophy', now unhappily revived in the reactionary thinking of a later day, and from the problems, grown inherited and 'academic', that those assumptions needlessly generated.

For the truth is that philosophy is not a 'discipline' that can steadily pile up an accumulated body of knowledge and thus 'advance'. It is not a nicely defined field, with a clearly demarcated subject-matter of its own. Mark Van Doren used to complain that philosophy had no subject-matter. He is right. Philosophy is rather like the trouble-shooter for ever on call, who can direct the shafts of his light towards any intellectual problem that is generating difficulties. When it has the occasion, philosophy examines the fundamental assumptions in any field or area of human concern whose consequences are leading to tensions or conflcits with other fields and their assumptions. Philosophy, in a word, is a process of criticism, of both what passes for knowledge and what passes for good and evil. It is the criticism of assumptions of fact and assumptions of value. Men have notoriously many interests and many values, and they are not all alike in those they make central. What the individual philosopher will be called upon to clarify and criticize will depend upon the caller—upon the social and cultural demands of the world in which he is living—and also upon the specific kind of clarification and criticism it seems important to him to undertake.

Sometimes teachers of philosophy have no interests and values of their own, and hear only dimly the demands being made upon them by a culture in intellectual distress. When they have arrived at that parlous state of mind, they are then apt to devote themselves to purely 'academic' problems, as we say—that is, to problems inherited from an earlier day, and an earlier stage of cultural growth, when they once presented genuine difficulties and live options. Now, because men have different interests, and because the centre of their concern may be located in many different areas of human activity, because some make one such area of living central, while others focus upon a quite different one, there will always be a number of different philosophies in the world at the same time, often competing for men's allegiance, more often coexisting in the same cultural world. No single one of them can rule the others all out of order; though there has recently been, unhappily, an increasing tendency to try.

My own historical interests, perhaps my inborn curiosity and my desire for synthetic constructions and visions, my delight in the inexhaustible variety of the intellectual perspectives of men, have given me a genuine concern for all such philosophies in our world today, as in the past. But though I am perfectly willing to coexist with philosophies whose problems I do not myself feel deeply, and whose generating assumptions I cannot but challenge, indeed welcoming this variety of human thinking, this does not mean I must take them all seriously in dealing with the intellectual problems which today do strike me as important. I may be behind the times, still dealing with the outgrown problems of my youth— though the philosophical problems first raised by Plato and Aristotle have been meaningful for quite a time now, and will doubtless seem still living to a few more generations, when those of Wittgenstein, and even of Bertrand Russell, have been forgotten. Indeed, Wittgenstein spent the latter part of his life forgetting the problems of his *Tractatus* period; and in his own career Russell has outlived his own problems a dozen times. Or I may be ahead of my day, dealing with philosophical problems that will come to seem important when present fads and fashions have faded away. Or it may be rather that I have been focusing my attention on perennial problems, the problems that have recurred in some fashion; though each time in a very different guise, in every generation since the Greeks. I do think I know something of the history of Western philosophy, and possess some historical sense. So I am inclined myself to judge that the third possibility is the most likely. This is the more true, in that I have directed my own thinking not to the surface problems of the passing present but to the central problems of metaphysics. To push the figure of the trouble-shooter, I have been concerned with devising the best possible flashlight with which to illuminate any specific problem of intellectual readjustment, and with mapping the terrain where I must use it. For metaphysics is primarily just such an instrument for criticizing philosophical and intellectual assumptions: and it is, as Dewey calls it, 'the ground map of criticism'.

And it must not be forgotten that my own teachers, whose problems still seem the most important to me, are not merely those from whom I learned in the flesh between 1915 and 1925. Those men introduced me to other teachers, the great Greeks, and all those thinkers in the philosophical tradition who have risen above the specific issues of intellectual policy in their own day, to a vision of what is, and how it may be understood. With that long line of teachers I feel at home: they have furnished me my insights and my working tools of distinction. For me they are a part of the living past. Much of my professional life has been concerned with disentangling what is merely local and dated in their thinking from what is of enduring value. I think I have done a good enough job at it to make that distinction clear at least to myself. To work with these ideas of the great thinkers of the living past strikes me as far less restricting than to confine oneself to ideas that first entered the world around 1935. I once heard a very intelligent philosopher read a brilliant paper on moral philosophy. But she mentioned no ethical teachers or writers before the G. E. Moore of 1903. Such a limitation may have its place in discussing the philosophical implications of present-day physical theory. But in moral philosophy, it is hard to justify. If this be not shutting oneself off from the major sources of our moral wisdom, I do not know what self-restriction may be. Russell not long ago warned us, in his *Wisdom of the West*, that philosophizing did not begin with his conversations with Moore in 1918, nor yet in 1637; it began with the Greeks, and he who deliberately turns his back on the roots of our intellectual being is doomed to be shallow and wholly lacking in dimension.

No, I have gone my own way with what I have learned from the many teachers in the rich intellectual tradition that stems from the Greeks. Like Dewey, I have always found more inspiration in Continental than in British philosophizing. I might have gone to Germany to study, had not the war intervened. That had been the original intention of both my father and myself. In that case, I might have accepted as my own the idiom of Cassirer, or even of Husserl. But given my starting-point at Columbia, I fancy that under whatever sky my philosophy would have been about the same. I doubt whether a first-class philosopher has appeared in England since Bradley, or in Germany since Dilthey, or in France since Brunschvicg and Lalande.

Some specification is doubtless in order. The fashionable philosophies of the day are, in America, Logical Positivism; in England,

Wittgenstein's later Linguistic Analysis; on the Continent, Existentialism. In the midst of these latest fashions, I still prefer to go my own way. I have today nothing behind me but the tradition of Western philosophy, and the Greeks.

With Logical Positivism or Empiricism, I have always felt much sympathy. For it has been concerned with the philosophy of science, and has done much of value there in clarifying scientific concepts. But it has been orientated towards the physical sciences, whereas my own orientation has been towards the biological and human sciences, as well as towards the humanistic tradition, for which the Logical Positivists have rarely shown much sympathy, or indeed understanding. And Logical Positivism has disclaimed all ability to deal intellectually with values, whereas my own philosophizing is fundamentally concerned with the criticism of values. Since migrating *en bloc* to the U.S.A. after 1938, the Logical Positivists have each gone his own way, and today it is difficult to speak of any common position.

But they all started with a phenomenalistic and sensationalistic conception of experience, derived from Ernst Mach, that showed no trace of having learned from Darwin and biology, or from William James and psychology. This was a conception of experience from which I was delivered in my freshman year, and emancipated from for ever, after as a sophomore reading Aristotle. At this late date, how can I take such a philosophy seriously? As Woodbridge used to say, the Logical Positivists seemed to be trying to do with words what John Locke tried to do with 'ideas'. And they got into the same difficulties and the same impasses. So long as they try to operate with such an antiquated conception of experience, all their virtuosity with the techniques of symbolic logic will not enable them to work out a consistent philosophy.

With the later Wittgenstein I have felt less sympathy. I have read diligently his *Philosophical Investigations*, and the prior Blue and Brown books. It may be merely the result of my lack of any personal contact with his charismatic personality, but I have never found in any of his writings a single idea that seemed to me both novel and true. How he could have become the inspiration of a movement surpasses my understanding. I have indeed great sympathy with his notion of the therapeutic function of philosophic analysis. But I have myself found that historical analysis—of the assumptions generating unreal problems, of why they were made, of the impasses they led to, and of why we no longer need make those unfruitful assumptions—is for me, and my students, a far better therapeutic instrument than his appeal to ordinary language and its usages.

And as for the Oxford 'analysts' of today, interested not so much in therapy as in the elucidation of linguistic usage for its own sake, I share that interest, and their passion for clear distinctions; and I can only applaud their increasing urges towards functionalism. But that has always, from Aristotle on, been the beginning of philosophy, its propaedeutic. I cannot myself but go on to its substance. Without sharing Russell's emotions, since I do not suffer his personal involvement, I agree thoroughly with his recent criticisms. I can see no reason, save intellectual laziness, for confining philosophy to the analysis of the meaning of terms. Philosophy today, as Russell eloquently puts it, must be saturated with the latest scientific thinking: it must know the concepts and the assumptions out of which our formulations of scientific knowledge are built. It must know the intellectual tradition stemming from the Greeks in which both our philosophy and our science have their roots. Far from being irrelevant to philosophy, as Oxford philosophers hold, or even a positive detriment, as some at least have maintained, science and scholarship are essential to any fruitful philosophizing today. So, even when an able thinker like Gilbert Ryle comes out with conclusions I can wholeheartedly endorse, in his *Concept of Mind*, I must still go my own way, duly noting that Oxford is outgrowing its initial limitations in men of wider horizons, as in Stuart Hampshire, Strawson, or the work of Friedrich Weismann.

Continental Existentialism, now happily retiring into a wider Phenomenology, I find both more and less congenial than these other philosophies. Dewey once remarked, after hearing G. E. Moore on perception, 'I have said some hard things about the Germans in my day. But at least they were dealing with important problems.' I do not mean French Existentialism. I enjoy its literary products with the next man, but intellectually it is very derivative, and so far as my reading in Sartre and Marcel and others goes, of little philosophical significance. For Heidegger I have immense respect, and only admiration for his many new metaphysical insights and distinctions. What in his thought I find more congenial than in that of the British or the Viennese is his metaphysical analysis of the Situation, phrased in his own distinctive language, but quite close to Dewey's analysis, and perhaps equally turgid— though German gives one an initial advantage. I am very glad that my colleague Herbert W. Schneider, with whose thought I have always felt I had more in common than with that of any other living philosopher, finds equal inspiration in Heidegger's metaphysics.

What in Heidegger I find less congenial is his addiction to Kierkegaard and the experience of crisis, perhaps above all his being hypnotized by the idea of death. With Sidney Hook, I find death a good and beneficent feature of human life, not the source of existential anxiety. The experience of Kierkegaard, which Heidegger embodies in his analysis, corresponds to nothing whatever in my own. Nor, I suspect, does it find any answering echo in the vast majority of Americans, even those who embrace it as a literary fashion or a theological apologetic. But once take the Kierkegaard out of Heidegger, and he is a suggestive metaphysician—though hardly a reliable politician. I have often been tempted to try to translate him out of the Danish into the Greek, in which tongue he would be most intelligible, since he is saturated with Greek philosophy.

My own understanding of Existentialism has come in good part from my association with Paul Tillich. I am not trying to perpetrate a jest in saying that for me, Tillich and Heidegger mutually explain each other, and both add further dimensions to Dewey's analysis of experience. Once take the later Schelling out of Tillich, and again you have a metaphysician of great suggestiveness. The overtones of Tillich's 'Power of Being' and of the '*Sein*' of the later Heidegger are very harmonious. This, however, is just that element in the thought of both that my own metaphysical pluralism makes it very hard for me to appreciate, or even to stomach. I must still go my own way, glad for whatever illumination I can secure from any quarter, but under whatever sky still faithful to the enterprises of my teachers, those living and those dead but immortal.

V

But I do not wish to conclude on such a negative note. Disagreement with some of the fundamental assumptions of philosophies with a wide appeal in the philosophic profession today is far from my central concern. Those philosophers to whom these programmes appeal are, in my estimation, philosophers still. They feel their problems deeply, they have done important work upon them, and they have much still to do. I could only wish they would all reciprocate, and freely grant that I, as a philosopher, and those who share my conception of the philosophic enterprise, may be freely permitted as philosophers to do the work we regard as important. In this respect the Wittgensteinians are the worst offenders, probably because their gospel is the newest and glossiest, and they have the enthusiasm of a fresh evangel. The Logical Positivists have grown positively mellow with the years, and are now almost content with a division of labour. And the Existentialists, now that their crisis is receding, have also broadened their horizons. They never broke with the tradition of philosophy as completely as the others; they merely reinterpreted it, discovering that all good philosophers, from Plato—or Parmenides—down, and even including St Thomas, had been really sound Existentialists at heart. Who can deny them their comforting perspective?

But the Oxford analysts have been prone to declare that those who are not 'doing philosophy' in their own way are not really 'doing philosophy' at all. In the world today, this links them with the doughty commissars of Diamat as the two philosophical movements to which the *odium philosophicum* is essential. They see themselves as God's chosen philosophers. This is hardly an enviable position for responsible men to find themselves in. Fortunately, there are many signs that even Oxford dons can have second thoughts.

No, I have merely wanted to make plain why my own philosophic development has not led me in any of these directions, despite their *actualité*. In philosophy, as in other forms of poetry and imaginative writing, and unlike the case in science, the latest forms to appear upon the scene are not necessarily the best. They may be all we poor contemporaries are up to and can manage. My historical interests have kept me from sharing this widely held and no doubt comforting illusion. A present-day composer does not have to use exclusively the twelve-tone scale, though doubtless he will, like Stravinsky, be tempted to try his hand at it. To do so is surely the easiest way to appear to possess originality. It is much harder to employ the more traditional techniques of the masters to surpass their work. But is it originality that we really crave most from a philosophy? Surely in the twentieth century we have passed beyond that Romantic ideal of the nineteenth.

As Homer, whoever he was, is still the greatest of epic poets, though he came at the very beginning of our Western tradition, so, I have long been convinced, are Plato and Aristotle still the wisest philosophers our Western world has ever managed to bring forth.

This does not mean a twentieth-century mind can continue to parrot their words. We have learned too much, about the world, about the conditions of human life, yes, about man himself. Even our adolescent psychology has revealed facts about human nature that even Plato hardly did more than suspect—though it is not without significance that a man like Freud, groping for words and labels for his fresh insights, was forced to turn to the Greeks and their experience for help. Would that his followers always employed those intellectual symbols with the imagination of Plato, or of Freud himself! With all I think I have myself learned in the past thirty years, I can still say, what I said in my youth, that though Plato and Aristotle did not say the last word, without what they first said all words would be meaningless, and when it is forgotten they usually are.

But I can myself hardly be accused of a mere repetition, even of Aristotle's words, which are important, still less of Plato's, for whom the word killeth but the spirit maketh alive. Quite the reverse. Classical scholars would rather say, I have not attempted to reconstruct the thought of Plato, or even of Aristotle, as it existed in ancient Athens in the fourth century BC. I have rather instead viewed both through twentieth-century eyes—as though a man today could find or use any others! The scholars are doubtless right; though I think I have incidentally done that preliminary job, too. For in the main I have not tried to reconstruct Aristotle's thought with objectivity in all its completeness. I have tried to understand it, and to use it for my own purposes, which, as those of a twentieth-century man, are surely different from what his own were. For I have attempted to use it to criticize two thousand years of philosophical tradition, manifestly unknown to the man who walked the streets of Athens and paced the porch of the Lyceum. He stood at the beginning of that tradition, establishing it on firm ground—though to a reconstructing scholar, he probably thought of himself as consummating the traditions of the early Greeks, of Empedocles and Democritus and the rest. I myself stand at the point at which we have arrived, using those same ideas to try to influence and modify that tradition, and to give it a new direction.

And such an enterprise involves selecting from Aristotle those ideas that promise to be fruitful for such purposes, content to leave the others in the hands of the 'objective' historian. Thus I am naturally interested in trying to understand what he may have meant by his mythical Unmoved Mover. But I find I cannot use that idea—very much! And I also find I have to reconstruct those Aristotelian ideas, giving them a novel, twentieth-century dress, to make them fit our own problems—something that seems often to horrify the scholars. In calling him a behaviourist and an objective relativist, I am fully aware that I am using terms he would not have recognized, terms designating issues in our own problems, not in his. I think I know the difference. My book on Aristotle is historically accurate, an objective reconstruction. But it is selective, of what seems today living in his thought. In my metaphysical enterprise, on the other hand, as sketched in *Nature and Historical Experience*, I go on to reconstruct that thought into tools I can use on twentieth-century intellectual problems. But I still think, as against his Platonizing detractors, that, in ordinary language, I am remaining 'true to his spirit'.

And what I have done with Aristotle I have tried to do also with another and less remote, though I hope no more intimate teacher, John Dewey. I think I can expound Dewey's thought with the best of them: I have boasted it seems to me I can understand his every word. But I have also confessed I have found it more fruitful to use his ideas as critical instruments than merely to expound them. And here, too, such employment demands selection. Thus, though I understand, I think, his instrumentalistic conception of knowledge as a construction of truth rather than a sheer discovery, I have never felt greatly tempted, save for polemical purposes, to make much use of this conception myself. My own caste of mind is far too realistic: I did not myself emerge from philosophical idealism. And so it is other ideas of his I have found it more fruitful to try to develop. And when I face my own philosophical problems, I find I have to reconstruct those ideas as well, restating them and reformulating them in my own language. Is this not indeed what philosophers have always done, from Aristotle down? Is it not what Dewey himself constantly urges us to do with the whole philosophic tradition? Certainly he would hardly object to a taste of his own medicine.

For of what use is it to a philosophical mind to reconstruct the past history of philosophy, with historical and scholarly accuracy, if he then finds in it nothing he can employ in dealing with his own issues, if it remain than a dead skeleton, bearing only the mouldering garments of another and remote and alien age? It is such a lifeless 'history', that inevitably turns into the record of human error, vain speculation, and the futility of human thought, that has brought historical interests, after much such exploitation in the nineteenth century, into disrepute with many twentieth-century movements, anxious to be relieved of the incubus of a dead past. From such a 'history' we do indeed need emancipation—though if we be humanists, even it can tell us much of the nature of man, as Cassirer would insist.

I remember once asking Arthur Lovejoy why he was so much interested in German intellectual history. 'Why,' he replied, 'the Germans have thought up ten times as many crazy ideas as the rest of them put together'. Such has never been my own interest in intellectual history. And this attitude has always led me to reservations as to Lovejoy's distinctive enterprise of 'the history of ideas', to the suspicion that he has been more concerned to trace the genealogy of 'crazy ideas' than to discover the history of important ones. In that sense, I fear, I have never been a true historian; nor does my theory of history permit me to be such a one. Rather, with Santayana, I should have to say, 'I am only a philosopher, almost a poet'.

No, the history of philosophy has always been for me, in Hegel's sense, 'pragmatic'. It has held lessons to teach: it has been the history of my teachers. One thing those teachers never taught me was to be an unquestioning disciple. Not that I have ever rebelled against any teacher; it simply never occurred to me that any one of them was demanding complete intellectual submission. They all had a rich store of ideas to offer me. I took what I could use—in my own thinking, or perhaps just as a useful foil. I left the rest, as historically interesting enough, but no more. Western philosophy since Descartes has in particular a great store of assumptions which, when able thinkers elaborated them to the bitter end, like Hume, were revealed as assumptions it were better not to make. These are important lessons I have taken to heart; I have learned much from them, much that I cannot but remember when I see contemporary philosophical movements light-heartedly and uncritically making those same old outworn assumptions once more.

The reconstruction of the living past—of those ideas that strike home to us, as suggesting answers to our own questions, the materials the long past enterprise of human reflection on man's life in the world has left as building-stones for us to use—in the light of the novel ideas of the best scientific knowledge today, that we may forge tools to use upon our own problems of cultural and intellectual tension, conflict, and readjustment—that is the way the philosophic enterprise has long looked to me. That is the way my teachers Woodbridge and Dewey tried to get me to look at it, when I was still too fascinated by the wealth revealed to take in the full import of what they had themselves learned about the function of philosophizing. That is the way I gradually came to see it myself, as I began myself to explore what the philosophers had been and what they had done, and why they had been driven to do it. That is the conception of the nature and function of philosophizing that took form for me with vivid realization, as I explored the living past of philosophy since Thales. That is the way intellectual history lookes to me, the pattern I tried to delineate in my course in the Theory of History, and in the relevant section of my *Nature and Historical Experience*. Indeed, with suitable enlargement as to the character of the problems faced, the nature of the inherited materials left as a deposit by the past, and the kind of fresh experience that generates the issues, that is the way all human history looks: the continuing reconstruction of the inherited past in the light of present problems and resources. I once called this a 'problematic' view of history, because I found in problems faced the 'focus' from which any history, of the present or of the past, has to be understood.

VI

But it is not the understanding of history I would here emphasize. It is rather the understanding of man's life in the world as it confronts us now—the understanding that is philosophy. To that understanding, historical knowledge is essential: it reveals the significance of what we have to work with and to work upon. But equally essential is scientific knowledge, the knowledge of what we have most reliably discovered about the world and human life in it. It is those discoveries, those fresh insights into the conditions of man's existence, that generate intellectual problems. For at the outset new knowledge usually seems to conflict with old, and the novel experience it makes possible and necessary generates our practical and cultural problems. How is Freud to be reconciled with Christian morality? How is atomic power to be controlled? How is relativity physics to be adjusted to the comfortable certainties of the Newtonian world? Here is where philosophy the trouble-shooter must be called in to cast its light.

And scientific discovery also injects new ideas with endless ramifications and implications, that cry aloud to be followed out and explored, ideas like evolution, like the field, like cultural pluralism, that demand the rethinking of all our previous thought. Philosophy explores such ideas, it makes the pioneering expeditions; the scientific settlers arrive only later to stake out their claims. This is the 'theoretical' or 'speculative' function of philosophizing, its imaginative generalization of new scientific concepts, or indeed of new concepts drawn from any field of human concern in which fresh experience is impinging on tradition, to see what they are worth, and what they can do when pushed. With such fresh perspectives, what is looks different, and familiar landmarks are thrown into novel relief. New metaphysical distinctions are formulated. For metaphysics is a growing, developing science, never more so than in the twentieth-century, and this is how it advances.

Historical knowledge of the living past, scientific knowledge of the most recently discovered and newly formulated ideas, these are both essential. Dewey used to counsel, a philosopher needs to know both the classical tradition and present intellectual realities. Without the classical tradition, his thinking will be meagre, pale, and barren; without the intellectual resources of the present, it will be short-sighted or even blind. And the bringing to bear of each upon the other is the ultimate function of philosophizing, of criticism.

The seventeenth century was so intoxicated at its discovery of the mathematical order of nature that it even fancied it could forget the past completely, and make a wholly fresh start: it needed only to work with the new. Men like Descartes, Hobbes, and Spinoza made the attempt. But we now realize their thought was soaked in tradition: they were actually bringing the whole medieval past to bear on the interpretation and generalization of the new science, for they had no other instrument to use. In that self-confident age, only Leibniz realized what he was actually doing: he had not tried to cut off his roots in the tradition. In consequence, of all those seventeenth-century pioneers, his thought alone seems still alive. Beginning with Locke, Hume, and Kant, philosophy became self-consciously an instrument of criticism: it appealed to 'experience' to adjust old to new. In Locke and Hume, it appealed to the only kind of experience conceivable in the Newtonian world, a mechanical sensationalism. In Kant, it appealed to the experience of the physicist, an interpretation of observations in terms of certain assumptions, and tried to adjust that experience to the experiences of the moral life and of the artist. In Hegel, it appealed to man's social and historical experience, which is more fundamental, since man's culture, his *objektiver Geist*, can give birth to physics, but physics does not generate culture, it only transforms it. With the coming of Darwin, philosophy appealed to biological experience; with James, to psychological experience; with Tyler and Frazer and Boas, to anthropological experience.

Since the eighteenth century all our philosophies have been critical philosophies of experience, appealing to 'experience', however variously conceived, to adjust old traditions to novel ideas. Even so, Aristotle in ancient Greece appealed to experience against the 'Platonism' of the Platonists, who in their Pythagorean enthusiasm had wellnigh forgotten it. But let him who thinks Plato himself had forgotten the experienced world, but read— really read—the dialogues. He will be unable to credit so fantastic a tale.

We have come the full circle. For what are all the philosophical movements of the twentieth century but just such critical philosophies of experience—dare I say, Aristotelian criticisms of abstract theories, much more radical and thoroughgoing than Aristotle's own, for whom experience was simply what 'we see'—*ōrōmen*. Bradley appealed to an immediate experience of 'feeling'; James, to an experience of consequences and to what all things are experienced as; Bergson, to an intuited experience of *durée*; Dewey, to a 'direct' qualitative and problem-generating experience, reflectively construed in biological and cultural terms; Whitehead, to durations of events, and to intuitions of values. The Logical Positivists have appealed to protocol sentences formulating immediate observations; the Wittgensteinians, to the experience revealed in the ordinary usages of language; the Phenomenologists, to the experienced world phenomenologically described; the Existentialists, to the experienced world of *Sorge*, *Angst*, and *Zeitlichkeit*. Our contemporary philosophies are all critical appeals to experience. Diverse as they seem, so diverse that they are often not on speaking terms with each other—for what existentialist could converse with a logical positivist, and what Wittgensteinian could talk profitably with either?—they are still parts of a common philosophical enterprise, the philosophical programmes of criticism of our day.

And I, too, belong here. I, too, appeal to experience. But, I hope, I appeal to an experience that consciously tries to embrace all these varieties. I appeal to the experience of process, of the universe of action that generates a universe of discourse, of the situation and its transactions. With Aristotle, I see a world of natural and human processes co-operating with each other, and impinging upon each other. With Dewey, I encounter a world of many distinguishable varieties of specific situation, running the gamut of all man's cultural activities. With Hegel, I attempt to embrace all these types of experience, all these revelations of the experienced world, in my critical vision of man in the universe, in nature.

ON WHAT THERE IS BEYOND
THE THINGS THERE ARE

PAUL WEISS

I

An exposition of a philosophic view is hard to separate from an account of other approaches to reality, for its justification in good part lies in the fact that it finds a place for basic truths which the others inevitably neglect. This fact becomes a little more evident when the positions of common sense, analysis, science, existentialism, and mysticism are surveyed and their limits indicated. The survey is followed by a summary of the position I developed primarily in the *Modes of Being* and the books that followed it. It then becomes possible to make an attempt to meet some of the current objections to the intelligibility, testability, or legitimacy of the enterprise.

II

Most of what men claim to know has been gathered in the course of daily living. Each learns almost untaught some of the crucial differences that separate the old from the young. Slowly and often painfully each learns the way in which men and women differ in outlook. Each, sooner or later, takes account of a telling difference in masculine and feminine demands, rhythms, and values. Gradually each learns to separate the plausible and the useful from the foolish and futile. Before many years have passed all men have come in some contact with birth and death, with fear, anxiety, and joy. Few are without the confidence that they can tell day from night, or what a change in the seasons portends.

None of this knowledge is pure; little of it is clear and precise. All of it is filtered through the language and customs of society. Indeed, men are deemed to be normal only so far as their speech and acts, and therefore what they claim, in fact, to know, is in consonance with what is acceptable to the rest. This is true even when one man affirms a singular truth which the mass reject. He might have considerable justification for saying that the sun never rises, that bodies all fall at the same rate, or that prayer is without efficacy, but most of the rest, even in the most advanced societies, will take it to be more sensible to think and to say something else.

Learning takes place more or less at haphazard. The contingencies of existence and the exigencies of life dictate in good part what it is that will be encountered. And what is encountered grounds whatever is known. No mind, though, is filled only with a miscellany of unrelated bits of information. Language and practice provide categories which determine how items are to be classified and used. Unfortunately, those categories are neither well bounded nor unalloyed.

Common sense observes carelessly and speaks loosely. Men testify under oath, with evident sincerity, about what they could not conceivably have seen; few know how to use technical terms or complex instruments with precision. Too often men overlay what they confront with conventions and hopes. What they experience is soon obscured by superstitions and arbitrary beliefs.

Were common sense more careful and more articulate men would not be inclined to analyse, except occasionally and then for a short time. Were it more precise and better organized, they would not so readily turn to science. Were its vision steady and its values keyed to man as he stands by himself, there would be less of a need to vitalize it in existentialistic and other personalistic ways. Were its items final or self-explanatory men might not be so tempted to look to mysticism and try thereby to get to whatever might lie outside and beyond it. And were all of it to form a single, self-critical, comprehensive system, there would be less reason to engage in speculative and dialectical activities, trying somehow to understand what is at the root of all that is and can be known.

Common sense has a vulgar muscularity which has prevented it from being crushed by any other agency. Reid, Moore, Peirce, and Austin have made the English-speaking philosophic community see how vital and sure-footed it is. But the more they insisted on the validity of common-sense claims and the soundness of common-sense discourse the more evident it has been that it is difficult for them to find room for abstract mathematics, formal logic, theoretical science, universal ethics, and a revelational religion. Each one of these challenges common sense at some crucial point. The necessities, the prescriptions, the unexperienceables, the ought, and the final judge of which the disciplines speak are not altogether within the grasp of common-sense experience and discourse. To be sure, common sense is sometimes pliable enough to accommodate faint versions of them. But it never finds a place for them in their full rigour or shows full respect for their austere beauty.

Common sense too often substitutes what is hoped for and believed for what is seen. It is too often dogmatic where it should be slow moving and detailed. One would feel less desire to abandon it if one could hold its impulses in check, refine its vocabulary, and give its attention steady and sure direction. Analysis is a sharp instrument enabling us to achieve these ends.

Analysis looks for the joints in things. It seeks to break up phenomena or discourse into more manageable and if possible more reliable and manipulatable parts. Today it depends considerably on the wit of men to use the distinctions of grammar or logic to tell them where to cut into things so that they can find the units in terms of which all else is to be understood.

Analysis enables us to know exactly what it is that we are claiming in what we say. It is a method which can be extended to embrace the assertions and objects of any discipline whatsoever. Wherever there is meaning, wherever there is something asserted, there evidently analysis can be used to lay bare the components and therefore the import of what is said.

Analysis waits for other enterprises to give it material on which to work. Though it follows its own bent, it is still a dependent enterprise. Nor does it examine the presuppositions on which its data rest; it does not know whether or not those disciplines on which it operates have anything answering to them in fact. And, of course, it knows no way of relating one discipline to another. The most it can do is to show that all are divisible into the same kind of elements.

There are analysts who boldly affirm that the elements to which they finally come are the atoms of the world or of language. Hume, the early Russell, and the early Wittgenstein take this position. But their justification is hard to find. Perhaps that is why these three acute thinkers soon turned from this position to attend instead to other subjects or approaches.

Analysis should be guided by the structure of things. That structure, because it is imbedded in the things, is most readily known by attending to what is encountered. An analysis which does this will more likely than not so divide entities that widely dispersed common factors will be found, enabling one to restate what had already been learned in a rough and uncritical way. But something more will be needed if what is sought is an explanation or a prediction, or if one wants to evaluate the claims of all disciplines without an antecedent judgment regarding their respective merits.

IV

Technology has transformed the shape of the West to give it a distinctive tone and drive. Behind that technology is science, a triple-pronged affair, more widely practised and praised than understood. One occupation of science has to do with the production of experiments, deliberately set in ideal and controlled situations so as to enable one to get precise answers to precise questions. Another occupation is with observations, usually achieved with the aid of tightly calibrated instruments. A third occupation is with the creation of theoretical formulations of the connections that hold between the law-abiding occurrences discovered in experiment and observation. When those theories are freed from their initial base and developed independently they assume the shape of comprehensive explanations and predictions of what can be known in other ways.

In all its guises science offers a challenge to the tacit claim of common sense to have reached foundational or inexpungeable truths. It does not therefore cast all common sense aside. In the end every scientific claim must be checked by common-sense men confronting common-sense scales, numbers, signals, lights, and photographs. What science does is to point to realities not within the province of common sense to acknowledge and sometimes even to understand. We need not, therefore, stand on either side of the barrier that separates some of the analysts from some of the positivists; we need not deny that what we know in commonsensical ways exists as surely as what we discover in controlled experiments, refined observations, and through the agency of theories. There are, however, other things to understand, not reachable by any of these methods. A strenuous effort should be made to try to attend to all avenues of knowledge, to reconcile their demands and claims, and to present the result in a single, well-organized, comprehensive account. Existentialism, mysticism, and metaphysics claim to know what is beyond the competence of common sense, analysis or science. They deserve some attention.

V

Science seeks cold, impersonal truth. It deals with items which occurred a long time ago, and with others scheduled to appear in the remote future. It interests itself as much in the composition of stars as it does in the appetites of men. This catholicity and objectivity some find offensive. Existentialists are among its most outspoken critics today. They object not so much to the results or the methods of science as they do to its attitude. For them there is little value, solace, or even truth in any view that does not express man as he authentically is. All else, they think, is desiccated, abstract, too alien to man to be anything more than an exhibition of the folly of detachment and the attempt to be objective.

Despite their conflict, the two positions share a common attitude towards common sense and analysis. Both find the first too crude and the second too naïve. But all four positions, I think, have a place in the civilized pursuit of knowledge. What science knows is on a plane different from that which interests the existentialist; both are concerned with aspects of the common-sense world and the meanings of both can be made clearer by having recourse to analysis.

VI

In their different ways these diverse approaches keep the mind focused on rather limited areas and tasks. None pays sufficient attention to the fact that men are constantly confronted with the wondrous, the perplexing, and the paradoxical. They do not seem to be sufficiently alert to the occasional moments of terror many experience, when the familiar world falls away to leave one confronting a vast, dark awesomeness. They also seem to be insufficiently aware of a continuity beneath the separated items that are dealt with by convention and practice, language, theory, and human concern. Such at least is the contention of some singular men over the course of history.

These men insist that there are realities which escape the mesh of other enterprises. They want to identify themselves with those realities, or simply to live with them. Methods which involve conceptualization they think, inevitably distort what everyone can glimpse, if only for a moment and only occasionally. They refuse to remain within the orbit of thought or even of human concerns.

What is real they assert is quite different from what is normally known.

These men are mystics, natural or supernatural. The natural mystic—a Schopenhauer or a Bergson—claims to be able to penetrate beneath phenomena to a quite different reality. He speaks of 'insight' or 'intuition' as means by which he can escape the thrall of daily discourse and understanding. His counterpart, the supernatural mystic, starts instead with a religiously grounded claim and tries to trace it back to its source, by cutting himself free from all restraining dogmas.

There seems to be a large core of agreement amongst these men, so far as one can judge from their somewhat diverse, metaphorically expressed claims. But there is no sure way of knowing this. They offer no definite criteria, no clear tests, no reliable evidence. That is, however, no adequate reason for dismissing them; they are evidently sincere and have something important to say. It would be wiser to try to see if it is possible to come to know in another way that to which they seem to point. This is one of the things a metaphysician tries to do. He thinks he sees in the heart of common sense, science, and existentialism indications of other basic beings which seem to be somewhat like what the mystics report. These he attempts to reach through the use of a distinctive philosophic method and tries to express through the agency of a fully integrated system, where item supports item and all is made subject to critically used criteria of clarity and completeness.

VII

This is a world in which there are many things of many kinds. I call them all 'actualities'. Some are known in a partially obscured or distorted form by common sense. Others, quite minute or startlingly. gigantic, are the topic of the sciences. It is conceivable that some of them might be reached by analysis; existentialists seem to get to the essence of a number of those which have considerable bearing on man's destiny. Were these approaches together to exhaust the universe, there would be little for a philosopher to do unless it be the relating of all of them, an examining of their presuppositions, or a forging of a language in terms of which one could discourse of any of their objects. But they do not seem to exhaust what can be intelligibly grasped. There is something about these approaches that remains inexplicable unless we take account of the presence of other realities which are distinct in location, nature, and function from any of the things they know or encounter.

All actualities seem to be subject to at least three compulsions. One of these is (1) *brute*, keeping them co-ordinate in time. Another is (2) *prescriptive*, dictating what actualities can be and do. A third is (3) *agglutinative*, affiliating some with others from which they diverge, sometimes quite radically, in nature, value, and function.

1. Some things are sluggish and others swift, but all enter the next moment together. What keeps them temporally abreast? An Aristotelian would say that they are all confined within a single area where they are temporally counted in a common way. A Leibniz would say that they had been preordained to be co-ordinate always. The one makes them move as a collection, though they had been taken to be independent in being and function; the universe seems to be far more open, larger, and peopled with beings which are more independent than those that Aristotle acknowledged. The other translates the temporal into the non-temporal, and therefore has difficulty with the question of the coming to be and passing away of things. It seems more correct to say that all things are swept along by the movement of a single cosmic, dynamic, extended Existence. This is not an area or a divinely instituted co-ordination, but a reality with a power of its own, compelling all things to enter into the next moment together.

2. Nothing will be unless it can be. But what can be is the possible. Because the possible determines the degree of freedom that is open to present actualities, predictions are possible and expectations plausible. Some of the possibilities are imperious and impose conditions to which all things must conform. It is these possibilities that concern mathematicians and logicians. Other possibilities promise enhancement to whatever will realize them; they are the possibilities which obligate. All are locatable in a single reality, an Ideal towards which all actualities point and which in turn makes them intelligible.

3. Some things attract one another; others are mutually repellent. Some of these attractions and repulsions are understandable by reference to electric currents. Some perhaps are adequately explained by a theory of chemical valency. But there are other

affiliations which occur without regard for the nature of the bodies of actualities. Those affiliations are most conspicuous in the commerce of human beings. Suddenly, but with confidence and certainty, men sometimes make contact with other men, and sometimes with animals or things, with whom they have no evident common background or experience. Attenuated forms of that attraction can be discerned throughout the animal kingdom; electric and chemical attractions seem to be special forms of it. In any case, it offers testimony to the presence of a power of affiliation which is strong enough to bring disparate entities into close concordance, even when they are quite remote in space and differ considerably in nature. One does not depart much from tradition if one speaks of this affiliating power as God, providing it be added that it is God as known in religion or some extension of this.

Though the *Modes of Being* speaks as though it intended to deal with four ultimate realities and the way in which they were interlocked, what it does, in fact, is to deal with actualities, the way in which they are related to the three sources of compulsion, and the effect of the interplay of these three sources on one another. Towards the end of the work, and more evidently in *Philosophy in Process*, it is seen that not only actualities but the three compelling powers are all encompassed by the single Being, *Actuality*, and that this is together with three other equally basic and ultimate Beings.

The nature and activity of a single Being, which grounds or encompasses all actualities and what they are subject to, has been touched upon by most of the great philosophers. Aristotle's Unmoved Mover, Thomas Aquinas's God, Spinoza's Substance, Whitehead's Creativity, Dewey's Nature, and even Bradley's Absolute have much in common with one another and it. All refer to a being that is final and real, and which exists in a different sense than that possible to actualities.

The things in this world are real. But they do come to be and pass away. All are oriented in Actuality, a permanent and final Being, not to be dealt with in terms appropriate to those actualities and that by which they are compelled.

The history of philosophic controversy offers ample evidence of the difficulty of coming to know and making intelligible the nature of the ultimate reality within whose confines actualities exist and within which there are also three powers that subject the actualities to inescapable compulsions. Those who have won an insight into the nature of that ultimate reality are understandably tempted to stop there. But then they stop too short. An all-encompassing permanent reality is strong enough—as the monists have seen—to swallow up whatever is within its confines. How could things maintain themselves over against it? Could the compelling powers be anything more than phases of that Being? Men like Bradley have seen the point and faced it boldly. Because, for them, there is only a single ultimate Being they find that they must affirm that no actualities have a being of their own. A single ultimate Being, they see, absorbs whatever else appears.

The conclusion is inevitable. To avoid it account must be taken of the reality of other Beings alongside of Actuality. The compelling powers to which actualities are subject can then be recognized to be specializations of Beings as permanent and as ultimate as Actuality is. The God, for example, that a religion acknowledges is a God for this world. In himself, and thus as only capable of functioning as a God for a religion and this world, he is equal in dignity and ultimacy to Actuality. The ideal contains what ought to be realized. This ought-to-be is, but only as part of a reality co-ordinate with, and, in fact, prescribing to the other Beings. And Existence, with its space, time, and dynamics, is and acts regardless of whether there are particular things or what they do. It, too, is final, irreducible, an ultimate mode of Being.

Each of the four final Beings acts on the others, giving them functions and features they otherwise would not have. God enables Actuality to stand away from its confined actualities, thereby permitting these to exercise a being of their own; Existence enables Actuality to spread over the entire reach of actualities, thereby enabling it to encompass them all. The Ideal gives Actuality a nature similar to that of its actualities; those actualities can therefore instance it, without losing their status as independent particulars. Actuality enables the other Beings to provide orientations for their distinctive particulars.

Actuality may be reached in a daring speculative or mystical move. The other modes of Being are not as readily attained. Whatever encounter one has with them is never more than fleeting, and is never clear edged. To know all the modes of Being with some clarity one must supplement insight with reasoned study. The agencies for accomplishing this are dialectic, the consideration of what would complete what one already knows, and system, the integrated articulation of the realities as they stand apart from one another, as they condition one another, as they affect one another, and as they manifest themselves in limited forms within the confines of each other, where they affect the activities of the particulars also encompassed there.

The result is rather complex and appears to be rather distant from anything plain men know or are usually interested in. As a matter of fact it enables one to understand a little better and to interrelate a little more coherently a whole range of inquiries which otherwise would seem to be without connection and without a rootage in the nature of things. Ethics and politics are individual and common ways of relating us to the Ideal; art and history are private and public ways of relating us to Existence; and religion, personal and communal, are ways of relating us to God. The Ideal, Existence, and God that are thereby known are qualified forms of ultimate modes of Being; they operate within the orbit of Actuality and there compel actualities to be contemporaries, to be ordered towards relevant possibilities, and to be affiliated. What those qualified forms of the modes of Being presuppose, it is the object of metaphysics to study and to systematize.

VIII

A view such as this raises two types of question: a substantive and a methodological. Have the realities been properly characterized in themselves and in interrelationship? Can these realities be known, understood, and spoken about intelligibly? Adequate answers to the first will lead one far into the internal workings of a rather elaborate system. Fortunately, they are adumbrated in the answers to the second.

It is common today to say that metaphysical assertions are at best poetic and at worst nonsensical, and surely vague and unverifiable. Neither the language of common sense nor that of science can accommodate them. I think this criticism is just in the main. Though unkind to poetry and overimpressed with science, it is surely right in remarking that metaphysics cannot be expressed in ordinary terms or in conformity to the criteria appropriate to the contentions of common sense, analysis, science, or existentialism.

Metaphysics speaks in a 'meta-language' which gives coherent and communicable sense to transcendental terms that are recalcitrant to our ordinary grammar. It forges a new language in which such terms as 'unity', 'being', 'possibility', 'truth', and 'the good' are intelligibly related by attending to the rhythms and nuances of compelling powers and what these presuppose. Those terms, shorn of that reference, take paradoxical turns, disruptive of conventional practice. Metaphysics starts with them as aberrational items and in a sense always leaves them that way as it moves on to understand how, in the light of what is ultimately real, they can be interrelated and significantly used.

Again and again the metaphysician, like everyone else, finds himself confronted with paradoxes and incoherencies. In the attempt to exhibit the rationale behind these, he alters his vocabulary and grammar. His discourse does not have a set of antecedently known and tried rules; it is a creative, freshly minted agent which is constantly altered to accommodate and quiet new perplexities. It does this by looking to the ultimate Beings and seeing what distinctions and stresses they demand of the accepted categories and claims.

There are some who hold that philosophy is economically, politically, or socially conditioned. What were problems once, they think, are problems no longer; what once was unknown is problematic now. Philosophy for them is a tentative, dependent, and relativized enterprise. They note that the nature and rights of slaves is not a major issue for us today, and that megalopolis, international law, space travel, and the rights of minorities are now to the fore. But the fact that there are problems that come and go does not mean that there are no problems which are always with us. Birth, death, joy, pain, love, hate, peace, war, and injustice, growth and decay, mind and body, man, woman, and child, explode into a multiplicity of issues and questions as soon as we refuse to accept without criticism the unexamined answers that common sense and science provide.

Philosophy begins with the wondrous. Whatever awakens surmise as to its ground or bearing on whatever else is or is known, can prompt the beginning of a long and hazardous dialectical journey. One knows that one has finally reached an ultimate Being when, upon returning to the world of things, one finds everything has now become wondrous—more wondrous even than the initial items had been before—and yet more clearly demarcated and understood. Wonder does not disappear as a result of philosophic inquiry; instead it becomes manifest everywhere. Philosophy does not dissolve or solve problems. It traces them back to their origin, and thereby discovers why the problems arise and are always with us.

4

THE PRINCIPLES AND CATEGORIES OF MORALITY

WILLIAM K. FRANKENA

In this essay two questions of moral philosophy will be discussed together. First, what are the basic criteria, standards, or principles of morality? What are the basic norms for making moral decisions and judgments? For example, should we take the Principle of Utility as our fundamental standard? Second, what are the main categories in terms of which our moral decisions and judgments are to be expressed? What kinds of predicates are to be used in moral deliberation and discourse? For example, should we use *deontic* categories or predicates like 'right', 'wrong', 'duty', 'obligation', and 'ought'; *aretaic* ones like 'morally good', 'morally bad', 'virtuous', 'vicious', 'admirable', and 'blameworthy'; or both? Just which categories of each kind should we employ?

Some explanations are necessary here. (1) These questions will be understood in a normative sense. I shall not be asking simply which principles and categories we do recognize, but which ones we should recognize. (2) Historically, the first question has long been a standard problem of normative ethics, but the second has not been much discussed in an explicit way until recently. (3) The two questions are interrelated, and that is why I discuss them together. I shall not try to show this, but it will appear in what follows that the acceptability of the Principle of Benevolence depends somewhat on the categories one is willing to recognize. (4) My discussion of these questions will not be exhaustive or rigorous, but only suggestive and exploratory.[1]

I

In order to answer the first question, I propose to begin with a conception of the Ideal, or rather, of the Ideal State of Affairs as far as human beings are concerned. Actually, it seems to me that there are two states of affairs that may be regarded as the Ideal: there is what may be called the Utopian Ideal, namely, the state of affairs in which everyone fully enjoys the ideally good or ideally best

[1] For more on the first question, *see* my *Ethics*, Ch. 2 and 3.

life, i.e. the best life that any human being might be capable of; and there is the more practically ideal state of affairs in which everyone has the best life he is capable of. I shall call this the Practical Ideal. These two statements of the Ideal are simply two ways of formulating the same basic conception, which seems to me to be implied both by our American democratic ideology and by the Marxist conception of the end of the dialectic of history in a classless society. In fact, I believe that it would be accepted by anyone who asks what the ideal human world would be and is free, impartial, clear-headed, and fully informed. Certainly the cultural relativists have done nothing to prove that it would not be.

In saying this, I do not mean that all such fully rational thinkers would have the same views in detail about the Ideal, though I believe that ultimately they would. But, if they would not, I think this would be because they have different conceptions, not of the *form* of the Ideal, which is what I have tried to describe, but of its *content*, i.e. because they have different conceptions of the good life. For example, one might be a hedonist, another an Aristotelian, and a third a follower of Kant or of G. E. Moore on the question of what is good in itself.

If we accept this view of the Ideal, we may derive from it an answer to our first question. It would be too much to claim that we ought to try to realize the *Utopian* Ideal. Even if we say that this Utopian Ideal ought to *be*, it does not follow that *we* ought to try to realize it. What we ought to do depends on what we can do, and we can hardly be asked to do more than to bring it about that everyone has the best life he is capable of. We cannot be asked to see to it that everyone has the capacities to live the ideally best life. *That* is up to Nature, which Kant once described as stepmotherly because she is so stingy. I do believe, however, that we may be asked to take the *Practical* Ideal as our end in life—or at least as the *moral* end in life. In fact, to say that it is the practically ideal state of affairs, not just for oneself but for the world, is equivalent to saying that the end of ideal, if not of actual, morality is the promotion of that state of affairs. In other words, it seems to me that, if we accept the above conception of the Ideal, then we must take as the first principle of morality: 'So act as to bring it about that, as far as possible, everyone has the best life he is capable of.'

Before one can use this principle, of course, one must first have some view about what constitutes the good or the best life—about what activities, experiences, etc., are good in themselves, which are best, and so on. This is important to remember, but we must now leave the question what is good to one side. For the purposes of our discussion we need not have an answer to it.

However, even if we do have a clear answer to the question what is good, better, and best in life, our principle still presents a problem as a basis of action. To reverse an old saying, it is a good wind that blows no one any ill. The point is that our actions often have consequences that are desirable or good on the one hand and consequences that are undesirable or bad on the other, good consequences for some and bad consequences for others. Where this is so we cannot proceed directly to the promotion of the Ideal. It may even be that the best life one person is capable of is not wholly compatible with others having the best lives they are capable of. We seem, therefore, to need a less ideal working principle to guide us in practice than the one formulated above.

Here is where the utilitarian would enter the argument. He would, or at least might, accept the Ideal as stated above and perhaps even the principle 'So act as to bring it about that, as far as possible, everyone has the best life he is capable of.' But he would argue that in practice we must compromise and rely on the Principle of Utility, i.e. we must do what will promote the greatest possible balance of good over evil in the world.

However, *this* Principle of Utility will not suffice. The problem is not just to bring about the greatest balance of good over evil in the world; it is to give everyone as good a life as possible. Some principle directing us to treat people equally, or to distribute good as widely as possible—some principle of justice— is also necessary.

At this point the utilitarian might reply, 'Yes, but let me restate the Principle of Utility. What it tells us to do is not to promote the greatest possible balance of good over evil, but to promote the greatest good of the greatest number.' This revised Principle of Utility, which is well known, tells us not only to maximize the balance of good over evil but also to distribute it as widely as possible. It is therefore more satisfactory as a working formula. But, notice, it is actually a combination of *two* principles: (*a*) Maximize the total balance of good over evil, (*b*) Distribute the good as widely as possible. Notice also that these two principles may conflict on occasion—we may have to choose between a course of action that produces more good but distributes it less widely and one that produces less good but distributes it more equally. It is not so magical a formula as its proponents pretend. Also, it is not a purely teleological or utilitarian principle, since it includes a principle of just distribution that is independent of the requirement to promote the most good.

It is, however, on the right track. For the ideal principle, 'So act as to bring it about that, as far as possible, everyone has the best life he is capable of', itself seems to me to break up in practice into two working principles, essentially the same as the two just formulated: (a) So act as to increase good and/or decrease evil, (b) So act as to treat people equally. Let us call the first the Principle of Benevolence and the second the Principle of Equality or Justice. Then it turns out that morality, in practice at least, rests on two principles, that of Benevolence and that of Justice. And, in answer to the first question, I wish to maintain that these two principles provide the guidelines of morality—for determining what we ought or ought not to do, for formulating our rights, and for defining the virtues and vices. Both are necessary and together they are sufficient, though I cannot try to show this now.

II

There are many problems about this answer to the first question, for example, that of a possible conflict between the principles of Benevolence and Justice. What concerns me here, however, is the fact that some recent British and American philosophers reject what I call the Principle of Benevolence.[1] These philosophers might accept my account of the Ideal State of Affairs. And they do agree that it is wrong to inflict evil on other people, i.e. they accept what might be called the Negative Part of the Principle of Benevolence: 'Refrain from doing evil.' But they deny its Positive Part; in other words, they deny that we have an obligation, even prima facie, to promote another person's good as such. Thus C. I. Lewis writes as follows:

'I would not say that benevolence beyond the call of justice has no sanction. . . . But the man of good will beyond the limits of obligation makes a *gift*, and it is to be appreciated as such, and not construed as a *requirement of the moral*.'[2]

[1] Some might also object to the Principle of Justice, arguing, for example, that one has no obligation to treat other parents' children equally with one's own. In part, my reply would follow the same lines as my defence of the Principle of Benevolence.

[2] Cf. *The Ground and Nature of the Right*, p. 84. The italics in this and the following quotation are mine.

M. G. Singer denies that one has a duty to do what would have good consequences, and then says:

'. . . In denying that one has the duty to do that which would have good consequences, I am not saying that such an action would be *wrong*. What I am saying is that one has the *right* not to, so long as the consequences of not doing so would not be undesirable. So what I am denying is that generosity or benevolence is a *duty*. No doubt benevolence is a *good thing* . . . and no doubt an act of generosity or benevolence is praiseworthy and admirable. But this does not mean that it is *obligatory*'.[1]

In a similar vein, Kurt Baier argues:

'We do not have a duty to do good to others or to ourselves, or to others and/or to ourselves in a judicious mixture such that it produces the greatest possible amount of good in the world. We are morally required to do good only to those who are actually in need of our assistance.'[2]

And finally, to give another example, J. N. Findlay maintains that:

'. . . So far from it seeming . . . evident that I ought . . . to seek to achieve the greatest possible sum of good . . . it seems rather to follow from the meaning of the words "obliged" and "good" that I am not obliged to seek the smallest particle of *mere* good of any sort whatsoever. Only to the extent that the absence of a good is regarded as evil, which is by no means always the case, does the notion of obligation, as ordinarily employed, enter into the discussion.'[3]

What objections do these philosophers have to the Principle of Benevolence, Positive Part? In general, they contend that its acceptance as a requirement of the moral would entail absurd or fanatical consequences in practice—that, in Jonathan Harrison's words, it would provide 'solace for obsessionals'.[4] To quote Singer again:

---

[1] Cf. *Generalization in Ethics*, p. 186.
[2] Cf. *The Moral Point of View*, p. 203.
[3] Cf. *Value and Intention*, p. 426, also 22.
[4] J. E. Harrison, 'Moral Talking and Moral Living', *Philosophy*, XXXVIII (1963), pp. 315–28.

'. . . If consistently adhered to, it would lead to moral fanaticism, to the idea that no action is indifferent or trivial, that every occasion is momentous.'[1]

As Baier put it:

'The view that we always ought to do the optimific act [even *prima facie*] . . . would have the absurd result that we are doing wrong whenever we are relaxing since on those occasions there will always be opportunities to produce greater good than we can by relaxing.'[2]

Much could be said at this point, but I shall content myself with two comments.[3] In the first place, it is not clear that matters are much more 'absurd' if one accepts the principle that we *ought* to promote *good* than if one accepts only the principle that it is *wrong* to promote *evil* or Baier's principle that we only ought to help those who need our assistance. One does have greater responsibilities, of course, if one must promote good as well as prevent evil or refrain from bringing it about, but it seems always possible to argue that if one relaxes of an evening one is omitting to do something which would prevent or help eliminate evil for someone, or that the consequences of one's relaxing are undesirable at least in the sense of including a failure to do something one might have done to remedy what is wrong with the world. There is so much wrong with the world that it is not clear that even Singer's 'Principle of Consequences'[4] permits us to relax—indeed, he himself allows that not doing what has good consequences usually has bad ones and hence is usually wrong. But, secondly, I am not eager to provide 'solace for obsessionals' either, and so I want to suggest that the Principle of Benevolence does not necessarily entail fanaticism. Its end is the promotion of goodness of life, and it seems at least plausible to contend that too great a devotion to duty day in and day out may have the effect of yielding less in the way of goodness of life— bringing us less near to the Ideal, paradoxical as it may seem—than a devotion which includes some relaxation. After all, the point of moral endeavour is to make the good life possible; it must then find

---

[1] *Loc. cit.*

[2] *Loc. cit.*

[3] One ought, for example, to discuss Singer's 'concert ticket case', *op. cit.*, pp. 185–6.

[4] Namely, that we ought not to do what has bad consequences.

some way of allowing us to enjoy the good life. Extremism in pursuit of the Ideal may not be a vice; but moderation in its pursuit may still be a virtue. After all, the Sabbath is made for man, not man for the Sabbath.

Thus it does not seem to me that the objection made by Baier and Singer to the Principle of Benevolence, Positive Part, is entirely conclusive. Still, it does have a point, and the rest of my reply will consist in showing that one may recognize its force without drawing the conclusion Baier and Singer draw. They are particularly insistent that one does not have a 'duty' or an 'obligation' to do good to others simply as such, and that one has 'a right' not to do it. And there is a sense in which they are surely right. As a number of writers have been pointing out recently,[1] the words 'duty', 'obligation', and 'a right' are most properly used in certain contexts: (1) when X has promised Y to do Z, then X has an obligation to do Z and Y a right to expect him to do Z; (2) when X has a certain office or role over against Y, e.g. if X is Y's father or secretary, then X has certain duties toward Y and Y has certain rights which he may press.

Now, it does seem pretty clear that one does not have a *duty* or *obligation* to do good to others in the same way that he has a duty or obligation to keep a promise or to care for his children. And others do not have a *right* to his beneficence; in this sense it *is* a 'gift', as Lewis calls it. Here we may recall J. S. Mill's distinction between rules of justice and 'other obligations of morality' like 'generosity and benevolence'.[2] The former, e.g. promise-keeping, are more essential or crucial for the very maintenance of society than the latter, and so are more properly demanded of us and labelled duty or obligation. Generosity and benevolence are principles of morality, but they do not have the same stringency, and need not be *demanded* of us or enforced as *rights*. So far Singer *et al.* are correct.

It would indeed be fanaticism to regard generosity and benevolence as duties or obligations in the strict sense in which keeping promises and fulfilling the duties of one's office are. Other people do not have a right to demand them of us; rather we have a 'right' not to be benevolent or generous. Yet it does not follow that gener-

[1] e.g. E. J. Lemmon, 'Moral Dilemmas', *Philosophical Review*, LXXI (1962), pp. 139–58; R. B. Brandt, 'The Concepts of Obligation and Duty', *Mind*, LXXIII (1964), pp. 374–93; J. E. Harrison, *op. cit.*
[2] Cf. *Utilitarianism*, Ch. V.

osity and benevolence are in no sense 'a requirement of the moral'.
For, as has often been pointed out, we do use the word 'ought' in
a much wider sense than that in which it is strictly correct to use
the words 'duty', and 'a right'—in fact, we use it in such a way that
it might be perfectly correct to say, as I did, that we *ought* to try to
bring it about that everyone has the best life he is capable of. Findlay,
whom I quoted as being on Singer's side, seems to recognize this
when he goes on to distinguish 'hortatory imperatives' or 'oughts
devoid of obligation, which delimit the upper reaches of what is
excellent', 'imperatives which urge, lure, or win us rather than goad
us into action by warnings and threats', from 'minatory imperatives'
which 'plumb the abysses of what is bad'. In recognizing, not only
'the essentially minatory imperative which warns us against creating evil or suffering', but also 'the largely hortatory imperative
which bids us spread happiness and other forms of well-being
among our fellows', he is admitting after all that there is an 'ought'
of some kind that attaches to the promotion of the Ideal—but
which clearly, to his way of thinking, does not entail any fanaticism
or absurdity.[1]

What I mean to say may be put as follows: when Portia says, in
The Merchant of Venice:
'Then must the Jew be merciful,'
Shylock asks (as Singer *et al.* might)
'On what compulsion must I? Tell me that.'
The answer is that there is indeed no 'compulsion'.
'The quality of mercy is not strained,
It droppeth as the gentle rain from heaven. . . .'
But nevertheless Shylock could be *expected* to be merciful—he
ought to be, even if he has a *right* to insist on justice and his pound
of flesh.

III

The above defence of the Principle of Benevolence, Positive Part,
has already included some discussion bearing on our second question, namely, 'What are the main categories or predicates to be used
in morality?' Let us now turn directly to this question. The chief
issue in recent British and American discussion of this topic has
been whether all voluntary actions or kinds of action can be classified morally under the following three headings: (*a*) the obligatory
or required, (*b*) the wrong or forbidden, (*c*) the indifferent (neither

[1] Cf. *op. cit.*, pp. 425 f.

obligatory nor wrong). And the main contention advanced is that they cannot—that we need at least one more category in morality, namely, the category of 'supererogatory' actions, i.e. of a class of actions that are not obligations or duties but are to be given a morally favourable predicate (not 'wrong' or 'indifferent'). J. O. Urmson, for example, maintains that the threefold classification of actions into duties or obligations, wrong actions, and permitted but indifferent actions is inadequate. An adequate moral theory must also allow for 'saintly' and 'heroic' actions, which go well beyond 'the call of duty', and acts of 'going the second mile', which are more ordinary, but also go beyond the limits of obligation. Recognition of such supererogatory actions, Urmson contends, is required by our ordinary common sense. He concludes that:

'. . . . We need to discover some theory that will allow for *both* absolute duties, which can be exacted from a man like a debt, to omit which is to do wrong and to deserve censure, and which may be embodied in formal rules and principles, *and also* for a range of actions which are of moral value and which an agent may *feel called upon to perform,* but which cannot be demanded and whose omission cannot be called wrong-doing.'[1]

Roderick Chisholm has also argued recently that, besides the categories of the obligatory, the forbidden, and the morally indifferent, one must recognize a fourth category of supererogatory action, actions that are morally good but not obligatory. But he contends further that we should add a fifth category of what he calls 'offences' —actions that are bad but not forbidden, or bad but excusable or permitted, e.g. trifling untruths or certain acts by informers. In fact, Chisholm points out that there are nine possible categories of action from a moral point of view, and that moral systems will differ according to which categories and how many they recognize, so that 512 different moral systems are possible. Just which one he means to argue for is not clear, except that it is one which recognizes at least the five categories mentioned and not just the usual three.[2]

Sometimes in the discussion it looks as if the debate is one about

---

[1] Cf. 'Saints and Heroes', in A. I. Melden (ed.), *Essays in Moral Philosophy,* p. 208 (my italics).

[2] Cf. 'Supererogation and Offense: a Categorial Scheme for Ethics', *Ratio,* 1963.

the nature of our *actual* morality, i.e. as if the question is whether it contains only three categories or not, whether we, in fact, recognize a fourth category or not. If this is the question, then the discussion is of concern to us only indirectly. But sometimes the question seems to be whether morality should contain only three categories or not, i.e. whether *ideal* morality should recognize more than three headings or not. It is really only in this form that the debate concerns us, since it is the principles and structure of ideal morality that we are interested in.

Now, actually, moral philosophers have for a long time recognized the existence and desirability of a fourth category. For they have used aretaic categories as well as deontic ones. More specifically, they have often spoken of actions and agents as being morally good, and have pointed out that an agent may be morally good, even when his action is wrong, and that his action may be morally good even though it is objectively wrong, e.g. when it is 'wrong but done from a good motive'. They would, therefore, have no difficulty in finding a place for 'supererogatory' actions, for they could admit (as they, in fact, have) that there are actions that are morally good but not obligatory. To this extent, much, if not all, of the recent debate about our second question has been misconceived. The real issue is not whether we should recognize another morally favourable predicate besides 'obligatory', but whether we should recognize a second favourable *deontic* category. One trouble with those who have attacked the threefold classification is that they have not made it clear whether the categories to be added should be deontic or aretaic.

To put the matter in another way; the concept of a supererogatory action is ambiguous. Saying that an action, X, is supererogatory may mean at least three different things:

(*a*) that X is morally good or virtuous, though not obligatory;

(*b*) that X is morally good or virtuous in an unusual degree, but not 'a requirement of the moral';

(*c*) that, although X is not obligatory or a duty, it is nevertheless something that morally *ought* to be done in some sense, not just something that is morally good to have done or something morally praiseworthy.

Since moral philosophers have in effect often recognized the existence of actions that are supererogatory in the first two senses, the only interesting question is whether we should admit that actions may be supererogatory in the third sense. Otherwise the debate about the trichotomous classification is much ado about very little. I have already suggested that, in so far as benevolent actions are supererogatory (i.e. fall under a favourable moral predicate without being morally obligatory), they are supererogatory in the third sense. Now I must make more fully clear the categorial scheme to which this commits me.

IV

We may notice first that Singer and his allies need not subscribe to the threefold classification, but can admit at least a fourth category. In fact, they must admit a fourth category if they are to find a place for acts of generosity and benevolence that go beyond the call of duty, since it is hardly plausible to say that such acts are morally indifferent or morally wrong, and they refuse to call them obligatory. But, if they admit a fourth category to take care of acts of benevolence and generosity, they must find some favourable predicate with which to characterize such acts. On their view, this predicate cannot be a deontic one, for they allow us only three deontic predicates, none of which apply to the acts in question. It may, however, be an aretaic predicate, and, in fact, Singer seems to be using such a predicate when he says that acts of generosity and benevolence are, no doubt, good things, praiseworthy and admirable.

On the other hand, my position requires me to hold that we *ought*, at least prima facie, to promote the good of others as such; I cannot be content with saying that such actions are permitted, morally good, or even praiseworthy and admirable. I must regard them not just as 'gifts' but as 'requirements of the moral'. I could then accept the threefold classification and argue that even positively benevolent actions are duties or obligations in the strict sense. As I have indicated, however, I agree with its critics that a simple threefold classification is inadequate, since it leads to a kind of fanaticism. That is why I must maintain that, although a fourth category is needed for acts of benevolence, we may still claim that such acts ought to be done and are a 'requirement of the moral', even though they are not strictly duties or obligations and even though we have 'a right' not to do them.

In order to maintain this I must make use of the distinction, made by many recent writers and already referred to, between (a) what is a duty or obligation in the strict sense, what it is strictly wrong not to do, what one has no right not to do, and (b) what ought to be done in a wider sense, but does not belong to that 'which can be exacted from a man like a debt'—the sort of thing of which one might say, 'You ought to do it, but you don't have to'. In fact, to my mind the difficulty with Singer and his allies, with the trichotomous classification, *and* with its critics, is that they either do not recognize this distinction or do not incorporate it into their categorial schemes.

If we do adopt this distinction, we obtain the following moral scheme, with at least five deontic categories in addition to aretaic ones:

A. Deontic categories
  1. What is strictly required or obligatory, duties in the strict sense.
  2. What is strictly forbidden or wrong, violations of strict duties.
  3. What ought to be done in a wider sense, but is not strictly a duty or obligation, what one has a right not to do.
  4. What ought, in a wider sense, not to be done, but is not strictly forbidden or wrong, e.g. what Chisholm calls 'offences'.
  5. What is deontically indifferent—not morally required in either the wider or the narrower sense, nor morally prohibited in either sense.

B. Aretaic categories
  1. What is morally good.
  2. What is morally bad.
  3. What is aretaically indifferent.[1]

Using this classification, I would put acts of positive generosity and benevolence under A3, as was indicated earlier, not under A1. This enables me to accept what is sound in the position of Singer and others, and to agree with them in holding that positive generosity and benevolence are not 'duties' or 'obligations', and yet to assert that they are, in an important sense, a 'requirement of the moral'. It may be that benevolent and generous actions are also normally to be put under B1, for the same action may fall both under a deontic and under an aretaic heading, though not necessarily under corresponding ones. Similarly, acts of equal or just

[1] It may be, of course, that we should also recognize more than three aretaic categories.

treatment, in so far as they go beyond the limits of obligation, may be placed under A3. Omissions of such actions, and omissions of acts of positive generosity and benevolence, again, I should classify under A4, not under A2. What about supererogatory acts of Urmson's two types, namely saintly or heroic acts and acts of going the second mile? I see no reason why they should not be put under A3 also, instead of under A1 or simply under B1. It certainly seems reasonable to me to say that we *ought* to do them, even though we cannot demand them of a man as we can a debt, instead of saying merely that they are 'good things' to do or 'gifts'. Urmson himself remarks that a man may himself feel 'called upon to perform' a supererogatory act, even though he might not call upon another man to perform one. To this extent, it seems to me, we may agree with Jacques Maritain when he writes that 'each of us is *bound* to tend toward the *perfection* of love according to his condition and in so far as it is in his power'.[1]

V

Many questions might be raised about what has or has not been said here. There is space only to say something about two of them. (1) Does my position provide 'solace' for obsessionals and fanatics?' It certainly makes fanaticism possible. But one does not become a fanatic in an objectionable sense unless one telescopes the wider into the narrower sense of what we ought to do, and thinks that everyone may be expected to do all of what he ought to do in just the same way in which he may be expected to keep his promises or to perform the duties of his station. And nothing that I have said requires one to think this. On the other hand, my position does allow for the fact—recognized by Urmson—that an agent may himself 'feel called upon to perform', i.e. feel a duty to do, actions which others would regard as supererogatory or even saintly and would not blame him for omitting. If this be fanaticism, I am inclined to cry, 'Let us have more of it!' Singer and his allies may be accused of being unfair to saints, but I prefer not to cross a holy picket line!

(2) Finally, it may be asked, 'Why should morality adopt the distinction between what is duty or obligation in a strict sense and what ought to be done in some wider sense, together with the resulting categorial scheme? Why should it not espouse the trichotomous classification or one of the more complex schemes that does not

---

[1] Cf. *The Responsibility of the Artist*, p. 42 (my italics).

acknowledge the distinction referred to?' The answer, which cannot be spelled out here, lies at least partly in arguing, much as Mill and Urmson do,[1] that even though we *ought* always to do what will promote the Ideal as far as possible, morality must in practice *insist* in a special way on certain practices and rules as being necessary for the very maintenance of a tolerable society, e.g. that of keeping agreements. Perhaps, too, it should insist that we should not harm one another. But, while proclaiming that we *ought* also to do whatever will bring good to them, and to treat them all equally, it may and perhaps should not always *insist* on this in the same way, but should be more relaxed in its demands (without giving them up entirely). In other words morality should, with the Ideal described earlier in mind, devise a system of rules, offices, roles, excuses, and extenuating considerations that will guide us in the determination of our strict obligations and rights and yet leave us scope for a more free response to a more ideal ought. It should always remember that its end is that everyone should enjoy the best life that he is capable of, so that, though it may *ask* much, it must not *demand* too much. In this way, it may provide 'solace' for idealists, heroes, and saints, and yet also have room for more ordinary folk, without giving them any undue cause for complacency.

[1] Cf. *loc. cit.*

5

THE RELATION BETWEEN NATURALISTIC SCIENTIFIC KNOWLEDGE AND HUMANISTIC INTRINSIC VALUES IN WESTERN CULTURE

F. S. C. NORTHROP

In *The Two Cultures*, C. P. Snow describes our present predicament with respect to this topic. It is not a very happy one. At best scientists and humanists find it difficult to communicate with one another. At worst, bitterness occurs. Witness the inhumane *ad hominum* attack upon Professor Snow by one of his humanistic colleagues at his University of Cambridge. It has not always been so. It need not be so today. To suggest why, for both the past and the immediate future, is the purpose of this essay.

The inability to communicate provides a sufficient reason for our unfortunate situation: Neither scientists nor humanists specify the more elementary common denominator factors which are necessary to relate the *specific contents* of successively generalized theories of naturalistic scientific knowledge in Western culture to the *specific contents* of its various humanistic intrinsic values.[1] Were this not so, bitterness at least could be avoided. And, although the reduction to common denominator factors and its communication present their difficulties due to (*a*) the various intrinsic values—aesthetic, moral, officially legal, and religious, (*b*) the successive increasingly generalized scientific theories and especially (*c*) the ambiguities of ordinary language, there need be no insurmountable *difficulty* in the way *in principle*.

The emphasis on specific content is very important. It makes the task of the philosopher of the sciences and the humanities much more laborious than most scholars and laymen suppose. Unfortunately, there is no trustworthy alternative. Otherwise with respect to Newton's *Principia*[2] one overlooks his warning, in its first

---

[1] By an intrinsic value is meant one that is elementary in the sense of not being instrumental to, or definable in terms of, some other value. This essay is dedicated to Professor Wilmon H. Sheldon, who suggested its synoptic concern. Similar indebtedness is due Professor Joseph C. Smith.

[2] Cajori Edition (NPCE), University of California Press, 1934, p. 6.

Scholium, against confusing (iii) the 'mathematical' functional meaning of its four elementary concepts, its eight technical defined concepts, its three universal laws of motion and their deduced theorems
with (i) *nothing but* their 'common' ordinary language 'reference to
sensible things'. Applied to Western legal science it has resulted
recently, as the professionally trained lawyer Jefferson, late in life,
forewarned, in the similar misinterpretation of its technical, legal
concepts, in terms of what Jefferson, earlier in his *Commonplace
Book,*[1] referred to as merely their 'attachment to sensible things'.
This 'nothing buttery' radical empiricism[2] makes nonsense, as the
sequel will show, of his *Declaration of Independence* principle and
of judicial review with respect to substance of legislative statutes
affecting religious and civil liberties in the American or any other
legal system. Of this, more later. Neglect of specific content also
results in countless treatises on The Good, The Good and The
Right, Hedonism, Rule Ethics, The Just, Self-fulfilment Ethics, or
Ought Implies Can which are likely to be vacuous. In short, the
goods, the rights, the pleasurables, the rules, the justice, the self-
fulfilments and the oughts as well as the cans are all empty. It is as
if in natural knowledge there were dull tomes about The Mathematically Physical True or The Directly and Indirectly Factually
Confirmed, but hardly a classic such as Newton's *Principia* or an
article such as Einstein's 1905 paper on The Special Theory of
Relativity concerning what the *specific content* is of the scientifically
true or the directly or indirectly confirmed for the naturalistic
subject-matter in question.

If such vacuity is to be avoided in value subjects, it may be wise
to follow the practice of comparative anthropologists, as described
in Clyde Kluckhohn's 'The Philosophy of the Navaho Indians'[3] and
Professor E. A. Hoebel's *The Law of Primitive Man.*[4] Kluckhohn
writes: 'The publication of Paul Radin's *Primitive Man as a
Philosopher* did much towards destroying the myth that a cognitive
orientation toward experience was a peculiarity of literate societies.
Speculation and reflection upon the nature of the universe and of
man's place in the total scheme of things have been carried out in
every known culture. Every people has its characteristic set of

---

[1] Gilbert Chinard Edition (JCBC), John Hopkins Press, 1926, art. 559, p. 111.
[2] With apologies to Professor Donald M. Mackay.
[3] *Ideological Differences and World Order* (IDWO), ed. F. S. C. Northrop,
Yale Univ. Press, 1949, p. 356. Hereafter F. N., *Philosophical Anthropology and
Practical Politics* (PAPP), Macmillan, N.Y. 1960, Ch. 6.
[4] *The Law of Primitive Man* (HLPM), Harvard Univ. Press, 1954.

"primitive postulates".' As Bateson has said: 'The human individual is endlessly simplifying and generalizing his own view of his environment; he constantly imposes on this environment his own constructions and meanings; these constructions and meanings are characteristic of one culture as opposed to another.' Hoebel's book shows, for its eight primitive legal systems, that their diverse values require eight different normatively worded postulate sets for their description. So normatively incompatible are the intrinsic values for the American Pueblo and the Cheyenne Indians, and also two American Plains Indian tribes in approximately the same environment, that the imposition of the specific content of the one on the other would cause a rebellion, though each group is pleased, and in all likelihood regards itself as self-fulfilled, with the specific content of its own intrinsic values. Furthermore, such primitive systems are different from that of Western legal science.[1]

These considerations point up two normative methodological maxims: First, values cannot be treated as abstract-nounish words in disjunctively related sentences, held up paradigmatically; instead, except when cultural diffusions occur, intrinsic values of any species form a system. For example, the first premise of Professor H. L. A. Hart's elucidation of the expression 'a legal right' is 'There is in existence a legal system'.[2] Hence, a deductive formulation in terms of value descriptive sentences, each system with its specific content must be used.[3] Where cultural diffusions and mixtures occur, analysis into the several systematically described, more elemental cultural components is necessary.[4]

Second, the method for describing the specific content of the value system of one particular introspecting person, legal system, religious institution, or any one of the world's cultures, must be different from that for *evaluating* the specific contents of one's and other, perhaps normatively incompatible, intrinsic values, once each is cognitively described. Clearly, to use the correctly described

---

[1] Paul Bohannan *Justice and Judgment Among the Tiv*, 1957, 69, 101, 104–5, 111, 120, 210, 212–14. For what those differences are: Joseph C. Smith, 'The Unique Nature of the Concepts of Western Law', *The Canadian Bar Review* (SCBR), Vol. XLVI 1968, 191–225.

[2] *The Law Quarterly Review*, Vol. 70, London, p. 49, and *The Concept of Law*, London, 1961 (HART).

[3] F. N., 'The Importance of Deductively Formulated Theory in Ethics and Social and Legal Science' in *Essays in Honor of Henry M. Sheffer*, ed. Henle *et al.* 1951 and (PAPP), Ch. 6.

[4] E.g. 'The Rich Culture of Mexico' in *The Meeting of East and West* (NMEW), *ibid*, 1946.

specific content (of the behaviour being evaluated), which is associated with one's own sensed pleasure, one's own content for a self-fulfilled life, or one's own official legal-political system to evaluate the incompatible specific content of some other person's intrinsic pleasurable values or legal system is to beg the evaluative question at issue as the sceptical Hume, Hobbes and other evaluative non-cognitive philosophers Professors Charles L. Stevenson, A. J. Ayer (and with respect to Bentham's hedonism), R. B. Braithwaite[1] and the English, American and Scandinavian lawyers Austin, Holmes, Hand, Karl Olivecrona and Alf Ross[2] have noted. Hence, to avoid confusing the cognitive character of the one with that of the other, we shall, following Professor Ayer's usage for ethics, call the former *descriptive*, and the latter *evaluative* intrinsic value theory.[3] We use the generic *value*, rather than its species, *ethical*, because aesthetic differ from ethical or legal intrinsic values and this essay must include both.

Notwithstanding the evaluative non-cognitivists' valid case against all traditional modern evaluative cognitivists, the non-cognitivists' own persuasive definitional method leaves their positive theory unpersuasive. Moreover, it is becoming intolerably so for many anthropologists and sociologists who initially (following Krober, Benedict and Mannheim) embraced it,[4] and for philo-

---

[1] Respectively, *The Treatise on Human Nature* (HTHN), eds Th. Green and T. H. Grose, London, 1886, vol. II, pp. 257–58; *Leviathan*, ed. Michael Oakeshott (HLO), Oxford, ch. 18; *Ethics and Language* (SEaL), Yale Univ. Press, 1944; *Language, Truth and Logic* (ALTL); 'The Role of Values in Scientific Inference', *Conference on Induction*, Wesleyan Univ., Conn., June 12–17, 1961.

[2] John Austin, *The Province of Jurisprudence*, 1832, with Introduction by H. L. A. Hart (HAPJ), London, 1954, 167–9, 132, 254 and esp. 261; 'Learned Hand on Holmes, Stone and Swan in *The Spirit of Liberty* (HSoL), ed. Irving Dilliard, Knopf, N.Y., 1953; K. Olivecrona, *Law as Fact*, 1939; A. Ross, *Towards a Realistic Jurisprudence* (RTRJ), Copenhagen, 1946. He shows that all Continental European Rationalistic or Existential *Sein-Sollen* (i.e. self fulfilment) theories entail self-contradictory is-ought 'facts'. The same is true for Lon Fuller's *Law in Quest of Itself* (FLoI), Chicago, 1940 and *Natural Law Forum*, Vol. 3, 68–76, 77–81. See Professor Ernest Nagel, *ibid*, 77–81 and vol. 4, 26–43. Cf. Hart, *op. cit.*, and F. N., 'Law, Language and Morals', *Yale Law Journal* (NYLJ), Vol. 71, 1017–48, 1962. To this should be added *is-ought* Hegelianism, Marxism, Neo-Darwinianism, or any historical determinism, as well as final cause Neo-Aristotelianism or voluntaristic 'courage to be' existential metaphysics.

[3] (ALTL), 103–6.

[4] International Symposium *Cross-Cultural Understanding* (CCU), eds F. N. and H. H. Livingston, Harper & Row, N.Y., London, Ch. 21; (PAPP), Ch. 6 and 7; C. Kluckhohn, 'The Scientific Study of Values', *Proc. Am. Philosophical Soc.*, Oct. 1958, and *Zygon*, 1966; David Bidney, *Theoretical Anthropology* (BTA), Columbia Univ. Press, 1953, Ch. 2.

sophers and lawyers as well.[1] Consequently, the present situation is that the *evaluative* (as distinct from merely descriptive) cognitivists and non-cognitivists establish merely their negative cases against one another. Conversely, both fail in their positive theses. Is there any escape from this predicament?

The normative cognitivists and non-cognitivists disagree only with respect to evaluative intrinsic ethical (or value) theory: the normative cognitivists affirming it to be cognitive, i.e. stateable entirely in terms of indicative sentences of which it is meaningful to say that they are true or false; the normative non-cognitivists affirming that evaluative intrinsic ethical theory entails at least one irreducible non-indicative sentence for its complete meaningfulness, such as 'Cheers!', 'Please like what I like', or 'Shoulder arms!' They agree, however, on two things: First, assuming a given intrinsic value with specific content, the question of which instrumental value is best to realize it, is answerable by indicative sentences which are directly or indirectly confirmable or disconfirmable. Second, although the language of naturalistic knowledge and descriptive ethical or legal theory is different (the former theories containing no normative words, the latter containing normative words such as sin, virtue, guilty, innocent, having a right with its correlative obligations, etc.), both naturalistic scientific theories and *descriptive* value theories are cognitive.

The latter fact permits us in later sections to use the cognitive method of descriptive intrinsic value theory with specific content in Western culture to answer the question whether, if *common denominator factors with the same specific content* can be found in both the cognitive natural scientific theories and the contemporaneous or later descriptive intrinsic values of Western culture, then perhaps evaluative intrinsic value theory may be more cognitive than recent anthropologists, philosophers and lawyers have been able to make meaningful and implement instrumentally.

Unfortunately, there is another difficulty in our way: It becomes evident when one notes that equally as important as the foregoing

[1] Brand Blanshard, *Reason and Goodness*, Allen & Unwin, London, Macmillan, N.Y., 1961, *ibid*, *The Nature of Thought*, Ch. X, 1941; Sidney Hook, 'The Nature of Intelligence', *School and Society*, Vol. 84, 1956; G. E. Moore, *Principia Ethica*, Cambridge Univ. Press, 1903; Felix Cohen, *Ethical Systems and Legal Ideas*, N.Y., 1933; Roscoe Pound (IDWO), Ch. 1, Harvard Law Review: Vol. 24, 591–619, Vol. 25, 140–68, 489–516 and 'Law and the Science of Law in Recent Theories', *Yale Law Journal*, Vol. 43, pp. 525 ff.; Edgar Bodenheimer, *Jurisprudence*, Harvard Univ. Press, 1962 and *Treatise on Justice*, N.Y., 1967;

emphasis on specific content are the three italicized words *'difficulty in principle'* above. They bespeak the historical fact that there is such a difficulty in principle in all Modern value theories, Neo-Aristotelian and Neo-Darwinian as well as Anglo-American and Continental European-Pan American.

It derives from both Aristotle's Greek Aryan ordinary language *logic of predicables* and the beginning of modern science and philosophy, when again misled by the two-termed subject-predicate (entity-property) syntax of any Aryan ordinary language[1] indicative sentence, its syntax was read into the nature of things, both naturalistic and normative. More specifically: (1) Descartes, Hobbes, Locke and also even Newton in his ordinary language thinking and writing (but not in his *Principia*, where he thought mathematical functionally) misinterpreted the many-entity-termed relational concept of inertial mass, and the different many-entity-termed relational concept of gravitational mass in Galilei's physics and Newton's Mathematical Laws of Motion, as a purportedly directly sensed two-termed entity property Aryan ordinary language material substance, or aggregate of such substances, each one with either (*a*) its Cartesian-Euclidian implicit topological,[2] and explicit metrical *extension* or (*b*) its purported Galileian-Hobbesian-Newtonian inertial free motion fastened to it, so to speak, Aryan prose-wise, as its intrinsic defining property or predicate. Contemporaneously, (2) Descartes, Locke, Berkeley, and Leibniz, also,

---

[1] I.e. any Western language, and also the Sanskrit of Aryan Hindu India and its Vaisesika Dualists. For the syntactical difference between any Aryan and the Burmese languages see Professor Khin Maung Win's Ch. 13 in (CCU). See also N. Chomsky, *Syntactic Structures* (CHOM), Th. Hague, 1957, *Aspects of a Theory of Syntax* (Cambridge, Mass.), 1965, *Cartesian Linguistics* N.Y., 1966, and 'Language and the Mind' in *Psychology Today*, Vol. 1, esp. p. 30.

[2] For the importance of the distinction between topological and metrical relatedness, see Leibniz on *analysis situs* in 'Leibniz' Theory of Space' (NLoS), *Journal of the History of Ideas*, Vol. VII, No. 4, 1946, 422–46, and Kant's 'incongruent counterparts' in their hearing on the relational theory of space as described in 'Natural Science and the Critical Philosophy of Immanuel Kant' in *The Heritage of Kant* (NHoK), eds G. T. Whitney and D. G. Bowers, Princeton, 1939, 39–64. Also Adolf Grunbaum's *Science and Zeno's Paradoxes*, 1967 (GZP), Allen & Unwin, London. Equally important is Kant's distinction in Newton's dynamical mechanics between the relations of 'co-ordination' and 'subordination' (NHoK). The former is the state functional relation between dependent and independent variables at any given moment of time. 'Subordination' is the causal relation of necessary connection between the independent variables at a present moment of time and their mathematically calculated empirical values at any specified past or future moment of time. This distinction will become important in a moment with respect to quantum mechanics.

and in their different ways, Hume,[1] Kant, Fichte, Hegel, Bradley, Husserl,[2] von Hartman, Freud, Heidigger, Sartre, and Tillich similarly misinterpreted the many-entity-termed relational (c) commonsensical and scientific observer, (d) the thinking theoretical physicist, the Continental Rationalistic *Cogito*, and (e) the humanistic evaluator as an Aryan prose entity-property, introspectively psychical mental or spiritual person called one's mind, spirit, windowless monad, Id, Ego, Super-Ego, or *Geist* (literally an irreducible disembodied person, or in short a *Ghost*),[3] thereby making everything 'for a mind', i.e. for such a ghostly disembodied me. With many-entity-termed relations irrelevant to the definition of the irreducible (1) material substances and (2) disembodied introspectively psychic Ghosts[2] the problem of specifying the *common denominator factors* for meaningfully relating (f) one introspective depth psycho-analytic or existential agonizing knower and evaluator to another, (g) the introspectively psychological knower to what he objectively knows, and (h) naturalistic scientific know-

---

[1] The non-sceptical Hume of the Norman Kemp Smith-Charles Hendel Editions of Hume's later ethical works. T. H. Green, in his *Introduction* to Vol. II of Hume's *Treatise* (HToN), sees the *non sequitur* from Vol. I; as did McTaggart in his lectures on Hume in 1922–3.

[2] Due to his 'bracketing' of the naturalistic object.

[3] Not in the relatively harmless *Deutsch* sense of *Kobold*, as instanced in the imaginative villager's belief in a disembodied person in a local haunted house, but in the sense of Locke and even the sceptical Hume's persisting blank-tabletish introspectively psychic atomic mental substance which having no built-in logic can merely feel, or in the sense of *Gespenst*, *Verstand* or (understanding) *Geist* as instanced in Descartes, Berkeley, the early McTaggart, the Smith-Hendel Hume, Leibniz, Lotze, Kant, Fichte, Hegel, Bradley, von Hartmann, Freud, Husserl and the agonizing Heidigger, Sartre and Tillich's belief that not merely one's own person but also that of everybody else is one or more disembodied Ghosts. Freud, for example, has four Ghosts in himself and each proper-named person: his conscious introspected ego and in its unconscious ghostly basement three other Ghosts named Id, Ego, and Super-Ego. Kant, writing probably with tongue in his cheek, see (NHoK), has in himself and everyone else at least five Ghosts: (1) The Transcendental Ego of the knower of nature. This Ghost is identical in all persons. Otherwise, each ghostly knower would not bring the same aforementioned topological and homogeneously metrical 'forms of sensibility' and Aryan ordinary language Category of substance to the Humian *a posteriori* data of the inner and outer senses. (2) The Regulative Moral Ego, which is synthetic *a priori* with respect to its Categorical Imperative. (3) The in part *a posteriori* legal Ego. (4) The Regulative Belief in the non-existing God and one's own proper-named Soul's religious *personal* immortality. And (5) the teleologically *Als Ob* (as if) Ego of the form-on-matter sculptor and the goal-guided local fellow who goes to the pub for a drink.

[4] See *Taschenwörterbuch der englischen und deutschen Sprache*, Vols I and II, von Prof. Edmund Klatt u. Dr Wilhelm Mosle, Vol. II, 1951, and von Dr Hermann Lindemann, Vol. I, Berlin-Schoneberg, 1912.

ledge to humanistic intrinsic values became *insoluble in principle*.

A second consideration supports this conclusion. With the exception of the American pragmatic evaluative cognitivists, such as Professor Sidney Hook and the sociological lawyers Professor Julius Cohen, Harold Laswell and Myres McDougal, whose pragmatic evaluative cognitivism has the merits of specific content, and of keeping man in nature,[1] but fails for a different reason;[2] most modern normative social scientists and humanists regard their respective subjects as autonomous. Practically all last-generation-minded Anglo-American lawyers study only their disjunctively related cases; many disdain jurisprudence and all theory, while surreptitiously smuggling in that of Hobbes, Hume, Austin, Thayer, and the late Judge Learned Hand. Kant's distinction between the *Naturwissenschaften* and the *Geisteswissenschaften*[3] turns the arts and normative social subjects into sciences, making each autonomous. The aforementioned evaluative non-cognitivists' distinction between indicative and non-indicative sentences is, in its different way, similar. Husserl's 'bracketing' of the natural object has the same effect. By virtue of its own concept of itself as autonomous, any such subject cannot relate itself in any meaningful way to any other subject. This also leaves the problem of this essay, of finding the *common denominator factors* necessary for meaningfully relating Western naturalistic scientific knowledge to its humanistic intrinsic values *insoluble in principle*.

There is a third difficulty in our way. It is the philosophical

[1] (HJI), *et al.*, *op. cit.*, Julius Cohen and others (COPA), *Parental Authority: The Community and the Law*, Rutgers Univ. Press, 1958; see also, with David Haber, *The Law School of Tomorrow*, *ibid.*, 1968, Symposium I; Harold Lasswell, *The Analysis of Political Behaviour*, Routledge & Kegan Paul, London, 1948; Myres McDougal, 'Law as a Process of Decision', *Natural Law Forum*, 1936; Harold D. Lasswell and Myres S. McDougal, 'Legal Education and Public Policy', *Yale Law Journal*, Vol. 52, 203–95. The late Professor Underhill Moore is equally important and realized that the pragmatic sociologically legal method does not warrant evaluative cognitivism with respect to Ehrlich's 'living law'. F.N. 'Underhill Moore's Legal Science', vol. 59, 196–213, and F.N. *The Complexity of Legal and Ethical Experience*, 1959, Little, Brown, Boston (CLEE). Ch. VI in relation to Petrazycki, esp. n. 81.

[2] *Descriptive* ethical or legal theory differs from naturalistic in containing normative and imputative (Kant, Kelsen) words and consequently measures the facts; rather than conforming to them, after the manner of non-normatively worded naturalistic theory. Hence the pragmatic test of workability *in fact*, as all the non-cognitivist philosophers and lawyers have noted, will not suffice to establish an evaluative cognitivism.

[3] Literally the science of persons conceived as Ghosts, Cf. n. previous page.

fashion of the moment to suppose that one can bypass epistemo-logy. Would that it were the case! The task of both the theoretical and the experimental physicist and the philosopher of science in its relation to the humanities would be much easier. Unfortunately for the philosopher's ease, but fortunately for the overcoming of the aforementioned *difficulties in principle*, such is not the case.

There are two reasons why. The first is contemporaneously scientific. The second arises from the ambiguities of ordinary language. As Whitehead emphasized, it is a very rich vehicle of expression, but also, because of the epistemological ambiguities of any one of its words, a most treacherous one.

The remarkable experimentally confirmed theories of twentieth-century mathematical physics depend as much on (*a*) an epistemo-logical investigation of ordinary, as well as more sophisticatedly scientific, natural knowing, as they do on (*b*) the Michelson-Morley experiment in the case of Einstein's Special Theory of Relativity and the black body radiation findings in the case of Quantum Mechanics, which initiated the speculative discovery of these two theories by Einstein, Planck, Schrödinger, Heisenberg, and Dirac, and the later diverse indirect confirmations by Eddington, Comp-ton, and many others. Einstein gives expression to this indispensa-bility of epistemology as well as observable data for science when he writes: 'The reciprocal relationship of epistemology and science is of noteworthy kind. They are dependent upon each other. Epistemology without contact with science becomes an empty scheme. Science without epistemology is—insofar as it is thinkable at all—primitive and muddled.'[1]

One such muddle, which Einstein found it necessary to clear up epistemologically before warranting the restriction of Newtonian mechanics required by his Special and General Theories of Relati-vity,[2] had to do with Newton's ordinary language thinking when he wrote that he had 'deduced' the elementary concepts and universal laws of his *Principia* from the experimental data. The epistemolo-gical name for this inductively described and *deduced* theory of human knowing is *naïve realism*, where *naïve* means directly sensed or introspected, and *realism* is the equivalent of *objective* knowledge, i.e. knowledge the *specific defining content* of which is *invariantly*

[1] *Albert Einstein, Philosopher-Scientist*, Vol. 7 (ELLP) in Library of Living Philosophers, 1949, ed. Paul A. Schilpp (SLLP), Evanston, Ill., p. 684.
[2] Albert Einstein Collected Papers, *The World As I See It*, Covici Friede, N.Y. 1934, p. 107 (EWIS).

the same for all frames of reference and all perceivers. For the specification of what Einstein found both ordinary and mathematical physical natural knowledge to be, see the articles entitled 'Einstein's Theory of Knowledge' and 'Einstein's Conception of Science', respectively by the physicist-philosopher Professor Victor F. Lenzen and the present writer.[1] For Einstein's judgment whether this is his conception, see his appraisal.[2] For evidence that this epistemology holds also in Quantum Mechanics, with Einstein's Special and General Theories derived as special cases, see the present writer's Introduction to Professor Werner Heisenberg's *Physics and Philosophy*.[3] (The revolutionary novelty of quantum mechanics consists in making the independent variables of the state function—Kant's relation of 'co-ordination' *supra*—at any given moment of time a function of probabilities, while keeping the Schrödinger time relation between states—Kant's relation of 'subordination'—thereby keeping physics classically causal, but because of the unique elementary probabilities definition of the state function, not deterministically so.)[4]

Einstein was greatly influenced by Mach's *Science of Mechanics* (1883) and by the secptical Hume.[1] Two years before the Michelson-Morley experiment, Mach demonstrated that the entities of mass, space and time of Galilei and Newton's dynamical mechanics are many-entity-termed relational elements; and not two-termed, single-entity-property material substances, moving after the imageful manner of colliding tiny *laissez-faire* billiard balls in a similarly self-sufficient container called space. Why? Because it is only from the relational mathematically functional meaning of the symbols m, d, t in Newton's equations that he can deduce the many theorems of his *Principia*, thereby permitting indirect cognitive tests which pay attention, following Bacon's dictum, to negative as well as positive instances and then generalize to a novel theory should even one negative instance turn up, as in the M-M experiment. Otherwise, the sting of the fallacy of affirming the consequent in indirect

---

[1] (ELLP), 355–408.

[2] *Ibid.*, p. 683.

[3] Allen & Unwin, London; Harper & Row, N.Y., 1958. Cf. R. Carnap, *Philosophical Foundations of Physics*, Basic Books N.Y., 1966, Ch. 30, esp. 288, and R. B. Braithwaite, *Scientific Explanation*, Cambridge Univ. Press, 1953, Harper Torch, N.Y., 7 ff., 76, 81–5, 115, 192.

[4] *Ibid.*, and *The Logic of the Sciences and the Humanities* (NLSH) (Meridian PB 71, 1959), Macmillan, N.Y., 1947, Ch. XI.

[5] Mach. English edn, 1893, Open Court, Chicago, London. Hume, Vol. I of HTHN).

confirmation is fatal. Whitehead expresses the same many-termed relational thesis as Mach, more after the manner of the pure mathematician, in his classic Royal Society paper 'On Mathematical Concepts of the Physical World' in 1905,[1] when, realizing the disconfirmation of Newton's relational theory in 1885, he put forward several possible many-termed relational alternatives, later developing one which failed to gain scientific acceptance for both physical and epistemological reasons. Avenarius, Mach, James and Whitehead's common error was the *non sequitur* that because persisting Aryan ordinary language material or mental substances do not exist, therefore, no persisting actual entities whatever exist. The consistently sceptical Hume is similar. This forced them to restrict themselves to successive perishing particular qualities ('adjectives') within radical empirical immediacy, and what can be 'extensively abstracted' therefrom.[2] As Whitehead noted, this left 'recollection' and memory meaningless, thereby generating the second *non sequitur* in Whitehead's case, of confusing nominalistic perishing particular qualities with 'eternal objects'. Unfortunately also, the abstractive method does not achieve its aim; placing a greater load on the deliverances of the senses, with respect to public nowness and the homogeneous metrical properties of space-time everywhere, than the senses are able to carry.[3]

Einstein avoids the *non sequiturs* of the sceptical Hume, Mach and Whitehead, while learning from the former two, and Berkeley on external objects, what radical empirical immediacy *alone* warrants.[4] After recalling the qualitative images of the Michelson-Morley experiment and Newton's *Hypotheses non fingo*, and turning epistemologist to re-examine afresh the relation, in anyone's human knowing, between the deliverances of the senses and any warrantable belief in persistent specifically defined entities and their laws,

[1] Trans. Royal Soc., London, Vol. 205, 1906. Abridged in *Alfred North Whitehead An Anthology*, Macmillan, N.Y., and Cambridge Univ. Press, 1953, 11–82.

[2] A. N. Whitehead, *The Concept of Nature*, Cambridge Univ. Press, 1920, Ch. IV, and *Process and Reality*, Ch. II, Sec. I.

[3] *Ibid.*, *The Principle of Relativity*, 1922, Ch. III; F.N. 'Whitehead's Philosophy of Science' in (SLLP), Whitehead, Vol. 3 and (ELLP). See also (GZP).

[4] *Berkeley's Complete Works*, ed. A. C. Fraser, Oxford, mdcccci, Vol. I, esp. 'Three Dialogues between Hylas and Philonous'. Realizing that the Humian positivists tended to smuggle in persisting naïve realistic objects to which the sceptical Hume's radical empiricism does not entitle them, Einstein frequently remarked: 'Bishop Berkeley was a genius. . . . Anyone should be able to see that we do not observe scientific objects but it took a genius to show that the same is true for ordinary objects.'

Einstein showed[1] that (1) the deliverances of the senses *alone* do not warrant either the layman's on the physicist's belief in external objects in public space and time. Why? (2) Because (*a*) to be an external object means to be in public space and time, (*b*) public time entails a meaning for the public (not merely Whitehead's privately sensed) simultaneity of spacially separated events, and (*c*) such publically meaningful simultaneity is not given through the senses. Hence, (3) the *naïve realistic* notion, defined above, of the meaning and warrant for anyone's belief in external objects in public space and time is false, and (4) although the radical empirical meaning of ordinary language words and scientific symbols, as described by Berkeley with respect to 'outer' sensed qualities and by the sceptical Hume and James introspectively, and also more generally, is a necessary condition for our cognitive knowledge of public objects and persisting neurophysiological selves, it is not a sufficient condition. Hence, (5) if the layman's and scientists' belief in public clocks and watches in public space and time, mathematically set and synchronized with astronomically calculated Greenwich time, is to be meaningful and necessary [even for pseudometaphysicians who bypassing science claim to know Reality directly], then the persisting objects and persons must be speculatively discovered, many-termed relationally defined, and indirectly confirmed by appeal to the directly observable (i.e. radical empirical) data. Finally, (6) because of the deliverances of the senses in the Michelson-Morley, Eddington's and many other experiments, and as described (in 2*b* and *c*) just above, the many-termed relational masses, space and time must be different from those of both Newton's mechanics and Maxwell's electromagnetics, with the latter deriving from Einstein's Special and General Theories of Relativity as very important and prevalent but restricted special cases.

Thus Einstein writes:

'Since . . . sense preception only gives information of the external world or of "physical reality" indirectly, we can only grasp the

---

[1] Albert Einstein, *Relativity, The Special and the General Theory*, Methuen, London, 1920, Ch. I–IX, for *ordinary observation*, esp. p. 22. For *ordinary heard*, rather than *seen* simultaneity, see F.N., Ch. 14 of *Man, Nature and God* (MNaG), Simon & Schuster, N.Y., 1962, esp. 211–12 (paperback paging different). *Annal. u Physik* 17 (1905) and 49 (1916); Einstein, Lorentz, Minkowski and Weyl, *The Principle of Relativity*, Methuen, London, 1923. F.N., *Science and First Principles*, 1931, Cambridge Univ. Press; Macmillan, N.Y., Ch. II. Also (EWST), (ELLP), (WLLP) and (GZP).

latter by speculative means. It follows . . . that our notions of physical reality can never be final. We must always be ready to change the[m]—that is to say the axiomatic substructure of physics—in order to do justice to the perceived facts in the most logically perfect way.'[1]

Note that the words 'external' and 'reality' express the fact that the layman and scientist's belief in an external world *with specified content* the same for all perceivers, requires for its meaningfulness a realistic epistemology. Neither a naïve realistic one nor a Kantian or Neo-Kantian one in which the external world and one's own persisting neurophysiological person is *strictly speaking* merely an 'unknowable *Ding-an-Sich*', will do. The adjective 'logical', in Einstein's last sentence above, indicates that the appropriate name for this cognitively testable realism is logical realism, or, more completely expressed, many entities termed logic-of-relations realism.

Investigations by Einstein and others show this epistemological clarification of cognitive natural knowledge to be more fully and precisely stated as follows: In the persisting analysis of the 'problematic situation' with which all inquiry begins, it supplements and step-by-step replaces[2] (1) the purported directly observed two-termed entity-property persisting entities (of both Aristolian-Medieval and Modern entity-property naïve realism), which generated the aforementioned *difficulties in principle* and 'primitive . . . muddle[s]', with (2) (i) nominalistic sensuously qualitative disjunctively relational radical empiricism in (ii) epistemological correlations with (iii) speculatively discovered (by theoretical mathematical physicists of genius), deductively formulated, indirectly and experimentally confirmed many-entity-termed logical realism, in which the epistemic correlations[3] implicit in the theory's deduced operational definitions[4] and accordingly constructed instruments

---

[1] (EWST), p. 60.   [2] (NLSH), Ch. I–VI.

[3] Present in the *Zuordnungen Definitionen* of Hans Reichenbach, *Philosophie der Raum-Zeit Lehre*, Berlin, 1928. The 'epistemic correction' usage was introduced first by F.N. at (*a*) the *East-West Philosophers Conference*, Honolulu, summer 1939, and published in *Philosophy: East and West*, ed. Charles A. Moore, Princeton Univ. Press, 1944, ch. VIII, and (*b*) the *International Congress of Unified Science* (ICUS), Harvard Univ., Sept. 1939, with Philip Frank in the chair and Bridgman a discussant. See (ICUS) abstract, more fully published later (NLSH) as 'Epistemic Correlations and Operational Definition'; the 'and'

[4] P. B. Bridgman. *The Logic of Physics*, Macmillan, N.Y., 1932. The realization of their indispensability is Bridgman's great contribution.

are two-termed, but not one-one two-termed relations.[1]

The reason for the non one-oneness is that the (i) *disjunctive* many-termed adjectival *relatedness* of the diverse successive qualities and their radical empirical perpetually perishing events *is not isomorphic* with the (iii) *logical realistic relatedness* of the more persisting, invariantly-the-same-for-all-perceivers-and-reference frames, public objects and their events. This non-isomorphism is the more fundamental reason why both Aristotle's two-termed property-entity and Whitehead's many-termed relational abstractive methods fail. Even so, the epistemic correlations *implicit in* the logical realistic theory's deduced operational definitions and their instruments are two-termed relations, because epistemologically they both distinguish and correlate the ordinary object, or the operated apparatus, in their (iii) logical realistically conceived and constructed meaning and in their (i) imageful directly sensed and felt radical empirical meaning. These *implicit* epistemic correlations (which Professor Henry Margenau noted in 1935 and called 'rules of correspondence') will become explicit and concrete in the later section on music: they vary from one sense to another of the same perceiver and from one speculatively discovered, indirectly confirmed publicly meaningful cognitive naturalistic theory to another. It is Professor Margenau's unique merit to have specified what they are for the many modern mathematical physical theories.[2]

The epistemic correlations have one other exceedingly important

---

not being the relation of identity or that, as in Reichenbach's *Zuordnungen Definitionen*, of a definition. Certainly, G. E. Moore showed that 'yellow' in the (i) radical empirical meaning of the directly seen colour is a simple, and hence it cannot be defined in terms of 'yellow' in the (iii) logical realistic meaning of the electromagnetic wave's frequency, and conversely to define the latter in terms of the former is to affirm nonsense—i.e. some electromagnetic wavelengths are yellow in the sense of (i). Hence, Reichenbach's Co-ordinative Definitional usage is a misnomer, combining and thereby confusing each of two different things: (1) Bridgman's operational definitions and (2) their *implicit* non-one-one two-termed epistemic correlations. Hence the title of (NLSH), Ch. VII. The necessity for this distinction between (1) and (2) was faced by Bridgman and others in physicist-astronomers' Symposium of the Princeton Bicentenial Conferences published later in *Physical Science and Human Values* with Foreword by E. P. Wigner, Princeton Univ. Press, 1947, 105–64.

[1] Otherwise the operational apparatus and procedures have no relevance to the testing of the theory in question.

[2] *Philosophy of Science*, Vol. 2, pp. 65 ff.; *Reviews of Modern Physics*, 1941, Vol. 1, pp. 176 ff.; and *The Nature of Physical Reality*, 1950, McGraw Hill, N.Y. 'Rules of correspondence' and 'epistemic correlations' are equivalent ways of denoting the non one-one two-termed relations. Important is the fact that the latter are not substantive 'correspondences' or 'correlations' of the usual kind, in

function. As noted above, all logical realistic entities receive their defining properties relational analytically from the substantive content of the many-entity-termed relations of which they are the relata or field. This is why all such physics is field physics. Consequently, these relational properties hold for all the relata of their field. This solves the problems of theoretically meaningful mathematical, mathematical physical, and legal obligational (NCEE) induction. This means, however, that the logical realistic propositions of (iii) above are tautologies. It is the epistemic correlation of their persisting entities and events with (i) the nominalistic disjunctively related radical empirical data which turns them into synthetic propositions, thereby making their cognitive confirmability or disconfirmability meaningful; always let it be re-emphasized paying attention to negative as well as positive instances.

It has been noted[1] also that the non one-one two-termed epistemic correlations vanish when the logical realistic object known is the logical realistic knower himself, since then the many-entity-termed relatedness of the one and that of the other is an identity. Thereby a realistic epistemological ontology is made meaningful, while also bridging the gulf between the knower and the known. This, too, will take on cognitively confirmable content in the next section and at this essay's ending.

So much for *warrantable* Western ordinary and scientific natural knowledge, which today is being spontaneously imported and slowly mastered by Japanese, Indians, Chinese and many others, while Oriental radical empirical aesthetic, psychological and religious ways are conversely transforming the West 'Towards a More Comprehensive Concept of the Person'.[2] What of Western intrinsic humanistic values? The sequel must limit itself primarily to its music and its legal science. If their differing specific contents are not to be misunderstood, both the writer and the reader must first face the following topic.

---

ordinary or scientific knowledge, between two factors in (i) the radical empirical nominalistic or (iii) the logical realistic, or (NR) the naïve realistic natural history, (iv) the circumstantial statistical world of discourse. Instead they are non-one-one two-termed *epistemological* relations of any substantive factor or symbol in its (i) radical empirical and its (iii) logical realistic meaning. Being epistemological, the epistemic correlation usage is certainly the briefest and perhaps the least misleading way to denote these unique non-one-one-termed relations.

[1] (PAPP), 110–11.
[2] *East-West Studies on The Problem of the Self* (EWPS), eds P. T. Raju, and Alburey Castell, Nijhoff, The Hague, 1968.

THREE DIFFICULTIES IN OUR WAY

Our first difficulty is that we have to use Aryan ordinary language to correct the countless errors its (a) two-termed entity-property syntax and (b) diverse confused and other meanings (picked up over the centuries by each one of its words) have produced. As Whitehead emphasized to me in 1922 and repeated annually afterwards: 'One cannot be too suspicious of ordinary language in science or philosophy.' Although it is a rich vehicle of expression, it is an exceedingly slippery and treacherous one.

In value subjects, the fatal dangers are much greater than in natural knowledge. For as noted above, Newton falls into grave error in his ordinary language writing, only to be saved by the different many-entity-termed relational syntax of his mathematical language. But most medieval and modern Western humanists at least use only one or another of the Aryan ordinary languages. Also, even though some lawyers have avoided the pitfalls of Aryan prose better, as the sequel will show, than other social scientists and humanists, these lawyers do not use the imageless relational symbolic language of mathematics. Consequently, if Einstein found physics 'primitive and muddled' due to the neglect of epistemology, we must not be surprised to find the humanities and 'social science' triply and quadruply so.

How are we to meet and overcome this difficulty? The answer has three parts. First, because all sensed or introspected qualities are disjunctively related rather than necessarily connected, as Hume showed, the logic of the (i) *differentiated* nominalistic radical empirical component of cognitive knowledge is the extensional propositional calculus of the Stoics[1] and *Principia Mathematica* with its 'material implication', the later Wittgensteinian truth-tables, and Peirce's *Secondness*.[2] This entails the ordinary language *Maxim I*: When referring to the (i) component of cognitive knowledge, all its words must be thought of, written, and read *only* in their nominalistic radical empirical meaning, as described best for the so-called 'outer' sensed qualities by Berkeley, and for introspected qualities by the sceptical Hume of Volume I of *The Treatise* and in William James's *Radical Empiricism* and other essays on the self.

Our second difficulty arises from the (iii) many-entity-termed

---

[1] B. Mates, *Stoic Logic* (MSL), Univ. of California Press, 1955; S. Sambursky, *The Physics of the Stoics* (SPoS), esp. 76–80.

[2] *Collected Papers* (CPCS), ed. Charles Hartshorne and Paul Weiss, Harvard Univ. Press, 1931–5.

logical realistic factor in warrantable knowledge of human and cosmic nature. Overcoming it gives ordinary language *Maxim II*: When referring to (iii), the noun in our ordinary sentence must be an irreducible many-entity-termed relation and its predicate the substantive content of that relation. This Maxim has some surprising consequences:

Corollary 1: Applied to the two-termed entity-property $\Phi x\ \Psi x$ symbols of *Principia Mathematica*, it entails that the Φs and Ψs must always be many entity termed relationally defined. This avoids the 'set-theoretical' paradoxes; without either the *ad hoc* restricted theory of types of Earl Russell and Professor W. V. O. Quine or the weak kind of self-reference of the unique *Symbolic Logic*[1] of Professor F. B. Fitch, which, when its propositions add the additional postulate necessary for specific content, loses sufficient self-reference and then falls back into the *ad hoc*ness of the theory of types. The unqualified validity of Godel's theorem needs also to be re-examined. Legal science will give reasons for this also.

Corollary 2: Necessary, too, is the construction (only now in process[2]) of an irreducible at least three-entity-termed logic of relations. Its intentional syntax is that of: the Stoics *Lekton*, Descartes's self-referential *Cogito*, Kant's Regulative moral Ego, Brentano and Husserl's act psychology, von Domarus's embodied psychiatry, and Drs (M.D.) Warren S. McCulloch, Arturo Rosenbleuth and Valentino Braitenberg's experimental cybernetic (i.e. self-referentially *helmsman*ing), circular ('feedback') mechanically causal neurophysiological systems, as well as the irreduceable three-termed relations of Royce's 'Principles of Logic' and Peirce's *Thirdness* (CPCP). Until such a constructed intentional three-termed logic is achieved, ordinary language will serve as a makeshift, providing we realize that it is 'unthinkable without epistemology', and follow *Maxim II* above.

Reference was made above to 'the (i) *differentiated* nominalistic radical empirical component' of human nature and natural knowledge. The word *differentiated* brings us to our third linguistic difficulty.

[1] Ronald Press, N.Y., 1952. See Appendix.
[2] See *Lekton* the Preface by Dr Warren S. McCulloch to the late Dr Eilhard von Domarus's (M.D. and Ph.D. Philosophy) *The Logical Structure of Mind* and its following *Commentary* published in *Communication: Theory and Research*, ed. Lee Thayer, Charles C. Thomas, Publisher, Springfield, Ill., Ch. XIV–XVI; 'On a Calculus of Triadas', W. S. McCulloch and R. Moreno-Diaz in *M.I.T. Research Lab. of Electronics*, Section *Neurophysiology. QPR No. 84*, pp. 333–46; *No. 88*, pp. 335–47. (Cambridge, Mass.)

Both James and Peirce (and also the ancient Oriental Nihilistic Mahâyâna Buddists and Unqualified Non-dualistic Vedantic Hindus) noted that the totality of nominalistic all-embracing existentially felt radical empirical immediacy is not everywhere and everywhen differentiated into successive 'perpetually perishing' qualities. Instead (for the radical empirical knower and evaluator as well as the known and the evaluated), it is, in James' words, 'at its periphery', and also in Peirce's statement about *Firstness*, undifferentiated and indeterminate, an irreducible 'spontaneous freshness' and 'creative potentiality' for successive somewhens and somewheres' differentiated qualities.[1] The late Professor Charles M. Bakewell, immediately upon his reading of *The Meeting of East and West*, called its author's attention to the equivalence of its language to that of his teacher and friend William James as quoted above.

The mathematical physicist Erwin Schrödinger comes to a similar conclusion in his *What is Life?*,[2] where, after stating 'that the pluralization of consciousness or minds . . . leads almost immediately to the invention of souls as many as there are bodies', he then adds that the 'only possible alternative is simply to keep to the immediate experience that consciousness is a singular'. Being, as Peirce notes, 'indescribable' (apart from its differentiated somewhens and somewheres), its logic must be that of the above Asians' Neti-Neti negative logic[3] (It is not this differentiated perishing particular quality. It is not that . . . quality.).

Otherwise, neither radically empirical feelingful man, nor even nature's beauty can be kept in nature,[4] instead of notioned to be

[1] (CPCP), Vol. 1, 357, and 6, pp. 190–225; cf. Charles Hartshorne, *The Philosophy and Psychology of Sensation*, Chicago, 1934, and 'the adumbrated' in Paul Weiss, *Reality*, Princeton, 1938.

[2] Macmillan, N.Y., 1946, 89–90.

[3] *Mahâyâna Sutras* in Max Muller, ed. of *Wisdom of the East Series* (MWES), Vol. XLIX Trans. Others and Junjiro Takakusu, and the latter's 'Eightfold Negation' (MPEW), p. 98, and his *Essentials of Buddhism*, Univ. of Hawaii Press, 1947. On Advaita Hinduism: (MWES), Vol. XXXIV; Sarendranath Dasgupta, *History of Indian Philosophy*, Cambridge Univ. Press, 1922; P. T. Raju, *Thought and Reality*, 1937; the English jurist Sir John Woodroffe's *Shakti and Shakta*, Luzac London, 1929, Ch. XIV; (NMNG), 20–4; for the non-identity of (*a*) Bradley's *Absolute* or the dialectical logic of negation of Hegel's *rationalistically differentiated Absolute Ego*, coming to self-consciousness in all too human (sinful, occasionally good, and indifferent) Western history, and (*b*) the Neti-Neti eight negations and its (i) nominalistic radical empirical naturalistic emotive consciousness 'without differences,' see A. C. Mukerji, *The Nature of The Self*, Allahabad, India, 1938.

[4] (NSFP), 256–62; (NMEW), Illustrations II–IV, XI, XIII–XVI; Jean Renoir, *Renoir My Father*, 1958, Little, Brown, Boston, 243–6, 147, 94, 106, 110.

superficial (*a*) Hobbes or Marxist phantasmic, (*b*) Kant or Neo-Kantian *als ob* un-Romantic, or (*c*) Fichtian, Kierkegardian, Sartrian,[1] and Tillichian[2] arbitrarily voluntaristic private projections. Otherwise also, as shown in 'To What Does Mathematical Physics Refer?'[3] the sufficient condition (as well as the indirect pragmatic ones described above) is not satisfied for the existential import of geological rocks or distant stars eons upon eons ago (when there were no humans aboard to project symbols, or lay down linguistic conventions about black marks on paper).

In any event, the way to meet our third ordinary language difficulty can now be stated: (i) radical empirical immediacy is not a projection of, or relative to, any introspectively psychic ego be it the Hegelian humanistic historian's Absolute or that of Berkeley and the other personalistic pluralists and voluntarists. Instead, it (i) is naturalistically and at least undifferentiatedly all-embrasive—a *First*, and hence one of the two elemental components of which all warrantably knowable naturalistic entities are composed; the other, being their (iii) speculatively discovered, experimentally and pragmatically confirmed, many-entity-termed relationally analytic logical realistic defining properties, conveyed by our ordinary language *Maxim II* above. Consequently, as Peirce noted tersely, the *Maxim III* for overcoming our third ordinary language difficulty with respect to undifferentiated (i) radical empirically immediacy *Firstness*, is: 'Only remember that every description of it must be false to it'. To this (1.357) one may add, 'Remember also that it is not in it.'

With *Maxims I, II* and *III* constantly in mind, we are at last prepared to describe Western intrinsic values in their relation to the foregoing descriptive epistemological analysis of cognitive natural knowledge. The agreement of evaluative non-cognitivists and cognitivists that descriptive intrinsic values are cognitive has been noted above. Hence, should the sequel show the descriptive analysis of Western intrinsic values to involve the same specific epistemology as its cognitive natural knowledge, then two things will be evident:

---

[1] Jean-Paul Sartre, e.g. *The Reprieve*, Knopf, N.Y., 1947.

[2] Henry Margenau, 'The Pursuit of Significance', *Main Currents*, Vol. 23, 65–76, and its Section V for its evaluatively non-cognitive Tillichian voluntaristic personal immortality notions; confirmed by Paul Tillich's (EWPS), 1965 address, 'The Problem of Immortality', published in (EWPS), 1968, Ch. 3.

[3] (MNaG), Ch. 15. Compare Professor Herbert Feigl's classic 'Existential Hypotheses Phenomenal and Realistic' in *Philosophy of Science*, Vol. 17 (1950), 35–62.

First, we shall have found the common denominator factors with specific content for relating the natural sciences and the humanities for which we have been looking since the beginning of this inquiry. Second, since this epistemologically analysed naturalistic knowledge is cognitive, to that extent the common denominator epistemological meaningfulness of the humanities is cognititive also. Restricting ourselves to Western music and then to legal science, we shall find even more than this to be the case cognitively; also that between aesthetic intrinsic values and moral, legally political, and religious ones, there is an important difference, which perhaps has not received the attention it merits.

INTRINSIC VALUES IN WESTERN CLASSICAL MUSIC

Whitehead noted that any thorough analysis of Western civilization tends to become a commentary on Plato. Although the sequel requires us to reject both Plato's and Aristotle's law and politics for that of the Stoics in what Jefferson called 'the pure form of Epictitus', in correlation with the 'hedonism of Epicurus' and to accept Einstein's epistemology rather than the abstractive method of either Aristotle or Whitehead; nevertheless, there is a generic sense with specific content common to the Democriteans, Platonists, the mathematics[1] of Aristotle, the Stoics, and the Moderns in which Whitehead's observation about Plato is correct.

Einstein tells one that 'If Euclid failed to kindle your youthful enthusiasm, then you are not born to be a scientific thinker', adding that in today's ordinary and scientific natural knowledge one 'can grasp reality in the sense of the ancient Greeks'[2]. Similarly Newton affirmed that he 'stood on the shoulders of the ancients'. His use in the *Principia* of Euclid's method of proving its theorems, and Euclid's metric for space, gives content to what he meant. But Euclid is little more than a systematic deductive presentation (with its assumed propositions, or 'axioms', and their deduced theorems) of the successively generalized observationally confirmed mathematically physical theories of Democritus, Theaetetus, Plato, Aristotle's mathematics, and the great Eudoxus who was a member of Plato's Academy. Recently, Professor S. Sambursky, the expert mathematical physical spectroscopist, talented Greek and Latin

[1] As distinct from his naïve realistic physics.
[2] (EWIS). 32 and 37.

classicist, and historian of Western science, has shown the same to be true for Chrysippus and the other Greek Stoics.[1] Tradition has it also that over the door of his Research Institute, Plato had the words, 'Nobody ignorant of geometry should enter my roof. . . .'[2] Certainly he is one of the world's greatest humanists and literary artists. These considerations suggest that to put the artistic component of Western civilization over against the scientific, branding the latter as slightly crude aesthetically, inhumane, and ethically neutral, if not positively evil, or to regard intrinsic values as autonomous, is a questionable practice. Plato's humanistic literary works confirm this conclusion.[3]

In his *Dialogues*, Plato refers frequently to 'the idea of the good' for measuring both personal moral and just political conduct. However, with but one exception, reported to us only by Aristotle and Diogenes Laertius,[4] he seems never to tell us quite what it is; except to say that it is identical with the idea of the beautiful in the arts and the idea of the true in the sciences. This, providing we take him literally, is, however, to tell us a great deal. Also, Plato has Socrates in Book VII of the *Republic* specify the subjects to which the method of human knowing (and its science of epistemology) has to be applied to arrive at the idea of the intrinsically good, or the intrinsically beautiful. If one examines these subjects with care, one finds that each is a mathematical science. There are at least four of them: (1) arithmetic, (2) acoustics, or what Socrates and all the Greek scientists and humanists called music, (3) stereometry, and (4) mathematical physical astronomy. The elemental mathematics necessary to understand these four mathematical natural sciences is contained in Euclid's *Elements*. Its Book VII is the prerequisite for understanding the first two of Socrates' sciences; as are Books V, X and XIII for the third and fourth. This means that Plato's (and his Socrates') humanistic philosophy of both the cognitively true, the good, and the intrinsically beautiful is likely to be but purring about empty words unless his *Dialogues* are read in conjunction with a thorough study of the specific content of the deduc-

[1] (SPoS), and *The Physical World of the Greeks* (SPWG), 1956

[2] As quoted in Professor Sambursky's 'Structural and Dynamic Elements in the Greek Conception of Physical Reality', 1964 (CCU), p. 239.

[3] As do those of the Democritean Epicurus, Lucretius, Eudoxus' hedonism, Aristotle, the Greek and Stoic moral, religious, and legal scientists, including even the scientific-minded humanists of Professor Sambursky's, *The Physical World of Late Antiquity*, 1962.

[4] See paper by O. Toeplitz in (MBGP).

tively formulated *relational analytically* defined *ideas* in the Books of Euclid's *Elements*.[1]

Briefly put, Euclid's Book VII constructs and deductively formulates the ratios and their proportions which relational analytically entail as their universally quantified entities the natural numbers of the Greek science of arithmetic. Such ratios and their proportions also define the experimentally and indirectly confirmed mathematical laws of its Democritean physics of acoustics. Book VII is credited originally to Theaetetus, the mathematical scientist after whom Plato named his *Dialogue* on epistemology. The discovery, mathematically functional statement and indirect experimental confirmation of the laws of acoustics, stated in terms of these Theaetetian (Book VII) ratios and proportions, is the achievement of the aforementioned experimental mathematical physicist, Democritus.

These laws are reconfirmed today in any elementary laboratory course on the physics of sound, and also at every symphony concert. For were the composer's, conductor's and all the players' scores not formally similar, in the mathematical logician's many-entity-termed *relationally analytic* sense of *similar relations*, the result would be auditory anarchy—a beatnik's brawl of noises instead of any piece of Western classical music in its diatonic or well-tempered scales.

The same is true for every one of the musicians' physical instruments. *Similar* ratios must be built into them so as to be instantly derivable as the one of the arithmetically ratioed acoustical vibrational *possibles*, specified by the conductor's arithmetically measured beat and the composer's black notes on every player's score. Such similarity of relations, called *isomorphism*, or proportionality, must also, by long practice, be made automatic for every professional player's reading of the score, fingers, and nervous system.

Theaetetus, Democritus, Socrates, Plato, Eudoxus and the Stoics' reason should now be evident for identifying (*a*) the [logical realistic] *idea* of indirectly and experimentally confirmed, and hence cognitive scientific knowledge, called ἐπιστήμη with the (*b*) idea of intrinsic beauty and its measure in the fine art of music, thereby

---

[1] The minimum reading required to connect Euclid not merely to the Platonists but also the Democriteans, Aristotle's mathematics, the Stoics and the modern calculus and real number theory is (1) *The Thirteen Books of Euclid's Elements*, Vols I, II and III, and the Commentaries by T. L. Heath, Cambridge Univ. Press, 1908; (2) the present writer's 'The Mathematical Background and Content of Greek Philosophy' (MBGP) in *Philosophical Essays for Alfred North Whitehead*, Longmans, Green & Co., London, N.Y., Toronto; and (3) for the Stoics, B. Mates, *Stoic Logic*, and S. Sambursky, *op. cit.*,

making such intrinsic values cognitive also. Not only do the Theaetetian ratios and proportions of Euclid's Book VII (1) specify the
mathematically functional *idea* of the true in the science of arithmetic and its experimentally confirmed mathematical acoustics,
but also (2) in the fine art of music they, and their Democritean
acoustical laws, theoretically define the intrinsic *ideal* of the classical musically beautiful conceived as (iii) the *relationally analytic*
logically realistic Theaetetian-Democritean ratio-proportioned
ordering of the (ii) epistemically correlated (i) *impressionistically
concrete* radical empirical sequence of perishing particular entity-
less tonal qualities and their associated tertiary qualities (called by
Democriteans, Epicureans, Platonists and Stoics alike, nominalistic
'sensibles') which one hears and feels at the symphony concert;
while also (3) *operationally defining* the score, the tuning fork,
the tuned players' instruments, and the neurophysiological and
behaviouristic professional skills which all must master.

Otherwise Toscanini, the maestro, could be waving his magic
wand and his players could be sawing and banging and blowing
away 'like mad' with nothing issuing forth but the disordered
arbitrarily voluntaristic irrational *Geist* of all too many of the
Geistenswissensschaftenlichen autonomously philosophical humanists
and the equally disorganized, demoralized, and agonized *Sorge* of
the similar epistemologically 'primitive and muddle[d]' autonomously pseudo-metaphysical[1] Neo-Aristotelians and Existentialists,
and their present youthful followers.

Since Plato's Socrates, in the *Republic*, identifies music with
acoustics, the ideal of intrinsic beauty in music in the same for
Platonists as for Democritus and the *Theaetetus* of Euclid's Book
VII, and for all musicians to date who use the Pythagorean diatonic
or its modified well-tempered scale. For all *similar* ratios not merely
measure (in the most literal sense of the word), intrinsic, or *ideal*,
beauty, but also, by way of the score, the instruments and the
players' behaviouristically conditioned neurophysiological motor

---

[1] Why pseudo-metaphysical? Because, as both Leibniz (LToS) and the Buddha
(NMEW) pointed out, it is the nominalistic *positivistic*, differentiated perishing
particular factor in knowledge which is the veridical existentially unique one.
But nominalistic positivism is anti-metaphysical, and not theistic, as the Buddha
affirmed. Hence, an existentialist metaphysics or theistic theology is a contradiction in terms. Such a 'God is dead', since it never was, nor can be. For the
difference between any Semitic theistic religion and Buddhist religion see
(MPEW) and logical realistically ratioed λόγος theism (MNaG) as compared
with the Buddhist religion of (i) Peirce's *Firstness* above; and (NMEW).

responses, they operationally define *instrumental* beauty. The prevalent notion that cognitive mathematical natural science can at best merely define instrumental values, but by its very cognitive nature cannot define the specific content of *intrinsic*, or *ideal*, values is erroneous. As Liddell and Scott's *Greek-English Lexicon* specifically states, art in the sense of intrinsic or ideal beauty, the Greeks called ἐπιστήμη, their word for cognitive science; whereas art in the operation definitional sense of instrumental beauty, they called τέχνη and applied the latter as much to the fine arts as to what we today call technology. Remove the ordering of the successive perishing directly heard qualities, by the mathematical physical experimentally confirmed ratios and proportions, and the ideal of the beautiful of Pre- or Post-Bachian Western music vanishes also.

Strictly speaking, the foregoing is *wholly* the case only for the one-dimensional Pythagorean, or Diatonic, scale in Western music. It is only in part the case in the one-dimensional well-tempered scale of Bach's Well-tempered Clavier, which he and his successors extended and exploited for organ and orchestra. The same is true for the music of Hindemith and the Post-Ives and Schönberg music of Berg, Ruth Crawford-Seeger's *Quartet* (1931), Milton Babbitt's *String Quartet No. 2* (1954) and the *String Quartet No. 2* (1965) by President Gunther Schuller of the New England Conservatory of Music.[1] This is equally the case for the ratios and proportions which are taken as elementary in defining the specific content of logical realistic intrinsic beauty in (*a*) the architecture of the Roman Arch, Byzantine Santa Sophia's cylindrical columns and semi-spherical domes, and (*b*) the Renaissance painting instanced in the Botticellian *Madonna and Child*, reproduced as Illustration XII[2] in the writer's *The Meeting of East and West*.

To see why, it is not irrelevant to turn back from the Democritean-Theaetetian arithmetical and acoustical logical realistic Special, or Restricted, Theory of Ratios and Proportions of Euclid's Book VII, to the more General Theory of Ratios and Proportions of Euclid's Book V, from which the theory of Book VII derives deductively as a special case; much after the manner in which Einstein's Special Theory of Relativity (1905) derives as a special case of his General Theory of Relativity (1914). The heart of the matter is contained in Definition 5 of Euclid's Book V.

[1] Centennial Symposium String Quartet Concert, Nov. 14, 1967, Jordan Hall, New England Conservatory of Music; also recorded symposium discussion.
[2] As analysed recently in F.N., 'Toward a General Theory of the Arts', *The Journal of Value Inquiry* (NJVI), 1967, Vol. 1, 96–115, esp. 101–5.

It is generally accepted that this remarkable achievement was initially that of Eudoxus in Plato's Academy. Whitehead remarked in 1922 that the two greatest achievements of the Western mathematically minded intellect were the ancient Greek discovery of the entity variable[1] and Eudoxus's Definition 5 Book V of Euclid's *Elements*. Proposition 1 in Book X of Euclid[2] and the subsequent proofs are also attributed to Eudoxus, as is the first deductive formulation of empirically confirmable mathematical physical astronomy.

As translated by T. L. Heath, Definition 5 Book V of Euclid is:

'Magnitudes are said to be *in the same ratio*, the first to the second and the third to the fourth, when, if *any equimultiples whatever* be taken of the first and third, and *any equimultiples whatever* of the second and fourth, the former equimultiples alike exceed, are alike equal to, or alike fall short of the latter equimultiples respectively taken in corresponding order'.[3]

What this definition does is to specify the formal properties of a four-entity-termed relation R whose specific content S relational analytically defines all the relational entities of the field of R, such that the two-entity-termed ratio r^1 of the first entity to the second and the two-entity-termed ratio r^2 of the third entity to the fourth are *equal* whether *any* four relational entities of the field of R take on whole number values or not. From this General Theory of Proportions and their Ratios, the Theaetetian equally relational Restricted Theory of Proportions and Ratios derives as a special restricted case, in precisely the manner in which Einstein's Special Theory derives from his General Theory of Relativity and both derive as special cases of Quantum Mechanics.

The important novelty of this definition appears in its words 'any equimultiples whatever'. What these three words do is to universally quantify two whole-number entity variables, usually expressed today as (m n),[4] with which respectively 'the first and third' and

---

[1] Also (SPWG), 182 ff.

[2] Its 'method of exhaustion' is the Greek's alternative to the modern differential calculus and its Weierstrassian logical realistic relational concept of limit (MBGP).

[3] Italics in lines 2 and 3 are mine.

[4] Where the properties of the whole-number entities are given relational analytically by the Theaetetian-Democritean R of Euclid's Book VII.

'the second and fourth' (magnitudinal) entities of the four-entity-termed overall relation R are multiplied, thereby restricting the substantive content S of R. Thus, in order to make the R of this Eudoxian-Platonic General Theory of Proportions and Ratios meaningful, not only are the four-termed entities of the field of R universally quantified on relationally analytic grounds, but also, within the substantive content S of R two universally quantified entity variables are required. This dual kind of quantification will become important in the next section on Western legal science.

Here, it remains to relate its Eudoxian instance to the intrinsic values of the well-tempered and more recent scales in Western music. Book XIII of Euclid is also involved. What it does is to generalize the Eudoxian-Platonic General Theory of Proportions of Book V to the three-dimensional case, proving that a three-dimensional Euclidean metric permits only five possible regular solids, all inscribable in a sphere, called the 'Platonic bodies', thereby creating the cognitive logical realistic science of stereometry, the third of Socrates' sciences necessary to arrive at the idea of the beautiful. This theory is reconfirmed today in crystallography and organic physical chemistry.

This remarkable Platonic scientific achievement, preserved in Euclid's Book XIII, is the original discovery of the same Theaetetus after whom Plato named his *Dialogue* on the theory of knowledge, and who deductively formalized the Democritean merely arithmetical theory of proportion of Euclid's Book VII. This means that the epistemology of the Platonists is identical with that of the Democriteans. Professor Sambursky has recently (1964 *op. cit.*) shown the same is true for the Chrysippean Stoics. The differences are in successive more factually inclusive generalizations, from which previous theories derive as still valid but specifiably restricted cases.[1] Moreover, since in Book VII of the *Republic*, Socrates identifies music with acoustics and its merely whole-number ratios, even the *specific content* of the ideal of intrinsic musical beauty is identical for the Democriteans and Platonists. In music, this ideal is, for both, the speculatively discovered, indirectly and experimentally confirmed cognitive (iii) many-entity-termed relationally analytic logical realistic Pythagorean Demo-

---

[1] The prevalent notion that recent discoveries render all traditional scientific theories, humanistic beliefs, and intrinsic values obsolete and even evil is quite erroneous. For any new generalization to establish itself, even for the scientific-humanist of genius who discovers it, it must specify the traditional theories as special cases of itself.

critean Theaetetian diatonic ordering of the (ii) epistemologically correlated (i) nominalistic differentiated radical empirical successively perishing auditorily sensed tonal and emotively associated qualities, called by Democriteans, Platonists and Stoics alike 'sensibles'; the *'ideas'* of (iii) being *universals* since relational analytically to be *any* entity in the field of R is to be defined by the substantive content S of R. The *implicit* (ii) epistemic correlations were covered up in ancient times by the metaphorical word 'participation' and the unspecific word 'analogical'.[1]

For the intrinsic ideal of the beautiful architecture of the Acropolis, the cylindrical columns and hemispherical domes of Greek Orthodox Santa Sophia and the Roman arch,[2] and also in the Renaissance Botticellian *Madonna and Child* painting referred to above, in all of which the ratio between the diagonal and side of a square or rectangle, and between the circumference and its diameter of a circle is elementary, the Eudoxian Book V-Platonic Theaetetian Book XIII ratios and proportions are inescapable (NJVI). The same is true in the basic novel fact of the slight acoustical shift from the Pythagorean Diatonic to the well-tempered scale. Here, the musical ideal of the intrinsically beautiful becomes rooted in one common arithmetically incommensurable, Eudoxian commensurable ratio of the General Theory of Ratios and Proportions. This key ratio is the twelfth root of 2 over 1, i.e. $\sqrt[12]{2}$.

I

To see why, let us begin with the completely arithmetically ratioed 12-tone Pythagorean or Diatonic scale of the piano, beginning with middle C' equal to 256 Democritean acoustical vibrations per second, and setting this equal to the arithmetical ratio $1/1$. Then the next higher octaval C'' is $2/1 = 512$ cps. All intervening tones are whole-number ratios also. Paying attention only to the white keys, they are, from left to right, for D' E' F' G' A' B' C'', respectively $9/8$ $5/4$ $4/3$ $3/2$ $5/3$ $15/8$ and $2/1$.

---

[1] Only with Aristotle and his followers, ancient, medieval, and recent, was the epistemology of natural knowledge and intrinsic values returned to naïve realism. This occurs, as specified in the Ross edition of Aristotle's *Physica*, where its elementary scientific objects, earth, air, fire, and water, are defined two-termed entity-property-wise, in terms of four pairs of the immediately sensed qualities: hot, cold, wet, and dry (W. D. Ross, ed. *The Works of Aristotle*, Oxford, at the Clarendon Press, Vol. II, Book IV, 5 n. 212b) and everything naturalistic and normative is arranged theocratic hierarchically by the *Sein-Sollen* natural history genus-species predicables.

[2] Jefferson showed his mastery of such architecture in his design of the arcaded *Lawn* and domed *Library* at the Univ. of Virginia which he also founded.

Whereas in the well tempered scale, paying attention to all twelve tones in the octave, and as in the diatonic, setting C' and C'' as 1/1 and 2/1 respectively, none of the intervening ratios is a whole-number ratio. Instead, they are the function of a real number geometrically commensurable ratios and proportions of the Eudoxian Definition 5 Book V of Euclid, or of Dedekind. The reason is that the well-tempered scale relates any octaval twelve tones of the piano to its immediate successor by the same ratio, thereby dividing the octave into twelve equally intervalled parts. This gives a piano, which without rebuilding it, can play a composition in any key. The consequence is that if the twelve-tone diatonic scale is to keep any octaval key notes, such as C' and C'' respectively equal to 1/1 and 2/1 as it does, while also keeping the ratio of each octaval note to its successor of the same ratio, then this immediate successor ratio must be the twelfth root of 2 over 1, i.e. $\frac{\sqrt[12]{2}}{1}$, since only then will the twelfth note to the right of the key note 1/1 have the ratio 2/1. This is confirmed by the expert on piano manufacture, H. A. Hutton in London's Imperial College of Science and Technology.[1]

Nor are the epistemically correlated radically empirical intervening heard tonal qualities identical either. This is the reason, even though some of them are near those of the diatonic scale, why Bach's well-tempered clavier, organ and orchestral music initially impressed his hearers as ugly and so shocked them. Brief reference was made above to the two-dimensional and stereometrically three-dimensional intrinsic values of Western architecture and certain Renaissance paintings. This raises an interesting contemporary question with respect to today's and tomorrow's music. The theory of both its diatonic and its well-tempered scales and also those of Hindemith and the Post-Ives Schönbergians is one-dimensional. Is not a two-dimensional or even a three stereometrically-dimensional arithmetically incommensurable Eudoxian ratioed and proportioned intrinsic musical ideal of the beautiful and its derived novel instruments possible also?

The answer is unequivocally Yes. It exists today in its (iii) experimentally confirmed logical realistic component in the Section on Music of *The Symphony of Life*[2] by the aforementioned professionally educated pianist and Gibbsian-minded mathematical physical chemist Professor Donald Andrews, as supported by Lord

[1] *Encyclopedia Britannica*, Vol. 17, 1945, p. 901.
[2] Unity Books, Lee's Summit, Mo., 1966.

Rayleigh's *Theory of Sound*[1] and Professor Walter Kauzmann's *Quantum Chemistry*.[2] In professional music today, it is exemplified quite independently in the unique stereometrical and parabolically waved instruments of the musician Lucia Dlugoszewski in her music and playing which accompanies the dancing of Erich Hawkins. Initially, her tones are as shocking as were those of Bach. All ratios are Eudoxian real-number ones and some specified by Professor Andrews involve Cantor's various trans-finite Alephs. Many of the graduate degree students of the pianist Professor John Spratt in the School of Music of Florida State University are also pursuing the implications for intrinsic musical beauty of a musical theory rooted in the aforementioned revolutionary Quantum Mechanical definition of state. In an otherwise causally disciplined dynamic sequence.

With respect to the intrinsic values of classical Far Eastern art such ratios and proportions are irrelevant. The same is true of a pure recent impressionistic painting such as Georgia O'Keefe's *Abstraction No. 3*, which is reproduced as Illustration XI in *The Meeting of East and West*. Another caution is necessary. Prall, who knew both his radical empirical Hume and French-American impressionistic painting and literature, showed in his *Aesthetic Judgment*[3] that the motif and criteria of intrinsic beauty in these arts is radical empirical in character. The transition from the painting and architecture of the Renaissance to the present moment has been described in the aforementioned essay entitled 'Toward a General Theory of the Arts'.[4] This section should be read within its place in 'the spectrum of aesthetic possibilities' of the latter essay.

THE RELATIONAL PERSONALITIES OF WESTERN LEGAL SCIENCE

They persist to the present moment, in every positive branch of this science, since the time of (*a*) the afore-described Greek Stoic logical realistic mathematical physicist and logician Chrysippus, who was among the first to affirm that rights-obligational moral,

---

[1] 1877, Ch. on membrane vibration, Dover, N.Y., 1945.
[2] Academic Press, 1957. The two-dimensional case, 274–5; the three-dimensional and Schrödinger wave equation, 162. The writer is deeply indebted to Professor Andrews for these references and all the musical ratios of this section. The errors are mine.
[3] Crowell, N.Y., 1936.
[4] (NJVI) pp. 105–113

legal, political and ethically religious man is cosmopolitan, ecumenical, or universal man, and (*b*) the Stoic lawyers and moral philosophers such as Quintus Mucius Scaevola and Epictetus. Many have been described in Henry Osborn Taylor's *Treatise on the Law of Private Corporations*[1]; the comparative lawyer Professor F. H. Lawson's *The Rational Strength of English Law*, *The Law of Property*, and (in their common-law relation to Stoic Roman, as well as civil law) *A Common Lawyer Looks at the Civil Law*;[2] and (*c*) more analytically in the Canadian lawyer Professor Joseph C. Smith's 'The Theoretical Constructs of Western Contractual Law', 'Law, Language, and Philosophy' and 'The Unique Nature of the Concepts of Western Law';[3] (*d*) Judge Littleton's *Institutes of the Laws of England*;[4] and (with respect to political sovereign-citizen persons) in *Magna Charta*; the *State Trial of Charles I*[5] before the High Court of Parliament in 1627–8; Jefferson's 'free and equal' *Declaration of Independence* legal and political persons; and the recent Mr Chief Justice Warren U.S. Supreme Court's *Brown vs. Board of Education*, in all of which judicial review occurred with respect to substance, of the theocratic political sovereign's commands, or of majority-approved legislative statues. A crucial inductive test of any legal theory is the obligated person p⁰ in the Stoic Roman and present-day real property law *jus in rem*.

Let us begin with Professor Lawson's findings, as analysed elsewhere:[6]

'Although his book shows little awareness of the epistemological distinctions at the basis of what he describes, he specifies the parts of Western law which have 'rational strength' and the parts which do not. The former he calls 'lawyer's law' and describes as having

[1] Banks Law Pub. Co., 5th edn. N.Y., 1902.
[2] Respectively, London, 1951, *ibid.*, 1958, and Univ. of Michigan Law Pub., Ann Arbor, 1953.
[3] Resp., S(CCU), Ch. 15, *op. cit.*, 1964, Brit. Columbia Law Jour. (SBCL), 1968, and Can. Bar Rev. (SCBR) 1968.
[4] As Trans. and *Commented upon* by Sir Edward Coke, with countless inductive case-law textual and marginal judicial references in its 394 folio-size pages. 'Twelfth Edition, corrected from the Errors of the former Impressions' (London), Fleet-Street, MDCCXXXVIII (CLILE).
[5] Vol. III, Charles I, 1627–40, London, Hansard. Cf. esp. 'Proceedings in Parliament relating to the Liberty of the Subject'. 59–190. See esp. the briefs of Mr Cresswell and Mr Selden as well as Sir Edward Coke. Cf. also C. H. McIlwain, *The High Court of Parliament*, 1910 and, *Constitutionalism Ancient and Modern*, Cornell, Univ. Press, 1939, *op. cit.*,
[6] F.N., 'The Epistemology of Legal Judgements' in *Northwestern Law Review*, 1964 (NELJ), 732–49.

concepts which are (1) 'intensely abstract' and 'perfectly defined', (2) 'completely generalized', (3) 'move among themselves according to the rules of a game', and form (4) 'a calculus remarkably similar to mathematics'. (1) and (3) insure that such legal language is neither completely radical empirical nor naïve realistic in its meaning. By (2) and (3) Professor Lawson means, as illustrated in 'England's most important rule governing the interpretation of statutes' that (5) the 'words must be interpreted according to their grammatical meaning'. (3) and (4) show this grammar not to be that of ordinary language, as does Professor Lawson's subsequent statement that the creation of such a legal language (6) 'made it necessary to devise a special form of logic or grammar . . .' He notes one very important judicial consequence: (7) 'Judges have no great power to control such written law'. Our epistemological analysis shows why. In logically realistic language, the words such as mass, corporate personality, or the *jus in rem* P[o] person derive their entire realistic meaning syntactically by way of the imageless, logically formulated many-entity-termed relations in which they function as the relata or field.'

Several important things follow: (*a*) The laws of such moral and legal science are analytic; since *all* their rights enjoying p[r]-obligated p[o] persons have only those defining properties *which* the literally specified and interpreted grammatical content S of their three-entity-termed relation R, relational analytically entails[1] that they possess in respect of the positive subject-matter *m* in question. Hence, (*b*) such science (reinforced by Professor Lawson's (6) and (7)) insures the necessary (but not the sufficient) condition for an interpersonal evaluative cognitivism with *specific content* S meaningfully the same for all evaluators. The sufficient condition occurs when the literally specified and interpreted substantive content S of R, *which is* relational analytically the same-for-all p[r]-p[o] persons, takes on existential import. This occurs by means of operational definitional procedural rules and the latter's implicit epistemic correlations, in which the (iii) S of R same-for-everyone imputative[2]

---

[1] This solves the problem of legal obligation induction (CLEE), 298–300, after the manner in which the afore-described Eudoxian-Dedekindian theory of mathematical entities resolves the problem of meaningful mathematical induction from some to all.

[2] Hans Kelsen, 'Causality and Imputation', *Ethics*, Vol. 61, 1–11; cf. review of his *What Is Justice?* Berkeley, 1957: Kelsen sees that 'the judge's judgment . . . is an imputative and imperative sentence; hence, law conceived solely in

and imperative p^r-p^o persons are (ii) *explicitly* correlated epistemically with the *public* birthday and place witnessed and 'of legal age'
officially notarized and registered (i) nominalistic *freely assenting*
and *existentially* self-committing, merely proper-named, *de facto*
naturalistic persons. Forthwith, (c) the bodily naturalistic person
not merely enjoys the p^r rights, but also his body is subject to *duly
processed* judicially authorized jail sentence, or other physical restraints, should he violate any one of the correlative p^o obligations
of this or any other positive branch S of R of the legal system.
Otherwise, his rights in the first instance would be interpersonally
and legally meaningless, to say nothing about being viably enforce-
able.

The epistemic correlations have three other important functions: (1) They prevent the wellnigh omni-prevalent present-day
ordinary language 'primitive and muddled' confusion of (a) the
same-for-everyone moral and legal person with (b) the different-
from-one-another proper-named private introspectively psychological, the existentially unique, or the public spatio-temporally
located (i.e. logical realistic) naturalistic persons. To avoid such
confusion, Coke translated the legal person in Littleton's Stoic
legal Latin interlarded Norman French text as the *he which* person
(*op. cit.*, Folio 1). *We must do likewise*; the nominalistic proper-
named *de facto* persons *being he who* persons.[1] (2) By restricting the
judicially *due processed* police power to the merely procedural role
in the viable instrumentation of the-same-for-everyone S of R *he
which* p^r-p^o persons, the physical police power is kept from entering

terms of a causal . . . relation between a present and future "is", will give only
indicative sentences'; Q.E.D., all deterministically causal theories leave ethics
and law meaningless, whether the cause be mechanical, historical, or *Sein-Sollen*
(is-ought) self-fulfillingful. F. N., *Virginia Law Rev.* V. 44, pp. 815–19.

[1] For this reason, the 1822 Hawkins and Rudall *Abridgement* of *Coke upon
Littleton* is most untrustworthy. Not only does it omit (1) Littleton's Stoic legal
Latin-laden Norman French text, and (2) the countless inductive cases in the
marginal references of Coke's 394 folio pages, which take one back, *as they did
Jefferson*, via Coke, Bracton, *Magna Charta*, Fleta and Azo of the Law School at
Bologna to the Stoic Roman legal scientist Scaevola, the Stoic Greek (former
slave-Roman citizen) moral philosopher Epictetus and his logical and cognitive
logical realistic naturalistic and cosmopolitan normative roots which came (his
English translator W. A. Oldfather, Loeb Class, Lib. I, xi, tells us) 'almost
entirely from the extensive collections of Chrysippus'; but also (3) *Hawkins &
Rudall Esq.'s* mis-state Coke's *he which* legal person on Folio 1 of the 1738
(CLILE) Edition as the 'he, who' person. [See their 'Eighth Edition', London,
1822, p. 1.]

into and thereby corrupting the *he which* moral and legal 'lawyer's law' Definition of Justice and its Liberty itself; as occurs with Hobbes, the distinguishing *a posteriori* mark of Kant's legal theory,[1] and Holmes's 'clear and present danger' dictum. Also (3) the epistemic correlations prevent the similar confusion of the quantifications of the (iii) entity variables of the *he which* p^r-p^o moral and legal persons, *which are* universally quantified on relational analytic grounds and hence singulars, with the (i) entity variables of the nominalistic proper-named persons, who in some species of positive law are existentially, $\exists p$, quantified and in other (p) universally quantified. A test case of the latter is the obligated person in the real property law *jus in rem* as instanced in the three-entity-termed sale of a woodlot *m* by A to B:

The interesting thing to note is that in any such Stoic Roman or present-day sale, only the buyer and seller sign the procedural duly witnessed, and notarized deed, yet not merely the seller B but also every other birthday registered citizen is obligated under duly processed police power penalty to respect A's *jus in rem* to the woodlot *m*. In the *Cornell Law Quarterly* (NCLQ), XLV, 1960, the present writer made this meaningful by pointing out that whereas the *he who* rights holding p^r *jus in rem* entity variable is $\exists p$ existentially quantified, the correlative *he who* p^o obligated entity variable person is (p) universally quantified, or what mathematical logicians call a 'bound' entity variable. In 1964 (CCU), the legal analyst Professor Joseph C. Smith noted that the latter 'fact was recognized by . . . Hohfeld . . . but . . . his definition does not accurately describe the right in rem, as [its] most fundamental character is that the holder of the duty need not be named . . . but [his] definition forces one to name every single person in the legal system as holders of similar duties in order to indicate the full range of the relation . . . . The only explanation which accounts for the fact . . . is that of [NCLQ above].'

The fact, noted under (3) just above, that all *he which* p^r-p^o moral and legal persons are *singulars*, is equally important:

For example, the criminal law *he which* p^r rights holding person is the criminal law S of R portion of the legal system itself. This shows in the fact that only the prosecuting attorney in his p^o obligational capacity as the official representative of the singular criminal law p^r personality can initiate a criminal law action: whereas in *tort* law, the injured party or his trustee can do so. The corporation law

[1] F.N., 'Language, Morals and Law', *Yale Law Jour.*, 1962, 1042–8.

he which p^r-p^o personality is similarly singular and also has one remarkable 'lawyer's law' property. In the legal system of the U.S., corporation law, like criminal law, (except where federal employees, buildings and interstate commerce are involved) is reserved to the States. Before me now is the 'Description of [an *he which* proper-named Corporation].' It reads, 'under the laws of the State of Delaware . . . its duration is perpetual'. Clearly, the *he which* moral and legal person and the born and dying 'he, who' introspectively psychological, existentially unique, or naturalistically behaviouristic persons are not to be confused; as Hawkins and Rudall's mis-statement in 1822 of the English lawyer's legal person as the 'he, who' person, made it easy to do ten years later, for Bentham[1] in his 'Theory of Legislation' and the radical empirical Humian piece of Austin in his 'Province of Jurisprudence Determined'.[2] The singularity of the Delaware corporate personality shows in two ways: (1) Although similar to the State of Maine *he which* rights-obligational corporate personality, there are differences. (2) Providing they are the same species of Delaware corporate personality, John Percival Kraut, Grocer; American Meter; and General Motors Inc. are identical corporate personalities, both rights and obligational-wise. The same is true of all birth certificate registered and 'of legal age' citizens in the overall federal legal system.

When combined with this essay's previous sections, several additional conclusions become evident: First, it is impossible to obtain an *interpersonal* evaluative moral or legal cognitivism the specific content S *of which* is even theoretical meaningfully-the-same for all evaluative persons, or solve the problem of obligational moral and legal induction unless the latter are literally specified and interpreted logical realistic rights-obligated persons *which are* relational analytically defined. Second, if this theoretically the-same-for-all specific content S of R is to take on existential import, epistemically correlated public duly-witnessed spatio-temporally located and dated cognitively objective (i.e. logical realistic) (i) proper-named naturalistic persons are also required. The same is true of admissible evidence and the facts of the case in the much-neglected minor premise of the judicial and the cognitively moral evaluative judgment of one person by another. Third, the epistemology of (1) such theoretically meaningful and existentially war-

[1] (SBCLR), 7–13.
[2] First ed., 1832. See (NYLJ) on Hume, Bentham, Austin, Holmes, and Hand. Also (CLEE), Ch. III, and (SBCLR), 13–15.

ranted evaluative moral and legal science is identical with that of (2) cognitively warranted objective ordinary and mathematical physical natural knowledge and (3) the intrinsic as well as instrumental humanistic values of the ratioed and scale-ordered beauty of Western music and its accompanying emotively felt 'sensibles'. Fourth, nevertheless, within this common-denominator epistemology there is an important difference between the specific contents of musical intrinsic values and moral, legal and religious ones, in their relation to the elementary Definitions and laws of the cognitively successive generalized theories of natural knowledge. As shown in the section on music, not merely is (a) its epistemology identical with that of natural knowledge but also (b) the specific content of its intrinsic values is defined in terms of the ordering of its (i) radical empirical auditory and emotive temporally successive perpetually perishing qualities in terms of the successively generalized (iii) elementary ratios and proportions of acoustical mathematical physical natural science. The latter condition (b) is not the case with the specific content S of the epistemologically similar intrinsic values of interpersonal moral, legal and religious science.[1] The reason is twofold: First, as just noted, the latter science's many-entity-termed relational *he which* rights-obligational persons are not those of the epistemologically similar *he who* naturalistic persons; instead, they are the legal procedural rules implicit epistemic correlates of the proper-named naturalistic persons. Second, although these epistemic correlations, implicit in the legal procedural rules, are a necessary condition for the existential import of the S of R 'lawyer's law' p^r-p^o moral and legal persons, they are not a literally stated sufficient condition. What is this positive lawyer's law-sufficient condition?

The importance of this question becomes evident when one asks with respect to the aforedescribed *jus in rem* p^o obligated person: Why should you or I, who have not signed the deed transferring the p^r right to the woodlot *m* from A to B, be obligated as much as is the signer A to respect B's p^r right to *m*. Part of the answer is the free-substitutability of anyone (including even you or me) for B in the right holder's p^r role in respect of some other *m*. Another more important part is one's birthday registered and of legal age status as the humblest of citizens. Apart from this, to talk about 'rights' or 'demands' is meaningless, if one means by them obligations of

[1] This possibility was noted first in *Philosophy of Science, The Delaware Seminar*, Ch. I (1961), Wiley, N.Y., and London.

everyone else in the legal system to respect and viably by procedural rules, implement one's rights. The deeper and more complete
answer is that all logical realistic science is not merely increasingly
generalized, as in the *1738 Edition of Coke upon Littleton's Institutes*,
to cover all past and present inductive judicial judgments and cases,
but also deductively formulated in terms of the minimum number
of Definitions and relationally analytic universal laws. Moreover, in
Western legal science later judgments derive from the earliest ones
not merely by generalization but also by its law of the conservation
of *he which* moral and legal p^r-p^o personality, called *stare decisis*. In
this connection, Professor Lawson's (1953) comparison of Anglo-
American common law with (*a*) civil law and (*b*) Roman law becomes important. Referring to (*a*), he says: 'I think it is time for the
English and American corporation lawyer to shed his pre-
conception and study more closely the chief components of the
substantive civil law.' He then shows that some branches of English
common law have more formal 'rational strength' than their opposite numbers in France; and that when to '*Williston on Contracts*,
Hohfeld's famous *Fundamental Legal Conceptions*'[1] is 'prefixed', we
obtain the type of legal thinking that is comparable to the later
Roman jurists and the modern civilians (pp. 68 ff.). Of the former,
Professor Lawson writes: 'The Romans taught the world—including even the common law—the possibility of forming a legal framework for society, composed of the smallest possible number of
elements.'

What are these elements? He then gives part of the answer: The
Institutes of Gaius and Justinian classify contracts 'into four species
[and] the general structure of the law of contract is best understood
if we examine . . . the stipulation and the consensual contracts.
. . . The stipulation contained two elements in a remarkably pure
state: form and agreement (114) . . . the content of the stipulation must have been infinitely variable [as it] was not a contract but
a contractual form, a mold for contracts (116). . . . It is as if the
Roman jurists of about 100 B.C. had said "Go where you will, you
will find that almost everything can be reduced to four (consensual
contractual) processes (127)." This led the reviewer in the *Michigan
Law Review*, Vol. 54, 1956, to add: 'Expressed in terms of mathematical logic, this . . . entailed two [mathematical] logical concepts: (1) the concept of the variable, designated . . . by the sym-

[1] Yale Univ. Press; Humphrey Milford, London, Oxford University Press,
MDCCCCXIX.

bol x and meaning "anyone", as opposed to the proper-name of a specific one, and to the entity-property class concept of all the sensuously similar ones . . .; (2) The concept of matrix, or propositional form, in which the material common-sense concepts . . . are replaced with variables (NMLR).'

To this must be added two things: (*a*) Reference to Jefferson's remarkable mathematical physical, modern and classical humanistic and professional legal education. (*b*) The few fragments of the Stoic Roman legal scientist Marcus Quintus Scaevola (?–105 B.C.) quoted in Justinian's *Digest*. (*a*) has been documented from Jefferson's *Commonplace Book* (pre-1776), *Autobiography*, and letters in the present writer's *UNESCO Journal of World History IX* essay 'Jefferson's Conception of the Role of Science in World History' (1966). Its conclusions are fourfold: First, before 1762 under the Professor of Mathematics at William and Mary College Dr William Small, whom J described as 'determining the destinies of my life', he concentrated on Euclid's *Elements*, Bacon's deductively formulated-experimental inductive method,[1] Newton's *Principia*, Barrow's *Fluxions*, and learned from French analytical mathematical methods and Lagrange's *Méchanique Analytique* that the entities of publically objective cognitive natural knowledge are relational analytically defined. Second, then Small persuaded the English common lawyer Whyte, who had a similar Baconian conception of the persisting entities of legal science, to take on J's professional training as a legal scientist. This occupied the years 1742 through 1746. It consisted in two things: (*a*) Working one way, with J's antecedent expertness in Latin and French, through the Stoic legal Latin-laden Norman French text (probably the 1738 edn.) of *Coke upon Littleton's Institutes of the Laws of England* (CLI-LE) and via its countless inductive case-law judicial judgements and marginal references back to its uncorrupted (of this more later) *stare decisis* origin with the Stoic Roman legal scientist Scaevola and the Stoic Greek moral philosopher Epictetus, whom the latter's *Loeb Classical Library* biographer describes 'as grounded in the systematic treatises of Chrysippus'.[2] Third, (*b*) simultaneously Whyte made J bring his Greek abreast of his 'expertness in Latin' and then read the Ancient moral, legal and philosophical classics in their original Greek and Latin. His conclusion was that only the Stoics in the pure form of Epictetus in correlation with the hedonism of Epicurus (recall also the hedonism of the Platonic Eudoxus) give us warrant-

---

[1] Bacon, let it be recalled, was by profession a legal scientist.   [2] Vol. 1, ix.

able *evaluative* moral or legal judgments. Why not Plato and Aristotle? The answer becomes evident when one reads Professor Joseph C. Smith's (CCU) description of the legal historical sequence in the converse direction from the Ancients to Brackton, Littleton, Coke, and Jefferson, together with the demonstration that some Chrysippian syllogistic judicial judgments occur in Justinian's *Digest*. This description notes that the [non-Epictetian] theocratic Roman politicians 'partially reconciled their legal theory with their governmental system through the fiction that by an implied contract the people confer upon the Emperor all power and authority over them'. Fourth, with J's reading of Coke's distinction between the *he which* moral and legal person and the different-from-one-another *he who* proper-named persons (and also Professor Lawson's Roman law contractual forms and entity variables in mind), it becomes likely that by his 'free and equal' *Declaration of Independence* principle, J meant the free substitutability of *any one* proper-named person for any other with respect to the singular *he which* p^r-p^o persons; the political sovereign's obligations being identical with that of the humblest citizens as settled in *Magna Charta* and the *State Trial* of Charles I in 1627–8.

To this must be added the Scaevolian fragments: In his *Ius Civil*, comprising eighteen volumes of case-law studies, the Stoic Roman legal scientist Quintus Mucius Scaevola is credited with systematically formulating the elements of Western legal science. Only some eight direct quotations from this legal classic are preserved for us as direct quotations in Justinian's *Digest*. Two suffice for our present purposes: Referring to the species S of R in respect of m, where m is that of wills and testaments, Scaevola says: 'Anything which is stated in a will in such a way that it cannot be understood is as if it had not been mentioned at all.' This doctrine of, 'literal interpretation', or what today is called 'strict construction' is the equivalent of 'England's rule for the interpretation of statutes'. The other relevant fragment is: 'No one can benefit another to the detriment of a third party, either by an agreement, by presenting a condition, or by entering to a stipulation.[1]

---

[1] *Quintus Mucius Scaevola: Digesta* (Corpus IURIS CIVILIS = IUSTINIANI DIGESTA RECOGNOVIT THEODORUS MOMMSEN, RETRACTAVIT Paulus Krueger Berolini MCMLIV apud Weidmannos), English translation by S. P. Scott, as checked against the Latin-English Dictionary of Lewis and Short by the Swiss professionally-trained lawyer Ekkehart Müller-Rappard in a research paper of January 1961 deposited in the Yale Law School Library, 1–69, esp. 8 and 9.

Stated positively, this gives the logically (as well as *stare decisis* historically, antecedent *sine quo non for* any meaningfully-the-same-for-all evaluative cognitivism with specific content S invariantly the same for all evaluators, which has the sufficient, as well as the aforementioned necessary, *existential import* to be *de facto* obligatory for all proper-named naturalistic persons. (2) As noted in (NYLJ), positive 'lawyer's law' itself contains one moral and legal categorical imperative. All are not hypothetical;[1] subject to change by the legislative majority or executive decree. (3) Applied to constitutional law and political science,[2] the generalized Scaevolian-Epictetian third party rule entails, in Jefferson's words, 'democracy, (the only pure republic, but impracticable beyond the limits of a town) . . . and elsewhere a republican, or popular government, of the second grade of purity . . . over any extent of country; [for] where the citizens cannot meet to transact their business in person, they alone have the right to choose the agents who shall transact it.'[3] Evident also is Lord Acton's observation, 'It is the Stoics who emancipated mankind from its subjection to despotic rule, and whose enlightened and elevated view of life . . . led the way to freedom.'[4] (4) A unique many entity termed relational definition of justice is also implied. Its import becomes clear when approached by way of contrast with Hobbes's definition of 'Liberty both Ecclesiastical and Civil' in his *Leviathan*.[5] It is: 'Liberty, or Freedom, signifieth, properly, the absence of opposition; by opposition, I mean external impediments to motion; and may be applied no less to irrational, and animate creatures, than to rational.'

Note what Hobbes has done: He has (*a*) taken the mathematically functional many-entity-termed relational concept of inertial

---

[1] Or what Kant called *maxims*, as with Austin, Kelsen and Kant's *a posteriori* legal, as distinct from his synthetic *a priori* moral, theory. Our moral and legal categorical imperative, unlike Kant's moral one, is an *analytic* universal proposition instead of *synthetic a priori*. The existential import of the analytic tautology coming, as in cognitive natural knowledge, via the procedural rules and their epistemic correlations, which turn the analytic tautology into a compound empirical synthetic proposition, which takes on *existential* import in the afore-described logically antecedent unique procedural ways.

[2] Cf. the political scientist Professor Joyotpaul Chaudhuri's 'Logical Realism and Rights', *South Dakota Law Review*, XII, also article in XI; and his 'The Elements of a Democratic Theory' in *Midwest Journal of Political Science*, XI, 45–72.

[3] (NMEW), p. 71.

[4] (CCU), p. 262.

[5] Thomas Hobbes *Leviathan or the Matter, Forme and Power of a Commonwealth Ecclesiasticall and Civil*, with an Introduction by Michael Oakeshott, Basil Blackwell, Oxford, undated, 136–7.

mass, deduced by Galilei, in Hobbes's day,[1] from Galilei's mathematical functional definition of force as that which exhibits its effect not as motion or velocity but as change of velocity, or acceleration, and then (*b*) conceived it (property-entity Aryan-prose-wise) as the intrinsic scientific defining property of an Aryan ordinary language syntactically entailed self-sufficient material substance, or aggregate of such substances. What he would do with Galilei, or the later Newton's equally necessary but quite different mathematically functional concept of gravitational mass, the Latin Aryan ordinary language Hobbes does not tell us. The conclusion drawn by him, however, is well known: The naïve realistic natural law[2] state of man in nature is 'a state of war'. This mythical natural law notion is then made the warrant for a mythical legal contract between the political sovereign and his subjects, after the manner of the pre-*Magna Charta* medieval theocrats described above, whose mythically contractual commands were absolute, and hence above judicial review with respect to substance in civil or religious liberties cases. Applied by nineteenth-century and present-day Austinians to a democratically political sovereign, this entails absolute 'legislative supremacy', again making judicial review with respect to substance illegal. See Learned Hand (HSOL), 228 ff. Thereby also was born the additional myth of the modern unilateral decision-making absolutely sovereign nation-state, whose proper-named legal and political personality is above judicial review with respect to substance by even a modicum of culturally or politically homogeneous regional or international law. Why? Because, if, as all Hobbes-Hume Austinians, as well as Marxists and Existentialists, affirm law and justice mean what such an absolutely sovereign nation-state commands and with physical force executes on those who dissent from its commands, then to speak legally and politically of international law is, as they correctly deduce, to utter a self-contradictory notion, identical with that of a Euclidian round square or a perpetual-motion machine in mathematically functional thermo-

[1] After fleeing with some other theocrats, following the trial of Charles I, Hobbes met Galelei in Florence in 1636.

[2] *Elements of Law Naturall and Politique*, Hardwick papers MS copy dated May 9, 1640. Hobbes's 1910 Camb. Univ. Press *Ency. Britannica* biographer adds that though Hobbes venerated Galilei, (1) 'The word Induction is never used by him with the slightest reminiscence of the import . . . of Bacon; and . . . he had nothing but scorn for *experimental* work in physics.' (2) In *De Cive*, 1646, he presented his mythical contractual natural law theocracy 'without its foundations in human nature'. Then (3) 'realizing the need for an exposition . . . comprehensive, concise and popular', produced the *Leviathan.*

dynamics. The criminal law consequences of Hobbes's Definition of 'Liberty' are even more remarkable: Taken seriously, it entails that if a rock, freely falling from a cliff, killed a freely moving pedestrian at its base, the local prosecuting attorney, upon the police report, would be *obligated* to bring a criminal-law action of at least 'accidental homicide' against the 'inanimate creature' for interfering with the legal and political *liberty* of the freely moving 'rational' pedestrian; conversely, should the rock merely injure him, bring a similar action against the 'rational' pedestrian for interfering with the rock's *liberty*.

What Hobbes also does in his use of Aryan ordinary language is to shift, from its entity-property naïve realistic materialistic natural law notion of each natural creature's *motion*, to private radical empirical *emotion* and its passion. Then one has the introspective association psychological theory of the meaning of any normative word of Hume, in which the specific content of the other person's behaviour being evaluated, as associated with the evaluator's intro-spected sensation of the pleasant or the approved, is, as Hume himself tells us, relative to each person's metaphorical 'human breast'; and it should be added to each person's perishing particular introspective moment. How on this theory there can be any mean-ing for a person entering into an interpersonal moral or legal contract or commitment of any kind today and then possessing tomorrow any 'rights' guaranteed by it, or obligation to fulfil it, should the contract or commitment become unpleasant or uninte-resting, these Hobbes-Humian Austinians and any of their latter-day saints such as Earl Russell, Thayer, the late Mr Justice Frank-furter or Judge Learned Hand never tell us. Moreover, this introspectively psychic theory, like that of the voluntaristic 'courage to be' existentialists for whom everything is privately unique, leaves one with nothing but disjunctively related private existentially voluntaristic atomic pseudo 'rights', bereft of any even momentary co-relative obligations (to say nothing about *publically meaningful* co-relative rights and obligations with specific content S the same for all evaluators). Certainly, to take such notions seriously would be for each person to take the law into his own hands, breaking down all its entailed procedural rules of *due process*, by insisting only on his 'rights' with no co-relative obligations. The name for this is anarchy. Then Hume 'in practice', and all Hobbes-Hume Austinians as well as the similarly naïve realistically materialistic Marxists, in their use of ordinary language, shift 'imperceptibly' to

Hobbes' natural law *motion* of heavier and heavier hardware. Forthwith, as the lawyer and legal philosopher Professor Alexandre D'Entrèves has aptly said, 'Clubs become trumps'.[1] Domestically, if taken seriously, this means that the individual anarchist puts a machine-gun on his shoulder. The name for this is *lynch law, or blackmail*, in which liberty is mistaken for licence. This magical use of the epistemological ambiguities of Aryan ordinary language is appropriately called 'the fallacy of the Hobbes-Humian oscillator'.[2] Its continental European equivalent is the afore-described *Sein-Sollen* historicism or existentialism. One such Anglo-American lawyer has recently faced this domestic as well as international bankruptcy with respect to any meaning for the word 'obligation' other than arbitrary naïvely conceived and used physical force.[3]

If Einstein thought the great Newton became 'primitive and muddled' epistemologically in his use of and thinking with Aryan ordinary language, even though no such confusion occurred in his *Principia* where he thought and carried through his proofs mathematical functionally, what is anyone to think of all this? Need one wonder also that Jefferson late in life deprecated the direction that moral and legal education was then taking because they were then following 'the honeyed Mansfieldism of Blackstone' (with his absolute political sovereign) instead of 'Coke Littleton' and Brackton.[4]

Such obligational bankruptcy and ordinary language oscillations only a relational theory of rights-obligation holding persons can remove, thereby restoring modern morals, law, religion and politics to moral, legal and linguistic integrity. It does so by retaining the (i) nominalistic radical empiricism of (*a*) Epicurus, Eudoxus, Locke of the *Essay*, the sceptical Hume and Jefferson, within (*b*) Peirce's *Firstness* and (*c*) substituting the (iii) many-entity-termed relational *he which* p^r-p^o logical realism of Chrysippus, Scaevola, Epictetus, Brackton, *Magna Charta*, Littleton, Bacon, Coke and Jefferson for (*d*) Hobbes and the Feuerbachian Marxist materialistic naïve

[1] *Natural Law Forum*, Vol. I.

[2] (PAPP), 106

[3] Professor Ronald M. Dworkin, *Univ. of Chicago Law Review*, Vol. 35, 14–15.

[4] Letter to James Madison, Feb. 17, 1826, *Selected Writings of Jefferson*, Mod. Library edn N.Y., 1944, 726. Note also in the *Declaration of Independence* version written in Jefferson's own hand, the wording is not 'life, liberty and [Locke's] preservation of property', but 'life, liberty, and the pursuit of happiness'. *The Writings of Thomas Jefferson*, ed. H. A. Washington, Taylor & Maury, 1853, Vol. I, opposite p. 26.

realism and (*e*) Kant's *a posteriori* legal and disembodied Ghostly moral persons. Roughly speaking, the (i) radical empirical factor gives the democratically elected majority approved 'representatively republican' legislative principle, *in which* the members sometimes are, but need not, be professional lawyers; and the (iii) irreducible three-entity-termed relational logical realistic factor provides the 'lawyer's law' literally specified and interpreted *evaluative* measuring-rod for the judicial review of executive acts or majority-approved legislative statutes with respect to their substance by jurists who are professionally trained logical realistic legal scientists. Generalizing the afore-positively-stated Scaevolian third-party rule with respect to any subject-matter *m*, this gives the following Definition of Intrinsic[1] Justice and its Liberty: To say that the positive 'lawyers law' rights p^r-obligated p^o *specific content* S of R in respect of any *m* is intrinsically good and just, either religiously or civilly, is equivalent to saying that (1) R is an irreducible three-entity-termed relation *which is* (p^r-p^o) universally quantified on relational analytic grounds and (2) the S of R is (p^r-p^o) universally quantified also.

Recall that the same is true for any person's moral judgment of another person's, or nation's, behaviour, which escapes relativity to the evaluator's metaphorical 'human breast'. Practically, (2) entails that the contracting executive parties or the legislative majority may put any specific content S they prefer in the act or statute, *subject to the condition* that if the substantive content S gives rights and correlative obligations to some proper-named *he who* persons, it must be such that any other person or citizen is freely substitutable for the contracting parties or majority with respect to those specific rights and their correlative obligations. The educational system of many U.S. states within their federal legal system antecedent to *Brown vs. Board of Education* (like the family law citizenship statutes of Hitler's *Reichstag* and many African and Middle Eastern nations today) met requirement (1), but not (2). This definition has additional merits: (*a*) Because relational rights are meaningless apart from obligations, it renders unnecessary the Kantian legal and Kelsenian *ad hoc* premise: 'the positive law ought to be obeyed'. (*b*) Because the epistemic correlations separate the judicially authorized police power of procedural rule implementation, from this logical realistic definition of Justice itself, the latter provides meaning and warrant for the inductive case law findings of the Queen's

[1] In the sense of the footnote of this essay's page 1.

Bench jurisprude Professor Arthur Goodhart, in his *English Law
and the Moral Law*: 'It is because a rule is regarded as obligatory
that a measure of coercion may be attached to it; it is not obligatory
because there is coercion.' (*c*) Because, similarly, the geographical
area occupied by proper-named naturalistic persons with their
tribal and racist folk geneologies are both (1) normatively meaningless, being an *is* rather than an *ought* and (2) irrelevant to this
Definition of Intrinsic Justice, it is a positive lawyer's law international legal principle, as people the world over are insisting.

This prepares us to understand why Professor Joseph C. Smith
is of the legal opinion that: 'Assuming this definition of justice, the
basic principles of democratic and responsible government such as
the liberty of the subject, equality before the law, the rule of law, due
process, freedom of communication, and judicial review of majority-
approved legislation under a religious and civil liberties bill of rights,
can all be logically defined or deduced in the form of theorems.
Equally, from one irreducible, at least, three-entity-termed relation
R, the formal properties of which are specified by this definition of
justice, any hypothetical logical realistic legal R, in either the Civil or
the Common law, can be defined, thus showing that Hohfeld's four
correlative relations with their eight concepts are not 'the lowest
common denominator'' of legal science. The basic divisions of law
into tort law, contract law, public law, criminal law, the law of real
property, and the law of personal property can then all be differentiated in terms of the quantifications of the epistemically correlated
variables, the value of which are nominalistic proper-named persons'.[1]

One final very important point must be noted about all naturalistic entities, be they elementary finite temporally persisting field
physical particles or logical realistic cybernetic neuro-physiologi-
cally self-regulating proper-named persons. As given in this essay's
three linguistic maxims, if Aryan ordinary language syntax is not to
corrupt our thinking about any entity whatever, the following
requirement, specified by Maxim 3, must be practised: Even
though an entity may be elementary in the naturalistic relationally
analytic universally lawful sense, it analyses further *logically* into
the radical empirically immediate cosmically all-embracing undifferentiated emotive *Quale* (as distinct from qual*ity* differentiated)
feeling which Peirce called *Firstness*, and also its naturalistic spatio-
temporally *invariant* (and hence, timeless) irreducible many-entity-

---

[1] This will be Professor Smith's concern in a forthcoming book.

termed analytically lawful relatedness. All invariant actual entities are therefore a logical γένεσις εἰς οὐσίαν of these two factors.[1] This has the merit of keeping naturalistic emotively moving beauty as well as aesthetic and empathetically sensitive human beings in nature.

[1] Cf. Plato, *Phileb.* 26 d8. See also 'Das Verhältnis von Mathematik und Ideenlehre bei Plato', Otto Töplitz in *Quellen und Studien zur Geschichte der Mathematik.* Abteilung B. Studien. Band 1, Heft 1, Berlin, 1929, pp. 3–33, esp. p. 15.

central# 6

THE DEFEAT OF GOOD AND EVIL[1]

RODERICK CHISHOLM

1. Looking for a topic that would be philosophically live, that would reflect my own interests, and that would be appropriate for the events of 1968, I kept coming back to the nature of evil. When the time came to submit a title, however, courage failed and I settled for 'The Types of Intrinsic Goodness and Badness'. Now I am able to compromise with 'The Defeat of Good and Evil'.

I shall discuss a distinction that seems to me to be of first importance to the theory of value. The distinction was seen by such theodicists as St Thomas and Hume's Demea. It was seen more clearly by Leibniz in his *Theodicy* and by G. E. Moore in the first and last chapters of *Principia Ethica*. And now, I think, we are able to see the distinction more clearly still as a result of recent work in the logic of preference—the logic of such concepts as *good*, *bad*, and *better*.

The distinction may be put by contrasting what I shall call 'balancing off' and 'defeating'. It is one thing to say that the goodness—the intrinsic goodness—of a certain situation is *balanced off* by means of some other situation; and it is quite another thing to say that the goodness of a certain situation is *defeated* by means of some other situation. Again, it is one thing to say that the evil—the intrinsic badness—of a certain situation is balanced off by means of some other situation; and it is quite another thing to say that the evil of a certain situation is defeated by means of some other situation.

Before I try to define the distinction precisely, I shall make certain general points about the logic of the terms 'good', 'bad', and 'better', when these are used in connection with intrinsic value. I shall assume that we can know, with respect to some things, that those things are good in themselves; that we can know, with respect to other things, that those things are bad in themselves; that we can

___

[1] Presidential address delivered before the Sixty-fifth Annual Meeting of the Eastern Division of the American Philosophical Association at Washington, D.C., December 27–30, 1968. To be published in *Proceedings and Addresses of the American Philosophical Association*, Vol. XLII (1968–9).

know, with respect to still other things, that those things are neither good nor bad in themselves; and that we can know, with respect to many things, that some of them are better in themselves than others. I shall also assume that we all know what is meant by the expressions I have just used. These assumptions may themselves be worthy of discussion, but they are not the topic of the present paper.

2. The word 'good', Aristotle said, is predicated in every category.[1] There is a sense in which we may say of a substance that it is good; there is a sense in which we may say of a quantity that it is good; and so, too, of a quality, a relation, a time, and a place. And similarly for 'bad'. But this is not true of the expressions 'intrinsically good' and intrinsically bad'—of 'good in itself' and 'bad in itself'.

Consider the things that are said to be intrinsically good or intrinsically bad. If we follow the great traditions in Western philosophy, we could readily make two lists—a good list and a bad list. The good list, the list of those things that are intrinsically good, would include such items as these: pleasure, happiness, love, knowledge, justice, beauty, proportion, good intention, and the exercise of virtue. The bad list, on the other hand, would include such items as these: displeasure, unhappiness, hate, ignorance, injustice, ugliness, disharmony, bad intention, and the exercise of vice. The things on the good list, one might say, are the sorts of things that ought to be. To the extent that they may be found in any possible world, that possible world could be said to rate a plus. The things that are on the bad list, one could then say, are the sorts of things that ought not to be. To the extent that *they* may be found in any possible world, *that* possible world rates a minus.

Without pausing to consider whether these lists are too long or too short, let us note one general point about all the items listed. The *terms* we have used in making up the lists are all abstract— 'pleasure', 'displeasure', 'love', 'hate', 'the exercise of virtue', 'the exercise of vice', and so on. What these terms refer to are not individuals or concrete things or substances. They are rather propositional entities, or states of affairs: there being happy individuals or there being unhappy individuals; there being individuals experiencing pleasure or there being individuals experiencing displeasure; there being individuals exercising virtue or there being individuals exercising vice. The things that are intrinsically good

[1] *Ethics*, I, 6.

and the things that are intrinsically bad are, all of them, states of affairs. We may also put this point by saying that states of affairs are the bearers of intrinsic value.

I am using the expression 'state of affairs' in the way in which Moore and Lewis used it—also, I think, in the way in which Frege used the word '*Gedanke*', in the way in which Meinong used the word '*Objektiv*', in the way in which Wittgenstein used '*Sachverhalt*', and in the way in which Russell once used the word 'proposition'. I am assuming, therefore, that there *are* states of affairs, some of which obtain and some of which do not obtain. There being horses, for example, is one that does obtain and there being unicorns is one that doesn't. In place of the verb 'obtains', we could use 'takes place', or 'occurs', or 'is actual', or even 'is true' or 'exists' (but if we use 'exists', then we should say 'There *are* states of affairs that do not exist' and not 'There exist states of affairs that do not exist'). I am also assuming that states of affairs stand in logical relation; to other states of affairs; one state of affairs, for example, may be said to imply or entail another, and every state of affairs has a negation.

Perhaps we ought to say that the only bearers of intrinsic value are *actual* states of affairs—just those states of affairs that occur, obtain, or exist. Everyone being happy is not a state of affairs that obtains and therefore we are not likely to say of it that it *is* good. We would be more likely to say of it that it *would* be good it if *were* to obtain. We would not try to comfort a pessimistic hedonist by telling him that everyone being happy is something that is intrinsically good. Yet we may say of it that it *is* such that it ought to be, just as we may say of everyone being unhappy that it *is* such that it ought not to be. And it is a useful shorthand to say, of non-actual as well as of actual states of affairs, that they *are* good, or bad, or neutral. It is also a useful shorthand to say, of non-actual states of affairs, that some of them *are* better, intrinsically, than others, rather than saying, more cumbersomely, that some of them are such that they *would* be better than others if only they were to exist.

A state of affairs is not intrinsically good unless it entails one of those states of affairs that are on our good list—unless it entails, for example, that there are individuals experiencing pleasure or that there are individuals behaving virtuously. A state of affairs is not intrinsically bad unless it entails one of those states of affairs that are on our bad list—unless it entails, for example, that there are individuals experiencing displeasure or that there are individuals behaving wickedly. These facts have a very important consequence which, I believe, has not been sufficiently noticed.

The negation of a state of affairs that is intrinsically good will not be a state of affairs that is intrinsically bad, and the negation of a state of affairs that is intrinsically bad will not be a state of affairs that is intrinsically good. There being happy Mexicans and there being Romans who are behaving virtuously are states of affairs that are intrinsically good. But their negations—there not being happy Mexicans and there not being Romans who are behaving virtuously—are not intrinsically bad, for they do not entail the existence of any of the items on our bad list. There not being happy Mexicans, of course, is very different from there being unhappy Mexicans, and there not being Romans who are behaving virtuously is very different from there being Romans who are behaving wickedly. On the other hand, there being unhappy Mexicans and there being Romans who are behaving wickedly *are* states of affairs that are intrinsically bad. And *their* negations—there not being unhappy Mexicans and there not being Romans who are behaving wickedly— are *not* intrinsically good, for they do not entail the existence of any of the items on our good list.

Good states of affairs and bad states of affairs, then, have this feature in common: they have neutral negations, negations that are neither good nor bad. I have used the word 'neutral' and not 'indifferent', since, if we take the word 'indifferent' in one of its familar philosophical senses, we must distinguish what is intrinsically neutral—that is to say, neither good nor bad—from what is intrinsically indifferent. An indifferent state of affairs, in this familiar sense, would be a state of affairs having the same value as its negation—a state of affairs such that it is no better than its negation and its negation is no better than it. There being stones, for example, whatever its instrumental value may be in this world, is intrinsically indifferent. So far as intrinsic value is concerned, there being stones is no better than there not being stones, and there not being stones is no better than there being stones. But the negations of states of affairs that are good and the negations of states of affairs that are bad, though they are themselves neither good nor bad, are not thus indifferent. For *they* differ in value from their negations. All indifferent states of affairs, therefore, are neutral, but not all neutral states of affairs are indifferent. And though we may say that every state of affairs is good, bad, or neutral, we may not say that every state of affairs is good, bad, or indifferent; for the negations of states of affairs that are good and the negations of states of affairs that are bad are states of affairs that are neither good, bad, nor indifferent.

Professor Sosa and I have worked out what we take to be the proper logic of these concepts and we have suggested how to define them all in terms of the relation of being intrinsically better. The gist of what we have said is this: Two states of affairs may be said to be the *same in value* if neither one is better than the other. An *indifferent* state of affairs, as just noted, is one that is the same in value as its negation. A *neutral* state of affairs, on the other hand, is one that is the same in value as some state of affairs that is indifferent. A *good* state of affairs is one that is better than some state of affairs that is indifferent. And a *bad* state of affairs is one such that some state of affairs that is indifferent is better than it. We have assumed, of course, that the relation of being intrinsically better is one that is asymmetric and transitive. And we have also assumed the following: that all indifferent states of affairs are the same in value; that all good states of affairs are better than their negations; and that all bad states of affairs are worse than their negations.[1]

With these simple points in mind, let us now turn to the difference between balancing off and defeat.

3. Balancing off is clear enough, but let us be explicit so that we may contrast it with defeat. Suppose there is one man, Mr Jones, experiencing a certain amount of innocent pleasure, and there is another man, Mr Smith, experiencing that same amount of innocent displeasure; Mr Smith is just as displeased as Mr Jones is pleased. Given a theory of value such as Jeremy Bentham's, we could say that, since the amount of goodness in this conjunctive state of affairs is the same as the amount of badness, therefore the

---

[1] See Roderick M. Chisholm and Ernest Sosa, 'On the Logic of "Intrinsically Better"', *American Philosophical Quarterly*, Vol. III (1966), pp. 244–9. We set forth a 'value calculus' with the following axioms, reading 'pPq', as 'p is intrinsically better than q':

(A1) (p) (q) [pPq ⊃ ∼(qPp)].

(A2) (p) (q) (r) {[∼(pPq) & ∼(qPr)] ⊃ ∼(pPr)}.

(A3) (p) (q){[∼(pP∼p) & ∼(∼pPp) & ∼(qP∼q) & ∼(∼qPq)] ⊃ [∼(pPq) & ∼(qPp)]}.

(A4) (p){(q) [(∼(qP∼q) & ∼(∼qPp)) ⊃ pPq] ⊃ pP∼p}.

(A5) (p){(q) [(∼(qP∼q) & ∼(∼qPq)) ⊃ qP∼p] ⊃ pP∼p}.

I now believe the following axioms should have been added:

(A6) (p) (q) (r) [(p v q)Pr ⊃ (pPr v qPr)].

(A7) (p) (q) (r) [pP(q v r) ⊃ (pPq v pPr)].

positive and negative values *counterbalance* each other. If the positive and negative values thus counterbalance each other, then the total state of affairs—Mr Jones in his innocent pleasure and Mr Smith in his innocent displeasure—is one that is neutral in value. If we think of the total conjunctive state of affairs as being a whole and of its conjuncts as being proper parts, we could say that one of the parts is better than the whole and that another of the parts is worse than the whole.

Or consider that whole which is Mr Jones experiencing a certain amount of pleasure and Mr Robinson experiencing a greater amount of displeasure. Applying Bentham's principles to this case, we could say that the whole is bad inasmuch as the goodness of one of its parts is *outweighed* by the badness of another one of its parts. Here, too, one of the parts is better than the whole. And here, too, the the whole, though bad, is better than one of its parts. The whole is worse than its good part and better than its worst part. For that state of affairs which is Jones experiencing a certain amount of pleasure and Robinson experiencing a greater amount of displeasure, though bad, is not as bad as that part which is Robinson experiencing that greater amount of displeasure.

And so it is easy enough to say what it is for goodness to be balanced off. There will be a whole with a good part and a bad part; these parts will exclude each other (neither one will entail the other); the whole itself will not be good, but it will be better than one of its parts. Actually, we needn't even say that the whole has a bad part; for if a whole is not good and is better than one of its parts, then the part that it is better than will be a part that is bad.[1] If the whole is neutral, then the goodness of the part will be counterbalanced; if the whole is bad, then the goodness of the part will be outweighed.

We may put the matter pedantically by saying that the *goodness* of a state of affairs p *is balanced off* by a wider state of affairs q provided that the following is true: q obtains; q entails p; p is good; q is not good; and q entails a state of affairs r such that p does not entail r, r does not entail p, and q is better than r. But it is simpler to say that when goodness is balanced off, then a whole that is not good has a part that is good, and, outside of it, a part that is worse than the whole.

When goodness is thus balanced off, we may be consoled at least by *its* presence in the larger whole.

---

[1] That this is so follows from the axioms and definitions of the value calculus referred to in the previous footnote.

The balancing off of evil is, of course, analogous. There will be a whole with a good part and a bad part; these parts will exclude each other; the whole itself will not be bad; but it will be worse than its good part. We needn't say, however, that the whole has a good part; for if a whole is not bad and is worse than one of its parts, then the part that it is worse than will be a part that is good. If the whole is neutral, then the badness of the part will be counterbalanced; if the whole is good, then the badness of the part will be outweighed.

We may put the matter pedantically by saying that the *badness* of a state of affairs p *is balanced off* by a wider state of affairs q provided that the following is true: q obtains; q entails p; p is bad; q is not bad; and q entails a state of affairs r such that p does not entail r, r does not entail p, and r is better than q.[1] But it is simpler to say that when evil is balanced off, then a whole that is not bad has a part that is bad and, outside of it, a part that is better than the whole.

When evil is balanced off, we may yet regret or resent *its* presence in the larger whole.

4. Now let us contrast *defeat* with balancing off. I shall first cite a number of examples, beginning with what Brentano called 'pleasure in the bad'.

Consider the sentence: 'Jones is pleased that Smith is displeased.' We may suppose that Smith being displeased is a state of affairs that is bad. Hence the sentence tells us, with respect to a certain state of affairs that is bad, that that state of affairs is the intentional object of Jones's pleasure. Let us interpret our sentence in such a way that it tells us that Smith's displeasure is, *as such*, the object of Jones's pleasure. That is to say, Jones relishes or savours Smith's displeasure in itself, so to speak, and not in virtue of, or merely in virtue of, what he takes to be its consequences. And refining to a certain extent upon ordinary language, let us so interpret 'Jones is pleased that Smith is displeased' that it does not imply that Smith *is*, in fact, displeased. Jones may be pleased, for all we know, about what he mistakenly thinks to be the fact that Smith is displeased.

---

[1] If, in our definition of the balancing off of goodness, we replace 'q is not good' and 'q is better than r' respectively, by 'p is better than q' and 'r is bad', we obtain a definition of the more general concept of the *partial balancing off of goodness*. And if, in our definition of the balancing off of evil, we replace 'q is not bad' and 'r is better than q', respectively, by 'q is better than p' and 'r is good', we obtain a definition of the more general concept of the *partial balancing off of evil*. Just as we may contrast balancing off with defeat, we may also contrast partial balancing off with partial defeat.

We understand 'pleasure in the bad', then, in such a way that we may say: first, that the intentional object of such pleasure is a state of affairs that is bad; secondly, that the pleasure is directed upon this state of affairs itself and not upon what are taken to be its consequences; and, thirdly, that the pleasure may be 'illusory' or 'unveridical'—that is to say, its intentional object may, in fact, be a state of affairs that does not obtain.

Pleasure in the bad is certainly an unseemly emotion. One *might* say, as Brentano did, that 'pleasure in the bad is, as pleasure, some-thing that is good, but at the same time, as an incorrect emotion, it is something that is bad'.[1] We may have our example, however, without being this rigid in our ethics. Let us suppose, for the moment, that pleasure in the bad, to the extent that it is pleasure, is good, and to the extent that it is pleasure in the bad, is neither good nor bad. Now we consider the state of affairs expressed by the sentence, 'Jones is pleased that Smith is displeased'. The state of affairs itself is neutral; it is neither good nor bad. It entails a state of affairs that is good; for it entails that Jones is pleased. It does not entail any state of affairs that is bad. (We are assuming, it will be recalled, that Jones's unseemly pleasure over Smith's displeasure may be illusory or unveridical. It may be that Smith is not dis-pleased at all.) And, finally, this neutral state of affairs—Jones being pleased that Smith is displeased—does not entail any state of affairs that is worse than it is. Hence we cannot say that the good-ness of Jones being pleased is in a way *balanced off* in the larger neutral situation that entails it. For the larger situation does not entail any *bad* state of affairs which outweighs or counterbalances the goodness of Jones being pleased. But, if the example is accept-able, we may say that the goodness of Jones being pleased is *defeated* by the wider state of affairs that entails it.

If pleasure in the bad illustrates the defeat of goodness, then displeasure in the bad may illustrate the defeat of badness. Consider what St Thomas says about righteous indignation. He defines the righteously indignant man as one who is 'saddened at the prosperity of the wicked'.[2] But let us modify his definition slightly and say that the righteously indignant man is one who is saddened at what

---

[1] Franz Brentano, *The Origin of our Knowledge of Right and Wrong* (London:. Routledge & Kegan Paul, 1969), translated by Roderick M. Chisholm and Elizabeth Schneewind, p. 90. Compare p. 115 n.

[2] St Thomas, *Commentary on the Nichomachean Ethics*, paragraph 356. See Aristotle's *Ethics*, Book II, Ch. 7, 1108b.

he takes to be the prosperity of the wicked. That he takes the wicked to be prospering, one might say, is a state of affairs that is itself neither good nor bad. That he is saddened is a state of affairs that is bad. But that he is saddened at what he takes to be the prosperity of the wicked, is, according to St Thomas, a state of affairs that is good, or, at any rate, not a state of affairs that is bad.

Or consider these types of feeling—pleasure in the bad and displeasure in the bad—when the intentional object that is bad is one's own wicked deed instead of the displeasure of another. Contemplation of what I take to be a previous misdeed of mine might be said to be a state of affairs that is neutral. If, now, we add to it that *good* state which is my taking pleasure in the object of my contemplation, then, some would be tempted to say, the resulting whole becomes *worse* instead of better. And so, if this is true, then, by adding a state of affairs that is good to a state of affairs that is neutral, we obtain a state of affairs that is bad.

Or suppose, again, that the added state is one of pleasure instead of displeasure. We have, as before, my contemplation of what I take to be my previous misdeed and this contemplation is ethically neutral. But now we add to it that *bad* state which is my taking displeasure in the object of my contemplation. Then the result, some will be tempted to say, is the virtuous activity of repentance and therefore the resulting whole is *better* because of the component that is bad. If this is true, then, by adding a state of affairs that is bad to a state of affairs that is neutral, we obtain a state of affairs that is good.

Let us add three further examples—two of them being very familiar. The unpleasant experience of fear, we may suppose, is a state of affairs that is intrinsically bad. But such experience is necessarily involved in the exercise of courage. And the exercise of courage, we may further suppose, is a virtuous activity that is intrinsically good. We need not pause to consider what else it is that goes with fear to make up courage. For the point of the present example is that the larger whole—the exercise of courage—is *better* intrinsically because of the badness of the part that is bad.

A certain combination of paints may be ugly. This combination may be entailed by a larger whole that is not ugly or that is even beautiful. And the larger whole may be preferable aesthetically just because of the ugliness of the part that is ugly.

I have said that, when evil is *balanced off* in a larger whole, we may, when considering the larger whole, regret or resent the presence of the evil there. But if these examples are acceptable, then one should say, 'Thank goodness for the badness of the part that is bad!' For in each case the badness of the part that is bad makes the whole *better* than what we would have had had the bad part been replaced by its neutral negation.

Finally, consider there being one wicked man and many men who are good. Presumably this state of affairs is one that is neutral or possibly even one that is good. Now consider there being one man who feels pleasure and many men who do not. Here we seem to have a state of affairs that is good—for we are saying of the many men, not that they are in a state of displeasure, but only that they are not in a state of pleasure. And now let us add these two states of affairs together, letting the wicked man be the one who experiences the pleasure and the many good men the ones who do not. I think one may well be tempted to say that this combination of a neutral state of affairs with one that is good results in a whole that is neutral. Here, then, we would have the defeat of goodness. We have a whole that is *worse* for the presence of a part that is good. Contemplating such a whole, we might well regret or resent the presence of the goodness there. For the goodness of the part that is good makes the whole worse than what we would have had had only the good part been replaced by its neutral negation.[1]

5. How, then, are we to define 'defeat'? We may do so by contrasting it with balancing off.

We said that when goodness is balanced off, then a whole that is not good has a part that is good and, outside of it, a part that is worse than the whole itself. But when goodness is defeated by a whole that is not good, then the whole does not thus contain any part that is worse than the whole itself. We may put the matter more exactly and more pedantically by saying that when the *goodness* of a state of affairs p *is defeated* by a wider state of affairs q, then the

[1] The following example is proposed by John Wisdom. Friendship is good; that is to say, two people standing in the relation of friendship to each other is good. Friendship is better for the exercise of tolerance, understanding, and forgiveness. But the exercise of tolerance, understanding, and forgiveness requires the existence of pain and sorrow. And the existence of pain and sorrow is intrinsically bad. Wisdom suggests there could not be 'sorrowing affection without pain nor lamenting affection without degradation'. And the important point is, he realizes, not merely that joint sufferings 'tend under certain circumstances to *cause* greater affection'; it is, rather, that a state of friendship that includes this evil is better, in itself, than one that does not. See John Wisdom, 'God and Evil', *Mind*, Vol. LXIV (1935), pp. 1–20; the quotations are from p. 19.

following will be true: q obtains; q entails p; p is good; q is not good; and it is not the case that q entails an r such that p does not entail r, r does not entail p, and q is better than r. And so when the goodness of p is defeated by such a larger whole, it will not be the case that the goodness of p is balanced off by that larger whole; we will not find elsewhere in the whole a part that is worse than the whole. When goodness is balanced off, and not defeated, by a whole that is bad, then we may be consoled at least by the presence of the part that is good. But if goodness is ever defeated by a whole that is bad, then we may well regret or resent the very part that is good.

Analogously for the defeat of evil. We said that when evil is balanced off, then a whole that is not bad has a part that is bad and, outside of it, a part that is better than the whole itself. But when evil is defeated by a whole that is not bad, then the whole does not contain any part that is better than the whole itself. More pedantically, when the *badness* of a state of affairs p *is defeated* by a wider state of affairs q, then the following is true: q obtains; q entails p; p is bad; q is not bad; and it is not the case that q entails an r such that p does not entail r, r does not entail p, and r is better than p. And so when the badness of p is defeated by such a larger whole, it will not be the case that the badness of p is balanced off by that larger whole; we will not find elsewhere in the whole a part that is better than the whole. When badness is balanced off, and not defeated, by a whole that is good, then one may yet regret or resent its presence there. But if badness is ever defeated by a whole that is good, then, as I have suggested, we may well be thankful for the very presence of the part that is bad.

It may be noted in passing that if, in our definition of the defeat of goodness, we replace 'q is not good' and 'q is better than r', respectively, by 'p is better than q' and 'r is bad', we obtain a definition of the more general concept of the *partial defeat of goodness*. And if, in the definition of the defeat of evil, we replace 'q is not bad' and 'r is better than q', respectively, by 'q is better than p' and 'r is good', we obtain a definition of the more general concept of the *partial defeat of evil*.

I would say, then, that the *concept* of defeat is entirely clear. It may well be that the examples I have given are not entirely plausible. It may even be, as some will doubtless urge, that the concept is not exemplified at all. Nevertheless I think the concept is of fundamental importance to the theory of value. Let us consider some of its applications.

6. We may now distinguish several different types of intrinsic goodness and intrinsic badness.

Consider a state of affairs that is intrinsically good. We may ask whether that state of affairs is defeasibly good or indefeasibly good. It will be *defeasibly good* if there is a wider state of affairs by which its goodness would be defeated. It will be *indefeasibly good* if there is no wider state of affairs by which its goodness would be defeated.

Consider, once again, Jones being pleased. According to Bentham's principles, this state of affairs would be indefeasibly good; although there are wider states of affairs in which its goodness would be balanced off, there are no wider states of affairs by which its goodness would be defeated. But according to certain other ethical views, the goodness of Jones being pleased is defeasible and it would in fact be defeated if Jones's pleasure were pleasure in the bad.

We should note that it is one thing to say that Jones's pleasure is only defeasibly good and it is another thing to say that its goodness has in fact been *defeated*. The goodness of his pleasure may be defeasible, since, let us suppose, it would be defeated if the pleasure were pleasure in the bad. But what if his pleasure is not pleasure in the bad? In this case, it may be that, though the goodness of his pleasure is defeasible, it is not in fact defeated.

What, then, of pleasure in the good? Suppose Jones is taking pleasure in Smith's innocent pleasure in the neutral—in Smith's innocent pleasure, say, in the being of stones. Shall we say that the goodness of this pleasure in the good is indefeasible? Kant would not agree. For what if Jones's pleasure were undeserved? Let Jones's pleasure in the good, then, be pleasure that is deserved. Here, surely, we have a state of affairs that is indefeasibly good. Though there are wider states of affairs in which its goodness would be balanced off, there are no wider states of affairs in which its goodness would be defeated.

Hence, with respect to states of affairs that are good, we may distinguish between those that are defeasibly good and those that are indefeasibly good. Then, with respect to those states of affairs that are defeasibly good and are also actual, those defeasibly good states of affairs that actually obtain, we may distinguish between those which are such that their goodness is in fact defeated and those which are such that their goodness is not in fact defeated. We may also distinguish between those which are such that their goodness is known to be defeated and those which are such that their goodness is not known to be defeated. (Hence we may provide a variety of possible uses for the technical philosophical expression, '*prima facie* good'. We could say that a *prima facie* good is a good that is defeasible; or we could say that it is a good that is in fact defeated; or we could say that it is a good that is defeasible and not known to be defeated.)

What we have been saying holds, *mutatis mutandis*, of evil. With respect to states of affairs that are bad, we may distinguish between those that are defeasibly bad and those that are indefeasibly bad. Then with respect to those states of affairs that are defeasibly bad and also actual, we may distinguish between those which are such that their badness has in fact been defeated and those which are such that their badness has not in fact been defeated. And we may distinguish between those which are such that their badness is known to be defeated and those which are such that their badness is not known to be defeated. (We could then provide analogous uses for '*prima facie* evil'. We could say that a *prima facie* evil is an evil that is defeasible, or that it is an evil that has, in fact, been defeated, or that it is an evil that is defeasible and not known to be defeated.)

Let us note in passing that it is now possible to distinguish still other types of intrinsic goodness and badness.

We could say, for example, that a state of affairs p is *absolutely good* provided, first, that p is good and provided, further, that *any* possible state of affairs entailing p is better than any possible state of affairs not entailing p, no matter how good or bad the other constituents of those states of affairs may happen to be.[1] Thus Pascal seems to have held that the existence of living things is such an absolute good: a world in which there is life, no matter how it is otherwise constituted, is one that is good and one that is better than any world in which there is no life.

Absolute evil would be analogous. A state of affairs p is *absolutely bad* provided that p is bad and provided that any possible state of affairs entailing p is worse than any possible state of affairs not entailing p. Thus Schopenhauer seems to have held that the existence of suffering is such an absolute evil: *any* world in which

---

[1] In *The Logic of Preference* (Edinburgh Univ. Press, 1963), G. H. von Wright envisages the possibility that a person 'actually welcomes a change to p & -q more than a change to -p and q, irrespective of all other changes which may simultaneously happen to the world', and says 'if this is the case, I shall say that he prefers p to q *absolutely*'. (p. 29).

there is suffering is one such that 'its non-existence would be preferable to its existence'.[1]

One could move on to greater heights, and depths. Thus there is, or may be, that which is not only absolutely good but also *diffusively good*. A state of affairs p is diffusively good if p is good and if any logically possible state of affairs containing p is also good. Hence if a state of affairs is diffusively good, it is not only indefeasibly good but it is also such that its goodness cannot be balanced off. Analogously, a state of affairs p is *diffusively bad* if p is bad and if any logically possible state of affairs containing p is also bad. Hence if a state of affairs p is diffusively bad, it is not only indefeasibly bad but it is also such that its badness cannot be balanced off.

I confess, however, that such distinctions as these are not likely to be of much use to most of us.

7. Before turning to theodicy, let us make certain general points about our *knowledge* of value and of defeat and defeasibility.

Propositions about *instrumental* value are, of course, *a posteriori* and contingent. To know with respect to some state of affairs that it is 'good as a means', or that it is 'bad as a means', is to know something about its causal properties; it is to know something about those states of affairs that would obtain as a result of its obtaining. What is instrumentally good on one occasion may be instrumentally neutral, or instrumentally bad, on another occasion.

Where knowledge of the instrumental value of a state of affairs thus involves knowledge of its *causal* properties, knowledge of the *intrinsic* value of a state of affairs may be likened to knowledge of its logical properties. For statements or propositions about intrinsic value may be said to hold in every possible world and therefore they may be thought of as being necessary. If pleasure is intrinsically good in this world, then it would be intrinsically good in any world in which it might be found. And if pleasure in the bad is intrinsically bad in this world, then it would be intrinsically bad in any world in which it might be found. Hence the kind of knowledge we have of intrinsic value is properly said to be *a priori*.

Statements or propositions about the defeasibility of value will also be necessary and *a priori*. But statements or propositions about defeat, as distinguished from defeasibility, are *a posteriori* and con-

---

[1] See 'On the Vanity and Suffering of Life', in the Supplements to the Fourth Book of *The World as Will and Idea*.

tingent. For to know that the value of a given state of affairs is actually defeated is to know, with respect to some state of affairs which would defeat its value, that that state of affairs in fact obtains.

There is no absurdity in supposing that a rational man might know *a priori*, with respect to some state of affairs p, that p is good, or that p is bad, and yet *not* know whether the value of p is defeasible. He might even believe, mistakenly, that the value of p is indefeasible. This could happen if every state of affairs q, such that q would defeat the value of p, were a state of affairs that he had never even conceived. Suppose, for example, that the goodness of pleasure would be defeated by the pleasure's being undeserved but otherwise not. And suppose there were a man who knew what pleasure is but who didn't know what it is to deserve anything or what it is not to deserve anything. Then he might know that pleasure is intrinsically good and believe, mistakenly, that it is also indefeasibly good.

Hence a reasonable man may be *dogmatic* with respect to questions of intrinsic value ('Is p a state of affairs that is intrinsically good?') and *agnostic* with respect to questions of defeasibility ('Is the goodness of p defeasible?'). If he conceives of some state of affairs q such that q would defeat the value of p, then, of course, he may be dogmatic with respect to the defeasibility of p. But if he does not conceive of any state of affairs q such that q would defeat the value of p, he may well withhold judgment about the indefeasibility of p. To know that the value of p is indefeasible, one needs to know that there is *no* state of affairs q such that q would defeat the value of p. Hence one would have to consider, for *every* possible state of affairs q, just what the total value of p and q would be. And this is hardly possible.

These epistemological observations have one important consequence. There is doubtless a temptation to say that a defeated good is not a good at all and thus to restrict the term 'good' to what I have called indefeasible goods. If we were thus to restrict our use of 'good', we would also restrict our use of 'evil', confining it to those things that are indefeasible evils.[1] Now if the only things that

---

[1] Although, as I have said, St Thomas seems to be aware of the concept of defeat (see *Summa Theologica*, I, 48, 2) he is also inclined to say, at times, that defeated goods and evils are not goods and evils at all. Thus he says: 'Initially and without qualification something may be judged to be good or evil, yet this decision may have to be reversed when additional circumstances are taken into account' (I, 19, 6); and '. . . something may be good according to a particular judgment which is not good according to a wider judgment, and conversely. . .'

are really good or bad are just those things that I have called in-defeasibly good or indefeasibly bad, and if we can never know, with respect to any state of affairs, that that state of affairs *is* indefeasibly good or indefeasibly bad, then it will follow that we cannot know, with respect to any state of affairs at all, that that state of affairs is good or that that state of affairs is bad. And this is an extreme that most of us would be unwilling to accept.

8. Finally, I shall make some brief observations about theodicy. For the concept of defeat has obvious application to the problem of evil.

We may assume that if an omnipotent, omniscient, and benevolent deity were to create a world, then that world would be at least as good as any other possible world. The total state of affairs which would make up such a world would be at least as good as any other possible set of states of affairs that would make up a world. We encounter the problem of evil when we try to answer the simple question: 'Is it possible for a world that is at least as good as any other logically possible world to include any states of affairs that are intrinsically bad?'

Perhaps we should remind ourselves that it would not be possible for there to be a world containing only states of affairs that are intrinsically good. For every state of affairs is such that every possible world contains either it or its negation. But some states of affairs—there being stones, once again—are intrinsically indifferent and therefore such that both they and their negations are neutral. Therefore every possible world will contain some states of affairs that are intrinsically neutral. Moreover, every bad state of affairs and every good state of affairs is a state of affairs such that its negation is neutral. Hence, for every evil as well as every good, that is *excluded* from a world that is good, that world will include its neutral negation.

Perhaps we should also note that, if God does not create at all, he will still function as a *causa deficiens*. For there will then be certain neutral states of affairs—the non-existence of stones as well as the non-existence of the various goods and evils we have dis-cussed—which he will thereby *allow* to exist.

I have said we encounter the problem of evil when we consider the question: 'Is it possible for a world that is at least as good as

---

(I–II, 19, 10). Contrast G. E. Moore: 'The part of a valuable whole retains exactly the same value when it is, as when it is not, a part of that whole'; *Principia Ethica*, p. 30.

any other possible world to include any states of affairs that are intrinsically bad?' There is an impressive list of philosophers who seem to believe, not only that the answer to this question is negative, but also that it is very obviously negative.[1] Yet if what I have said about defeat is correct, then the answer to this question is at least not *obviously* negative. For it would seem that a world that is at least as good as any other possible world could contain states of affairs that are intrinsically bad—provided that the badness of each of these states of affairs is defeated.

What if the evils of the world were defeated by some wider state of affairs that is *absolutely good* in the sense we have defined—what if the evils of the world were defeated by a certain state of affairs q such that q is good and such that any possible state of affairs entailing q is better than any possible state of affairs not entailing q? Epicurus said that if God is able but unwilling to *prevent* evil, then he is malevolent. But if the evil in the world is defeated and contained in a larger whole that is absolutely good, one should rather say that, if God had been able but unwilling to *create* such evil, then he would have been malevolent. (What, though, if there were a possible world having the same value as this one but containing no evil? One is tempted to say that God should have created that world instead of this one. But why so, if this one is just as good? Creation of the other world, one might say, would be very much like an act of supererogation.)

It is clear, I think, that this is the sort of thing that has been intended by the great theodicists in the history of Western thought. It is also clear, I think, that the theodicist *must* appeal to the concept defeat—that he can deal with the problem of evil *only* by saying that the evils in the world are defeated in the sense that I have tried to describe.[2] The other familiar moves just don't work at all.

[1] For example: John Stuart Mill, F. H. Bradley, J. E. M. McTaggart, C. J. Ducasse, Henry Aiken, Antony Flew, J. L. Mackie, J. J. McCloskey, and W. T. Stace. See the references in Nelson Pike's anthology, *God and Evil* (Englewood Cliffs, N.J., Prentice-Hall, Inc., 1964), pp. 86–7.

[2] Discussing some unpublished statements of mine on this problem, Terence Penelhum writes: 'Chisholm's suggestion that a theist can hold that every evil is defeated without claiming to know by what, must contend with the fact that in a given form of theism the range of possible defeating factors may be specifically understood and incorporated in its moral requirements.' See Terence Penelhum, 'Divine Goodness and the Problem of Evil', *Religious Studies*, Vol. II (1966–7), pp. 95–107; the quotation is on p. 107. Many theists, I would think, could accept the epistemological point made above—namely, that a reasonable man may be dogmatic with respect to questions of intrinsic value and at the same time agnostic with respect to questions of defeasibility.

But we must not let the theodicist have the last word—not this year anyway.

What possible state of affairs *could* thus serve to defeat the evil that is in the world? The wise theodicist, I should think, would say that he doesn't know. It is at least *logically* possible with respect to the evil that does exist that that evil is defeated? The most the theodicist has a right to say, I believe, is that it is *epistemically* possible. It may be, for all we know, that the evil in the world is defeated in some state of affairs that is absolutely good. And it may also be, for all we know, that the goodness in the world is defeated in some state of affairs that is absolutely evil.

7

PRAGMATISM AND THE TRAGIC SENSE OF LIFE

SIDNEY HOOK

In the realm of thought and culture America has largely been a colonial dependency of Europe. Its own authentic history—the conquest of a virgin continent, the bloodiest of all civil wars, the technological revolution, the extension of social democracy—has not been reflected in a characteristic philosophy of life. As the pioneer settlements struggled across river and mountain, New England divines were still wrestling with age-old problems of freedom and predestination. When the nation was locked in arms over the issue of slavery, its leading teachers were still justifying the ways of God to man while the more daring were beginning to unwind the cobwebby speculations of German idealistic philosophy. Only towards the end of the nineteenth century did a distinctively American philosophy emerge. The names associated with it were Charles Peirce, William James, and John Dewey. This philosophy was labelled pragmatism or instrumentalism or experimentalism.

Pragmatism was regarded as a distinctively American philosophy, despite its European congeners, because it stressed three things: the universe was open—therefore possibilities were real; the future depended in part upon what human beings did or left undone—therefore man was not a slave of scientific or theological necessity; ideas were potentially plans of action—therefore thinking could and did make a difference to human affairs. This emphasis on action became central in the interpretation of pragmatism and before long action was identified with practice and—fateful step!—practice with usefulness. Since Americans were considered a practical people with a highly developed sense of the concrete and useful, pragmatism was played up abroad as the American philosophy par excellence. Its claim that all thinking which aimed to win new knowledge involved some practice or experiment was transformed into the belief that all thinking was for the sake of practice. And since the chief practice of Americans seemed to be in the eyes of their poorer neighbours the making of money, pragmatism was cried down as the typical philosophy of a *parvenu* people, insensitive to tradition and culture, and devoted only to the invention of machines to make more machines by human beings who acted as if they were themselves only complicated machines.

This European conception of pragmatism reached American shores and infected some of the more tender-minded intellectuals who attributed their ineffectuality not to their own failings but to the addiction of the American people to the philosophy of pragmatism. It is now an almost unchallenged commonplace that pragmatism is a superficial philosophy of optimism, of uncritical adjustment and conformity, of worship of the goddess success. Such an interpretation of pragmatism not only runs counter to what we know of the personalities of Peirce, James, and Dewey, but is based upon a tendentious reading of their work.

What was overlooked in this caricatured account is that the very nature of philosophy, as the pragmatic philosophers conceive it, makes it a method of clarifying ideas and therefore pre-eminently a method of *criticism*. It is death on bunkum and pretentious abstractions especially when they are capitalized as Success or Historical Destiny or Reality. It clarifies the meaning of ideas by uncovering their consequences in use—not merely consequences in linguistic use but in the behaviour of things and people in the concrete situations in which language functions. Long before Wittgenstein, pragmatists believed that language was a form of life. They sought to reduce differences concerning supposed first principles and ultimate necessities to their varied fruits and consequences in experience.

Pragmatism was not only a method of clarifying ideas by exploring their consequences in behavioural use. It was also a temper of mind towards the vital options which men confront when they become aware of what alternative proposals commit them to. It stressed the efficacy of human ideals and actions and at the same time their inescapable limitations. It forswore the promise of total solutions and wholesale salvation for piecemeal gains. Yet far from embracing easy formulae of the ultimate reconciliation of conflicting interests and values, it acknowledged the reality of piecemeal losses even when we risk our lives to achieve the gains. No matter how intelligent and humane our choices, there are, William James insists, 'real losses and real losers'. We live in a dangerous and adventurous and serious world and 'the very "seriousness",' James goes on to say, 'we attribute to life means that ineluctable noes and losses form part of it, that there are genuine sacrifices, and that something permanently drastic and bitter always remains at the bottom of the cup'.

This aspect of the philosophy of pragmatism has been almost completely ignored by its critics. It seems to me, however, to be central in pragmatism, and to provide an illuminating perspective from which to survey the problems and predicaments of men. It is grounded in a recognition of the tragic sense of life.

Despite its criticism of the detailed claims of traditional philosophy, pragmatism has a certain kinship with some classical conceptions of the role of philosophy, but not with their methods and manners of thought. Although it recognizes the importance of precision in the analysis of problems, it is not a 'minute' philosophy charting the refinements of linguistic usage while other disciplines stride forward. And although vitally concerned with normative problems of individual and social ethics, it does not seek necessarily to reform or revolutionize the world. It tries to undercut the rather tedious disputes about what philosophy is or should be by calling attention to its plural historic roles. 'Logic is the essence of philosophy', some philosophers of our times have declared. Yet Plato is surely more notable for his vision and as a dramatist of the life of reason than for his logical analyses. 'The function of philosophy is not to understand the world but to change it', say some other philosophers. But neither Aristotle nor Hume was a reformer or revolutionist. Yet each enriched the stores of human wisdom even if we believe that we have gone beyond them.

Pragmatism is a philosophy which does not rule out the right of other philosophies to be legitimately regarded as philosophies on the basis of some 'proper' definition of philosophy which cannot be defended without circularity. It does not take as its own norm the positivistic criterion of whether philosophy is a science or a body of knowledge of comparable objectivity. It asks only whether what passes for 'philosophy' in any historical period is worth doing, whether there is sufficient illumination in pursuing certain themes, ignored by other thinkers, to justify continuing concern with them, especially in the light of their bearing on basic issues in other disciplines, and on the conduct of social and personal life. Sufficient for its importance is that it makes a difference, good or bad. After all, no one really believes that only science is a self-justifying enterprise.

In this sense pragmatism is as catholic in its conception of philosophy as the great classical views of philosophy, although it regards the *a priori* and deductive methods employed by most philosophies of the past as inadequate, their conclusions false or misleading, obstacles rather than aids to the extension of knowledge and the further enrichment of experience. Because of current misconceptions of the nature of pragmatism it may be helpful to call attention to some of its neglected aspects.

For many years I have concerned myself with problems of social and political and legal philosophy, with 'problems of men' as authentic as any of those recognized by thinkers who would reform modern philosophy. But I find myself increasingly out of sympathy with those who have impugned the whole philosophical enterprise because of its failure to serve as a beacon to mankind in distress. When I ask myself why I feel uncomfortable and at odds with those who attack philosophers because they have nothing of immediate, practical moment to say, I find that my conception of philosophy although stated sometimes in words similar to theirs, differs in important ways. Put most succinctly, although I believe that philosophy is a *quest* for wisdom, many of those who cite this phrase, too, speak and act as if they already had it. The difference may be only of nuance and emphasis, but it has a profound bearing on one's conception of the appropriate role of the philosopher in the culture of his time. It is the difference between being a moralist and being a moralizer. The moralizer may be called 'the shouting moralist', of whom Santayana somewhere says that he 'no doubt has his place but not in philosophy'. It is a difference, on the one hand, between *analysing* specific and basic social problems and conflicts, and *clarifying* the issues in dispute with all the tools at one's command—and, on the other, *proclaiming* solutions and programmes on the basis of antecedent commitments which one shares with some faction of his fellow men. It is the difference between approaching problems of human experience in terms of one's vocation as a philosopher, which is to do intellectual justice to the varied and conflicting interests present or discovered, and one's vocation as a citizen limited by specific duties he must fulfil. It is the difference between intellectual concern which may or may not lead to programmes of action and commitment to programmes of action which by their very nature estops self-critical thought.

In the course of its history philosophy has been many things. But its distinctive concern at all times *has* been the quest for wisdom. Otherwise there would be no point in including thinkers like Descartes or Leibnitz in the history of philosophy in addition to the history of science or mathematics. What distinguishes the philosopher as a moralist from the philosopher as a mathematician, logician or natural scientist, and from the ordinary man as a philosopher, is his sustained reflective pursuit of wisdom. This means two things. The systematic study of the knowledge which is relevant to wisdom: and the analysis of the commitments we assume and rule out when knowledge is related to policy. All of us know that wisdom and knowledge are not the same thing, but we sometimes mistakenly speak as if they are opposed. A man may have knowledge of many things and not be wise, but a wise man cannot be ignorant of the things he is wise about. He must have knowledge of the nature and career of values in human experience; knowledge of the nature and history of the situations in which they develop and conflict; knowledge of the minds and emotions of the carriers of value; knowledge of the consequences of actions taken or proposed. The wise man is not one who merely recites moral principles and applies a ready-made schedule of moral obligations to the problems and perplexities of value conflict. He is one who on the basis of what he already knows, or believes he knows, makes fresh inquiry into the situations which define alternatives and exact their costs. 'Only the conventional and the fanatical', observes Dewey, 'are always immediately sure of right and wrong in conduct'. This means that a philosopher must earn his title to be wise not by right of philosophical tradition or philology but by the hard work of acquiring relevant knowledge and by hard thinking about it.

Here lie important tasks for the philosopher. To be wise he must immerse himself in the actual subject-matters (not necessarily experiences) out of which life's problems arise. To be wise about economic affairs he must study economics, to be wise about problems of law he must study law, to be wise about politics he must study history, sociology and other disciplines. To be wise about war and peace he must study military technology and the theory of and practice of communism, including its strategic exploitation of peace movements to disarm the free world. Indeed, these subjects are so interrelated that to be wise about any one of them he must study them all. And I might add, in view of some current writing, to be wise about education it is not enough merely to rebaptize the ends of the good life as ends of a good education, too, as if without operational application to concrete historical situations, they had any but a peripheral bearing on the great, current problems of education. One must study social history, the psychology of learning, the methods and techniques of pedagogy to achieve educational wisdom. To enumerate the ends of the good life is not enough. Nor is a primer on logical analysis which can serve as an introduction to the study of *any* subject, a primer to a philosophy of education.

All of these problems are of tremendous complexity because of the number of independent variables they contain, because they rarely permit of controlled experiment, and because the community must sometimes act upon them in desperate urgency before the analysis is complete. This should make for humility among philosophers even as they bring to the study of these problems the methodological sophistication, the arts and skills of analysis which are the hallmarks of their profession. This is what *I* mean by 'the problems of men'. It is philosophy not as a quest for salvation but as a pursuit of understanding of great cultural issues and their possible upshot. It does not start from a complete stock of philosophical wisdom which it dispenses to others with hortatory fervour but with an initial sense of concern to meet the challenge of the great unresolved problems of our time, offering analysis of these problems which will win the respect of the specialist and yet command the attention of everyman, e.g. how to preserve peace *and* freedom, achieve adequate production and meaningful vocations for all, design patterns of creative leisure, effect desegregation if possible without coercion, establish a welfare state and a spirit of enterprise, preserve national security and the right to dissent. It is philosophy as *normative* social inquiry. And it is *not* social reform. How could philosophy be identified with social reform in view of the existence of many esteemed philosophers from Aristotle to Santayana whose judgments of wisdom were conservative, hostile to social reform? Such identification would be comparable to defining a physicist as one who was committed to a specific hypothesis in physics.

At this point my inner ear senses unspoken murmurs of surprise. 'Surely', some of you must be saying, 'this constitutes a repudiation of John Dewey's conception of philosophy, for, after all, does not Dewey call upon philosophers as philosophers to do precisely what is being urged they should not do? Does not Dewey call upon philosophers to play the role of social reformers?' My answer is: 'Not as I understand him and not as he is to be understood in the light of all he has written.'

Here is not the place to provide the documentation. I content

myself merely with saying that Dewey has a very *complex* conception
of philosophy. Philosophy is indeed concerned primarily with what
I call normative problems of social inquiry. But its function is also
to provide leading, speculative ideas in science—natural and social.
And a third function is to weave together certain families of ideas
into a philosophical synthesis. 'There is a kind of music of ideas,'
he says, 'which appeals, apart from any question of verification, to
the mind of thinkers!' Nor is this all. The philosopher must bring
some perspective or vision to bear upon the world which is related
to issues of value and hence makes the analysis of normative problems of social inquiry more sensitive. 'Philosophies', declares
Dewey, 'are different ways of construing life. . . .'

There is more, then, than problems of normative social inquiry
which falls within the province of the philosopher's concern. There
is the illuminating perspective in which they are seen which is
metaphysics. 'If philosophy be criticism,' Dewey asks in *Experience
and Nature*, 'what is to be said of the relation of philosophy to
metaphysics?' His answer briefly is that metaphysics is a description of those gross features of the world which constitute the back-
drop of the theatre of human activity against which men play out
their lives. The conduct of life and the analysis of its problems,
however indirectly, will reflect what we believe to be the generic
features of human experience in the world. In this sense, as ultimately related to the human scene and the adventure of human
life, but not to ontology, metaphysics is 'a ground map of the province of criticism establishing base lines to be employed in more
intricate triangulations'.

This brings me finally to my theme of the tragic sense of life
as a feature of human experience which provides an illuminating
perspective upon the analysis of man's problems. The juxtaposition
of the expressions 'pragmatism' and 'the tragic sense of life' may
appear bewildering to those who understand pragmatism as a narrow theory of meaning and 'the tragic sense of life' as the hysterical
lament that man is not immortal—the theme song of Unamuno's
book of that title. To speak of pragmatism and the tragic sense of
life is somewhat like speaking of 'The Buddhism of John Dewey' or
'The Dewey Nobody Knows'.

I am not aware that Dewey ever used the phrase 'the tragic sense
of life', but I know that growing up in the shadow of the Civil War,
he felt what I shall describe by it and that it is implied in his account
of moral experience. At any rate nothing of moment depends upon

whether the view is actually Dewey's or Hegel's or William James's or Nicolai Hartmann's in all of whom it can be found. I take the responsibility of the interpretation and its application. It is a perspective which seems to me to illumine the pragmatic view that problems of normative social inquiry—morals in the broad sense—are the primary—not exclusive—subject-matter of philosophy, and that reason or scientific intelligence can and should be used to resolve them.

By the tragic sense of life I do not understand merely sensitivity to the presence of evil or suffering in the world, although all tragic situations to some degree involve one or the other. And since I have mentioned Buddha I should like to say that the presence of the evils in the world which led Buddha to surrender his Kingdom in order to seek salvation for himself and mankind are not to me the realities fundamental to the tragic sense of life. There were three things in Buddha's experience, reflection upon which led him to a renunciation of his princely lot and a quest for liberation from desire and incarnate existence—sickness, old age and death. One can very well understand why in the world in which he lived and for many centuries thereafter until our own, these phenomena loomed so large in the over-populated and poverty-stricken areas of Asia. None the less if we are to distinguish between the sense of the *pitiful* and the sense of the *tragic*—sickness, old age and even many forms of death, despite their numbing effect upon human sensibility, are not necessarily to be classified as tragic.

First, given the rapidly expanding horizons of knowledge in our age, there is nothing in the nature of things which requires that the sick, any more than the poor, must always be with us. If scientific medicine develops at the same pace in the next few hundred years as it has in the last century, it is not shallow optimism to anticipate that the most serious forms of sickness will disappear and not be replaced by others. Even where sickness is present it may be the occasion of tragedy, but by itself is not an illustration of it. In relation to the forces of nature man's lot may appear pitiful. The tragic is a moral phenomenon.

What is true of sickness is true of old age. The aged arouse our compassion because of their feebleness and fragility—and the multiplicity of their aches and pains. When these are absent—and this, too, is a concern of scientific medicine—there is a chance for serenity, wisdom and beauty of spirit to manifest themselves. There is sometimes a grandeur and stateliness about an old tree which aged

persons do not possess because the processes of physical degenera-
tion, and the consequent weakening of the vital powers, make man
pitiful. There is no tragedy in growing old biologically, but only
sorrow; the element of the tragic enters in the defeat of plans or
hopes, in the realization that in much grief there is not much
wisdom, and that we cannot count merely upon the passage of time
alone to diminish our stupidities and cruelties.

But what of death—Buddha's third appalling discovery—pre-
occupation with which has become so fashionable today among
some European existentialist philosophers that their philosophy
seems to be more a meditation upon death than upon life? Is not
death the ultimate source of whatever is tragic in life? I cannot
bring myself to think so. Nor can I convince myself that its nature
and significance in life waited to be discovered by Kierkegaard and
Heidegger and their modern disciples.

It is the reflective attitude towards death, not the popular attitude
or the one displayed by those in its last agonies, which throws light
on its nature and place in life. The attitude exhibited by Socrates in
facing it seems wiser than that expressed by the contemnors of the
rational life who, not content with talking about what they find when
they look into themselves, inflate it into a universal trait of the
human psyche. So Tolstoy, who is quoted by existentialist writers,
writes: 'If a man has learned to think, no matter what he may think
about, he is always thinking of his own death. All philosophers are
like that. And what truth can there be, if there is death?' Logically,
of course, this makes no more sense than the even more extreme
statement of Sartre that 'if we must die then our life has no meaning', which to those who solve some problems in life and therefore
find some meaning, might be taken as a premise in a new short
proof of human immortality. All this it seems to me expresses little
more than a fear of death and a craving for immortality. It is a
commonplace observation, however, that most human beings who
desire immortality desire not unending life but unending youth or
other desirable qualities which life makes possible. The fable of
Juno and her lover in which Juno petitions the Gods to take back
the gift of eternal life they had conferred upon a mortal indicates
that the Greeks knew that a life without end could be a dubious
blessing. In this respect the Hellenes were wiser than the Hebrews,
whose God drives Adam from Paradise after he had eaten of the
fruit of the tree of knowledge to prevent him from eating of the
fruit of the tree of eternal life. Agony over death strikes me as one

of the unloveliest features of the intellectual life of our philosophic times—and certainly unworthy of any philosophy which conceives itself as a quest for wisdom. It has never been clear to me why those who are nauseated by life, not by this or that kind of life but any kind of life, should be so fearful of death.

Wisdom is knowledge of the uses of life and death. The uses of life are to be found in the consummatory experiences of vision and delight, of love, understanding, art, friendship and creative activity. That is why in a contingent world of finite men, vulnerable to powers they cannot control which sometimes robs them of the possibility of any justifying consummations, death has its uses, too. For it gives us some assurance that no evil or suffering lasts for ever. To anyone aware of the multitude of infamies and injustices which men have endured, of the broken bodies and tortured minds of the victims of these cruelties, of the multiple dimensions of pain in which millions live on mattress graves or with minds shrouded in darkness, death must sometimes appear as a beneficent release not an inconsolable affliction. It washes the earth clean of what cannot be cleansed in any other way. Not all the bright promises of a future free of these stains of horror can redeem by one iota the lot of those who will not live to see the dawn of the new day.

It is nobler to exist and struggle in a world in which there is always a vital option to live or die. The fear of death, the desire to survive at any cost or price in human degradation, has been the greatest ally of tyranny, past and present. 'There are times,' says Woodbridge, 'when a man ought to be more afraid of living than dying.' And we may add, there are situations in which because of the conditions of survival, the worst thing we can know of anyone is that he has survived. We have known such times and situations. They may come again.

Even in a world in which all injustices, cruelties and physical anguish have disappeared, the possibility of withdrawing from it makes the world in so far forth a better and a freer world. So long as we retain possession of our faculties, our decision to remain in the world indicates a participating responsibility on our part for those events within it which our continuance affects. If human beings were unable to die they would to that extent be unfree. Man shares a *conatus sui esse persevare* with everything else in the world or at least with all other sentient beings. But just because he can on rational grounds give up his being, choose not to be, he differentiates himself most strikingly from his fellow creatures in nature. I conclude therefore that death as such is not a tragic phenomenon and that its presence does not make the world and our experience within it tragic. It would be truer to call tragic a world in which men wanted to die but couldn't.

What, then, do I mean by the tragic sense of life and what is its relevance to pragmatism? I mean by the tragic sense a very simple thing which is rooted in the very nature of the moral experience and the phenomenon of moral choice. Every genuine experience of moral doubt and perplexity in which we ask: 'What should I do?' takes place in a situation where good conflicts with good. If we already know what is evil the moral inquiry is over, or it never really begins. 'The worse or evil,' says Dewey, 'is the rejected good' but until we reject it, the situation is one in which apparent good opposes apparent good. 'All the serious perplexities of life come back to the genuine difficulty of forming a judgment as to the values of a situation: they come back to a conflict of goods.' No matter how we resolve the opposition some good will be sacrificed, some interest, whose immediate craving for satisfaction may be every whit as intense and authentic as its fellows, will be modified, frustrated or even suppressed. Where the goods involved are of a relatively low order, like decisions about what to eat, where to live, where to go, the choice is unimportant except to the mind of a child. There are small tragedies as there are small deaths. At any level the conflict of values must become momentous to oneself or others to convey adequately the tragic quality. Where the choice is between goods that are complex in structure and consequential for the future, the tragic quality of the moral dilemma emerges more clearly. And when it involves basic choices of love, friendship, vocations, the quality becomes poignant. The very nature of the self as expressed in habits, dispositions and character, is to some extent altered by these decisions. If, as Hobbes observes. 'Hell is truth seen too late', all of us must live in it. No matter how justified in smug retrospect our moral decisions seem to have been, only the unimaginative will fail to see the possible selves we have sacrificed to become what we are. Grant that all regrets are vain, that any other choice would have been equally or more regretted, the selves we might have been are eloquent witnesses of values we failed to enjoy. If we have played it safe and made our existence apparently secure, the fascinating experience of a life of adventure and experience can never be ours, and every thought of a good fight missed will be accompanied by a pang. It is a poor spirit,

William James reminds us, who does not sense the chagrin of the
tardy Crillon, who arriving when the battle is over is greeted by
Henry IV with the words: 'Hang yourself, brave Crillon! We fought
at Arques, and you were not there!' On the other hand, if we have
scorned to put down our roots, hugged our liberty tightly to ourselves by refusing to give hostages to fortune, become crusaders or
martyrs for lost causes, we have thrust from ourselves the warmth
of sustained affection, and the comforting regularities which can
best heal the bruised spirit.

There is a conflict not only between the good and the good but
between the good and the right where the good is a generic term for
all the values in a situation and the right for all the obligations. The
concepts of good and right are irreducible to each other in ordinary
use. We are often convinced we must fulfil a certain duty even when
we are far from convinced to the same degree that the action or the
rule it exemplifies will achieve the greatest good. The 'good' is
related to the reflective satisfaction of an interest: 'the right' to the
fulfilment of a binding demand or rule of the community. There is
no moral problem when in doing the right thing we can see that it
also leads to the greatest good or when striving for the greatest good
conforms to our sense of what is right. But the acute ethical problems arise when in the pursuit of the good we do things which
appear not to be right, as, e.g., when in order to avoid the dangers
of war a nation repudiates its treaty obligations or when in order to
win a war non-combatants are punished who are in no way responsible for the actions of others. They also arise when in doing what is
right our actions result in evil consequences, as, e.g., when a dangerous criminal, set free on a legal technicality, kills again or when
the refusal to surrender to the unjust claims of an aggressor results
in wholesale slaughter. Many have been the attempts made to escape
the antinomies between the right and the good by defining the good
as the object of right or the right merely as the means to the good.
All have failed. To act upon the right no matter what its consequences for human weal or woe seems inhuman, at times insane.
The thirst for righteousness has too often been an angry thirst
satisfied if at all by long draughts of blood. On the other hand, the
attempt to do good by *any* means no matter how unjust, is sub-
human and usually irrational.

As compared to traditional ethical doctrines, ideal utilitarianism
reaches farthest in our quest for an adequate ethics, but in the end it,
too, must be rejected. And it was the pragmatist and pluralist,

William James, long before Pritchard and Ross, who indicated why in the famous question he asked: 'If the hypothesis were offered us of a world in which Messrs. Fourier's and Bellamy's and Morris' Utopia should all be outdone, and millions be kept permanently happy on the one simple condition that a certain lost soul on the far off edge of things should lead a life of lonely torture, what except a specifical and independent sort of emotion can it be which would make us immediately feel . . . how hideous a thing would be its enjoyment when deliberately accepted as the fruit of such a bargain?' The situation is unaltered if we recognize that there are other goods besides happiness and that justice is itself a good, because in that case the conflict breaks out again between good and good. In this connection I would venture the statement that it is the failure to see the radical pluralism in the nature of the goods which are reckoned in the consequences of an action which accounts both for Moore's view that it is self-evident that it can *never* be right knowingly to approve an action that would make the world as a whole worse than some alternative action and for Kant's view that there are some duties that it would *always* be right to perform, even if the consequences of the action resulted in a worse world or in no world at all. No specific rule can be laid down as absolutely binding in advance either way. Nothing can take the place of intelligence; the better or the lesser evil in each situation can be best defined as the object of reflective choice. Even the decision in the stock illustration of the textbooks whether to execute an innocent man or turn him over to be tortured in order to save the community from destruction—would depend upon a complex of circumstances. It is perfectly conceivable that an unjust act will sometimes produce the greater good or the lesser evil. It is sometimes necessary to burn down a house to save a village. Although when applied to human beings the logic seems damnable, few are prepared to take the position of Kant in those agonizing moral predicaments that are not uncommon in history, especially the history of oppressed minority peoples, in which the survival of the group can be purchased only at the price of the pain, degradation and death of the innocent. No matter how we choose, we must either betray the ideal of the greater good or the ideal of right or justice. In this lies the agony of the choice.

Many have been the attempts to escape the guilt of that choice. I cite one from the past. During the Middle Ages, Maimonides writing on the Laws of the Torah to guide his people discusses what a community is to do when it is beset by enemies who demand the life of one man with the threat to kill all if he be not turned over to them. Maimonides teaches that they are to refuse to turn over any man even if all must die in consequence, except if their enemies call out the name of a specific person. I had heard this teaching defended on the ground that if the community itself had to make the decision who was to die, it would be taking the guilt of an innocent man's death upon itself, which is impermissible. But if the enemy names the man, then he can be turned over because the guilt and sin fall now on *their* heads. By this miserable evasion it was thought that the tragic choice could be avoided. But it turns out that Maimonides has been misread. What Maimonides really taught is that only if the name of the person who has been called out is of one already under the death sentence for his crimes should he be surrendered. But never an innocent man. 'Never', however, is a long time. It is problematic whether the Jews would have survived if they had always abided by Maimonides' injunction.

If anything, human beings are more readily inclined to sacrifice the right to the good than the good to the right especially in revolutionary situations which have developed because of grievances too long unmet. It can easily be shown that it was Lenin's conception of communist ethics which implicitly defined the right action as consisting in doing *anything*—literally anything that would bring victory in the class struggle—which explains the transformation of a whole generation of idealists into hangmen. In fact, the health of the revolution whether in the times of Robespierre or Castro never really requires the holocaust of victims offered up to it. But no revolution including our own has ever been achieved without injustice to someone. However the conflict between the principles of right and the values of good be theoretically resolved, in every concrete situation it leads to some abridgment of principle or some diminution of value.

The most dramatic of all moral conflicts is not between good and good, or between good and right, but between right and right. This in its starkest form is the theme of Sophoclean tragedy, but the primary locus of the tragic situation is not in a play but in life, in law, and in history. Innocence in personal matters consists in overlooking the conflict of moral duties and obligations. Innocence in political matters, the characteristic of ritualistic liberalism, consists in failing to see the conflicts of rights in our Bill of Rights and the necessity of their intelligent adjustment. In our own country we have witnessed again and again the antinomy of rights revealed in divided loyalties, in the conflict between allegiance to the laws of the state and allegiance to what is called divine law or natural law or the dictates of conscience. On the international scene it is expressed in the conflict of incompatible national claims, each with *some* measure of justification, as in the Israeli-Arab impasse.

One of the noteworthy features of moral intuitionism as illustrated in the doctrines of Ross is this recognition that *prima facie* duties conflict and that every important moral act exhibits at the same time characteristics which tend to make it both *prima facie* right and *prima facie* wrong, so that although we may claim certainty about these *prima facie* duties, any particular moral judgment or action is at best only probable or contingent. As Ross says, 'There is therefore much truth in the description of the right act as a fortunate act.' From this the conclusion to be drawn, it seems to me, is that the most important *prima facie* duty of all in a situation requiring moral decision is that of *conscientiousness*, or reflective assessment of all the relevant factors involved, and the searching exploration of our own hearts to determine what we sincerely want, whether we really wish to do what is right in a situation or to get our own scheming way come what may. As much if not more evil results from confusion of our purposes and ignorance of our motives than from ruthless and clear-eyed resolve to ignore everyone's interests but one's own. This emphasis on the importance of reflective inquiry into the features of the situation which bear on the rightness of an action seems to me to be more important than Ross's conception or interpretation of the intuitive apprehension of our *prima facie* duties. It is easier to doubt that we have this faculty of infallible intuition than that our intelligence has the power to discover our conflicts and mediate between them.

Irony is compounded with tragedy in the fact that many of the rights we presently enjoy we owe to our ancestors who in the process of winning them for us deprived others of their rights. In some regions of the world the very ground on which people stand was expropriated by force and fraud from others by their ancestors. Yet as a rule it would be a new injustice to seek to redress the original injustice by depriving those of their possessions who hold present title to them. Every just demand for reparations against an aggressor country is an unjust demand on the descendants of its citizens who as infants were not responsible for the deeds of aggression. That is why history is the arena of the profoundest moral conflicts in which some legitimate right has always been sacrificed, sometimes on the altars of the God of War.

The Christian and especially the Buddhist ethics of purity which seeks to transcend this conflict and avoid guilt by refusal to violate anyone's right in such situations, can only do so by withdrawing from the plane of the ethical altogether. This may succeed in God's eyes, but not in man's. The Buddhist saint or any other who out of respect for the right to life of man or beast refuses ever to use force, or to kill, even when this is the only method, as it sometimes is, that will save multitudes from suffering and death, makes himself responsible for the greater evil, all the more so because he claims to be acting out of compassion. He cannot avoid guilt whether we regard him as more than man or less than man. No more than we does he escape the tragic decision.

There are three generic approaches to the tragic conflicts of life. The first approach is that of history. The second is that of love. The third is that of creative intelligence in quest for ways of mediation which I call here the pragmatic.

The approach of history is best typified by Hegel precisely because he tries to put a gloss of reason over the terrible events which constitute so much of the historical process. Its upshot is woefully inept to its intent. It suggests not only that whatever cause wins and *however* it wins, is more just than the cause which is defeated, but that the loser is the more wicked and not merely the weaker. Further, it calls into question the very fact of tragic conflict from which it so perceptively starts. No one has seen more profoundly into the nature of the tragic situation than Hegel and its stark clash of equally legitimate rights. But his solution, expressed in Schiller's dictum *Die Weltgeschichte ist das Weltgericht*, as Hegel develops it, makes the philosophy of history a theodicy. It thereby vulgarizes tragedy. For it attempts to console man with a dialectical proof that his agony and defeat are not really evils but necessary elements in the goodness of the whole. The position is essentially religious. No monotheistic religion which conceives of God as both omnipotent and benevolent, no metaphysics which asserts that the world is rational, necessary and good has any room for genuine tragedy.

The approach of love is incomplete and ambiguous. It is incomplete because if love is more than a feeling of diffused sympathy but is expressed in action no *man* can love everyone or identify himself with every interest. Empirically love has produced as much disunity as unity in the world—not only in Troy but in Jerusalem. Injustice is often born of love, not only of self-love but of love of some rather than others. Love is not only incomplete but ambiguous. There are various kinds of love and the actions to which they lead may be incompatible. An order of distinction is required. A man's love for his family must be discriminatory: his love of mankind not. He cannot love both in the same way without denying one or the other. The quality of love is altered with the range of its generalization. In one sense love always shows a bias which reinforces some conflicting interest; in another it gives all conflicting values its blessing without indicating any specific mode of action by which conflict can be mediated. Love may enable a person to live with the burden of guilt which he assumes when he sacrifices one right to another. But it is no guide to social conflict as the last two thousand years have shown. Because the Lord loves man equally nothing follows logically about the equality of man before the Law. 'The *Agape* quality of love', says Tillich, 'sees man as God sees him.' But what *man* can tell us how *God* sees man? 'Agape', continues Tillich, 'loves in everybody and through everybody love itself.' Karl Barth speaks more simply and intelligibly, and with a basic brutality which is the clue to his crude neutralism, when he claims that such love has no bearing whatever for the organization of any human society.

Finally there is the method of creative intelligence. It, too, tries to make it possible for men to live with the tragic conflict of goods and rights and duties, to mediate not by arbitrary fiat but through informed and responsible decision. Whoever uses this method must find his way among all the conflicting claims. He must therefore give each one of them and the interests it represents tongue or voice. Every claimant therefore has a right to be heard. The hope is that as much as possible of each claim may be incorporated in some inclusive or shared interest which is accepted because the alternatives are less satisfactory. To this end we investigate every relevant feature about it, the conditions under which it emerged, its proximate causes and consequences, the costs of gratifying it, the available alternatives and *their* costs. Every mediation entails some sacrifice. The quest for the unique good of the situation, for what is to be done here and now, may point to what is better than anything else available, but what it points to is also a lesser evil. It is a lesser evil whether found in a compromise or in moderating the demand of a just claim or in learning to live peacefully with one's differences on the same general principle which tells us that a divorce is better for all parties concerned than a murder. In every case the rules, the wisdom, the lessons of the past are to be applied, but they have presumptive, not final, validity because they may be challenged by new presumptions. 'The pragmatic import of the logic of individualized situations', says Dewey, 'is to transfer the attention of theory from pre-occupation with general conceptions to the problem of developing effective methods of inquiry', and applying them. It is a logic which does not preach solutions but explores the suggestions which emerge from the analyses of problems. Its categorical imperative is to inquire, to reason together, to seek in every crisis the creative devices and inventions that will not only make life fuller and richer but tragedy bearable. William James makes essentially the same point as Dewey in the language of ideals. Since in the struggles between ideals 'victory and defeat there must be, the victory to be philosophically prayed for is that of the more inclusive side—of the side which even in the hour of triumph will to some degree do *justice* to the ideals in which the vanquished interests lay. . . .' But prayer is not enough. He goes on: '*Invent some manner* of realizing your own ideals which will also satisfy the alien demands —that and that only is the path of peace.' To which we must add, provided there is a reciprocal will to peace in the matter. And even then, your own or the alien demands or both must be curtailed.

As you may have gathered by this time, I have been concerned to show that this pragmatic approach to the moral problem can not only be squared with the recognition of tragic conflicts, of troubles, minor and grave, which dog the life of man in a precarious world, but that it gets its chief justification from this recognition. Intelligence may be optimistic when it deals with the control of things but the moral life by its very nature forbids the levity and superficiality which has often been attributed to the pragmatic approach by its unimaginative critics.

Indeed, I make bold to claim that the pragmatic approach to tragedy is more serious, even more heroic, than any other approach because it doesn't resign itself to the bare fact of tragedy or take easy ways out at the price of truth. Where death does not result from the tragic situation, there are always consequences for continued living which it takes responsibly without yielding to despair. It does not conceive of tragedy as a pre-ordained doom, but as one in which the plot to some extent depends upon us, so that we become the creators of our own tragic history. We cannot then palm off altogether the tragic outcome upon the universe in the same way as we can with a natural disaster.

Contrast this attitude towards tragedy with the Hegelian fetishism of history which in the end is but the rationalization of cruelty. Contrast it with the Judaic-Christian conception which offers at the price of truth, the hope that the felicities of salvation will both explain and recompense human suffering. Contrast it with the attitude of Unamuno whose hunger for immortality is so intense that he sees in intelligence or reason the chief enemy of life, both in time and eternity. For him the joy and delight of life is the conflict of value and value no matter what the cost. 'The very essence if tragedy', he tells us, 'is the combat of life with reason.' And since the Inquisitor is concerned with the eternal life of his victim's soul, the potential victim must defend the Inquisitor's place in society and regard him as far superior to the merchant who merely ministers to his needs. 'There is much more humanity in the Inquisitor', he says. Crazed by this thirst for the infinite, Unamuno glorifies war as the best means of spreading love and knowledge. He illustrates the dialectic of total absurdity and caprice in thought which often prepares the way for atrocity in life. Here is no quest for the better, for the extension of reasonable controls in life and society, for peace in action.

To be sure, Unamuno is so horrified by the flux of things in which all things are ultimately liquefied that he expresses pity for the very 'star-strewn heavens' whose light will some day be quenched. But this cosmic sentimentality is disdainful of the vexatious, unheroic daily tasks of mediating differences, even of mitigating the consequences of irreconcilable conflicts, of devising ways to limit human suffering whose ubiquitous presence is the alleged cause of spiritual agony.

No two thinkers seem so far removed from each other as Miguel de Unamuno and Bertrand Russell—and as philosophers they are indeed related as a foothill to a Himalayan peak. But this makes all the more significant the similarity of their attitude towards the arts of social control which require the extension of man's power over nature. For Russell, any philosophy, and particularly one like Dewey's, which interprets ideas as implicit guides to activity and behavior, and knowledge as dependent upon experimental reconstructive activity in the situation which provokes it, exhibits 'the danger of what may be called cosmic impiety'. It is an arrogant power-philosophy whose insolence towards the universe is hardly less objectionable when it stresses social power than individual power.

It is fortunate that Russell's attitude—in which he is not always consistent—towards scientific power and control of our natural environment has not prevailed, otherwise the whole of modern civilization including modern medicine would never have developed. The charge of megalomania against any view of knowledge just because it is not a pure spectator view is absurd. For the pragmatic view accepts the Spinozistic dictum that nature can be changed only by nature's means. The problem is to discover or devise these means. This cannot be intelligently done without experimental activity. According to Russell's own position, power itself is neither good nor bad but only the uses and ends of power. But since he also tells us that there is no such thing as a rational or irrational end, that intelligence or reason is helpless in determining what we should do with our power, one can argue with much better warrant that it is *his* view, *if acted upon*, that increases 'the danger of vast social disaster' rather than the pragmatic view which believes that by changing nature and society, man can to some extent change themselves in the light of rationally determined ends. No humane person can read history without being moved more by man's failures to use the knowledge he has had to remove the evils and sufferings which were remedial than by his attempt to achieve too great a control or power over nature. It was not science which was responsible for the use of the atomic bomb. It was politics—a failure of politics to understand the true situation. The pitiful disparity at any particular time between what we know and what don't know is sufficient to inspire a sense of humility in the most intellectually ambitious. But it is only in the most vulgarized sense of the term 'pragmatism', a sense which Russell helped to popularize by flagrant misunderstandings, that the adequacy of a thoery of knowledge, whch regards activity or experiment as integral to the achievement of knowledge of fact, can be judged by its alleged social consequences.

I am more interested tonight in stating a position than establishing it. As I understand the pragmatic perspective on life, it is an attempt to make it possible for men to live in a world of inescapable tragedy—a tragedy which flows from the conflict of moral ideals,—without lamentation, defiance or make-believe. According to this perspective even in the best of human worlds there will be tragedy—tragedy perhaps without bloodshed, but certainly not without tears. It focuses its analysis on problems of normative social inquiry in order to reduce the costs of tragedy. Its view of man is therefore melioristic, not optimistic. Some philosophers belittle man by asking him to look at the immensities without: others belittle him by asking him to look at the perversities and selfishness within. Pragmatism denies nothing about the world or men which one truly finds in them but it sees in men something which is at once, to use the Sophoclean phrase, more wonderful and more terrible than anything else in the universe, viz. the power to make themselves and the world around them better or worse. In this way pragmatic meliorism avoids the romantic pessimism of Russell's free man, shaking his fist in defiance of a malignant universe, and the grandiose optimism of Niebuhr's redeemed man with his delusions of a cosmic purpose which he knows is there but knows in a way in which neither he nor anyone else can possibly understand.

To the meliorist the recognition of the gamut of tragic possibilities is what feeds his desire to find some method of negotiating conflicts of value by intelligence rather than war, or brute force. But this is not as simple as it sounds. There is no substitute for intelligence. But intelligence may not be enough. It may not be enough because of limitations of our knowledge, because of the limited reach of our powers of control. It may not be enough because of the recalcitrance of will—not merely the recalcitrance of will to act upon goods already known and not in dispute, but because of unwillingness to find out what the maximizing good in the situation is. And although we are seeking to settle conflicts of value by the use of intelligence rather than by force, is it not true that sometimes intelligence requires the use of force?

Let us take this last question first. Faced by a momentous conflict of values in which some value must give way if the situation is to be resolved, the rational approach is to find some encompassing value on the basis of some shared interest. This, as we have seen, involves willingness to negotiate—to negotiate honestly. The grim fact, however, is that there is sometimes no desire to reason, no wish to negotiate except as a holding action to accumulate strategic power, nothing but the reliance of one party or the other upon brute force even when other alternatives may exist. In such cases the moral onus rests clearly upon those who invoke force. Their victory no more establishes their claim to be right than a vandal's destruction of a scientist's instruments of inquiry has any bearing on the validity of his assertions, evidence for or against which, could have been gathered by the instrument destroyed. The intelligent use of force to *prevent* or crush the use of force where a healthy democratic process, equitable laws and traditions and customs of freedom make it possible to vent differences in a rational and orderly way, is therefore justifiable even if on prudential grounds one may forgo such action. This means that tolerance always has limits—it cannot tolerate what is itself actively intolerant.

There is a tendency in modern philosophical thought which, in rejecting too sweeping claims for the role of intelligence in human affairs, settles for too little even when it does not embrace a wholesale scepticism. Of course, a man may know what is right and not do it just as he may know what is true and not publicly assert it. In neither case is this a ground for maintaining that we cannot know what action is more justified than another or what assertion is more warranted than another. The *refusal* to follow a rational method, to give good reasons, is one thing: the claim that there are different rational methods, different *kinds* of good reasons each with its own built-in modes of validity, is something else again—and to me unintelligible. To be sure, the acceptance of rational method is not enough. Men must have some non-rational element in common. Hume is on unquestionably solid ground in asserting that reason must always *serve* a human need, interest or passion. But his mistake outweighed his insight when he contended that rational method could only be a servant or slave of what it served and that needs, interests and passions could not be changed or transformed by the use of intelligence. In our flights into space if we encounter other sentient creatures capable of communicating with us, it is more likely that their logical and mathematical judgment will be the same as ours than their ethical judgments, because we can more readily conceive creatures of different needs than of different minds.

At any rate the world we live in is one in which men do not share all their needs and interests and yet it is one in which they have sufficient needs and interests in common to make possible their further extension, and to give intelligence a purchase, so to speak, in its inquiry.

The most difficult of all situations is one in which even the common use of methods of inquiry seems to lead to conclusions which are incompatible with each other although each is objectively justified. There is always an open possibility of ultimate disagreement no matter how far and long we pursue rational inquiry. We can conceive it happening. In such situations we must resign ourselves to living with our differences. Otherwise we must fight or surrender. But it is simply a *nonsequitur* to maintain that because no guarantee can be given that there will not be ultimate disagreement, penultimate agreements cannot be validly reached and justified.

In any case we cannot in advance determine the limits of reason or intelligence in *human* affairs. So long as we don't know where it lies, it is sensible to press on, at the same time devising the means to curb the effects of the refusal to reason when it manifests itself. Above all, we must avoid oversimplifying the choice of evils and encouraging the hope that to be unreasonable will pay dividends.

We are moving into another period of history in which freedom once more is being readied for sacrifice on the altars of survival. The Munichmen of the spirit are at work again. The stakes are now for the entire world. Our task as philosophers is not to heed partisan and excited calls for action, but rather to think through the problems of freedom and survival afresh. In a famous pronouncement two years ago Bertrand Russell declared that if the Kremlin refused to accept reasonable proposals of disarmament, the West should disarm unilaterally 'even if it means the horrors of communist domination'. Although he no longer believes this, there are many others who do. I know that common sense is at a discount in philosophy, but in ethics it should not be lightly disregarded. A position like this obviously can have only one effect, viz. to encourage the intransigence of those who wish to destroy the free world without which there cannot be a free philosophy. You cannot negotiate successfully by proclaiming in advance that you will capitulate if the other side persists in being unreasonable. Our alternatives are not limited to surrender and extinction of freedom on the one hand and war and the danger of human extermination on the other. There are other alternatives to be explored—all tragic in their costs but not equally extreme. The very willingness, if necessary, to go down fighting in defence of freedom may be the greatest force for peace when facing an opponent who makes a fetish of historical survival. On pragmatic grounds, the willingness to act on a position like Kant's *fiat justitia, pereat mundus* may sometimes—I repeat—sometimes—be the best way of preserving a just and free world—just as the best way of saving one's life is sometimes to be prepared to lose it. The uneasy peace we currently enjoy as a result of 'the balance of terror' is tragic. But it may turn out that it it is less so than any feasible alternative today. If it endures long enough and it becomes clear to the enemies of freedom that they cannot themselves survive war, they may accept the moral equivalents of war in the making. The pragmatic programme is always to find moral equivalents for the expression of natural impulses which threaten the structure of our values.

I have perhaps overstressed the sense of the tragic in human life in an effort to compensate for the distortions to which pragmatism has been subject. There is more in life than the sense of the tragic. There is laughter and joy and the sustaining discipline of work. There are other dimensions of experience besides the moral. There is art and science and religion. There are other uses for intelligence besides the resolution of human difficulties. There is intellectual play and adventure. But until men become gods—which will never be—they will live with the sense of the tragic in their hearts as they go in quest for wisdom. Pragmatism, as I interpret it, is the theory and practice of enlarging human freedom in a precarious and tragic world by the arts of intelligent social control. It may be a lost cause. I do not know of a better one. And it may not be lost if we can summon the courage and intelligence to support our faith in freedom—and enjoy the blessings of a little luck.

8

THE NEED FOR A PHILOSOPHY
OF DEMOCRACY

JOHN WILD

As a philosopher still impressed by the *historical* importance of political theory, and as a human individual participating, to some extent, in the life of a so-called democratic nation, I have been disappointed and even depressed by recent literature devoted to democracy, and even more by the general attitudes which seem to prevail in public arguments and debates on this topic. In such arguments, the notion of democracy seems very generally to be taken for granted with little sense of the need for distinguishing between what is essential and what is incidental or derived. And in the literature on the subject, which is relatively slight in comparison with that on socialism and communism, less attention is paid to basic philosophical patterns of thought and feeling than to more evident, but perhaps more superficial, matters of formal procedure.

The terms *free country* and even *free world* are often used. But it is rare that one finds any serious discussion of the different interpretations to which this term (freedom) is open, of the relation of freedom to responsibility, and of individual to political, or social, freedom. These terms seem to have fallen into the obscurity of the obvious which covers many problems. In this paper I shall try first of all to raise some of these problems, which, in my opinion, are not pseudo-problems of pure theory but real difficulties and confusions which affect actual political policies. In the second place, I shall make a few suggestions as to how some of these difficulties might be corrected.

THE FORMALIST VIEW OF DEMOCRACY

In more general discussions of the subject, democracy is commonly identified primarily with formal procedures of a certain kind.[1]

[1] Cf. David Spitz, *Patterns of Anti-democratic Thought*, Macmillan, New York, 1965, and Mayo, H. B., *An Introduction to Democratic Theory*, New York, Oxford Press, 1960. I am not singling out these works for special criticism. Each of them contains valuable insights and some high-level philosophical argument. But in *this respect*, each is representative of a widespread present tendency with which I am in disagreement.

Three of these are of particular importance: regular elections, majority rule, as I shall call it, and the existence of opposition parties. I shall not argue that these procedures are not needed in large-scale democratic groups. My point will be that they are not essential, that exceptions may be found, and that they do not penetrate to the heart of what those who believe in democracy really mean.

Turning now to regular voting procedures, this is no doubt a need for large democratic groups of millions of individuals. But it is easy to think of large-scale nations, like Russia, where regular elections are held, which we would not call democratic. What is evidently missing here is an opposition party. The formality of voting is insufficient. It makes a difference what one is voting for and what one is voting against. But this is not the only difficulty. When we think of democracy, most of us think primarily of the nation-state and of the procedures by which the ruling officers of such vast corporate structures are chosen. But we know of the importance attached by De Tocqueville and other keen observers to the role played by smaller groups of different kinds from governmental departments and provinces, down to business corporations, special interest groups, and the family.

There is strong justification for holding that unless the normal individual can play an active democratic role in the processes of such small subordinate groups, the large-scale national democracy cannot be sustained. It is in these smaller groups that the individual may in some cases be on the winning and in others on the losing side, so that permanent frustration and embitterment may be avoided. It is here also that he may learn by direct confrontation to tolerate and to respect those holding attitudes different from his own—an essential aspect of democracy. But many of these smaller groups can carry on democratically with only rare, or even no elections, because a consensus can be achieved. So for this reason also, it would be a mistake to think of regular elections as essential to the democratic process. It is needed in gigantic organizations, but even here exceptions may be found. So it is secondary and derived.

Let us next turn to the principle of majority rule. There is to be no discrimination between equal individuals. Each vote is to count for one. This idea of equality is a fundamental value of democracy, as we shall see, and it is the first premise from which the principle of majority rule is derived. When the group is divided, the opinion of a majority, when freely expressed, shall prevail. When examined in abstraction, this certifies itself as a genuinely democratic principle of equality and justice. But the facts of actual practice point to certain qualifications which show that this principle is not fundamental but derived. Majority is a relative term. So we must ask what kind of a majority? A majority of whom? In principle, we are inclined to say a majority of those qualified or eligible to vote. But we all know that this does not agree with procedures generally recognized as democratic.

For presidential elections in the United States in recent years, a turnout of more than 70 per cent of the eligible voters is unusual. This means that a 'majority' of 36 per cent of those properly qualified can win. When we use the term here we are, therefore, referring to a majority of those not only qualified but with sufficient concern to take the trouble to vote. This factor of concern is even more evident in the procedures of smaller special interest groups, like associations for specific reforms, learned societies, etc. Here it is well known that the common affairs of the society are run by a small number of those with special qualifications and an exceptional interest in these affairs. As long as the more indifferent majority makes no vigorous protest, performs certain minimal functions like the paying of dues, and grows in number, few of us would want to say that it is being governed in a non-democratic manner. But it would be highly dubious to identify this procedure with majority rule, since the important decisions are made by the voting of a very small minority, with the general consent of the rest. This indicates the weakness in any attempt to identify democracy with the principle of majority rule.

This weakness becomes even more evident when we think of those instances, like the well-known case of Germany in 1933, when a majority, or plurality, of the citizens voted to establish the Hitler dictatorship. Surely it is a mistake to identify the essence of democracy with a procedure that can be used to destroy it. This principle of majority rule is not essential. It is secondary or derived.

When we come to the third procedural principle, the right to disagree within limits, and the existence of loyal opposition parties, we are getting closer to something essential, but we have not yet arrived. Opposition groups struggling for a different kind of dictatorship can exist in countries which no one either here nor there would view as democratic. Has China now become a democracy because of the opposition of Liu Shao-chi and his followers?

Here again we are dealing with a formal procedure and abstracting from all content. It makes a difference what the opposition party stands for, and what it is that is being opposed. What are the distinctive meanings and values of democracy? The essence lies here, not in formal principles.

If the presence of recognized opposition does not ensure democracy, we need to examine more carefully the widely held assumption that the absence of such opposition ensures non-democracy. In many of the developing countries of Africa, for example, we now find a condition of one-party rule with no recognized opposition parties. Hence it is believed that this is a great setback for democracy. But under the conditions now prevailing, is this necessarily true? With two or more tribal groups, each opposing the rest in free elections and parliamentary conflict, might it not happen that they would cancel out each other so that no decisions could be made? This might conform to certain traditional conceptions of minimum government. But would such a perpetual stalemate be what we now mean by democracy? All the formal procedures might be there. Only nothing would be done. Is it not possible that under one-party rule with a small group of leaders or only one, decisions might be made that would move the country by improved education and industry, for example, in a democratic direction accepted without serious protest by the more passive majority? This may be an imperfect condition. But is it anti- or even non-democratic? We cannot hope to give definite answers to such questions unless we get away from formal procedures, and approach more closely to the essential meaning of democracy. What is its basic aim? What is it moving towards? What is the underlying philosophy of democracy?

NEGATIVE FREEDOM AND GOVERNMENT

We come closer to an answer to these questions when we turn to the content of the American Bill of Rights and to the corresponding attitudes embodied in the British and the French traditions. These are concerned with the weak and fragile individual. First, they try to protect him in his weakness against the paralysing influences of uncontrolled group power, against arbitrary arrest, seizure, and torture. Then in an affirmative way they aim at fostering and promoting the free and responsible activities of thinking and choosing which he alone can perform, and which have an essential value for the democratic community. Thus he should have access to reliable information through freedom of publication, of the press, and other public media. It is only on this basis that he can develop sound and responsible beliefs. He should have the right to express these beliefs whatever they may be, and the right to meet in free assemblies where opposing views are defended and criticized.

In the *United Nations Declaration of Human Rights*, a document of major importance for democratic theory, these rights of the individual are further extended. He has a right to domicile in a country where he may be supported by the powers of a full community so that he may live his own life, and pursue his projects without arbitrary deprivation or restraint. He has a right, furthermore, to periods of rest and leisure, and to adequate medical care to protect him, in his weakness, against the constant dangers of physical breakdown and ill health. Finally, since he is born in abysmal ignorance, he has the right, not specifically recognized in the American constitution, to an education, so that he may learn to think and to choose responsibly without avoidable impediments.

From these democratic articles and declarations, we may infer that a primary concern for the peculiar powers and dignity of the fragile and ephemeral human individual belongs essentially to the meaning of democracy. Any violation of these so-called rights, wherever and however it occurs, is undemocratic. Here we are confronted not with a mere formal procedure, but with a principle having actual content, and ruling out certain ways of thought and action of specifiable kinds. Disrespect for the individual person is always undemocratic. This is not a derivative, or instrumental, principle, but one that is true essentially and without exception. This, I believe, is correct. But further questions need to be asked, two of which are especially important.

The first is concerned with individual freedom. Does this freedom have no limits? Does the free individual have a right to do or to think anything he pleases, so long as he does not interfere with the similar rights of others, as J. S. Mill maintained? If this is not true, and if democracy is committed to certain stable values and meanings, how can it be defended against the charge of dogmatism or fanaticism of some kind?

The second question concerns the nature of democratic rule. Does it mean merely the minimum of government, or does it possess distinctive features which mark it off from other forms of rule? The liberal tradition in nineteenth-century political theory, which is still dominant, has given answers to these questions which are oversimple, and which have dulled the image of democracy in the minds of many in the West.

This tradition, throughout its history, has defended a negative conception of freedom as *freedom from* restraint of any kind, including that of self-imposed responsibilities. When conceived in this way, freedom bears no affirmative connotations favouring one mode of thinking or acting over another. This conception has no doubt served an important function in criticizing fixed views of liberty put forth by dogmatists who knew exactly what the free man should do in any circumstances. But it has now led to a negativistic view of democracy as standing for no affirmative aims, but only for endless criticism and dissent. If a society is to maintain itself in time, however, its affairs must be ordered affirmatively in one direction rather than in another, with little interest in arriving at justifiable agreement on affirmative goals, the decisions of actual practice will be dominated by the drift of power. Thus, as the critics of modern democracy have cogently argued, this show of negative freedom is a convenient and self-righteous mask for the rule of force.

Liberal thought has consistently opposed the continental conceptions of a general will over and above the wills of the individual members of a group, and of a group soul or substance with a life and unity of its own in which the individual members participate. There is certainly some truth in this rejection of group mythology, which has enabled traditional liberalism to avoid many pitfalls of totalitarian political theory in the past. But it is also a one-sided view which has dangers of its own. Whether or not there is such a thing as a group substance, it is clear that every child is born into a society which is ordered and structured in certain ways. The child is necessarily assimilated into these structures which tend to drift, and in a certain sense live a life of their own. Otherwise, it is impossible to understand what a democratic Bill of Rights is protecting the individual against. The liberal conception of a democratic society as a set of atomic individuals free to set up a minimal government to pursue their private wishes without external compulsion is a self-destructive myth. This negative freedom is not enough. Affirmative action must be taken, or freedom will be submerged in the drift of social power.

Similar objections may be raised against the liberal answer to the second question concerning democratic action and government. When society is conceived as a mere association of atomic individuals, each entitled to the exercise of a purely negative freedom, it becomes impossible to distinguish sharply between democratic and non-democratic governments. Any common order, or rule, infringes on the individual's negative freedom. The democratic ideal is, therefore, identified with the maximum possible anarchy of the individual units, and the minimum possible government to sustain it without criminal violence and revolution. But this negative ideal of political action has turned out to be mistaken and irrelevant to the mass societies of our time. Social patterns and institutions are constantly drifting in unforeseen directions to produce unforeseen and often unjust consequences. Hence in politics, to do nothing is a form of positive action leading to positive and often evil results. The idea that these evils of drift may be quickly corrected by the legislative decrees of popular representatives has been shown to be fantasy. As critics once more have pointed out, it has contributed to that notorious self-righteousness which so often cloaks the drift of American social and political power.

To many thinkers who understand the force of these objections, it appears that the whole traditional ideal of democracy, which they identify with traditional liberalism, must be abandoned. We must give up the notion of a negative freedom for the individual, and must recognize the priority of objective social patterns, which Hegel called *objektiver Geist*, over individual opinion and desire (*subjektiver Geist*). This means that traditional individualism must be abandoned. These notions are taking us closer to Hegel and Marx than to anything that can properly be called *democracy*, which is indissolubly bound up with the independence of the free individual (*subjektiver Geist*) and his control over the powers of the group (*objektiver Geist*).

In my opinion these critical statements are oversimple and open to serious question. Democracy is bound up with the dignity and social power of individuals. But it is not necessarily committed to traditional individualism. I shall now try to show this by indicating democratic ways of answering these two critical questions concerning negative freedom and negative government without falling into the mistakes of traditional liberalism.

AFFIRMATIVE FREEDOM AND DEMOCRATIC ACTION

The liberal ideal that democracy means only endless criticism and dissent, and that it stands for nothing affirmative has weakened it basically and dimmed the image of it in many contemporary minds. As a result, it is now widely taken for granted as a mere procedure, indifferent to affirmative meanings or values of any kind. In this sense, it may appeal more to intellectuals, professionally engaged in the task of criticism than to living men who are constantly forced to make vital decisions for themselves and others. As a matter of fact, it has recently been ably defended precisely on the ground that it is entirely open, committed to nothing, and radically relativistic in its point of view, no one belief being really sounder than any other.[1] The individual and the group, are therefore, free at any time to doubt any view, to believe anything, and to try out any way of life they may arbitrarily prefer. Hence the dogmatism and fanaticism attaching to other political theories are avoided.

This relativistic position is open to several serious objections of which we shall consider only one. If this view is to guide our thought and practice, does it not commit us to a firm belief in the value of free inquiry, and an open way of life not constrained by arbitrary dogmatism? To this the defenders of relativism may reply that inquiry and openness are not specific values in the sense of something to be done. They are only instruments by which such values may be found. Therefore, they still remain free and uncommitted —seekers only and not finders. But is this isolated seeking not an artificial abstraction? Can we seek without any hope of finding? If it is serious and not a mere game, does this seeking not commit us to a belief in what we may find, and ultimately to action on the basis of this belief? Here we must drop the argument.

But perhaps we have carried it far enough to justify the following statements. The founders of democracy in the West, who acted in the British, French, and American revolutions, believed in free inquiry and the open life as values, superior to those achieved by the suppression of meaning, dictatorial authority, and arbitrary action. Furthermore, they did not hold this belief irresponsibly with no concern for the evidence available in human experience. Perhaps a stronger case can now be made for this belief. If so, there is an alternative to the negative conception we have been discussing.

Democracy cannot be reduced to a mélange of scepticism and relativism. It stands for certain values of which freedom of inquiry is certainly one. Responsible action in the light of what is revealed,

[1] Cf. T. L. Thorson, *The Logic of Democracy*, Holt, Rinehart & Winston, New York, 1962.

imperfect though it be, is another. In spite of the dangers and risks involved, such action is better than the drift of blind power. Since it is the fragile human individual alone who is able to engage in such inquiry, democracy requires respect for any individual, and a concern for protecting him against the constraints of arbitrary power. Hence the democratic bill of rights, which have far-ranging implications for social action with respect to education for all, social welfare, the elimination of discrimination, etc. This view is far from relativism. Let us now consider two objections.

According to the interpretation of democracy we are suggesting, freedom has both a negative aspect, freedom *from*, and an affirmative aspect, freedom *for*—what is seen to be required by the human situation, that is, obligations and responsibilities. It is easy for us to think of these aspects as being essentially incompatible and opposed. Hence two sets of questions can be raised, first by those, like Sartre, who identify freedom with negation, and second by those who identify it with the positive fulfilment of certain obligations. The former will say that by subjecting the free individual to various obligations imposed by facts, by nature, and by other extraneous factors, the democratic theorist is infringing on his negative freedom which transcends any fact, and any obligation supposedly required by nature or by other external factors.

To this we may reply that human freedom is not absolute but limited, and that we do not become free by ignoring these limits. Furthermore, a theory which expects of man that he transcend all facts, including those of his own existence, cannot be distinguished from nihilism, for nothingness also transcends the given facts. We may also point out that the responsible man understands these obligations and imposes them on himself. They are not simply imposed from the outside. They involve a factor of autonomy which is not the same as negation. Finally, it must be emphasized that there is no freely accepted responsibility which is not open to further questioning, revision, correction, and even abandonment by the free minds of men. So the negative element is still present, though the possibility of finding and creating meaningful answers is not ruled out *a priori*. But this brings us to an opposed type of question that will be raised by those who are partial to a rigorous affirmative freedom.

They will say that obligations which are still open are not binding. How can we really believe in principles that we are questioning as we lay them down? This reduces the whole enterprise of democracy, as we are explaining it, to a mere game that calls for no un-qualified commitment, and cannot, therefore, be taken seriously. Our answer to this must here take the form of a brief reference to the phenomenology of belief which must play an important role in the philosophy of democracy if this is ever fully formulated.

The opinions that we have *about* various matters are unstable and easily come and go. They may even be forgotten. Hence it is only an exceptional opinion that can survive a period of serious doubt, and here the objection holds good. But what we call belief, or conviction, is a different phenomenon. My belief *in* a friend or a principle is the permanent basis for my acts. I have assimilated it into my being by a long process of criticism and habituation which involves an element of doubt. In fact, it is fair to say that until I have seriously doubted a belief, it has not really become my own. So the notion that doubt is necessarily destructive of belief is simply false. Doubt may destroy ungrounded conviction. So the fanatic is afraid of being questioned. But it will not destroy a grounded belief which is aware of the uncertainties and the evidence against. Here we must remember that belief and life in the concrete world always involve elements of vagueness and risk.

Politics rests on beliefs of this kind. Hence it is perfectly possible to believe very firmly in the many values, obligations, and responsi-bilities of democracy in spite of a constant doubt that is always open to revision and correction. Such a believer certainly believes in constant negation and criticism. But he also believes firmly and affirmatively in the possibility of finding patterns of meaning which can survive such criticism, in the responsibility of all individuals to realize them, in so far as possible in the concrete, in the widening of this field of responsibility and autonomy, in the dignity of all individuals everywhere, and in the need for protecting them against the arbitrary restraints of group authority and power. This brings us to the second question concerning the traditional liberal theory of negative government. Is there a democratic alternative?

NEGATIVE GOVERNMENT AND DEMOCRACY

Liberal thought was right in attacking the conception of a group soul or substance, which has turned out to be a myth without empirical foundation. But strong doubt may be raised as to whether liberalism has really freed itself from this notion, which, as we shall see, still hovers in the background. There is no group substance.

This is correct. The liberal mind then infers that society is composed exclusively of individuals acting with different instruments in various ways for various ends. This is also correct as far as it goes. When society decides to act, it is always an individual who makes the decision in behalf of the group. When the state executes a criminal, there is always an individual executioner who presses the button.

But who, or what, is this individual?

The liberal mind is still apt to think of him as an isolated thing, or substance, enclosed within his body, and to think of society as a group, or collection, of such separated substances. This assumption is based on trends in our intellectual history that go back to ancient Greece. But it is basically one-sided, and when expressed without qualification, is mistaken. This is because it ignores certain relational patterns, like those of family life, in which the 'individual' is involved continuously from the beginning, and which are not collective in character. Thus the family is not a mere collection of individuals. It is a 'collection' acting in accordance with certain formal patterns which we indicate by such relational terms as husband and wife, brother and sister, parent and child. These patterns order and form the individual's life in certain stable and determinate ways.

Thus the family speaks a language, and from infancy on, the child is both taken over by the language of his parents and actively takes it over until he learns to speak it for himself. Now, this language that he learns is not a mere collection. The English language, for example, is not a collection of all the words spoken at different times and places by English-speaking individuals. It is an ordered collection with a unity and wholeness of its own. It has a history, a beginning and an end, and in a very real sense lives a life of its own, not *apart from* the successive generations of individuals speaking it, but *in them* and *through them*. This is true not only of language and the family but of hunting, fishing, industry, exchange, art, government, and every purposeful activity in which the individual is engaged.

It is the failure of the liberal mind to focus these patterns of social life that leads him, and most of us, to think of the social as something out there, over against us as individual substances, which can influence us from the outside and oppress us in various ways. Having made the mistake of regarding individuals as initially separated things or substances, and of society as a mere collection, he is then forced to regard social patterns, so far as he recognizes them too late, as other things outside of him with powers that can compel him to do things that he does not wish to do. This lies at the root of the negative theory of government and social control as an infringement of the rights of isolated individuals. On this liberal view, it is impossible to identify any distinctive features of democratic as against non-democratic forms of social control. Democracy has to be negatively conceived as the maximum absence of government or its minimum necessary degree.

But if there is no such *thing* as a group soul apart from the individual members, a mistake has been made. There are no social patterns or powers which exist apart from the individuals, and which help them or hinder them from the outside. Individuals exist only in and through these power-structures which, in turn, exist only in and through their individual carriers. The control, or lack of control, over such structures, which are always in change, is something to be exerted, or not exerted, by individuals over something not outside but *in* themselves. What is this something? It is an ordered set of habits, attitudes, and modes of understanding in each individual which enables him to perform his allotted tasks and to co-operate with the others. This *is* the club, the labour union, the industry, the army, the nation, or whatever the 'group' may be. When these individual habits and attitudes become confused, the group becomes confused; when they disintegrate, the group disintegrates; when they operate smoothly and coherently the social life is maintained, and radiates the tremendous power that results from organized co-operation. But now we must note two ways in which this social life may be maintained. This will shed some light, I believe, on the distinctive features of what we now mean by democratic government and action.

The first way is the way of drift, as we may call it, which is an ever-present factor in human life. Under this condition, the individual members interiorize the group patterns only to the degree that is required to carry on their separate functions, and no further. In learning to perform their functions well, they must also develop a certain flexibility which enables them to adapt to unexpected situations, but this is not carried very far. They have some understanding of the whole enterprise in which they are engaged, but this is usually dim and confused. They do not raise questions about the common purpose, and are not interested in mutual discussion and debate. They are satisfied with the *status quo*, and this attitude is encouraged by the decision-makers in positions of power.

These leaders, too, are loyal to the institution as it is, rather than to the members. They believe in *it* rather than in *them*. They do not rely exclusively on the force of habit to ensure conformity, but seek to enforce it by the laying down of rules, and by threats and punishments of various kinds. They discourage mutual discussion and the formation of small pressure groups. Aside from the interchange that is required for the efficient performance of their interlocking functions, they are interested in keeping the individuals separate and alone as the lonely members of an effective system.

Power structures of this kind have maintained themselves with great efficiency by drifting in this way for centuries under accidental autocratic control. Many of the gigantic power systems of our time are sustained by such drift. Nevertheless it is against power systems of this kind that the individual must be protected if he is to become responsible. This, I believe, is the reason for the Bill of Rights, inspired by a different ideal of democracy, which points towards another way and in another direction.

Those who are moved by this ideal see that unguided power corrupts. They see the dangers of blind power-structures, the conflict of power, the manipulation of power for its own sake, power politics, and the rule of power. They do not seek the elimination of power-structures, for this would mean the elimination of human life. Existence is power. But they seek for the responsible control of such power by individuals who alone are able to find meaning, and to give a meaningful response. Hence in their weakness they must be protected against the power systems which always surround them and must carry them into a senseless drift unless they are constantly watched and infused with meaning. This is the democratic ideal as it should be understood in the age of power.

But protection is not enough. Individuals are not innately free and responsible. If they are to become free, they must decide for this on their own. They may be helped, however, by the processes of formal and informal education to develop a flexibility which goes beyond the special functions they perform. They may be encouraged to internalize not only these but the whole public world that surrounds them on their fringes—to raise questions where it is obscure and confused, and to criticize its injustices and distortions. They should be encouraged to think for themselves and to form their own beliefs. As adults, they must be given the opportunity to meet together in small and large groups for the discussion of opposed views of common interest, in the hope that patterns of meaning may emerge which may survive criticism and elicit agreement. When this happens, common action may be taken, first of all in the form of protest, which is an essential factor in the ethos of democracy too often unduly subordinated or neglected.

Modern democracy, as a dynamic self-amending process, has always recognized the right to criticize and to form loyal opposition parties which can vote against the government. But in the mass societies of the present time, these voting procedures may ignore vital issues, and may simply conceal blind drifts of power. In recent years, therefore, minority groups in 'democratic' countries, facing the distortions and corruptions resulting from such drifts, have had to devise new techniques of protest, in order to call attention to their grievances and to have them seriously discussed. This democratic development has not been sufficiently studied. But we may note here how strikes, boycotts, sit-ins, and public demonstrations, only fifty years ago in the United States regarded as illegal infractions of the law, have now been recognized as an authentic expression of democratic freedom, and, therefore, as legal. This is indeed right, since democracy rests on the resolution of differences in the light of free and open discussion by the electorate. But people cannot be expected to consider those blind tendencies and their unforeseen effects of which they are unaware. When these inequalities and distortions are clearly focused through the agency of protest they may be widely and seriously discussed and debated. Out of this open debate and criticism, acceptable ways of controlling the drift may be devised. Then democratic action may occur.

But this will be quite different from what the liberal tradition has envisaged. It will not take the form of legislating social patterns into existence *de novo*. This is only a dream. It will always take the form of correcting and controlling social institutions that are already in existence. Such action will never be undertaken by isolated individuals interested only in living their private lives. This is the condition of the lonely crowd, or the lonely technicians, who are precisely in the state of drift.

When the believer in democracy speaks of the individual and his dignity, as he must, he will be referring not to a separated substance, originally complete in itself, nor to a set of such substances. He will be referring rather to many individuals, all individuals, ultimately the whole of mankind, in so far as they are capable *with each other* of controlling the drift of nature and habit into which they have been thrown. They need not be, and probably never will be, a majority in the strict sense of this term, for the majority is usually lethargic and indifferent. But this private lethargy will prevent them from interfering not only with the miseries and abuses which arise from drift, but also with the justices that correct them. So the task is not completely hopeless, for in history we find examples of concerned minorities who have changed the destinies of small groups as well as of larger ones while the majorities have gone along. But such responsible action requires leadership of a special kind.

Traditional liberal theory has failed to focus the distinctive traits of democratic leadership, and has even questioned the notion of a democratic élite as inconsistent with the whole ideal. This is certainly a mistake. If anything like democracy is ever to be worked out, it demands an élite, but an élite of a peculiar kind. Such leaders must care not so much for the technical majority which is content to drift as for the major minorities who really care for the common interest. They will be loyal not so much to the institution as it is, as to its real possibilities in the direction of greater freedom, responsibility, and opportunity for all.

They will pay attention to the concept of mankind, and will recognize it as a democratic ideal based on the worth and dignity of the individual wherever he may be. For when we think of mankind, we do not think of power complexes, nor allied states, nor leagues of nations. These are not mankind. When we use this term we are thinking rather of all individuals everywhere, including the various power patterns by which they live, but using them and controlling them for the sake of a meaningful human existence on this earth. This type of leader will be more interested in positive purposes than in laying down rules and punishments. He will try to stir up free discussion and criticism even when this is directed against policies he supports. He will encourage the formation of special interest groups both small and large, and will listen to their demands.

He will oppose the disintegration that leads individuals into the drift of the lonely masses, and will help them to communicate and to unite. When the drift of power-structures ends in conflict, as it ultimately must, he will try for negotiation, since the unleashing of blind power is the end of responsibility and, if it persists, of the democratic enterprise. He will seek to avoid this at any cost. So when overarching meanings cannot be found, he will seek for a balance of power which at least checks it and holds it in leash. But as a democratic leader he must seek for something more, not subservience to power but control over it for the interests of mankind. This is the aim of democratic action.

THE TRADITIONAL VIEW AS CORRECTED

If negative freedom is only a moment in such action, and if it is essentially concerned with the fostering of certain existential values like freedom and equality of opportunity for all individuals, we can understand the proper, but subordinate, place which is to be assigned to voting procedures in democratic theory. In large-scale groups, like the nation-state, regular elections for the choice of rulers and the broad outlines of policy by those who are concerned is always advisable. But they are not essential to democracy. For example, in those small-scale groups which play a necessary role in the democratic process and where a consensus can be achieved, they are not required. The principle that each vote should count for one is valid as an ideal, for it is based on the capacity of the individual to interiorize the whole public world and its patterns, if he cares to do so, and to arrive at sound and informed beliefs on basic issues. But procedures are still democratic if such decisions are made by a majority of those who are really concerned, and are accepted by a largely indifferent majority. The protection of minorities and their right to organize opposition parties is sound and democratic so far as it goes, for it is based on the dignity of the individual person and his capacity for responsible thought and action. But under modern conditions, it must be extended to include the right of minority groups to protest against deprivations and injustices to which both the government and loyal opposition are indifferent.

Without these qualifications, the voting procedures of so-called democratic states may be high-sounding disguises for a power drift of selfish interests, as the Marxists have pointed out. And even with these qualifications, such drift is a constant danger, which has been accentuated by individualistic interpretations of democratic theory. On these views, both individual freedom and social action are negatively conceived. The former is identified with the absence of all constraint, including that of self-imposed obligations to authentic values, even those of freedom and democracy. The individual is, therefore, negatively free to do anything, even nothing, if he likes. Social action is also regarded negatively as a necessary evil which is to be checked and reduced to a minimum. But since power is an inescapable fact of life, this must lead to an inadvertent drift produced *in* the individuals not by outside forces but by their very indifference. This drift, I believe, is contrary to the basic aim of democracy—the deliberate control of group power, not subservience to it. This traditional, liberal view is not only internally inconsistent, but inconsistent with the facts.

In this paper I have tried to suggest, in outline, an alternative philosophy of democracy which might free it from these inconsistencies. It cannot be properly understood negatively as a form of scepticism and relativism concerning value. It is a definite point of view basically concerned with the dignity of every human individual, and with certain values which he alone can achieve, including those of free inquiry, the finding of grounded meanings, and, in the light of these, responsible action to control the drift of power. The checking and balancing of power are often necessary, but they are half-way measures which cannot be equated with control. This cannot be achieved by the voting procedures of isolated and indifferent individuals. It can be achieved only by the constant action of concerned individuals who accept a joint responsibility for what is being done.

As over against the drift of power under autocratic rule, this mode of democratic action has at least four distinctive features. First, it arises from the free discussion and choice of a majority of those who are actually concerned. Second, each individual accepts a real share of responsibility for the decisions of rulers he has helped to select, and keeps a constant watch over what is being done. Third, these rulers remain in touch with the currents of public desire and belief as they emerge from larger and smaller groups in the community—both leading them and being led. Finally, they are responsible not to any fixed power-structure, but to the people and their ideals of equality and freedom in the control of power.

According to democratic philosophy, this mode of democratic action is not only an instrument by means of which other intrinsic values, like peace and social welfare, are to be attained. It has an intrinsic value of its own which takes precedence over other interests, and is to be preserved at any cost. Under any conditions and at all times it is good for individuals to care for their common destiny, and to control the blind drift of power by free and responsible action.

9

THE DEVELOPMENT
OF MY PHILOSOPHY

CHARLES HARTSHORNE

In my intellectual development, four principal periods may be distinguished. In the first (age 15–22, or 1912–19), the only philosophers in anything like the strict sense whom I can recall as having influenced me directly were the Quaker mystic and teacher, Rufus Jones (I had one course with him at Haverford College, where I studied for two years), Josiah Royce (solely as author of *The Problem of Christianity*), William James (*The Varieties of Religious Experience*), and Augustine (*Confessions*). Otherwise the chief stimuli during this period were Emerson's *Essays*, Matthew Arnold's *Literature and Dogma*, Coleridge's *Aids to Reflection*, H. G. Wells's novels *Mr Britling Sees It Through* and *The Bishop*, and Amiel's *Journal*. I also read an encyclopedia article on Berkeley's philosophy—which seemed to me rather silly, though some years later I enjoyed challenging people to refute it. Two years working as an orderly in an army base hospital in France gave considerable time for reflection. In spite of the limited philosophical fare, I reached (about 1918) some metaphysical convictions which I still see as sound—in part for the reasons which I then had in mind. The convictions reduce in a way to two.

The *first* is that experience (any possible experience) has an essentially social structure, meaning by this that what is directly given as *not oneself*—or not simply one's own sensations, feelings, or thoughts—is feeling which belongs to other selves, or more precisely, other sentient creatures. Besides one's own feelings and sensations (and I thought then and think now that these are essentially akin), experience literally contains feelings belonging to other individuals. In short, I arrived on phenomenological grounds (not then so characterized) at the denial of the alleged truism: X cannot feel Y's feelings. On the contrary—I have held for nearly fifty years now—X *always* feels feelings not X's own, but those of other creatures. Of course, secondarily these feelings thereby become X's, but not in the same simple sense as they were previously Y's. In the language I learned many years later from Whitehead, experience is always 'feeling *of* feeling', where the first and the second feeling are distinct and involve at least two feeling subjects. The first feeling is X's 'subjective form' of feeling or 'prehension', the second is X's 'objective form' but Y's subjective form. Thus experience is essentially and literally and always in some degree sympathetic, a *participation* by one subject in the experience of other subjects. The concrete data of an experience are simply other experiences. These are not necessarily human experiences (except in immediate personal memory) or anything closely similar to the human. During my entire career I have rejected the assumption that psychical terms can refer only to animals. Rather, I found long ago that inorganic nature as experienced consists of non-human and non-animal feelings. That most people are not conscious of this has never seemed to me decisive. There is apparently almost no limit to the lack of consciousness which can be involved even in human experience. Here I agree in one way or another with Leibniz, Peirce, Whitehead, Wordsworth, Freud, the English psychologists Spearman and Aveling, etc. Moreover, the carelessly formulated, never really tested, psychological theory of 'association' is ideally fitted to safeguard this unconsciousness. In my first book (1934), *The Philosophy and Psychology of Sensation*, I tried to argue on both *a priori* and empirical grounds for the essential identity of sensation and feeling, and for the social or participatory character of both. (But by that time I was in the third of the four periods above referred to.)

The other main conviction was that the social character of experience has a monistic aspect, in that the many selves, sentient creatures, or 'wills' as I recall terming them, are somehow included in one supreme Will or purposive being. This belief, too, had a partly phenomenological basis. We experience a sympathetic overlapping of selves or experiencing subjects, in such a way that any attempt to derive all motivation from reference to long-run personal advantage, 'self-interest', is contradictory of the essential structure of experience. But if self-interest is not *the* motive, what is? To say that there is no one motive to which all others can be referred for their evaluation is to give up the quest for a rational theory. (In *this* respect the self-interest advocates are in the right.) Mere altruism is not the answer; for it commits us either to an indefinite multiplicity of interests, or else to an abstraction like the greatest happiness of the greatest number, a happiness which no one enjoys. The only satisfaction to further which can furnish a rational or all-inclusive aim is the satisfaction of an inclusive self, whose joy fully includes ours and that of all those about whom we could possibly care. In identifying with our fellows we do not lose our own self-identity, since we are all essentially expressions and constituents of the One All-inclusive Life. In this reasoning I was no doubt unconsciously influenced by Emerson and Royce; I was also treading, in my own way, a path taken ages before in India, China, Egypt, Greece, and Palestine. But it did not occur to me that the view implied, as it does for so many Hindus, that the plurality of selves is anything like an illusion. The many selves I took to be genuinely distinguishable from each other and from the inclusive self. Nor did it occur to me to suppose, with Royce, that what I will is also willed by the inclusive Being. My volition is *in* God, but not by God, it is in him not as his volition but as mine. I have *never* accepted the ultra-simple notion of 'omnipotence' as sheer determination of events by a single agent.

For a time I did incline to accept James's idea of a deity finite in power. Only much later did it become clear to me that there is no point in supposing that divine power falls short of some ideal of completeness. Rather, one must see that a monopoly of decision-making is not an ideal at all, and that the ability to manipulate puppets, or to make others' decisions for them, is nothing very glorious, compared to the ability to inspire in others a creativity whereby their decisions transcend anything otherwise determined. To think this out was a matter of decades. I am glad, however, that my clergyman father never preached the conventional doctrine of omnipotence and always took for granted that many things happen not because God has decided that they shall, but because creatures decide as they do. In this my father was influenced by a liberal theological professor at the seminary where he studied. My gratitude to that professor! There was also, in my earliest form of natural theology, no inclination to identify God with an unmoved mover or with anything complete once for all, incapable of any sort of increase. I do not recall ever accepting this view, except for a short time while in Hocking's metaphysics class, before he made clear to me the reasons for rejecting it.

The *second* period was four years of study (half of them as an undergraduate) at Harvard, followed by two years of postdoctoral study abroad, mostly in Germany. My thesis on 'The Unity of Being in the Divine or Absolute Good', not a page of which has ever been published, was written during the fourth year at Harvard.

It embodied a more qualified monism than the title might suggest, by no means identical with views like those of Bradley, Sankara, or Royce, since I not only, with Royce, asserted the reality of relations but unlike him accepted truly external as well as internal ones. To be sure, I agreed with the monists that every relation is internal to *something*, but I also held that it must not be internal to everything. I believed in genuine contingency or chance, and had been convinced by William James that God is not the only agent making decisions which can be attributed neither to any other agent nor to any complex of antecedent causal conditions. I thought then and think now that the deterministic theory of freedom is unacceptable, and this both for some of the reasons James gives and for still others. (I must by now have read fifty essays trying to reconcile determinism and freedom. They all miss the real problems.) Freedom is more than voluntariness; it is creation—and while aspects of a voluntary act, which is free in the sense of being unconstrained and consciously satisfactory to the agent, may be causally determined, the entire concrete experience must always have some aspects of creative self-determination, of causally optional 'decision', whereby the antecedent determinateness of the world is increased. Reality is in the making in the sense that causes are *less determinate* than effects, therefore less rich in value. This is the very point of causal production, without which, as James shrewdly saw, it has no point. Perhaps Bergson also helped me to see this. I had certainly at one time been a convinced determinist.

In writing the thesis, I was, so far as I know, uninfluenced by Peirce, and only slightly influenced by Whitehead, of whom I knew only what a hasty skimming of *The Concept of Nature* and an enthusiastic report by Northrop of his studies with Whitehead in London could teach me. I immediately accepted the view that the most concrete form of reality is the event. This seemed not to conflict with any conviction I had previously entertained. However, without the clarifications later introduced by Whitehead this was for me only a somewhat vague suggestion.

The two years abroad produced no very explicit new convictions, in spite of exposure to Husserl and other famous philosophers. Neither Husserl's method nor his results seemed to me convincing. He was largely blind to the social structure of experience, as were the philosophers he took most seriously, e.g. Descartes, the English empiricists, Kant, Leibniz, and Brentano. Besides, Husserl had a naïve Cartesian confidence concerning the possibility of being absolutely clear and certain about phenomenological reports, whereas I thought that obstacles to such clarity and certainty are to some extent insuperable, and that, so far as they can be over-come, the way to do it is not through 'bracketing the world' (which seems to amount to denying the intrinsically social character of experience) but in quite other ways—above all by trying out various logically possible formulations of what experience may be thought to be, looking to direct experience for illustrations. And one needs to be aware that the interest in direct experience is aesthetic rather than ethical, practical, or scientific. Husserl wanted to set aside speculations until pure and certain reports upon the given had been attained. I believed that there can be no wholly non-speculative descriptions of the given, somewhat as there is no such thing as mere assembling of facts prior to the formation of hypotheses in natural science. We start with beliefs. We cannot start with assump-tionless description. This is the Baconian fallacy in phenomenology. All philosophizing is risky: cognitive security is for God, not for us. And Husserl was by no means without assumptions; for one thing, assumptions concerning the aesthetic aspect of experience, since he took for granted the usual view that value qualities are tertiary, mere reactions to the secondary sense qualities. I have denied this for nearly fifty years. I deny it now. Nothing is more primitive or pervasive in experience than intuitive valuation or feeling. Sensa-tion is but a sharply localized aspect of this. Later I found this view in Whitehead, Bosanquet, Croce, and others.

The *third* period began abruptly in September, 1925, when I became a humble member of the Harvard philosophy staff, and was asked at one and the same time to begin editing the writings of C. S. Peirce and to assist Whitehead in grading papers. Thus I was simultaneously exposed to intensive influence from two great minds, one (Peirce) of whom had been hitherto almost unknown to me and the other only slightly better known. Both philosophers immediately appealed to me more than any third, except perhaps Plato, had previously done. Where Husserl, Heidegger, Kroner, Ebbinghaus, Rickert, Hartmann, Natorp, and before that my Harvard teachers, taken singly, had seemed to offer somewhat thin philosophical fare, Peirce and Whitehead were to my understanding thinkers who combined great technical competence with a rich, subtle sense of reality in its manifold aspects, and extraordinary power of intellectual invention. They were obviously aware of the social structure of experience and reality and also of its monistic aspect; and they seemed less naïve than Husserl about the method of philosophy. They had a matchless sense of the range of human concerns. They were humorous as well as deeply serious; and Whitehead at least (unlike some of the professors I met abroad) was almost miraculously free from vanity. On the other hand, Peirce of the two was more adequately aware of the nature of science on its empirical side. For example, Peirce was a pioneer in affirming the importance of behaviourism in psychology. (Here Whitehead was amazingly aloof from science in its working procedures.) Yet Peirce was as convinced as Whitehead that the reality of the world is in feelings, not in mere matter. I cannot but regard the simultaneous exposure to two such philosopher-scientists as a wonderful stroke of luck. That it came after I had had opportunity to face the problems of philosophy for nearly ten years, and had had the benefit of more than a dozen skilful teachers of the subject, was probably all the better.

An additional piece of good fortune was that after a year or so of my solitary struggling with the Peirce papers, Paul Weiss volunteered to help. Thus a job too big for one man became manageable. I shudder to think of having had to do it single-handed. Weiss was just the person the situation called for.

During the three years as instructor and research fellow at Harvard, and for some years thereafter, I considered myself as both a 'Peircean' and a 'Whiteheadian', in each case with reservations. It would be only a guess if I were to say now which influence was the stronger. My partial acceptance of Peirce I can see to have been in some respects uncritical, particularly with respect to his Synechism. As to Whitehead, I never could assimilate his notion of 'eternal objects', and for a good many years I rejected entirely his doctrine that contemporary events are mutually independent. On the last point I have come to change my mind, but to make up for this have become more aware of difficulties in other parts of his system. It does not seem so very important that one encounters some philosophers in the flesh and others not. If Peirce has perhaps influenced me less than Whitehead, it is chiefly because his writings are on the whole less congenial to the philosophical attitude I already had when I encountered the work of the two thinkers. And after all, I learned Whitehead's philosophy chiefly from his books, as I did previously that of Emerson, James, and Royce—three men without whom I cannot imagine my intellectual development.

A good part of the effect of Peirce and Whitehead was to encourage beliefs already adopted, such as the self-creative character of experience, implicative of real chance; the ultimate dispensability of non-physical categories (the emptiness of the notion of mere matter); the two-aspect view of God (which I got from Hocking if from anyone) as both eternal and yet in process (hinted at by Peirce, asserted by Whitehead—or as both absolute and relative, infinite and finite; the necessity for admitting internal as well as external relations between events; the immediate givenness ('prehension') of concrete realities other than one's own experiencings (I had been confirmed in this by reading Lossky); the priority of the aesthetic aspect of experience (perhaps due to Wordsworth more than to any philosopher, but confirmed by Rickert and Heidegger and later by Croce and others, including some psychologists).

While doing the Peirce I began to write the book on sensation. This led me in time to intensive study of psychological monographs and journals. This exploration of an empirical science was enjoyable. With the publication of the book, however, I largely dropped this line of study, and to this day have not been able to make much further advance in it. I came to understand why psychologists in general found this book little to their liking. On the other hand, like some psychologists, I believe it embodies insights which must sooner or later be incorporated into science as well as philosophy. With the sensation book (a development of one theme of my thesis), as well as the Peirce editing, out of the way I began to work out my version of metaphysics and natural theology, the central theme of the thesis. But now I had to try to incorporate what I had learned from Peirce and Whitehead, also what I was learning at the University of Chicago by association with pragmatists and positivists, including many scientific friends with positivistic leanings. (For twenty-seven years I listened to papers by members of the 'X Club', an association of scientists, and came to know some of the members rather well.)

Since I was teaching about Peirce and Whitehead, as well as attempting to present my own views, my thinking and writing fluctuated between exposition and, to some extent, defence of the views of these men and the effort to build my own system independently. Probably my contemporaries found themselves a bit puzzled as to how to classify me. Was I essentially a disciple of Whitehead, secondarily of Peirce? Or was I essentially what Husserl suggested I would be, an 'independent philosopher'? In my thesis and in Germany I did not think of myself as a disciple of anyone, nor so far as I know did anyone else. True, I was perhaps closer to Hocking, among my teachers, than to the others, but Lewis, Perry, and Sheffer had had strong influence, and so had the writings of Russell, Moore, Bergson, Bradley (in good part by way of disagreement), and even Spinoza. But from 1928 to, say, 1945, it was plausible to think of me as Peirce's and even more as Whitehead's disciple. (Some even imagined I had been enrolled as a pupil in Whitehead's classes.) If, however, I have often defended Whitehead, and also Peirce—especially before Whitehead's *Adventures of Ideas* had rounded out that writer's great speculative period—and have indulged in one-sided or exaggerated praise of their philosophies it was partly because of the conviction that anyone taking the systems of these famous and eloquent writers seriously would at least be in the general neighbourhood of basic metaphysical truth, which would not equally hold, in my judgment, of those taking Moore, Hume, Hegel, Russell, Ayer, Bradley, Wittgenstein, Austin, Ryle, Dewey, Lewis, and Carnap seriously.

It seemed obvious that truths so ultimate that they hold of all possible realities can have no necessary connection with any one human being, whether Whitehead, say, or myself. Without claiming to have been free from egoistic cravings, I can perhaps claim to have had a genuine and persistent ambition to enrich human consciousness, an ambition strong enough to make me at least partially indifferent to the question of who is credited with discovering certain conceptual means for appropriating the truth. Once in Germany (1949) a professor complimented me upon a speech concerning Whitehead's philosophy and added something like the following: 'The modesty with which you avoided stressing your own views as distinct from Whitehead's made your talk all the more appealing.' I wish to add to this some remarks overheard from students:

A. 'What is Hartshorne teaching this quarter?'
B. 'Whatever it is, it will be Whitehead.'
C. 'Whatever it is, it will be Hartshorne.'
D. 'The trouble with Hartshorne is, he's so damned original.'

Of my former students, one, John Cobb, is an important young theologian whose book, *A Christian Natural Theology Based upon the Philosophy of Whitehead*, is perhaps the best critical outline of Whitehead's system we have. Another, Schubert Ogden, is an important young theologian whose philosophical base is my philosophy. He is one of a number who will see to it that my ideas will not be forgotten—no matter what happens to me personally. I am not greatly excited by the difference between these two, but proud of them both. For either way the 'Neoclassical' tradition, the natural theology of creative becoming and divine relativity, will persist.

The change to what I term my *fourth period*, one of greater independence, or greater stress upon my own intellectual devices and spiritual convictions, was gradual. The sharpest shift probably occurred in 1958 while I was in Japan. Here by request I taught my own views, not Peirce's or Whitehead's. And here I began to think out with a new thoroughness the conviction expressed in my thesis (a conviction scarcely hinted at by Peirce, and not even hinted at by Whitehead or my Harvard teachers), that Anselm's ontological argument is one of the most truly essential discoveries ever made in metaphysics, even though a discovery which, like so many others, was partly misinterpreted by the man who made it, as well as by most of his critics. This line of inquiry is carried almost as far as I am likely to carry it in *Anselm's Discovery*, together with Chapter Two of *The Logic of Perfection*.

It has seemed more and more clear to me that both Peirce and Whitehead tend to blur the important distinction between metaphysics, or *a priori* ontology, and empirical cosmology, the latter subject but not the former making essential appeal to empirical evidences. The distinction can be found in both men, but inadequately emphasized and clarified. The clue to a more adequate way of dividing the *a priori* and empirical elements in philosophy is provided by Popper's great theme of observational falsification as the decisive feature of empirical knowledge. Not 'Could it be verified?' but 'Could it conceivably be falsified?' (by observation) is the primary question to ask if one wants to classify statements as belonging to science or merely to philosophy. I *define* metaphysics, or *a priori* ontology, as the search for truths which, though 'about reality', could not conflict with any conceivable observation.

The dogma that if no experience would count against a statement it 'says nothing about reality' is, to me, just antimetaphysics posing as self-evident. I think, on the contrary, that there are statements true of reality which no observation could conceivable falsify. For example, 'Deity (defined as the property of being unsurpassable by another) exists' conflicts with no conceivable observation, yet implies this, for instance, about reality: that it is completely known to the being who could not conceivably be surpassed by another. That this statement cannot conflict with any conceivable observation is deducible from 'unsurpassable by another', as I have shown in various writings. I also take the statement, 'Every event includes properties not deducible from its causal conditions and the valid laws applicable to these, but yet every event has some features thus deducible,' to be true of reality as such, while again conflicting with no conceivable observation.

Of course, a statement which no observation could count against says nothing *contingent* about reality. It does not discriminate one possible world state from another. This does not prevent it from being true of any and every such state, hence also (trivially if you like) of the actual state. Thus if the divine existence is necessary, as I hold, then no possible experience could negate it. It is therefore trivially true that it fits our actual experiences, and it is true of the actual world that it is divinely known. 'Trivially' here means, 'as anyone who fully understood the terms of the problem would see to be self-evident'.

It is a strange logical lapse to infer 'describes no possible experience' from 'conflicts with no possible experience'. What could not be false under any circumstances is either nonsense or it is true under any and every circumstance. The notion that the 'non-existence of deity', or existence either of an 'absolute causal order' or of a 'causeless chaos', must describe a conceivable circumstance or 'state of affairs' is just the assumption that neither theism nor the idea of creative or indeterministic causality is metaphysically valid. If we ask how this invalidity is known, I think we must answer, 'In no way.' Rather, we have sheer assumption. The 'non-existence of deity' is, of course, a possible verbal formula, as is 'the existence of pure chaos' or 'an absolutely deterministic causal order'; but every attempt to provide consistent and unmistakable significance for the formulae will, I think, fail. We can conceive a world resting upon and known to divine power, but only in a fashion applicable to *any* conceivably observed world as well as to ours. No observational criterion for separating divinely ordered and known worlds from those not so ordered and known is conceivable. If you doubt this, tell me the criterion. The very idea of God itself implies the impossibility of such a distinction. 'Dependent upon God', like 'creative yet casually conditioned', is a metaphysical expression, definitive of possible experience in general, neutral between alternative forms of experience.

Theism, Creationist Causalism, are true of reality, but not empirically true. They are descriptions of reality which are neutral to alternatives other than verbal. Of what use are they, some will ask, since the alternative in such a case is only verbal absurdity or vacuity? Answer, of no use to anyone whose understanding is superhumanly penetrating enough to grasp immediately and surely the absence of a real alternative, but quite useful to confused human beings (that is, all of us) easily able to confuse sense and nonsense. Metaphysical truths are truistic—if one is sufficiently clear-headed enough to see them as such. But who is? Wisdom's disjunction concerning metaphysics, 'paradox or platitude', would be applicable perhaps to an angelic intelligence. But for ours there is a third possibility, termed by an Indian philosopher (J. N. Chubb) 'luminous tautology', evident when and so far as we grasp the meanings of terms which express features too profound to be humanly apprehended without difficulty. Of course God exists for you, if you understand 'God'. But why should that understanding be altogether easy, or exempt from danger of confusion or subtly hidden contradiction? Perhaps 'God' cannot be understood, having only a noncognitive or essentially confused import, a vague association of pictures incapable of being definitely true or false. But if this positivistic tenet is rejected then theism becomes obligatory. For 'deity can be conceived not to exist' is demonstrably confused or self-contradictory.

Apart from my stress on the *a priori* status of metaphysics and upon the ontological argument, I have various differences from Peirce and Whitehead. Some of these are rather additions than rejections. I make great use of the idea of asymmetrical relativity, and of asymmetry as a logical concept, in a way that seems to have no precedent in the history of philosophy. Here Peirce (especially in his account of secondness) was partly mistaken, and Whitehead, though correct, failed to make the point explicit. I believe that all philosophers have in this respect neglected a powerful key to metaphysical truth. But I have yet to publish an account of this line of reasoning.

Whitehead's 'eternal objects' in my opinion fail to do justice to the force of nominalistic arguments. Here I find Peirce's view of the continuum of possible qualities, and of continuity as a merely potential rather than actual 'multitude' (or set), a superior line of thought. This doctrine was one aspect of what Peirce called Synechism. In this aspect, Synechism coincided with a view of qualities which I had worked out partly in my thesis and partly during the two years preceding my work on Peirce. This is one example of the pre-established harmony by which, from 1925 on, I found myself related to Peirce and Whitehead.

The other aspect of Synechism puts Whitehead in definite opposition to Peirce. Here I have long followed Whitehead, and at this point particularly I am indeed his 'disciple', for without his influence I might never have felt the force of the reasons favouring his quantum principle of unit instances of becoming which are neither instantaneous nor do they involve real internal succession, in spite of his dubious talk of 'earlier' and 'later phases'. Where Peirce thought present experience was 'infinitesimal' in time length, Bergson and Dewey are vague or ambiguous on the issue, but Whitehead opts for a definite succession of unit events, never more than finite in number in a finite time. There is, in short, no continuity of becoming. (This has nothing to do with the Humian notion of a mere succession of events without intrinsic connectedness or partial identity. Confusing these two vastly different ideas is a common error in the criticism of Whitehead.) A continuum has no definite finite number of segments, but a stretch of actual becoming always has such a number, according to Whitehead. The mathematical continuity of time, as of space, refers to time as order of possible, not of actual, happenings. Peirce confuses the two orders: exactly the mistake he ought not to have made, since he himself holds that continuity is the order of possibilities. To make it also the order of actualities is to abolish any clear distinction between actuality and possibility. Moreover, this denial of objective modal distinctions is a clear case of what Peirce attacked as 'nominalism'. The penalty was that whereas he ought to have anticipated quantum mechanics in principle, Peirce in effect rejected it in advance. Yet to furnish a guide to the development of physics was one of his declared objectives.

Another point that is obscure in Peirce, and also in my thought prior to studying Whitehead, is the temporal structure of perception. Is the directly experienced always—or even ever—simultaneous with the experiencing? In short-run memory—here Peirce and Whitehead agree, and I think I might in any case have held—previous experiences are directly given (in spite of the 'mistakes of memory', really of memory judgments). But only Whitehead states clearly that the given is no less temporally prior in perception than in memory. It was, I think, a flash of genius in Whitehead to generalize the element of immediate givenness—'prehension', a word used by Leibniz, incidentally—so that the given is always temporally antecedent to the prehending experience. This solves at one stroke a host of metaphysical problems. Perception and memory on this assumption have the same relation to time, both giving us the past, immediate or remote, but whereas memory gives us our own personal past, perception gives us the impersonal past, the past of other individuals, including those individuals constituting our own bodies. In both cases, by a natural and pragmatically harmless illusion, we may seem to ourselves to be experiencing the very present. In the case of memory the illusion is called introspection—really very short-run retrospection. Some other philosophers have avoided this form of the illusion but nearly all have fallen into it in interpreting perception. I know of no philosopher before Whitehead in East or West who viewed with complete clarity all immediate experience of the concrete as experience of past happenings. I do not believe I could have seen this clearly without help from him. And, unless it is seen, the asymmetry of awareness, its one-way dependence upon its objects, cannot be clearly grasped. The concept of prehension as the basic form of dependence, the link between successive moments of process which Hume could not find, is a contribution second to none in modern metaphysics. It presupposes the concept of actual becoming as discontinuous; for without this concept the issue tends to remain incurably obscure, as Peirce's example nicely shows. The temporal structure of his Secondness or Reaction, and indeed its logical structure—is it symmetrical interdependence or one-way dependence?—is never made clear, with all Peirce's wrestling with the subject. It could not be clear, for in sheer continuity there are no definite units, whether objects or subjects, to act or to interact.

Both Peirce and Whitehead have affirmative things to say about God. The one hesitantly and inconsistently, the other more definitely and coherently, posits a divine Becoming rather than mere Being—an idea which duplicated a conviction I had acquired from Hocking's metaphysics class about 1921. But even Whitehead seems partly inconsistent on the issue (in speaking of God as *an* actual entity rather than a personally ordered society of entities, also in sometimes speaking as though God were simply 'non-temporal', and in still other ways), so that it is in my opinion impossible to accept his exposition of this theme as it stands.

I agree precisely with Chubb's contention that the idea of God, fully developed, is the entire content of non-empirical knowledge (including arithmetic and formal logic). Neither Peirce nor White-head say this with any explicitness; there is nothing in metaphysics (or *a priori* knowledge) not also in natural theology. They are essentially the same. A non-theistic metaphysics—as Comte held—is a confused and arbitrarily truncated natural theology. If I have concentrated upon natural theology more, probably, than any other recent writer, it is partly because I learned long ago from Plato, Spinoza, and Royce, that this subject coincides with metaphysics, and partly because I was shocked at the carelessness with which, as it seemed to me, the subject of 'God' was being treated by my philosophical, and to some extent theological, contemporaries. It has seemed clear that unless I took pains to work out certain things in this connection no one else was likely to do so in the near future. It was for the same reason that I wrote the book on sensation. No one else was doing much (by my standards) with either topic. Many good minds were grappling with philosophy of science, formal logic, ethics, perception, even aesthetics, but the two neglected mysteries, sensation as such and deity, seemed to demand an attention far beyond what anyone with adequate training was giving them. In both cases there was a vacuum into which my interest almost automatically moved. That as a result I might gain a wider circle of readers than philosophers alone, and, for instance, become an influence in contemporary theology and religion, was not, I think, particularly foreseen and did not furnish the main motive. Nor did mere religious feeling or piety. What I thought I saw was an intellectual mess needing clarification.

It is a question of some moment how far a philosopher, even one rather young, can be induced by another to change his opinions. Hocking did convince me in a very brief discussion, but once for all, that my perhaps only momentary toying with the idea of an immobile deity, devoid of an open future, was a mistake. Whitehead did convince me that the becoming of experience and of reality generally is in quanta, in unit cases which correspond to finite stretches of time, not to instants. He did convince me, when I was no longer very young and he was no longer alive, that contemporary events are mutually independent, and that perception gives only antecedent happenings. Peirce did convince me, backed up by Dewey and Mead, if I needed any convincing, that nameable quali-ties such as colours are not eternal but emergent. Moore did con-vince me, again if I needed convincing, that it cannot be correct to say that an experience can be its own object, that the data of mental states can be those very states. (Here Russell is wrong, Berkeley at best ambiguous, and Moore right.) Hocking or James convinced me that determinism, which I had for a time strongly affirmed, was an error. Later confirmation came from Peirce, Whitehead, and Popper. Influences I cannot trace led me to give up the belief I held for a time in my twenties in personal immortality (apart from Whitehead's 'Objective Immortality, of all events).

Many influences convinced me that 'proving' the rightness of a philosophical position was much more difficult than I still hoped, even in my early teaching days, and that having a right to be confident of one's views was much more problematic. At the least one must be able to state the counter-arguments in as close to their strongest form as possible. The basic giveaway in philosophy, apart from the ignoring of opposed positions, is the straw-man argument systematically resorted to. I know a philosopher, a former fellow student of mine, who told me not many years ago that in his courses the students read only the textbooks of which he is the author. How then, I asked him, do they learn about other views than yours? 'Oh,' he replied, with every assurance, 'the other views are all in my books.' This is not (I trust I can say) how my students are treated. And I have tried to argue with able opponents, not just with sympathizers or callow, obsequious, or cowed students. To this extent, at least, any confidence of rightness I feel has some justification. Although I have written over sixty reviews, no one, whether author or another reader, has accused me of misrepresenting the views expressed in the book which I have reviewed. There is a reason for this. After writing the review I have taken pains to go over the criticisms (and usually I did disagree at some points with the author), looking up once more the passages to which my review took exception to see whether they really did express the views I found objectionable. Usually they did, but now and then they did not, so that I had to delete or alter the criticism. I wonder if this rule is generally followed. If not, that alone is enough to account for many of the misrepresentations which disfigure the journals. My own books have sometimes suffered from this insufficient care to avoid the straw-man procedure in the one place where, if anywhere, it is inexcusable, in reviews. One's memory of passages one has an inclination to dislike is particularly apt to be creative in an unwittingly malicious fashion. Only careful rechecking can be relied upon in such cases.

The disciples of Wittgenstein have taught me at least something. I have lately been coming to see that my criticisms of 'classical theism' and 'classical pantheism' (technical terms which I have tried to define with care) are really in substantial degree linguistic, and amount to accusing the partisans of these doctrines of employing words taken from ordinary meaning (or significantly related to words that are so taken) to express esoteric meanings whose relation to the ordinary meanings has never, and really never, been carefully set forth. I refer to 'absolute', 'relative', 'infinite', 'finite', 'ultimate', 'transcendent', 'immanent', 'perfect', 'real', 'omnipotent', 'omniscient', 'necessary being'. These terms, I hold, have been systematically misused almost throughout the history of metaphysics, Occidental and Oriental. I deny that this is inherent in the metaphysical use of words as I define that use. One can be careful; but for whatever reasons metaphysicians have usually not been.

If I have any regrets about the development sketched above they are two. First, I might have taken more seriously than I did James Haughton Woods's wise injunction: 'Study logic; it is the coming thing in philosophy.' I took it somewhat seriously and learned a good deal from Lewis and Sheffer, but I might well have gone further, and have kept up the habit of thinking in mathematical ways better than I have. Second, I would have done well to make my writings more readable than I sometimes have. Style is important in philosophy. The extraordinary influence of some recent English writers not only in England but in the United States and many other countries is owing in no small measure to their readability. Clumsy sentences are resented, sometimes unconsciously, and neat or witty sentences are enjoyed and promote a good opinion of the thought as well as of the writing.

Apart from these two points I am tolerably well pleased with the way my career has gone. Unfortunately, there seems no way in philosophy to escape altogether from the dilemma: either remain in a state of uncertainty about the basic correctness of your position, or else protect yourself from exposure to hostile views. I do not find in the usual varieties of 'linguistic analysis' much to arouse doubt concerning my essential tenets or methods, but I am less easy when confronted with the contentions of 'finitistic' logicians concerning the vacuity of the notion of infinity, apart from the merely potential infinity of 'for ever more and more'. On the one hand, with G. E. Moore, I do not see that we can dispense with an actual infinity of past events, but on the other hand I feel the force of neo-Kantian objections to such an infinity. My guess at present is that this is merely a particularly clear-cut form of the basic mystery of meta-physics, as the exploration of luminous tautologies, truths that would be self-evident if we could grasp them with sufficient clear-ness, but which cannot humanly be grasped quite in this fashion. Will mathematicians ever come to agree concerning infinity? Perhaps no more than philosophers can agree concerning God. And if we cannot agree, can any of us have the right to be sure? There is one way in which, on 'neo-classical grounds', one can soften the dilemma, 'numerically finite or numerically infinite' with respect to past events. The entire value of reality is exhausted in the qualita-tive richness by which harmony of feeling in God is intensified. Granted an infinity of past events, all but the most recent events are already synthesized in the divine receptivity. They thus form a single though infinitely complex feeling. If reality is finite in space, as I take it to be, then only a finite number of items needs to be synthesized in any given case. Thus in a sense no 'infinite synthesis' is in question. Does this solve the problem? Perhaps.

I feel moved to express immense gratitude, first to my philoso-phical teachers at Harvard, 1919–23, who presented a wonderfully sharp and invigorating challenge by the intensity and diversity of their intellectual and spiritual values: J. H. Woods (the scholar in Indian philosophy), Demos, Eaton, Perry, Hocking, Lewis, Sheffer, Bell (who left philosophy for gentleman farming in Nova Scotia, but whose insight into modern philosophy was remarkable), Lévy-Bruhl, De Wulfe; also the psychologists Troland (that superb prematurely deceased scientist), Langfeld, and McDougal. Second, my gratitude goes to the group of scholars and thinkers who taught me as a post-doctoral student at the University of Freiburg 1923–5: Husserl, Becker, Heidegger (I heard him also in Marburg), Kroner, and Jonas Cohn. Third, to Peirce and Whitehead, two men who sought truth incomparably more than success or popularity, and who in inborn genius have perhaps never been surpassed. From Tillich and Karl Popper I have also learned, and to Berdyaev and Paul Weiss I owe at least the encouragement of their sturdy inde-pendence and vividness in the exploration of metaphysical issues. These, with Rufus Jones, after my intelligent and intellectually honest preacher-father, are the persons who have chiefly taught me (if anything has) to think philosophically, or to react creatively to the history of ideas.

Once when in Paris I told Lévy-Bruhl that my interest was in metaphysics he replied, 'I believe, with David Hume, that our line is too short to sound such depths. However [he graciously added] it is an honour to try.' Have I succeeded in sounding the metaphysical depths? I only know that I have tried, and have usually, though not perhaps always, felt that it was a privilege to do so.

10

A PHILOSOPHICAL OUTLOOK

DANIEL DAY WILLIAMS

Philosophical concerns are an integral part of my work in Christian theology. The Christian faith has always been articulated in relation to philosophical outlooks. The process begins in the New Testament with the Greek and gnostic background of the Logos doctrine, the theme of incarnation, and the stoic elements in Paul's ethical outlook. To be a philosophical theologian is to carry on the task of seeking that understanding which arises from faith and which is coherent with the data of human experience and the rational intelligibility which philosophy seeks.

The service of theology and philosophy to each other must arise from the common search for a truth which lies beyond any particular achievement of either mode of inquiry. Philosophy which is merely the handmaiden of theology is philosophy exploited and divorced from its proper function. Theology which is only philosophical thought in the guise of traditional language is theology divorced from its responsibility to the community of faith. The problem of the proper relationship of the two disciplines has concerned me for many years. I have concluded that there is no single methodological answer. We must tackle our problems of faith and truth in the cultural and philosophic situation in which we find ourselves. Theology may work in various ways in relation to philosophic inquiry and in relation to a particular philosophical outlook. In my own case I have found a new possibility for theology in the philosophy of Alfred North Whitehead and the general point of view of process philosophy and it is with this point of view that I am concerned here.

Critical issues have always arisen for theology and religion on the question of the nature of God and our knowledge of God. The modern questions are those raised by the critical analysis of empirical knowledge beginning with David Hume, and pressed in our time through an analysis of the possible range of language about 'God'. There are also the issues concerning the relevance of any meaning of God to the values and decisions which press upon us in the twentieth century. This latter point was put forcefully by

Professor Alisdair Macintyre in his Bampton lectures in Columbia University in 1966. He argued that whereas questions about God were relevant to the world-view of the eighteenth century and the nineteenth with the new sciences of Newton and of Darwin, in our time the problems posed by the scientific aspect of nature do not involve issues which are resolvable by appeal to God. The pressing issues of our time concern the achievement of viable human modes of living together, and to these issues traditional meanings of God are not relevant.

Theology in my view must meet the philosophical issues which are thus posed for any belief in God. This is not primarily for apologetic reasons. It is for the sake of the self-understanding within faith itself. Believers in God are also contemporary men who live in the same world which scientists, social strategists, and logicians inhabit. We are all responsible for engaging with human problems. I reject the view that theology can be satisfied with a private and parochial truth which bears on no concern for the common life.

Two theses about God will be defended here.

First, the critique by positivism of assertions about God is directed against the traditional conceptions of God. As a criticism of traditional doctrine it has validity. What is required is the reconception of the metaphysical aspect of traditional theology and the development of a concept of God in which his transcendence and immanence, his being and becoming, his power and his participation in the world's life are held together. Theology which holds the traditional conception of God's being is not able to interpret the world's life as a continuing evolutionary activity, and the life of man as a realm of limited freedom and originality within which man has power to shape his environment and his existence.

Second, God conceived as metaphysically creative activity, as becoming, does enter into the processes of human society, and his being lends its structure and value to the forms of human relatedness. The task is to show how the actuality of God does qualify and give both judgment and hope to the quest for social justice.

It is astonishing in the discussion about God among the philosophical critics of traditional theology how little attention has been paid to the conception of God in process philosophy even though that conception has had such major contributions as those of C. Lloyd Morgan, Henri Bergson, S. Alexander, Alfred North Whitehead, Henry Nelson Wieman, and Charles Hartshorne. So far as I can tell, practically the entire discussion about religious language has gone on as if the only conception of God which can be offered is that of traditional Christian theism especially in the form it takes in Anglican orthodoxy. Paul Tillich's theology is suggestive on the side of metaphysical doctrine; but on every crucial question such as God's relation to time, his impassibility, and his relation to the ontological categories Tillich sides with the tradition.[1]

It is my purpose here to state the theistic philosophic outlook which I find developed in process thought, especially that of Alfred North Whitehead and Charles Hartshorne, and to explore one way upon which this point of view may be fruitfully developed as a philosophy directly relevant to the task of living together and achieving a tolerable environment for significant human living.

What Whitehead has made possible in his metaphysics is the statement of an authentically social doctrine of reality. It is perhaps the first truly social doctrine of being ever stated. I perfer the term social to organic in speaking of metaphysical structure, for organism suggests a monistic view which Whitehead explicitly disavows though there is a type of organic relatedness of all actualities to each other in his doctrine. Whitehead proposes his metaphysics as a way of unifying an intelligible world view based on the data of modern science, and as a critical instrument for appraising traditional ethical and religious systems, including the Christian doctrine of God. His critique of Christian theology is profoundly important and I have elsewhere analysed it at length.[2]

I shall here state my own philosophical convictions about this view of reality and the theory of metaphysical knowledge which it involves.

The statement of a metaphysical outlook involves a twofold requirement. There is the establishment of the basis on which metaphysical assertions can be made and justified. That is the epistemological and methodological problem. Second, there is the elaboration of the metaphysical doctrine. It is a cardinal tenet of my position that these two tasks are inseparable. Our understanding of the way we know cannot be separated from our view of what we know, and what we know involves judgments about what things, and minds, and statements are. These are metaphysical judgments,

---

[1] I have elaborated this critique in 'Tillich's Doctrine of God,' *The Philosophical Forum*, Vol. xviii, 1960–1.

[2] Daniel D. Williams, 'Deity, Monarchy, and Metaphysics; Whitehead's Critique of the Theological Tradition', in Ivor Leclerc, ed. *The Relevance of Whitehead*, New York, Macmillan, 1961.

or at least they have metaphysical aspects. Bertrand Russell certainly cannot be accused of any strong bias toward metaphysics, but he says in *An Inquiry into Meaning and Truth*:

'. . . Complete metaphysical agnosticism is not compatible with the maintenance of linguistic propositions. Some modern philosophers hold that we know much about language, but nothing about anything else. This view forgets that language is an empirical phenomenon like another, and that a man who is metaphysically agnostic must deny that he knows when he uses a word. For my part, I believe that, partly by means of the study of syntax, we can arrive at considerable knowledge concerning the structure of the world.'[1]

Since one thing must be said before another, I will state first the conception of knowledge which I hold and then outline the main points in a social doctrine of reality.

The epistemological doctrine might be called an organic empiricism. It has affinities with the idealist's rendering of experience, and with American pragmatism. We know through the grasping of our environment by the psychophysical organism which displays for mental reflection its patterns, qualities, and interactions. The experience from which we derive knowledge is not in the first instance the sense-data. They are important but superficial elements in the organic process. The experience is the concretely felt bodily being-in-the-world and grasping the aliveness, the becoming, the give and take with a real world in the total complex functioning of the animal body and its conceptual apparatus. The flow of experience is the stream of qualities coming into our bodily perceiving. We 'cut up' the world through the functioning of our perceptive apparatus. We screen out much of it. Our bodies take in more than our consciousness ever grasps. But we really perceive the world of things which have their life, their qualities, their impingement upon our receptive organism.

There are two modes of perception; presentational immediacy and causal efficacy, as Whitehead calls them. The first is the end-product of the total bodily functioning as it produces the sharp specific qualities on the sense-data. The second is the deep organic bodily process of 'non-sensuous intuition' through which we feel our being in the world in interaction with other real things. Hume

[1] Bertrand Russell, *An Inquiry Into Meaning and Truth*, New York, W. W. Norton, 1940, pp. 437-8.

attends only to presentational immediacy and can find no relations there, but Whitehead denies that the flow of atomic sensations is the only mode of experience. There is an organic flow of feeling from the past into the present. Each new occasion of experience grasps the immediate past as now efficacious in its conditioning of the new occasion of experience. Hence causality is directly experienced when we attend to the ground stream of becoming.

Each occasion of experience involves the grasp of the structure of possibility in the form of aim at a new pattern of completed satisfaction. Hence into our knowing there enters always some laying hold of the realm of possible structures as qualifying present experience, and luring us towards a future where possibilities become realized. Hence our knowledge of the world has its 'conceptual pole', our feeling of the realm of structures which may or may not come to be exemplified in spatio-temporal realities. By calling this 'conceptual' we do not say that we always consciously attend to it. The body-mind organism may grasp the structure of the future more clearly than does the conscious mind in particular moments. Psychological clinics give abundant evidence here.

Our knowledge of the world is a knowledge of the structures exemplified in the actual world as we take it in through its structures for definition, analysis, and logical development. The fundamental process of knowing is the bringing of abstract structures to concrete experience for verification. There are degrees of precision, of course, and there are kinds of questions we can ask which concern the possibility of conceiving the most general characteristics of the world. Here we come to the possibility of metaphysical knowledge; but one further point about the epistemological doctrine must be made.

All knowing is evaluation. There is no knowledge without selection, affirmation, and negation of specific possibilities in our relations to the world. Our bodies select and our minds select. We give attention or we refuse it. We judge importance and triviality.

Every formulation of an hypothesis involves judgments of relevance and precision which have an aspect of evaluation. Some human adjustment to an on-going process is involved in all knowing. This is what the pragmatists have clearly taught us. All the implications of this view cannot be developed here, but it is worth while pointing to its significance for ethics, since the question of ethical judgments is raised anew by contemporary analytic philosophy.

The problem of value judgments viewed from this perspective is not a special problem involved in some types of judgments. It is involved in all judgments whatsoever. To be is to value, and to judge is to value some mode of thought and form of expression over others. To be sure all value judgments are not ethical. They may be aesthetic, organic, or purely utilitarian. Ethical judgments arise where a value judgment involves the principles of valuation which a responsible person accepts as relevant to his use of his freedom, and in which his relationships to the significance of other persons and their needs is involved.

METAPHYSICAL KNOWLEDGE

Of course we know something; but do we have knowledge of 'reality', the kind of knowledge which philosophy has sought in metaphysical inquiry? There are types of metaphysics which it seems to me cannot be brought within the scope of the kind of knowledge I have been pointing to. What we can know is the generic traits of existence. The position I take is that metaphysical inquiry depends upon the relating of conceptual structure to experience just as does scientific inquiry, but what marks off metaphysical inquiry is that it must treat all experience as evidence. This generality of aim gives metaphysical inquiry its special character and constitutes its central problems. My position concerning metaphysical method is as follows.

The question of what constitutes evidence for any assertion has received intense discussion in contemporary philosophy. Empirical theories of verifiability hold that evidence consists of specific observations of the behaviour of things as that behaviour is predicted in hypotheses. General theories contain elements not directly confirmable in this way; but they are indirectly confirmed in so far as they are logically related to hypotheses which involve specific predictions. Evidence derived from observations can justify the claim to knowledge, at least to probable knowledge, in so far as experience yields specific confirmations or disconfirmations. While there is a necessary caution in holding that what has taken place in a certain way will do so in the future, science proceeds with a pragmatic expectation that prediction is possible.

Metaphysical statements have a different character from scientific statements because they refer to structures which are found in everything, or they may refer to the 'whole'. The object of metaphysical inquiry has been differently understood in philosophy.

Broadly speaking the three possibilities are to define metaphysics as the search for 'being itself', or for the 'whole', or for the most general structures which characterize everything that is. The question of what constitutes evidence cannot be satisfactorily answered apart from a clear position on the object of the metaphysical inquiry. For the purpose of the present discussion we can acknowledge that these three views of metaphysical inquiry have this in common, they seek evidence which will justify assertions about what is real which go beyond the description of any particular area of experience. Metaphysics seeks the characterization of everything that is. This holds whether the reality is conceived as 'being-itself' beyond existence, or the 'whole', or the generic traits of all processes. In each case the question of the logic of validity involves the question of how a limited experience can justify statements about what characterizes every experience. How can we go from some experience to 'every possible experience'?

It is understandable that metaphysicians and their critics sometimes take the position that metaphysical doctrines appeal to intuitions which cannot be justified by anything beyond themselves. They must be accepted on faith or as visions which satisfy, guide, and enrich life, but which are not subject to confirmation or disconfirmation as scientific statements.

Against this view I argue that there is evidence which may count for or against every metaphysical assertion because every statement about what is 'real' or about the traits of all experience is a statement about some part of reality. All experience is potentially evidential with regard to metaphysical statements. We say 'potentially' because for something to function as evidence it must be related to an hypothesis and to some prescribed mode of investigation, so that the statement to be confirmed is logically related to the resolution of the inquiry which is going on. The metaphysician does not simply stare at the world, or turn his gaze inward. He inquires in relation to a set of concepts and their logical and existential implications. What he is seeking is a structure of interrelated categories which in principle can be verifiable in every experience, and in every type of datum yielded by human investigation. He seeks the structures which are involved in the description of everything that is, and in the way things go together to make up one world.

It may seem trivial to stress that for the metaphysician everything gives evidence of the structures which characterize everything; but the real point now becomes clear that the difficulty in metaphysics does not lie in the absence of evidence but rather in the wealth of evidence. Concepts such as those of space, time, cause, freedom, value, possibility, structure, process, matter, mind appear in every metaphysical doctrine in some form. The problem is to clarify their meaning and their relationships and therefore to gain some knowledge about the way the world is. We experience a common world or at least a world which has some traits in common. Whitehead says, 'Metaphysics is nothing but the description of the generalities which apply to all the details of practice'.[1] Metaphysical systems vary greatly because there is so much evidence and it is subject to alternative types of analysis.

Are there, then, criteria for the validity of metaphysical doctrines? Whitehead states three: consistency, which is defined in logical terms; applicability, that is, the metaphysical scheme must be exemplified in some area of experience; and adequacy, that is, it must express and illuminate what is found in its extension to every possible area of experience. Whitehead recognizes, of course, that completeness in any of these aspects is a limit to guide inquiry and is never attained. He pleads for the widest possible understanding of the range of experience:

'Nothing can be omitted, experience drunk, and experience sober, experience sleeping and experience waking . . . experience anticipatory and experience retrospective . . . experience normal and experience abnormal.

And he then comments:

'The main sources of evidence respecting this width of human experience are language, social institutions, and action, including thereby the fusion of the three which is language interpreting action and social institutions.'[2]

Every doctrine of the nature of being is in some sense a synthesis of concepts which taken together are asserted to characterize what is really there presented to us in experience. Traditionally metaphysical systems have not only sought this synthesis but have made

---

[1] Alfred North Whitehead, *Process and Reality*, New York, Macmillan, 1936 p. 19.
[2] Alfred North Whitehead, *Adventures of Ideas*, New York, Macmillan, 1933, pp. 290–1.

extravagant claims for their completeness and finality. Sometimes they have appealed to a special kind of experience for the ultimate knowledge which unites the whole, as in mystical neo-Platonism. Sometimes they have held that the rational structure which embraces the whole of reality can be philosophically exhibited as in Hegel's unguarded claims. Often religious apologetics have been constructed to show that the religious conception of the divine being provides an adequate unifying principle for metaphysics.

Against any claim for metaphysical omniscience a cautious assessment of the nature of metaphysical knowledge is in order. Rather than treat metaphysical systems as having a special privilege in access to knowledge of reality, they should be recognized as explorations of an infinitely complex reality, and the attempt to reach an adequate system of categories for interpreting it. All systems are abstractions. While religious experience and valuations have their rightful place in the inquiry, they cannot claim some privileged access to final truth apart from the general justification which they sustain in the inquiry as a whole. Evidence is present in abundance which confirms or disconfirms metaphysical statements, but there is always a limit on the process of verification, and therefore on the claim we should make for the adequacy of the conclusions.

Such a metaphysical method does not rule out reference to religious experience. There is no *a priori* reason why religious experience should not count towards our ultimate judgment about what things are. But the method does not permit the use of metaphysical argument to reach conclusions congenial to a particular religious outlook regardless of what the range of evidence in human experience will sustain.

There are always commitments and valuations in the perspective of every inquirer. These elements do not arise from the evidence alone apart from personal response, and cultural conditioning. There is no metaphysical inquiry without some implicit valuations which arise in the faith or the personal commitment of the inquirer. But the evidence which justifies a conclusion must be what is gathered from as faithful a discrimination of the whole range of experience as possible. And if it be said that the evidence for a metaphysical outlook cannot be conclusive since differences of interpretation are possible, it needs to be pointed out that in that respect scientific theories are in no different situation.

From this point of view the metaphysical inquiry after God is no longer a search for a cause outside the world, but for that reality which is involved in the structure and becoming of everything that is, and which is necessary to give coherence, relatedness, and an ultimate valuation to each occasion of experience. Either God is immanent in the metaphysical situation as its supreme and necessary participant, or rational experiential knowledge of him is impossible. I agree entirely with contemporary humanists and atheists that the problem of knowledge of God requires us to ask what difference God as an actual entity makes in the flow of events and our understanding of their structure. Traditional metaphysics has generally looked for God as an external 'cause' of the world and has therefore been baffled about how to apply the term cause to this relationship, and has required God as responsible for everything that happens. Hume's critique stands clearly justified.

In process metaphysics we require God not as external cause but as the immanent structure-giving actuality, participating in all becoming, and moving from actuality to new possibilities with the life of the world.

There has developed among Whiteheadians an issue concerning the relation of the ontological argument to the kind of metaphysical description which we can give of that supreme actual entity which is God in his primordial nature as the structure of all possibility and in his consequent nature as the supreme experiencer of the objective outcome of every actual occasion. Charles Hartshorne has taken the position that the only argument for God is the ontological argument.[1] While he once found the traditional arguments in various forms in Whitehead, he now rejects all forms of empiricism in the knowledge of God. The ontological idea is the statement of what is required for a rational understanding of anything; for the standards of perfection must be accessible to reason, and the absolute standard of perfection implies its own existence. To be sure the perfection of God is that of a continually creative and 'self-surpassing' perfection. Hartshorne holds to the doctrine of God's continual becoming as process theologians hold it. But he believes that all reliance on experiential knowledge for affirmation of God's existence is futile.

The ontological argument stands as the permanent challenge of conceptual rationality to a metaphysical system. I am one of those

[1] Charles Hartshorne, *The Logic of Perfection*, LaSalle, Open Court, 1962; *Anselm's Discovery*, LaSalle, Ill., Open Court; and *A Natural Theology for our Time*, LaSalle, Open Court, 1967.

who hold that affirmations of existence require some kind of experience of what exists. I cannot see what use the ontological argument is to our understanding of God and the world apart from our experience of that 'most perfect being' which enters into every thought. Is the idea of God equatable with an experience of God? William Ernest Hocking put it this way in *The Meaning of God in Human Experience*. But if this be so then the ontological argument does not move simply from concept to actuality but from a concept which involves experience to a description of what is experienced.

The service of reason to metaphysical understanding involves the clarification of what is involved in understanding God as that being whose actuality is necessary to the existence of every other actuality. But I keep my reliance for the reality of our knowledge of God on the conviction that in every experience we are, however dimly, aware of the sustaining, value-producing, goal-ordering reality at work in all things. I am not sure I am saying something different from Charles Hartshorne here. He continually refers to experience in giving concrete content to the idea of perfection. I am concerned only that preoccupation with the ontological argument does not deprive empirical theism of its claim that God is experienced. What Hartshorne has done is to show that the logic of perfection can apply to God in a way which undercuts the traditional monarchial absolutism in the doctrine of God, and this is an achievement of epic proportions in the history of man's vision of deity.

Process metaphysics proposes to elaborate an authentic doctrine of the *social* character of reality. The elaboration of the structure of sociality is one of the pressing requirements for metaphysics and theology relevant to contemporary man's experience. Here surely the issue about the significance of God for human relationships must be met. In the concluding part of this article I outline the point of view which I am trying to elaborate, and indicate some main lines along which further work in process philosophy may go on.

THE LOGIC OF SOCIALITY

One way of exhibiting the meaning of a position is to identify the kinds of problems to which it leads. For process philosophy the metaphysical task is the elaboration of the social doctrine of the world and of God. We have had an implicit monarchianism in the metaphysical tradition in which all meaning is finally determined by one omnipotent source whether that be God, or the scientific method, or reason, or sense data. It has been opposed by a nominalism in which nothing is necessarily related to anything else, and relations are merely names for accidental arrangements of items in experience. These two poles offered as exclusive alternatives have dominated and I believe corrupted much of the philosophical discussion of being.

There are ethical implications of this monarchianism. The source of responsibility is either some supreme and external law given before whom there is no response save that of an absolute obedience which adds nothing creative to the universe, or there is anarchy without any basis of responsible relatedness. A social doctrine of reality in its ethical dimension would be one in which individual creativity and significance has its place in the context of a social process, with means and ends, conditions and consequences, freedom and responsibility, in some organic mutual interaction.

Such a statement can, of course, be more easily made than expounded. But it indicates the overall direction. The task which is imposed upon us is elaborating such a conception of how the world and its possibilities, God and the creatures are together in an ongoing process. From this point of view we can explore the nature of man's relation both to the natural order and to God who enters into every relationship as the supreme member of the society of being. God functions in his eternal primordial aspect as the structure of possibility, and in his concrete consequent aspect as participant in the society of free creative beings. The entire society depends upon him in a way which does not apply to the creatures. He is necessary to them, but no particular creature is essential to him for his being. Charles Hartshorne has suggested the analogy here of the human personality, which is in Whiteheadian terms a society with a dominant member. A route of actual occasions of experience forms the ruling thread of continuity which mobilizes, informs, and sustains the integrity of the person. This is only an analogy when used to describe God's relationship to the world, but it does point towards that kind of structure which we shall have to describe if we are to have a theistic account of the pattern of the social. Every relationship of things to each other in the world will reflect their participation in a structural order and a supreme experience which is in the actual process in which both participate. For one being to respond to another is to create a new situation to which God must respond, and the divine response enters into the qualification of each new occasion of experience between the finite members of the society.

Two persons, A and B, are in conflict with one another. Each asserts himself in the relationship, and communicates his interests, his feelings, his indignation. What A does creates a new situation for B, and B's response to A reconstitutes the situation for A. But neither A nor B has the meaning of his action solely within himself. Each appeals to standards of judgment, meaning, right and wrong, which he asserts as the true meaning of the conflict. Each tries to change the other, or destroy the other according to an image which he holds, not only of himself but of life and being. So the meaning of the relationship brings each to the boundary of that which gives shape to the being of both, which holds before each a structured future with certain delimited possibilities, including, perhaps, the possibility of reconciliation. The appeal to a good which embraces both, or to a possibility beyond the present state of either A or B is, metaphysically speaking, an appeal to recognize the larger context in which the conflict takes place. It is, though it may be mute and unrecognized, an appeal to God.

God is present in the relationship first as the order of possibility which gives logical structure to every element in the experience. Without God there would be no conflict. Chaos leads to no decision. Only where there are meanings to be appealed to, satisfactions to be derived can there be a clash. The conflict may be over the meanings of words and their interpretation. It may be over the appropriation of items of value, property, ideas, or institutions. It may be the dark background of hostile feeling which arises out of past history and resentments and colours the present perception of each by the other. In every case there is the immanent structure of the order of valuation of which each participant must be aware in order to discover the meaning of his relationship to the other.

God is also present as the supreme appropriation in a unity of experience of the actual feelings and decisions of the participants. No human experience is self-contained. It has depths of awareness of the issues of truth and error, fact and illusion of which we are not the standard but for which a standard must exist. Being known by another has within it a tangent which reflects an awareness of what being fully known by another would mean. 'God knows', we say, piously or profanely, giving linguistic testimony to our sense that what is actual must be known as actual in some experience, and that ours is fragmentary.

In this doctrine the conflict between A and B means something for them, but it also means something for God. It presents to God new data to be brought into his experience of the world with its suffering, its becoming and its possibilities. The meaning of the conflict, therefore, is not only what A and B find it to be for themselves, but what it is for the larger society of which they are a part and that society includes the divine experience. What we are for ourselves and one another is both judged and adjusted by what we are for God. The meaning of any life is not complete in itself, it is what it is for the society of being. 'For the love of God', we say, appealing in agony or pity or joy to our sense that what we are and do has a destiny in something beyond this present enjoyment or suffering.

Professor Findlay has recently written that the idea of God 'has unique logical properties'.[1] From the process point of view, those properties have to do with God's unique metaphysical status; but they do not require the complete separation of God's being or the content of the divine experience and its value from what happens in the world. The use of the phrase 'acts of God' for 'inexplicable catastrophes' reflects the implicit monarchianism in much of our religious language. The affirmation 'God with us' fully interpreted has profound implications for a more adequate language of value judgments. The good society is not the society beyond all struggle, suffering and incompleteness, but the society most open to the widening creative life which moves through it, which reaches toward a good it can never fully embody, but with a confidence in its ultimate worth because it involves the life of every member, and this includes the life of God which appreciates, judges, and is enriched by every finite good.

A social metaphysics will ultimately lead to the transformation of religious language because every language includes the adumbration of modes of metaphysical thought.

It is to the elaboration of the implications of the social vision of reality that process philosophy can address itself. Metaphysics, ethics, aesthetics, and religion are all aspects of the total task. My own thought has turned towards the logical formulation of the structure of social relationship. Can we set forth the complex of inter-relationships which is invloved in the way in which things come into being in relation to their own past, to other entities, to future possibilities? Can we formulate the structural relationship which holds

[1] J. N. Findlay, *Language, Mind, and Value*, London, Allen & Unwin, 1963, p. 9.

between God as the supreme member of the society of being and all the finite members? The simple logic of one and many will not suffice for this, nor will the traditional notion of God as being itself which absorbs all particular beings into one transcendent unity. A society is both one and many, it compromises individual members with their freedom and spontaneity, yet each individual participates in the ground of all possibility and is related to the supreme participant, God. It is the problems involved in stating the abstract aspects of such a view which I have called the logic of sociality. The use of the term 'logic' here may produce some perplexity. How far can we identify the analysis of forms of existential relationships as a 'logical' problem? Carnap seems to believe this is possible. He indicates that Russell and Whitehead began the application of logic to existential relations, but did not carry it very far.[1]

I shall here summarily set forth what would seem to be some requirements of an adequate logic of our speech about social relationships.

A first requirement would be that all existential relations would involve both the freedom and individuality of each member of the society as well as the participation of each member in the life of the others, drawing upon them and contributing to them. To be is to become, but to become is to draw upon the achieved becoming of other things, including the events in one's own past, the becoming of other things. It is also to draw upon the structure of possibility which embraces all becoming. In Whitehead's universe to some extent 'we are one another'. Absolute individuality is as meaningless as the absolute unity of all things. What each appropriates from another never exhausts the uniqueness of the other, but uniqueness is always a contribution of value or disvalue to a society.

But in a society where there is a supreme participant necessary to every other member, to be related to other individuals is to be related to that structural order which enters into every individual determination. In personal terms, to be related to another person is to be related to that person as he is related to other persons and to God. To value another person is not only to appreciate his being in itself but his being as it contributes to every other experience including the value of the unifying experience of all things which is the experience of God. From this point of view we can state in clear if abstract terms the answer to Professor Macintyre's chal-

[1] Rudolf Carnap, *The Logical Structure of the World*, Chicago, University of Chicago Press, 1967, p. 8.

lenge as to whether the idea of God is relevant to contemporary social problems. The problem of our time is the problem of how men can find a free, humane, just relationship to one another. The issues of what kind of being and value men assign to one another, the sources of ultimate human valuation of life, and the kind of freedom which belong to persons are all questions to which theism contributes an answer. The discovery of God is the discovery of a metaphysical order which binds life to life, in a dynamic community and that surely is relevant to every social issue.

A second requirement of the logic of sociality is the working out of the insight that all action involves being acted upon. Monarchianism again dominates much of our language here. To be 'free', we say, is to dispose of the other, to be invulnerable, to brush aside all obstacles. But metaphysically this is false. Nothing acts effectively without being conformed to the world. To act toward another is to enter into a mutual interaction. What the employer does toward his employees remakes the employer. What the revolutionary does to the established power reshapes the mind and being of the revolutionary. This is not a moralistic prescription that we ought to take account of consequences. It is a metaphysical analysis which reveals that all action is self-transformation through relationship to the other. Much moralizing actually overlooks this metaphysical insight. It forgets that the moral stance itself remakes the being of the person who holds it, for better or for worse. One remembers Kierkegaard's astute analysis of the puritanical conscience. Being afraid of falling into guilt, we fall into guilt.[1] The art of self-control is always the art of discovering the conditions of self-transformation.

The third requirement is the elaboration of the logic of value judgments in the context of social relatedness in which values occur. Contextualism in ethics and value theory is one of the pervasive movements of thought in our time and process philosophy agrees to a considerable measure with the contextualist thesis. Things are good in so far as they serve the increase of a certain kind of being and creativity in the context in which they occur. What is relevant, releasing and effective for the increase of social communion in one situation may become obstructive habit in another context. Every present good must be appraised in relation to what is now given, but also in relation to the continuum of means and ends, conditions

[1] S. Kierkegaard, *The Concept of Dread*. Eng. trans. by Walter Lowrie. Princeton University Press, 1946, Ch. 11.

and consequences, which stretches into the future. Morality which is simply the imposition of abstract law without this concrete responsibility for the future consequences of acts is truncated and legalistic. It becomes destructive.

The logic of value judgments thus becomes involved in the pattern of social relationship. And again we are brought to the question of an ultimate standard of value judgment which is not outside of but pervasive in every particular context. It is the question of God raised at the point of value judgments. I must mention here the important contribution of Henry Nelson Wieman, who points out that the problem of value judgment in the context of a genuinely social metaphysics leads to a distinction between two kinds of good: *created goods*, which are achieved desirable things or situations, and *creative good* which is the living process of creativity, the creative event bringing new structures of meaning and value into existence. Wieman's doctrine is a major contribution to value theory.[1] It suggests a new problem in the logical analysis of value judgments. *Creative* good is good because it produces new *created* goods, but *created* goods are good as they serve the working of creative good. Here is significant dialectic in value judgments. Clearly the supreme standard of value, God, must value both kinds of good, but in different ways. For Wieman God is identified with the *creative* good, but the creative good must seek and value the created results of its activity.

We see here again that the theistic outlook is relevant to the question of human commitment within social processes and conflicts. The creative good can claim absolute commitment, but it is not identical with our human ideals and structures of value as we now hold them. All present judgments are held subject to the working of the creative good which they serve.

Finally, the logic of a genuinely social relationship must include the logic of an ever-enlarging experience. It must embrace past, present, and future. A society requires new being, freedom, spontaneity of the members bringing new value into the increasing life of the whole. Perfection identified with static completeness is the apotheosis of monarchical values and culture. The logic of perfection needs to be radically restated so that the conception of perfection itself, that is the aim of all striving, includes the continual search for new good beyond present actua-

[1] Henry Nelson Wieman, *The Source of Human Good*, Chicago, The University of Chicago Press, 1946, Ch. III.

lity. The adventure of life is involved in the meaning of fulfillment.

Such a doctrine of perfection does not in one sense solve the problem of evil. There is no answer to the question why the world is the way it is, why goods and evils are mixed as they are. But the doctrine of social relatedness does not impute the cause of all imperfection to the creator of the society. To create a society (and we speak of God as the creator, for without him there is no society) is to create creators with their spontaneity and freedom. It is to make even the creator vulnerable to the accidents, the distortions, and the perversities of free and finite beings. If God is to have a world in which love has any meaning, he must have a world where evil is risked. Thus far the logic of social relatedness can take us. It is not an explanation of how the world came to be what it is; but a discovery of what is required if the supreme value of communion among things is intelligible at all.

Abstractions have just as much meaning as comes from their power to illuminate the concrete realities of human experience. The search for a new logic of sociality, abstracted from the complex of relations of God and the world seems to me a necessary and revolutionary philosophical task. It would contribute to the illumination of the human struggle to find viable forms of social existence. It is not a substitute for empirical social analysis, for historical understanding, or artistic sensitivity. Logic and metaphysics are not the climax of the search for reality, but only indispensable modes of analysis of the concrete.

The logic of sociality needs therefore to be put alongside other modes of interpretation of human experience. I am concerned with the possibility of a phenomenological understanding of human experience. Such studies of man as those of Paul Ricoeur from a phenomenological point of view surely supplement metaphysical analysis, and I have attempted one such analysis of suffering.[1]

Phenomenology without a metaphysical doctrine of being, however, seems to me to fall short of what phenomenologists are seeking, that is, the meaning of the forms of human experience. For the meaning is not only in intuited essences. Man is in a world, and his meanings arise between him and his world. The question of what is real is ultimately a metaphysical question. Hence the abstrac-

[1] Cf. Paul Ricoeur, *Philosophie de la Volonté* I, II, Paris, Aubier, 1950, 1960. My analysis is in a paper on 'Suffering and Being in Empirical Theology' to be published by the Divinity School of the University of Chicago in a volume of essays on empirical theology.

tions of metaphysical inquity are instruments for detecting the ground patterns in the real world and thus illuminating experience.

The question of how the logic of sociality can enter into Christian theology is a separate topic; but it is not hard to see that when the Christian faith has affirmed that God is love, and has seen the divine life as a self-giving redemption of the world through suffering, it has anticipated the social view of reality which has all too often been obscured by the failure of traditional metaphysics to see that God must share the life of the world and its becoming if he is to be relevant to it.

11

THE PERSPECTIVE OF A
TELEOLOGICAL PERSONALISTIC
IDEALIST

PETER A. BERTOCCI

I

In this essay I shall first set down the direction of my philosophical pilgrimage, and then try to justify several predisposing steps that move me in that direction.

I am a personalist. I believe that everything that is depends ultimately upon a *self-existent Person*. This tenet unites many thinkers—Thomistic realists, some absolute idealists, and most theists.

But I am a personalistic idealist. Idealism in its dominant historic stance is, first, the contention that the Good, as Plato said, is the source of everything's being, and being known. However, in accordance with the Judeo-Christian vision, I conceive the ultimate aim of God to include the creative growth of persons in a responsive-responsible community.

Many theistic idealists would agree thus far. But they would reject a second historic thesis of idealism: the *qualitative structure of all being is psychic or mental as well as goal-directed.* While I find a form of Leibnizian-Whiteheadian pan-psychism very attractive, in this teleological personalism the inorganic space-time world is the energizing of the cosmic Person. This cosmic Person creates, sustains, affects and is affected by, the myriad forms of somato-psychic being that range from the lowest forms of life to the highest forms of personal unity anywhere in the universe. This qualification of Berkeley, Hegel, Lotze, Bowne, and Brightman, on the one hand, and of Leibniz, Fechner, James, Whitehead, and Hartshorne, on the other, ultimately leans heavily on the nature of personal unity, with special reference to the mind-body problem, to be suggested below.

It makes considerable difference what model of a person is used by a personalist as his basis for analogy to other forms of mental beings or substance-causes, sub-personal and super-personal. On my view, a person is a complex unity *of* activities: feeling-wanting, sensing, remembering, thinking, willing, oughting and appreciating (aesthetic and religious).[1] Further, a person is a self-conscious agent, free within limits to develop in accordance with ideals of truth, love, and of aesthetic and religious sensitivity.

This model of the person needs much defence. But the important effect is a reconsideration of the meaning of *creatio ex nihilo*.[2] For without *creatio* I see no way of accounting for the limited freedom or creativity of persons, or of conceiving of the person as a mode, centre, or focus of some other being. I hold that to be a person is to have the capacity to create what was not (*ex nihilo*), without losing one's own identity in the change. At the same time, creative actualization or fulfilment on the part of any finite person is impossible without responsive-responsible interaction within a community of persons.

If each person enjoys delegated spontaneity and creativity, he is not a part of some whole. The part-whole model of the universe, even as contemplated in the dynamic philosophy of organism does not enable us, as I see it, to account for that quality of individuality and sociality which characterizes personal existence especially. More adequate is a telic Purposer-purposers model. The Creator-Purposer creates and sustains purposive selves (possibly in a relative continuum) who are creatively free, but cannot actualize their potential apart from a mutual responsive-responsible community.[3]

What I have set out so boldly issues from a synoptic view of human experience. My guiding principle in the search for truth is the reasonable probability envisioned in the criterion of growing experiential coherence. My faith in reasonableness keeps me both from what seems to be irrationalistic tendencies in existential personalism, and from rationalistic reduction of the individuality and freedom that I find in personal experience.[4]

I turn now to critical turning-points in this philosophical *excursus*.

---

[1] See 'A Temporalistic View of Personal Mind', *Theories of Mind*, edited by Gordon M. Scher, New York: The Free Press, 1962, pp. 398–421, and 'Foundations of a Personalistic Psychology', *Scientific Psychology*, ed. by B. B. Wolman and E. Nagel, New York. Basic Books, 1964, pp. 293–316.

[2] 'Towards a Metaphysics of Creation', *Review of Metaphysics*, Vol. 17 (1964), pp. 493–510.

[3] See 'An Impasse in Philosophical Theology', *International Philosophical Quarterly*, Vol. 5 (Sept. 1965), pp. 379–96.

[4] See 'Free Will, The Creativity of God, and Order' in *Current Philosophical Issues* (Essays in Honor of Curt J. Ducasse), ed. Frederick C. Dommeyer, Illinois, Charles C. Thomas, 1966, pp. 213–35; and 'The Moral Structure of the Person', *Review of Metaphysics*, Vol. 14 (1961), 369–88.

II

In a class, one day in 1932, Alfred North Whitehead said, as I recall: If you want to understand a philosopher, try to understand and examine what he has unwittingly taken for granted. In my last year in High School I had begun to question the faith in the infallibility of Scripture that had indeed given needed focus and direction to my adolescent years. In my own experience I had already discovered the value of that forgiving love which, as I saw it, the life and teaching of Jesus exemplified. This experience had transformed a life prey to the influences of a slum in greater Boston. But did the experience have to be interpreted in Catholic or Protestant authoritarian fashion?

In my junior year in college the life and teaching of Socrates joined with that of Jesus: the unexamined life and the unloving life are not worth living. The experience of loving, and the experience of examining, a particular fusion of the practical and the theoretical, constitute my peak experiences.[1] My motive in philosophizing has been to examine whether the value judgment involved in such experiences could be warranted.

I was to discover increasingly how momentous philosophically is the decision to accept a method and a criterion of truth as one's guide in examining. Another remark of Whitehead's, in the first year of my graduate study—'the purpose of philosophy is not to explain mystery but to corner it'—actually reinforced much that had been taught me by Edgar S. Brightman, who was, as my teacher first, and then as my colleague, my Socratic gadfly. That remark was to be further reinforced by F. R. Tennant who guided my doctoral dissertation. In the attempt to corner the mystery, in the attempt to stay relevant to the question: What is the good? I was to see that no one phase of human experience can be neglected or given arbitrary priority.

This 'radical experientialism' is sensitive to the possibility that a method which has been successful in one segment of experience may be irrelevant to another phase. It forces me to be problem-centred rather than method-centred. This tenet entails the kind of experientialism in which each area of experience is inspected both by a method appropriate to it, on its own terms, and by being confronted with what the other areas of experience suggest. What I

[1] See the eloquent exposition of this theme in Edwin A. Burtt's *In Search of Philosophic Understanding*, New York, New American Library, 1965.

wished to avoid at the outset was a methodological imperialism or dogmatism in the name of any one phase of human experience. My pervasive act of faith—not blind faith but faith informed by my own and, as I see it, man's experience with methodological imperialism—is to let each dimension of man's experience speak for itself and to suggest bases for some illuminating pattern and meaning relevant to every dimension.

Hand in hand with this experiential synopsis goes a *definition* of truth as the correspondence of a proposition about a state of affairs with that state of affairs. What I mean by 'correspond' is best illustrated in an experiential situation. As I listen to someone else tell me what I said, I decide whether what he says 'corresponds' to what I was trying to convey. I decide he is mostly correct but partly incorrect because I know what I said and what I meant. His error consists in not describing accurately or asserting what 'corresponds' to what I meant. Again, I often decide that the word I use to express a feeling or thought does not quite 'say' or quite 'correspond' to what I am feeling and thinking. I have no better instances of what I would mean by the truth of a proposition.

I am willing to generalize from such situations where I have access both to the experience or event and the referent. When I seek 'the truth of the matter', I seek the statement or proposal that corresponds to the state of affairs referred to in the sense just mentioned—not as copy, not as identical with, not as partial fulfillment of my experience or object, but as expressing in sign or symbol, verbal or otherwise, what I would recognize as 'corresponding' could I have access to both the referent and the meaning-media agreed upon. Similarly, I am expressing the truth about another's experience when my expression would be adopted by him as leaving nothing out that he is feeling or intending. I know the truth about an apple, or a gremlin, or a God, *if*, assuming each could respond to my claims, each could say 'yes'.

But even in the ideal cognitive situation, my own expression of, or another's assertion about, my experience, I am impressed by the limited range within which I can be confident that correspondence can be checked. My past is involved in all statements I make and yet here my attempts at checking correspondence are frustrated. I conclude that my claims to truth must leave room for fallibility.

It is at this point that I find a distinction very desirable between *psychological certitude* and the truth of any proposition. For while there are relatively few, if any, occasions when I am capable of any direct checking of assertions about my past or about the non-self, I still find myself psychologically certain that I mailed that letter this morning, and that the noise I hear is that of a passing automobile. Further reflection on this fact, that I seem to be correct 'psychologically' despite different degrees of confirmability, makes me all the more cautious about assigning to any one experience and description arbitrary, dictatorial cognitive power over the import of other experiences. Nowhere is the caution the more imperative than when I am dealing with the crucial cognitive situation that I call the experience of objective reference.

What I mean by 'objective reference' is a pervasive experience without which the word 'knowing' would be meaningless. In any experience of cognitive-claim, or objective reference, I *refer* the object experienced beyond itself (not necessarily beyond myself). 'Refer' here is an ultimate; I can only give examples. The 'red' I undergo is, as an experienced state, undeniable; it is cognitively innocent as such. But when I say, 'That is red', I am referring beyond the experience as experienced and claiming to know that 'that' is red. Again, the experience of kindness is cognitively innocent of the cognitive claim I make when I say 'Kindness is better than unkindness.' Objective reference, I am suggesting, is not restricted to any one dimension of experience.

No objective reference, then, no knowing. But more: no objective reference, no *problem* of knowing. What distinguishes a human mind is the fact that it is not only capable of experiencing a state but *referring* that state as experienced, thus claiming to know by way of it something other than it. At the moment of objective referring the knower may be convinced (psychological certitude) that his reference is correct. The 'red' I experience is the book's. The kindness I now experience is judged to be a state better than unkindness I experienced. The experience of objective reference renders all of us 'inexpugnable realists', to borrow Arthur Lovejoy's term, for we are prima facie convinced, when we are cognizing, that what is before us *is* as we experience it. It does not occur to us initially that we could be wrong, that experiencing 'it' may not be knowing it.

Yet my thinking about my experiencing cognitive certitude soon teaches me that I have the same experience of objective reference about the snake that turned out to be rope and the rope I claim not to be a snake. In short, this experience of objective reference, intrinsic to every cognitive claim, and yielding psychological certitude at the moment, cannot *by itself* be depended upon as justifying any cognitive claim. I am indeed *referring* beyond the experience as experienced, and I need to look further for *cognitive assurance* (in varying degrees). What seems clear is that in itself objective reference cannot be used as favouring either the view that in knowing the knower is, or that the knower is not, identical with the object known. However, what renders me an epistemic dualist is the fact that the psychological certitude I experience in objective reference does not keep me from error. And here several other conclusions are suggested to me that are decisive for my pilgrimage.

First, there is no objective reference without a referrer, an experient, a proposer. Objective reference is not an event like any other event. A stone falls, a finger bleeds. But only a proposing-referring self, an experient-knower, can experience red *and refer it* beyond itself as a claim to truth.

Second, if I had no other ground for believing in myself as (at least) a mental being, the fact of objective reference is decisive. For like any other being or event, I can undergo something. But in addition I can refer any particular experience beyond itself in a cognitive claim. A brain cell, or a magnet (or any event in the physical and biological world as usually defined), cannot do this. I can make a mistake, I can be in error, only because I can refer to another what I later discover is not 'its' but 'mine'. An error, in other words, must be located. Only within me, as undergoing and referring what I experience, can my erring be located. The error is not in the rope but 'in me' as proposing on the basis of an experience that this experience of snake does correspond to a snake.

Whatever else it means to be a mind, it means that kind of being who can experience objective reference and its certainties and still turn out to be correct or incorrect. Apropos here is H. H. Price's inimitable remark: 'Let us rather take off our hats to any creature which is clever enough to be caught in a trap. It is the capacity of making mistakes, not the incapacity of it, which is the mark of the higher stages of intelligence.'[1] To know that I can be in error is to know that I am an experient-proposer—indeed an agent-proposer who cares to know what degree of correspondence, what kind of relevance, my experience has to what is not myself.

[1] H. H. Price, *Thinking and Experience*, Cambridge, Mass., Harvard University Press, 1953, p. 87.

III

I have opted for the definition of truth as correspondence, and, in analysing the knowing situation, found that the very search for correspondence defines my nature as an experient-purposer who must justify his claim that any claim to truth, whatever certitude his immediate 'objective' experience gives, needs further justification. I would agree with Whitehead: 'The elucidation of immediate experience is the sole justification for any thought; and the starting-point for any thought is the analytic observation of components of this experience.'[1] But my elucidation cannot assume that the immediacy of experience is the immediacy of truth. It might well turn out that some immediate experiences are true, but I can be justified in believing this only because other experiences, including action, indicate that my description is reliable. Any analysis I give of experiences will not be acceptable if my claims about experiences are contradictory; yet my experiences are my point of departure and my point of confirmation.

What this means is that my 'experiential hospitality' is to eventuate in hypotheses that follow the norms of formal, logical consistency; if my thought is contradictory I cannot 'go' anywhere theoretically. But it also means that my search for logical coherence must begin in, and return to, the *erlebt* experience and not 'think' or 'logicize' the givens in experience away.

When I try to articulate what this respect for logic and experience demands concretely, I come upon *growing, experiential coherence* as my test for any truth-claim. An hypothesis must, once it is logically possible, be relevant to such variety, quality, and relations as are given in experience. What I find myself doing as I seek experiential coherence is developing an interrelated system of hypotheses that are both mutually consistent and of aid in comprehending my experiencing in its variety and connections. While hypothesis and theory must not dictate to experience, an experience, simply because it is my experience, cannot hold back an otherwise theoretically illuminating hypothesis (especially since a certain amount of uncritical or critical theory is probably involved in what I would

---

[1] A. N. Whitehead, *Process and Reality*, New York, Macmillan, 1929, p. 6. Note Royce's remark: 'Without experience, without the element of brute fact thrust upon us in immediate feeling, there is no knowledge. . . . The whole problem of our knowledge, whether of Nature, of men, or of God, may be condensed into the one question: What does our experience indicate?' *The Conception of God*, New York, The Macmillan Co., 1897, p. 16.

call 'pure' experience). Any hypothesis that is experientially coherent must remain open to revision and in competition with other hypotheses.

Accordingly, as I see it, one never reaches *the* hypothesis that is completely coherent experientially. He reaches an hypothesis—be it about his own present, past, or future, be it about the nature of other minds, of things, values, and God—that is more coherent with the available data, and 'established' theories about them, than is any other hypothesis.[1] Hence, any 'naturalism' or 'theism' or any other 'ism' constitute hypothetical systems which purport to inter-relate the relevant considerations, both for theory and practice, more completely than any other system. The art of truth-finding always involves more than theorizing; it involves a practical as well as appreciative sense of what the alternatives involve. It is in this context that I wish to say, with Bishop Butler, that probability is the guide of life. I do not expect to find, in virtue of the accumula-tion of experience and knowledge, a system of hypotheses that is logically certain and experientially complete. But when hypotheses are born within the context of my desire to weed out inconsistency in the commitments that are the stuff of my existence, I find myself 'willing to believe' the system that keeps the arteries of experience feeding the whole of my life.

My basic faith, if you will, is that whatever truth is available to man takes root in the various aspects of human experience when they and their import are gathered together in a comprehensive system. It may be that some one aspect of experience is *the true* path, or that some one seemingly trustworthy segment is the de-monic error. But the safest way of learning this is not by excluding that segment just because it does not fit in with some more 'estab-lished' segment, but by seeing whether it stands condemned by the synoptic search for coherence. If the religious or the moral con-sciousness, for example, seem to lead to conflicting conclusions, the settlement of the conflict may come by asking how their claims can *also* be supported by the sensory, the aesthetic, and the theoretical. Only thus, as I see it, can methodological imperialism, dogmatic pluralistic empiricism, or confining logical coherence be adequately challenged in the name of both experience and reasonableness.

The life of reason is not the life of logic but the search for such

[1] See Edgar S. Brightman, *Person and Reality*, ed. Peter A. Bertocci in collabo-ration with J. E. Newhall and R. S. Brightman. New York, Ronald Press, 1958, pp. 22–33.

connections, not barring the logical, as the complexities of human experience warrant. Logical and semantic clarities are not enough. We need both accuracy and adequacy in our hypotheses. Our motives—including the need for objectivity—must themselves be judged in the context of our need as human beings to know what *we* can do and become in the world as we come to know it.

IV

I move from basic epistemic contentions to two critical metaphysical tenets when I assert that the agent-proposer involved in the being of objective reference, of truth and error, is at least a unity of conscious activities. First, whatever else I am, I am what I am *consciously aware* of being in introspection. I am always amazed at the spectacle of psychologists and philosophers who are willing to give up, or soft-pedal, the only evidence that is unique to them as persons—especially since they can only reasonably give it up *after* they have inspected it and found it wanting. The words 'immediate experience' have no meaning except for an experiencing agent that can inspect its own awareness—whatever difficulties crop up as he *self-consciously* evaluates any given interpretation of his experienc*ings* and experienc*eds*.

Both on the basis of such inspection and reflection, I go on to assert the undeniable conscious unity that I call *I*. What is this non-probable, undeniable I? I am a multi-phased unity of feeling-desiring, emoting, sensing, remembering, thinking, willing, oughting, appreciating, and worshipping—all activities interpenetrating with each other. The nature of each of these experienc*ings* or activities needs careful description, their epistemic import needs critique, and their relation to each other careful tracing. But I go on to say that they are *my* activities, or mine, both because they define what I am in the immediate scope and 'tone-quality' of my existence, because their particular organization distinguishes me from other beings, *and* also because I can direct them (within limits).

It should be noted here that I have not said that I am aware of *my self*, as if the self could be an object like red, or anger, or pleasant, to be found alongside of experiencings and experienceds. I have said that *I*, or person-self, am the unity of these activities-experiencings (not of the experienceds, since these objects of the experiencings come and go). This unity is not a blend or concoction, a fusion or a collection; to be a self or person is to be a unity of these activities-experiencings which can be distinguished within the whole but not separated from it.

I am trying to avoid two errors, and to do so in the name of what I actually experience. There is no homunculus behind and unifying my activities, a soul-substance that 'has' its experience but is not identifiable with any of them individually, or with them as a whole, nor am I a collectivity of processes or activities, for then I could not understand such unity as I find. In order to give a probable account of my unity and process, self-identity and change, the following view has increasingly recommended itself to me.

To be a personal self is to be an active, self-identifying being. It is the very nature of this unity of activities to wax and to wane within the limits of their potential. A personal self will never become an animal or sub-personal self because its activities, maturing and responsive to each other and to the environment, nevertheless do maintain their self-identity. And by 'identity' I do not mean a mathematical equality, for I find no experiential referent for such equality. This 'mathematical' conception of permanence as sheer identity seems to me to be the core-mistake in thinking about permanence and change; it is nowhere more unexperiential than in thinking about self-experience.

As I see it, then, the experiencing and experienced fact is that I change and recognize myself as changing. This is the existential ultimate at any present. It must not be lost in any attempt to explain 'how it is possible', for this self-identity change is presupposed by any such attempt. Such a loss occurs when we try to fuse the concept of identity or permanence with that of change. We then are tempted to say, as many have, that I am an unchangeable *I* that transcends 'its changes' or 'its activities', But in so doing we invite such contradictory conclusions as: thinking experiencings have their being in a non-thinking, non-changing, activity-unity; or we urge the unity of experiencings is developed or learned without making clear what gives continuity to the unity we find in our varied experiencings and experienceds.

This is not to say that the problems of unity, continuity, and change do not haunt me even as I hopefully make the following suggestion. I at any moment—far from being a non-temporal or a timeless 'point'—am a complex telic *durée* of such activities as those mentioned above; unity is intrinsic to the very being of that filled-moment. Again, a personal being, is minimally, a *now*, experiencing a 'saddle-back' unity of activities that I may telescope here as wanting-knowing activities. Every irreducible *now* is engaged in some form of wanting-knowing; it is related to but not reducible to its inner (unconscious), and outer, environments. These environments do not push it around as a billiard-ball might be pushed around. The wanting-knowing unity is always accepting and rejecting within the actuality-potentiality of its constitutive nature, as permitted by its regnant telic thrust.

However, if this saddle-back unity were all I could not even speak of continuity. Yet it is within it that I find evidence for continuity. In my personal now, I am constantly aware of some 'again'; I say that I am remembering an earlier now in my experiencing now. I can be wrong about the interpretation I give an again-experience, but, as H. H. Price says, the awareness of resemblance is irreducible to recollection, since it is more fundamental and primitive. So much, then, for the cross-section view of personal unity—a complex, unified, *now* of activities (and their potential), within which the connective activities of remembering and thinking are at work.

But this cross-section of I-experience is indeed a specious present if it tries to understand itself without reference to a not-now and a not-self. The telic ferment in a present, referring to a past (again) and to a not-yet, issuing from a past *now* and changing into a future *now*, *is* a continuity-in-change. I can wrongly interpret what I am and will be, but the continuity-in-change is primitive as the base of any specific interpretation. In short, I propose that the continuity of personal being is a self-identifying concrescence that may be said to be selectively pregnant with its past in any present as it labours for its future. A future self is the by-product of the self's own original telic nature in selective interaction with *its* circumambient environment (however we finally define the latter).

So important for the telic personalistic idealism I propose is this model of personhood that I restate. The essence of personhood is an intrinsic unity of permanence and change. For neither permanence nor change is, I suggest, ever experienced as such; their mixture or fusion to make a self is certainly not experienced. 'Permanence' and 'change' are conceptual abstractions intended to focus on two ways of describing what each person does experience. What is *erlebt*, be it in a specious present, or in an experience *of* succession, is the kind of being that can be called one because it—as an actual-potential, temporal unit—is *one now*. At any moment in its history, owing to internal inability to stay alive or to maintain continuity in change, it may cease. To cease for a person would be for him to lose his initial unified-change, or his self-identifying change.

For (and here I veer from Whiteheadians as I understand them) personal continuity is not to be seen as a passing of identity from moment to moment in what might seem a series of moments. This model is much too mechanical (and almost any model will seem mechanical). The continuity is self-identical not because of 'passing on' of identity but because whatever happens *within* the original unity of activities, or whatever happens *to* it, can be accepted by the unity in such a way that self-identity is not lost. I am not a monad without windows or without a permeable membrane; but my windows and my membrane do not simply 'let in' or assimilate anything that comes along; nor do they merely 'sponge up' in the interacting situation.

I can say no less than this: I am a complex active unity that is responsive to my environment and my own changes in a way that keeps my self-identity in my varying contexts. Continuity is possible because this does happen. My original unity does not remain identical in the logico-mathematical sense; it is identical in the sense that I can know that ten strokes of Big Ben are successive as *my* experience even as I fuse their qualitied content into my experience. My memory is never mere retention. 'Retention' is the word for the fact that the self at stroke one is able to be modified and yet keep its self-identity, even as stroke two affects the self-identity without destroying it.

This, I suggest is the model of personal being, of dynamic mental substance-cause, of agent-proposer, of wanter-knower, at the human level. I am a personalist because I find in it, when proper allowances are made, the most helpful model for understanding everything around me that I understand, namely, telic-unities-in-change in a world that is defined by the continuities and unities that make up 'the many'. Can this view of personhood be accommodated to the existence of an unconscious self, and to the facts of intermittent consciousness? Several suggestions regarding an approach can be made here.

V

Were 'againness' never experienced in any way, I would have no epistemic ground for belief in my part. The experience of that-pain-*again*, that-red-*again*, is as much given as is pain and red; 'again' is not an addition to, not an interpretation of, an experience.

This does not mean that a specific again cannot be false—just as a specific set of sensory experiences can turn out to be 'hallucinatory'. *What* I know about the cognitively innocent 'again', just as *what* I know about the cognitively innocent red, is an interpretation, which may later be seen to be incoherent with other evidence. In a word, any conception I develop of what constitutes my total self—and in this instance my past self—will be the most coherent interpretation of my agains and the remainder of my experiences.

A comment on grounds for belief in an unconscious will indicate the interesting epistemic problem we face there and also serve as a transition to the knowledge of our bodies. Often others tell me about events in my past of which I have neither recognition nor recall; there is no experienced 'again' about them. Yet it is more coherent to believe that a certain view of my unremembered-by-me-past is correct because it is more coherent with agains I do experience. Of my 'unconscious', however, I have no 'again' experiences at all. My belief that my unconscious exists (and any theory of its nature) must be based on coherent connections that *can* be made with what I do consciously experience. For example, the view that my consciousness is the small visible segment of the iceberg is an hypothesis based on what is consciously experienced in the segment, but I have no again experiences to guide me here.

I myself am willing to postulate a telic unconscious that will help me to understand conscious and subconscious experiences, and to provide psychic continuity despite consciousness discontinuity and intermittency, as in sleep. However, my first purpose here is simply to indicate that if there is a matrix of unconscious telic activity, we can only hypothesize about it on the basis of evidence in consciousness and in observable behaviour. But the unconscious is *my* unconscious only as its nature explains *my* conscious experience and behaviour and no one else's.

Second, while I cannot expand on the matter here, I find it probable to suppose that, during periods of unconsciousness, I still exist as a telic mentality active at a different level of my total potentiality. Again, it is *my* sleep-phase, and my state of unconsciousness (or *my* sleep-phase), because what is hypothesized as occurring then is needed for me to understand the kind of continuity-unity in my conscious-self-conscious phase. My unconscious states allow me to interpret more clearly what my total nature is. The continuity between these states is not experienced as such but what is said about deep sleep and dreaming and unconscious states has coherence only when they are hooked together in waking states. The unconscious is postulated and described in order to explain what appears and goes on in consciousness. The particular views taken on these matters will be affected by how the body is conceived, and we are now ready to note the methodological situation we face in this connection.

What reasoning leads me to believe in my body? There is a kind and order of data—that I ordinarily call sensory data—which we do not experience *ab initio* in an episodic 'again-context'. It is these data, as we shall see in the next section, that help me to identify the being I call my body.

A methodological and an epistemic warning are in order here. I cannot define these data as those I experience by way of my bodily senses. For they do not come with the labels 'bodily'; they are refractory qualities in certain complexes and patterns of order. It is already a theory about them to assert that they are mediated by, or constitute, a body that is different from other bodies. It is already a theory about them to say that their source is in a particular kind of spatio-temporal world mediated to us by our 'bodily senses'. It is already an interpretation to say that they are 'no more than' manifestations of what we know as non-spatial activities. For again, what is given within the complex matrix of what I have called self-experience are variegated qualities—not the colour-red-by-way-of-my-eyes but experienc*ed* 'red' distinguishable from 'green' (and the affective-emotive tones that go with it). It is after much inspection, learning, and thinking that I come to distinguish and classify the various kinds of sensory experiences and to develop the hypothesis that they are 'mediated' by certain events in bodily organs.

VI

I pass swiftly, then, to suggesting how I come to mean what I do by 'my body'. In the first place the qualitied-experiences I come to call 'sensory' are different from each other—'blue', 'hard', 'cold'. is not 'burnt' or 'sweet'. They do have a spatio-temporal matrix in common, I discover. Some, however (visual and tactual experiences, for example), are intrinsically extended, and in 'next-to-each-other' relations within my *durée*. Others (olfactory and auditory experiences) may not themselves be extended, but they are most readily related to the extensive matrix. Characteristic of these qualitied experiences is their intrinsic 'brute' quality and a re-

fractory succession and pattern. Henceforth I shall call these refractory experiences, appearing in some refractory order, *qualia*.

Secondly, the *qualia* that I finally identify as 'my body' are no
different prima facie from the family of qualia that I identify as an
apple or a chair. What I call *my bodily* qualia do not come with
tags on them differentiating them immediately as my body. I
am governed by the refractory pattern of their own qualitied-
order as I differentiate them as my body, but they are not immediately different from the refractory, extended-qualia-in-extension-
relationships that I call the sensible extended world. For most
practical purposes I find it possible and convenient (but not
arbitrarily practical and convenient), to distinguish the extenso-
durational patterns of qualia (like colours, sounds, smells, kin-
aesthetic and somaesthetic qualia) from essentially durational and
non-extended experiences (like ideas, emotions, volitions, obligations, and values).

It was the extended character of the sensed world, a character
he could not find in the remainder of his experience, that led
Descartes to reject the identification of mind and body. To this
extent, it seems to me, he was correct. But a faulty epistemology
and inadequately criticized assumptions led him to separate his
non-extended unitary *Cogito* from the body which he assimilated to
the rest of the extended world and its presumably mechanical
nature. Furthermore, even his heroic attempts to see his mind and
body as a functional unity, did not succeed in indicating why his
body should be *his* body. Recent phenomenologists and existentialists have, on the other hand, tried to avoid Descartes's separation,
but ended up, as I see it, in blurring both the distinction and some
of the inescapable differentiations between bodily and mental processes. I believe it is possible to be fair to the non-extended without
separating the extended and shall now outline a view of the person
that may also become a working model for understanding the way in
which the cosmic Mind and the world (including persons) are related.

If I stay close to my actual experience and do not allow either
Cartesian or phenomenological interpretation to overwhelm me, I
think I can say that what I call *my*self (from the beginning of any
awareness of myself as myself) is a larger *unitas multiplex* within
which I come to identify a certain family of qualia as my body. But
this family of qualia in turn is also distinguishable from a larger
spatio-temporal matrix I call 'the world'. But how then do I come
to *my* family of qualia, *my* body? I find that I can divest myself of

such families of qualia as 'my clothing' and substitute other *qualia*-families for them. But such divesting and substitution is not possible with relatively stable interrelated *qualia*-families I gradually identify as my body.

There are degrees of divesting and substitution possible, I discover. The spectacles I wear (that is, the *qualia*-family I can 'isolate' as eyeglasses) are as foreign in one sense as the splinter in my finger or my false teeth. But I come to learn that while my spectacles are important to me, I never experience them as I experience my eyes or my own teeth or the place where the splinter is lodged. *My* body then—and it is no simple matter for me to know its 'circumference' exactly—is at any stage and moment in my being that again-and-again matrix of qualia which has been gradually weeded out from the vast 'manifold of qualia' I call the sensory world. I can weed these 'body'-qualia out because they go together with a relative constancy not characterizing all the other given and learned families of qualia that I call not-mine and not-me.

But even this would not suffice to justify 'my' or distinguish *me* and *not-me*. A stone-qualia-family, for example, also comes to me with certain refractory regularity, and by virtue of that fact, I can relate myself to it (pick up the stone) in a very limited way. But because this qualitied-order is always beyond my control, because these qualia come into and go out of my life without my say-so, I can readily assign them to an order governed from beyond myself.

This is not quite the case with my-body-qualia. Despite their variations and changes as 'I' grow, they form an identifiable continuant matrix that leave me in little doubt about their belonging with me, or 'I' with them. In a manner of speaking, we cannot escape each other. We can affect each other within the larger matrix, the total *erlebt* I, that includes both my sensory and non-sensory qualia and activities.

All of what I mean by myself and my body is never a neat bundle of identical continuities. To illustrate, let me say that 'my' arm falls 'asleep'. The first time I felt it, *as asleep*, it seemed a foreign object, for strange sensations afflicted me. But as I moved that arm I gradually found 'my' arm coming back, for the familiar qualia 'returned'. After repeated experience of having *that* arm fall asleep I came to know what it meant for *that* arm to be asleep within the larger family of body-qualia. I recognize my arm normally as the continuant family of activities and contents within the larger matrices I identify as *I*.

The import of what I am suggesting so far comes to this. I, as a total person (not a now only) at any one stage of my development am a complex unity of activities and their respective content-objects (sense-data, objectives, memories, ideas, obligations, and so on). My body, is that relatively persistent and continuous matrix of sensory experiences which, co-existent with the rest of my activities and their content, is learned to be the base and intermediary for other sensory experiences that I learn to call the world beyond, yet related to my body. This experienced family of bodily-qualia (that is, the only 'body' I know *experientially*) is the one that coexists with my being and I am involved in its changes and it in mine in ways that call for further understanding.

Indeed, it is my thinking about this experienced body that leads me to theories about it. But these theories, however rooted in my immediate experience may change without alteration in my immediate experience. Hence when my doctor tells me that the ache (the qualia) I feel in my head is due to changes that he notes in my shoulder or my brain, he is introducing theoretical constructs, event-patterns, of which I have no immediate experience. There is no reason, at this point in the argument, for my denying that what I experience as self-body is the epiphenomenon of 'physical' electrical vibrations, or of 'biological' changes, or that it is a mode of Spinozistic Substance, of Hegelian *Idee*, or one among a society of Leibnizian monads. Whatever I conclude to be the ultimate status of my self-body is theory based on the experienced activities-*cum*-content I cannot escape as being myself.

Furthermore, I do not first identify myself and then 'the beyond'; my experiencing, desiring, theorizing go on together as I act in the light of presumed knowledge. I feel or am aware of myself as a wanter-knower, whose limits and nature become clearer as I discover what I can and what I cannot control, and in what way and to what degree. On a certain morning I find that I have a stiff neck, that if I persist in trying to turn it, all I can be assured of is pain; on another day I find certain ideas persisting in my consciousness despite every effort to dislodge them. But sooner or later these are definable within a larger, more continuous context that stays mine because I can effectively control what takes place regarding them, and do not stay 'mine' as that contextual unity does.

It now becomes clear that my agency, my capacity to initiate and influence changes that take place 'in' me, and 'beyond' me is crucial in defining what I am, what is mine and not mine. I define myself basically as the kind of person who, within limits, can initiate changes, within the circumference of my own being as I relate it to what seems no part of me. I do not create the basic patterns of order-in-change that constitute the complex experiencings and ex-perienceds that I experience myself as, but I come to know what I am by initiating patterns of order-in-change and waiting to see what happens 'to' me and 'in' me.

For example, when I turn the wheels of my automobile, I *am taken* where the motor and the physical forces operative on the wheels take me. I experience another order of constraints once I introduce food and liquid into my body. I experience the con-straints of reasoning in still another way. If I decide to reason I do not make up 'the laws of thought as I go along'. Nor can I control the flood of memories associated with the problem. But I can be selective in using these associations in accordance with the laws of thought and evidence.

In general, then, what is mine, what I identify myself with, is what I discover to be my inescapable and continuant pattern of activities-*cum*-content. What I learn to identify as my bodily-*activities*—activities connected with the sensory realm, basic to actions like eating, talking, walking—are mine just as my wanting-oughting-thinking activities are mine. That is, they are distinctive aspects of the confluence of activities that I am. These activities and their qualia are not 'outside' my mind, belonging to a non-me world; they are interpenetrating aspects of my being, but no more exhaustive of my being than are my desiring, willing, oughting and appreciative activities. In sum, 'my' body is that complex unity of activities-*cum*-qualia that define one phase or pole of my being.

What is being denied in this view is, first, that my body is given *to* my cognitive-conative being as the manifold sensory qualia I call a stone is given. Descartes was correct. There is a non-extended part of my being that is not reducible to, and not identical with, the extended. But Descartes's severing of the body from the complex 'thinking being' and assimilating it to the world of things was a mistake that need not be repeated. The view here is that while it may be doubted that the total activities-cum-qualia that I call my body are coextensive with, or the cause of, the non-extended and non-sensory dimensions of my being, *they are part of what I am and not added to a non-extended 'soul'*. Of course, I may be incorrect in describing or interpreting somatic activities and qualia (just as I may be wrong about the exact nature of my non-somatic functions).

But in principle, I am not definable apart from either roughly circumscribable area of my being.

What is also being denied in this view is that my body *incarnates*, to use the term some phenomenologists prefer, my being. The incarnation view does emphasize what is true, that what I do, in and through my body, is more intimately expressive of my thought and volition than any dualistic view recognized. A violinist, to be sure, must learn to play his body as well as his violin; but when he touches his body—as opposed to the violin—there is a recognition of the co-responsive continuity with himself that is absent when he touches his violin. His total being—in its sensory-nonsensory nature—is, as it were, already alive with the burden he wishes to convey through, or give further completion to, through potentialities of the violin-world. Hence, it is, I suggest, more accurate to say, not that I *am* incarnate in my body, but that I am a sensory-nonsensory unity who can express his intent through his body, and through his use of the sensory beings and events in the world beyond his own being.

I wish, then, to avoid at one swoop the notion that I am an incarnate I, and nothing more—for I am more than what I can express with, and in, *this* spatio-temporal complex. I wish also to avoid the notion that my body is an instrument—however important—of my mind as the violin is an instrument that defines a violinist as a violinist. My 'embodied' being is in a together-relation (to be more accurately defined) with the other dimensions of my being; I am not a mind in a body, a body with the capacity for mind, or mental activities with point for point parallelisms with bodily activities.

I am a continuant-unity-of-activities-cum-qualia the nature of which is capable of identifying itself in and through time. I am a continuant-unity whose constant problem is that of defining exactly what his total activities (conscious-unconscious, somatic-nonsomatic activities) embrace as he interacts with a world which comes and goes in an order over which he has little control and upon which he depends for large areas of his fulfillment.

VII

In this section, without arguing for idealism, I wish to suggest that the concept of the person briefly outlined provides a model for understanding the relation between the cosmic Mind and 'the inorganic world'. For my purposes here let me assume that the cosmic Mind creates *ex nihilo* the person and sub-personal selves of the organic world. Let me also assume that the person in particular has a delegated freedom that cannot be adequately accounted for if the person is conceived as a centre of, or embraced in, the cosmic Mind. As I shall suggest in the next section the universe is ultimately a telic order guided by the purpose of compossible creative growth and satisfaction. But here I wish to suggest an alternative to what I understand to be Berkeleyan, Leibnizian, and even Whiteheadian, views of God's relation to the events in the complex unity we call the physical world.

The cosmic Mind, as I envisage it, bears analogy to the intellect and will of the finite person. God's willing is guided by norms of reason and goodness that are intrinsic to his very being (what E. S. Brightman has called the Rational Given).[1] In other words, the cosmic Person enjoys an unchanging 'formal' structure that is expressed in the essential unity and continuity in any world. In him as a Person, in him as a Purposer involved in creating and sustaining the specific orders that express his purpose, there is no change. The cosmic Mind will never be less than a Person or more than a Person.

What I now wish to suggest is that eternally co-existent with God's formally distinguishable structure is a non-rational Given (again to use Brightman's term). This non-rational Given, like the body of the finite person as outlined above, is not an expression of the Person, although his purpose can be expressed through it. The non-rational Given is as much a phase of the total Person as is the rational Given, and together they form the total being of the Person.

To explain further, I do not mean that we have here a Platonic *ananke* or Receptacle that is co-eternally independent of God; I do not mean an amorphous, 'bastard kind of being', that is *ab initio* to be persuaded to take on forms presumably alien to it. Rather am I suggesting that within the total unity of the cosmic Person, interpenetrating with all the other phrases and activities of his being, is his 'body', the analogue of the person's spatio-temporal body. To say that this order of being within the Person has distinctive activities-content does not mean that the cosmic Person is partitioned into un-spatial and non-spatial being, as if one were given

---

[1] *Person and Reality*, 3, 4, and 17. While the view I am suggesting here is not identical with Brightman's, it is much influenced by Brightman's thought.

to the other—any more than a finite body divides a human person.[1]
The cosmic Person is not dealing with a 'content' essentially alien
to his being, either imposed upon him from without, or self-
imposed by creation.

On this view, the cosmic Person's non-rational Given provides
the ontic base, or the 'standard', ontic activity-content-pattern that
we come to know as Nature. But this non-rational Given does not
exhaust God's being. Indeed, what we hypothesize as the evolution
of the natural world is the history of the cosmic Person's altering
of the concrete situation in his own ontic being in accordance with
his purposes (and allowing for the changes effected by the relative
autonomy of man and sub-personal selves). Again, the order-in-
change, the developments within cosmic history, may be regarded
as developments in the history of the Person himself as he works
out his aims.

In even more specific terms, what we refer to as the formation
and evolution of the physical order, what we refer to as the impersonal (not non-personal) common matrix for the orderly becoming that we classify as the inorganic realm, may be viewed as a telic
creative change movement toward even greater plentitude of compossible beings.

It must not be thought, however, that the spatio-temporal world,
as we conceptualize it, has a *one-to-one* correspondence with what I
prefer to call the 'ontic realm of eligibility', or the standard extenso-
temporal aspect of the cosmic Person's being. Finite selves, personal
and sub-personal, interact with that realm; their lives converge
with it, are threatened by it, and are sustained and challenged by it,
but they are not identical with it, 'embraced', or 'comprehended'
in it. A Kantian agnosticism, nevertheless, is not consistent with the
fact that our humanized phenomenal world is sufficiently relevant
to the ontic realm to allow probable knowledge and the relatively
successful practical response human beings can make. The phenomenal world is a human joint-product born of interaction and interchange between man and the realm of eligibility.

We may compare the realm of eligibility to the sounding-board
of a piano. The strings there allow many patterns of response; not
every musical pattern is 'eligible' for its support. The pianist in

---

[1] In order to explain non-disciplinary evil not accountable to human free
choice, it may well be that within the total being of the Person there is a recalcitrant factor that poses problems for the creative purpose of the Person. But I
shall not deal with the problem of evil in this essay.

expressing himself must learn to respond, to shape his own potential to what the piano-realm-of eligibility makes possible. Furthermore, no one, and not even all of the pieces played on the piano can be said to be identical with the sounding-board; we know not what possible aesthetic possibilities can yet be realized by the self-disciplined and creative pianist. Analogously, the 'realm of nature', as we conceive it at this point in history, is a theoretic-practical system that finds support in the realm of eligibility (that we are calling the non-rational Given aspect of the cosmic Person's being, in which He is at work in accordance with his own plans, without defaulting the freedoms delegated to all selves). But our present scientific hypotheses, accepted as fact (or, as I would put it, as the most coherent interpretation of the refractory data we experience), may give way to other hypotheses that allow us to respond to, and understand more completely, what the realm of eligibility has in store. In the realm of value, interpenetrating with the natural realm, the human task is to find hypotheses and the ways of living that will be more fully relevant, and find greater support, within the realm of ontic eligibility. In so doing there will be more creativity and fulfillment in the divine-human co-responsive community that is here envisioned.

VIII

On what grounds, then, can such an objective idealism be interpreted teleologically, and what is the nature of the cosmic purpose?

A basic methodological caution, consistent with the theory of knowledge suggested above, is crucial here. We cannot first assume a particular theistic or non-theistic view of the inorganic and organic world (the realm of Nature) and then insert man into it. We cannot, for example, assume a telic or a non-telic view of Nature and then wonder how man's experience of freedom and purpose, his moral, aesthetic, and religious experience can be fit into that? Our knowledge of the world is human knowledge and our human knowledge is not unaffected by human values; at the same time, both our knowledge and our values are related to our natures and their potential in relation to what is beyond us (in the realm of eligibility). If this caution is observed, two basic steps toward a teleological personalistic idealism suggest themselves.

First, the epistemic dualism embraced above cannot profess to the kind of cognitive grasp that is crucial to realistic and rationalistic epistemologies. Nevertheless, such probable knowledge as we have does enable persons to survive and develop as they interact with each other and with the realm of eligibility. Short on certainty, this dualism is clearly not short on relevance. Our knowledge is more like the map of a terrain than any picture, but the fact that we can draw, live with, and improve the map means that our cognitive equipment is not at odds with the realm of eligibility.

In a word, if man is held to be an ontic alien in the world, the fact that he can know the world even with such probability as we have, is left in an odd theoretical suspense, and the success of his actions becomes a constant surprise. To speak as if man's nature and knowledge are addenda to 'a world' that is complete without him is both to conjure up an unexperienced situation, and to court a discontinuity we abhor in any other cognitive situation. The inexpungeable fact is—man, a knowing-caring, a knowing-valuing agent who understands both himself and his world in interactive relation. (To say that this is not so is to claim to know the situation as it is!) Man-discovering-such-truth-as-he-has is a fact about the world with man's activity-potential and growth in it. Why treat the fact that man can know, that man's knowledge increases as he adheres to cognitive ideals, as an unilluminating fact about the realm of eligibility? The fact that man can both arrive, can survive, and can grow, gives us some insight into what is more, and what is less, and what is not, eligible in this kind of universe.

Second, man's knowing does not go on in a value-vacuum. Knowing itself is an activity that man values and that takes place only with self-discipline. Philosophers, artists, prophets, scientists, statesmen, are persons who in acquiring a certain quality of being which they prize intrinsically have been able to accept the cost for their peak-experiences and achievements. In their agonies and in their ecstasies they have disciplined their freedom and their desires by logical considerations and evidence, they have been willing to see loved ones hurt as they held fast to conclusions justified by their disciplined probings. And in these very experiences and achievements they have been telling us about the conditions under which man, in this realm of eligibility, can fulfil himself.

We cannot continue to neglect or minimize the fact that the responsibility for truth-finding presupposes the knower's willingness to develop not only the methods of investigation relevant to his problem but the moral courage, the mutual tolerance, the humility and meekness, the sense of humour, without which his cognitive abilities are ineffective. In a word, man's knowledge is an ethical achievement; and this fact, too, is an index to the nature of things. Man does not know simply *as* a knower; he knows as a person caring about, committed to, and 'enjoying' moral, aesthetic, and religious meanings that are 'soundings' of the realm of eligibility.

To rephrase: human cognitive insight and accomplishment in any area may seem at first sight to be the joint-product of human cognitive capacity interacting with the realm of eligiblity. But what actually goes into this joint-product is not only the nature of the realm of eligibility that responds negatively and positively to man's soundings, but the developing nature of man's moral-aesthetic-religious response. Persons are still discovering that unless they consciously come to appreciate and control their own potential-actual natures, unless they develop guidelines for increasing warranted knowledge and mutual respect for all their ventures in value experience, there can be no wisdom—in this kind of world!

Consequently, if we have discovered, for example, that belief in the uniformity of nature and belief in the norm of creative love are in some degree the conditions not merely of personal growth but of knowing at its best, are we not saying that so far as we know these norms express goals in the structure of Being? This correlation of knowing and valuing is what could not escape Plato when he said that the Good is the source of everything's being and being known.

In the last analysis, I would wish to argue,[1] to know is to love; and to love is to be guided *by what is and can be* in the concern for mutual creativity. For as persons we find what we are, where we are, and what we can be most fruitfully, when we act-in-knowing as creative within a community of responsive-responsible persons.

This essay suggests an ontology in which the person, a responsive-responsible being in the world, is not an addition to the world but the most illuminating clue we have to the nature of its being. Once we leave man the knower-actor in the world, once we see his cogni-

[1] This whole argument, influenced in large measure by F. R. Tennant's 'wider teleological argument' in *Philosophical Theology*, Vol. II, has been restated in my *Introduction to Philosophy of Religion*, and been supported by 'Free Will, The Creativity of God, and Order', in *Issues in Contemporary Philosophy*, Essays in Honor of C. J. Ducasse, ed. F. Dommeyer, and in 'The Impasse in Philosophical Theology', *International Philosophical Quarterly*, Vol. 5 (Sept. 1965), pp. 379–90, and 'The Cosmological Argument Revisited and Revised'.

tive venture as rooted in cravings and commitments to personal and social values, once we see that the only world we know about is one within which certain qualities of cognitive-moral-appreciative effort are the ones that are mutual supporting, we can live with some confidence as fighters for these ideals in a Realm of Ends.

12

CARTESIAN EPISTEMOLOGY AND CHANGES IN ONTOLOGY

RICHARD RORTY

Many philosophers nowadays ignore or ridicule traditional ontology, but few are happy with the breezy 'refutations' of metaphysics which were fashionable a decade or two ago. On the one hand, quarrels between Absolute Idealists and Physical Realists, inter-actionists and epiphenomenalists, process philosophers and sub-stance philosophers, seem as inconclusive as ever. Even streamlined versions of old ontological theses (for example Strawson's claim that material objects are basic particulars or Quine's that we can get along with physical objects and classes) do little more than excite a certain languid admiration of their authors' ingenuity. On the other hand, few of us can swallow the notion that Plato, Aquinas, Spinoza, Kant, Russell, and Whitehead were simply 'confused about language'. Even if one suspects that the systems they erected simply worked out the absurd consequences of a few blunders,[1] one wants a longer story about how some of the most intelligent men who ever lived made such blunders, and about why they devoted their lives to piling paradox upon paradox.

I do not think that a satisfactory story of this sort has yet been told. Most such stories either blithely dismiss pre-twentieth-century philosophy or else make what is, I suspect, a serious mistake. The mistake is the assumption that there is a single discipline called 'ontology' or 'metaphysics' which was practised by Aristotle, Aquinas, Descartes, Hegel, Whitehead, and Russell, and which is still being practised by Quine, Strawson, Sellars, and J. J. C. Smart. It is tempting to think that we shall always come back to the good old metaphysical problems despite changes in jargon, for this way of viewing the matter also suggests that no radical change has occur-red. On this view, the rise of 'analytic' philosophy is *just* a change of idiom, and the positivistic rejection of metaphysics was just juvenile rhetoric, on a par with Descartes's self-deceptive attacks on the scholastics.

---

[1] Cf. Austin's remark (in conversation) that 'Plato thought that all general terms were proper names, and Leibniz that all proper names were general terms'.

Only time will tell whether a genuine world-historical change is now going on in philosophy. It may be that the present split between 'metaphysicians' and 'analysts' is a mere provincial squabble which will strike our descendants as comic, but I doubt it. Self-deceptive as Descartes may have been concerning his relation to his scholastic teachers, it was no small change that came over men's notions of what it was to do philosophy at the end of the seventeenth century. Self-deceptive as the positivists may have been, I believe that no smaller change is taking place now. To appreciate this change, I think we have to see that the ways of answering the ontological question 'What is really real?' are very different at different epochs. Specifically, the criteria for a satisfactory answer to this question changed in the seventeenth century, and are changing now. A full-blown history of these changes would offer a comparative account of the criteria used by the Greeks and the medievals, those used by philosophers between Descartes and Russell, and those being invoked nowadays, in say, controversies between Strawson and Quine. I shall not attempt this, for two reasons. First, I do not think that I understand the Greeks well enough to get them right. Second, I do not think that the most recent discussions of 'ontology' have lasted long enough for criteria to have emerged.[1] I shall, however, try to offer an account of the criteria used in what I shall call the 'Cartesian' period of philosophy —the one which stretches from the end of the seventeenth to the middle of the twentieth centuries. If my account is right, then it will at least be clear that present-day motives for doing ontology and present-day criteria for having produced the true ontology are altogether different than in earlier periods. One can, of course, use the term 'ontologist' to cover Aristotle, Hegel, and Quine, for they all are concerned with what there is; but this is about as helpful as using 'atomic physicist' to cover Leucippus, Dalton, and Gell-Mann.

---

[1] For an exploration of criteria which might be invoked by a reductionist programme like Quine's, see Gilbert Harman, 'Quine on Meaning and Existence, II' *Review of Metaphysics*, XXI, pp. 362–7. As Harman notes, treating ontology as subject to the same sorts of requirements as a scientific theory raises problems about how we decide which of the purposes served by the 'reduced' entities we want to continue to be served, as opposed to those we want to repudiate. I think that more would have to be said about criteria for such decision before we could do much to adjudicate disputes about what there is between philosophers like Quine, Davidson, Strawson, Martin, and Sellars. More would also have to be said about the criteria for the validity of 'transcendental' arguments and about the relation between such arguments and reductionist programmes.

So much for prefatory remarks about my aims. The claims which I want to make are as follows:

1. A necessary condition for participating in ontological discussion during what I shall call the 'Cartesian period' was that an answer be given to the question: Given that we have incorrigible knowledge only of the contents of our minds, how is it that we can know about anything else?

2. The paradigm of an answer to this question was the claim that the nature of the object of knowledge—reality as opposed to appearance—was different than either common sense or science conceived it.

3. The justification for the existence of ontology as a distinct discipline came to be the fact that neither science nor common sense could offer an adequate reply to the epistemological sceptic. Giving such a reply became the *paradigm* of what it was to do philosophy.[1]

4. The refusal of many contemporary philosophers to take seriously the suggestion that reality is different from either common sense's or science's picture of it is due to the fact that they no longer accept or find it necessary to answer the epistemological sceptic.

5. The reasons why this premise is no longer accepted can be traced back to the abandonment of certain more general principles.

6. These principles are such that, once they are accepted, it is not clear why there need be a discipline called 'ontology' over and above empirical science. The justification of the existence of such a discipline thus requires to be rethought.

I should like to argue for all of these, but as regards the historical claims, (1)—(3), I can do no more than suggest how they *might* be argued for. Specifically I shall make some dogmatic remarks about the Cartesian period in philosophy as a suggestion of how I would meet *prima facie* objections to these historical claims. On the last

---

[1] The science of a given period tends to take *one* solution as a paradigm, whereas since Descartes philosophers have argued about which of the 'classical' solutions was correct. This helps account for the 'unscientific' character of philosophy as a discipline. For this reason, however, it is perhaps more fruitful to say that scientific epochs are defined by the *solutions* they take as paradigmatic, whereas philosophical epochs are defined by the *problems* they take as paradigmatic. (As may be obvious, I am here drawing upon a terminology and an outlook put forward by T. S. Kuhn in his *The Structure of Scientific Revolutions*, Chicago, 1962.)

three points, the reasons why epistemological scepticism no longer seems a live issue to many philosophers, and the implications of these reasons, I shall be able to actually do some arguing, and thus be more susceptible to refutation.

One might object to my first claim—that the answering of an epistemological question was, in the Cartesian period, a necessary condition for a satisfactory ontology—by saying that the task of ontology is, after all, just to tell us what there is—or what things are really real. One would think this could be done, and has been done, even if by those who never heard of a problem about our knowledge of the external world. I think that one can meet this objection by asking how, in such a view, one would distinguish ontology from the empirical sciences. In the sense in which pre-Sophistic philosophers like Anaximander and Democritus were asking about what is really real, modern science is a satisfactory answer to the question. If by 'what there is' or 'what is really real' one means anything like 'that by reference to which we can explain everything else, in a relatively simple and elegant way', then, in Sellars's words 'Science is the judge of the things that are that they are and of the things that are not that they are not'. If explanation and prediction are the only purposes to be served by the construction of an ontology, there is no excuse for an armchair substitute for science. One can only make sense of ontology as an armchair discipline if one sees the ontologists' definition of 'really real' or 'what there is' as something like 'what there would have to be if certain principles which we do not wish to give up are to be maintained.' The principles referred to will have to be generalizations at a level not evidently susceptible to empirical refutation—such principles as that 'We can know what colours things have', 'We can tell right from wrong', 'We can communicate with each other', and 'Tables are solid objects'. To say that we need better answers to the question 'What is there?' than either science or common sense gives us makes sense only if we see some such principle endangered by either science or common sense. If to be a philosopher who does ontology is to be something different from an armchair scientist, the difference will only appear by isolating the questions which impelled him to become an ontologist. What sets apart the ontologies of professional philosophers is that they are created in response to questions arising within other areas—specifically, epistemology, ethics, logic and semantics. This is the reason for the notorious difficulty of drawing a line, within a given philosophical system, between ontology and these other areas, and the difficulty (or pointlessness) of answering questions like 'Is Aristotle's doctrine of substance an answer to a logical or an ontological question?' Typically, the scientist's (and the man in the street's) view about what really exists is not influenced by questions about how we can know what we know, or name what we name, nor (except when the existence of God is under discussion) by questions about whether we should value what we value. By and large, the man in the street, the scientist, and pre-Sophistic philosophers are not bothered by such questions. Typically, post-Sophistic philosophers are. When we go through the history of thought and try to divide off the scientific from the specifically philosophical elements (in, for example, the works of Aristotle, Descartes, Newton, Freud, or Quine) we do so by putting the doctrines which can be evaluated without reference to such questions under the heading 'science' and the rest under the heading 'philosophy'. I would argue that such an historically-oriented approach is the *only* way in which we can catch the felt difference between science and philosophy, once we grant Quine's point that Carnap's internal-external distinction has to be reformulated and made a difference of degree. To use a loose analogy, we can only define the class of philosophical theories by enumerating a set of philosophical problems, just as Quine can only define the class of logical truths by enumerating the logical constants. To practise a discipline called ontology, as opposed to simply having a set of beliefs about what exists, one needs to be motivated by one or another of the ethical, epistemological, or semantic questions which provide part of the enumerative definition of the term 'philosophical problem'.

If there is any point at all in classifying philosophy into periods, this classification must be done by picking out the, as it were, pre-ontological questions which made it seem necessary to create a third view of what there is over against both common sense and science. I do not think that the questions raised by epistemological scepticism are the *only* questions which moved philosophers during the Cartesian period; one cannot neglect the Platonic notion of ontology as a way of justifying our claims to be moral which persists in Spinoza and Hegel. I think that inspection of the controversies between philosophers in this period would show that a philosopher who put forward a competitor to common sense and to science (as Spinoza, Leibniz, Berkeley, Kant, Hegel, and Russell did) always argued for this theory by claiming that if his ontology were not accepted we could not have the knowledge we appeared to have. Philosophers who put forward no such competition (e.g. Locke and Hume) were sceptics, the men who were prepared to admit that we knew less than we seemed.

I turn now to a more concrete form of the objection I have just discussed. Surely, it might be said, the great metaphysical issue of the period was the mind-body problem. Doubtless this problem is intimately linked to the problem of the possibility of knowledge of body by mind, but why suggest that one is more fundamental than the other? Here I want to claim that a certain view of knowledge— the one which engenders epistemological scepticism—just *is* fundamental; there would have been no mind-body problem without it.

The mind-body problem is an offspring of the theory that knowledge consists in the having of certain representations of reality (including perceptual ones), by the subject. As Matson has recently pointed out,[1] the Greeks had a soul-body problem but not a mind-body problem—or, at least, not the mind-body problem which has bothered philosophers from Descartes to Feigl. Before *this* mind-body problem can be made to seem urgent (as Matson also notes) one has to have the notion of 'immediate awareness', and to believe that the things we want to know about (tables, other men, stars, the moral law, and the gods) are not things which we are immediately aware of. Once one believes all this, one will have to grant the existence of a realm to contain the objects of immediate awareness. This will be the Mind, or the Subject *qua* Subject. Psychophysical dualism follows from epistemological dualism.[2] In the great systems of the Cartesian period, the primary task of ontology was to get the Subject and the Object back together. Solutions to the mind-body problem appear as simple corollaries to solutions of the Problem of Knowledge.

Thus the ontologies of almost every important non-sceptical philosopher from Spinoza to Russell consisted in a redescription of the Object—that which we want to know about—according to which the Subject and the Object turned out to be much the same. The concomitance of the modes of the two known attributes of Spinoza's God, the pre-established harmony of Leibniz's monads, the variations on what Austin calls 'the ontology of the sensible

[1] Wallace Matson, 'Why Isn't the Mind-Body Problem Ancient?' in *Mind, Matter, and Method*, ed. Feyerabend and Maxwell, Minneapolis, 1966, pp. 92–102.

[2] The genesis of the latter dualism from the former is well displayed in Lovejoy's *The Revolt Against Dualism*, Ch. 1.

manifold' (Berkeley, Kant, Russell), the perfect union of appearance and reality in Hegel's or Royce's Absolute, and Whitehead's panpsychism are so many ways of showing that if you know enough about the sort of thing you are directly aware of (the contents of your mind) you will know everything there is to know about everything. In short, the mainstream of ontology has been a redescription (specifically, a 'subjectivizing') of the Objects—a redescription which would not have been thought necessary had not the original claim about direct awareness been swallowed.

If it is admitted for the sake of argument that the problem of overcoming epistemological scepticism was the original motive which, during the Cartesian period, called ontology into being, one might still be tempted to say that as soon as ontology got going a host of further problems were revealed. There are, after all, plenty of metaphysical issues other than the relation of the knower and the known, or of the mind to the body. So it might be objected that the initial justification for doing ontology is no longer needed once this whole range of urgent problems becomes visible. In replying to this, I should want to make two points.

First, the other metaphysical issues which have found their way into the textbooks could hardly have occurred to anyone who had not had the conception of the relation between the mental and the physical which created the mind-body problem—*viz.*, the mind as the home of representations of which the knower is immediately aware. Since the Realm of the Mental was not spatially locatable, and maybe not even temporal, it was easy to go on to postulate as many Realms of Being as might seem necessary to contain anything which we wanted to talk about, but which did not fall within the purview of either common sense or science. Propositions, values, numbers, the True, the Right, the Absolute, and unicornhood were all admitted as candidates on the ground that if ideas could be real, then anything 'spiritual'—*viz.*, anything which was like an idea (in not being a physical object)—could be real, too. With the introduction of these candidates, the game of ontology became more complex, for new rules were added. Instead of simply getting the Subject and the Object back together again, you had to spell out what you proposed to reduce to what and what you were going to make irreducible. (Were numbers, for example, reducible to ideas about quantities of physical objects? Were they objects of which we had mediate awareness? If the latter, did God have to have immediate awareness of them? If so, did we have to be immediately aware of God? etc.) Again, the Realm of the Mental had to have some sort of unity, and thus it was discovered that there was a problem about the Nature of the Self. (Could it know itself directly? If so, then the subject of ideas would have to be an idea. So perhaps it was a kind of Idea of Ideas? etc.) Given this more complicated problematic, philosophers won points for elegance of reduction and lost points for paradoxicalness. Roughly speaking, the best ontology was the one which did enough reducing so that the universe looked reasonably neat, but not so much that one had to say such *outré* things as 'Numbers are really inscriptions' or 'Pains are really neural events' or (but this one was hard to avoid) 'Physical objects are merely permanent possibilities of sensations'.[1]

The second point which I want to make in reply to the above-mentioned objection emerges if we ask why philosophers were so concerned about what could be reduced to what. One might reply that it is simply an aesthetic delight to find a system in which appearances are saved with just the right balance between number of entities countenanced and degree of paradoxicalness. But this aesthetic attitude towards ontology, though presently flourishing,[2] is a very recent development. To explain three hundred years of ontologizing, it will not suffice to dwell on the familiar pleasures of finding, or proving the impossibility of finding, necessary and sufficient conditions for this and that. I think that the way to explain it is to realize that for philosophers during the Cartesian period it seemed as if there were only four possible answers to the question 'How do we justify claims about Xs?', *viz.*:

(1) We are directly acquainted with (have immediate awareness of) Xs.

(2) To talk about Xs is just a relatively misleading way of talking about Ys, which we *are* directly acquainted with. (E.g. Berkeley's phenomenalism, Kant's identification of 'nature' with the ordering of intuitions by concepts.)

(3) To talk about Ys, which we are directly acquainted with, is just a relatively misleading way of talking about Xs. (E.g. Spinoza's identification of our ideas with modes of the One Substance, Hegel's identification of everything with an appearance, or facet, or stage, of the Absolute Spirit.)

---

[1] I owe this way of looking at the matter to Milton Fisk.

[2] See Goodman, 'The Significance of *Der Logische Aufbau der Welt*', in *The Philosophy of Rudolf Carnap*, ed. P. A. Schilpp, La Salle, 1963, especially pp. 551-3.

(4) Appearances to the contrary, we *can't* justify claims about Xs. (Scepticism.)

As long as these seemed the only answers, reason tottered every time it looked as if something else (the moral law, God, numbers, meanings) was neither an object of immediate awareness nor somehow identical with such objects. To show that Xs were really real was a matter of showing that they could be known, which in turn was a matter of showing that somehow we were directly aware of them. This coalescence of reality and knowability was the reason why no one—not even Kant himself, in some passages—could put up with the notion of 'things-in-themselves'. The identification of knowability with being an object of immediate awareness is less easy to see, but I think that an analysis of particular cases would show that 'the quest for certainty' which was initiated by Descartes, combined with the lingering influence of Plato's principle that only what is a matter of knowledge, rather than opinion, is fully real, produced just such a coalescence.[1]

I have now done all I can in the space at hand to support the first three points I listed—my historical remarks about the character of ontology during the Cartesian period. Nothing, of course, can substitute for detailed inductive argument when one is trying to establish an historical thesis, but I hope that I have given some plausibility to my claim that ontology during this period centred around problems raised by epistemological scepticism, and more specifically by a certain notion of 'incorrigible knowledge'. I know that 'centred around' is horribly vague, and I should prefer to put my thesis as 'had these notions not been held, there would have been no such thing as ontology during this period'—but this seems on a par with such a pointless counter-factual as 'if there had been no quarrels between the popular and aristocratic parties in Rome, the Republic would not have been replaced by the Empire'. (Pointless because the Republic would not have been the Republic, nor the period the period, if the antecedent had held.) So I have stuck to the more modest claim that an attempt to get the Subject and the Object together again constituted the paradigm of doing ontology.

I turn now to defending my last three points—points which can

---

[1] George Pitcher, in a forthcoming book on perception, has analysed the role of this 'Platonic principle' in the creation of sense-data theories; I owe a sense of its importance to his discussion, and I was greatly helped by his comments on an earlier version of this paper.

be summarized as the claim that contemporary philosophy no longer sees the point of the question 'since we have incorrigible knowledge only of the contents of our minds, how can we have knowledge of anything else?' and that the principles which lead to denying sense to this question make it difficult to see why there need be a discipline called 'ontology'. The lynchpin of my argument here is the claim that the most important element in contemporary philosophy is the adoption of what I shall call the Principle of the Relativity of Incorrigibility—or, bowing to Sellars, the Principle that the Given is a Myth. I shall mean by this the following thesis:

That a given sentence is used to express incorrigible knowledge is not a matter of a special relation which holds between knowers and some object referred to by this sentence, but a matter of the way in which the sentence fits into the language of a given culture, and the circumstances of its user, at a given time.

If this principle seems too innocuous to have such importance, I would point out the phenomenon of epistemological scepticism itself. Why, after all, should the fact that we have incorrigible knowledge only of the mental cast doubt on the claim that we have corrigible knowledge—but still *knowledge*—of the non-mental? The first stage of answering this question is simply to cite Malcolm's point that the epistemological sceptic trades on an assimilation of 'know' to 'know for certain'—where 'known for certain' is equated with 'indubitable', and the latter is illustrated by reference to our knowledge of our own mental states, or our knowledge of how things appeared to us. But why was such an assimilation ever accepted? I don't have a really good answer to this, but I think that one can begin by noting that no one would have been tempted to make such an assimilation had they not believed that the fact that no doubt was possible about these matters was a clue to the *nature of knowing*. To put it another way, no one would have been tempted to this assimilation had they not believed that knowledge is the sort of thing that *has* a nature. One must further believe that this nature can be isolated, thereby segregating cases of true knowledge from cases of pseudo-knowledge, not simply in the common-sense way in which we tell the wise man from the fool, but in some deeper and more interesting way. An epistemological sceptic cannot think of knowledge-claims as cultural phenomena like marriage ceremonies; for viewed *that* way a universally-accepted knowledge-claim is automatically a sound one—at least until further evidence comes in (not evidence of some new and deep sort—but evidence of a sort which would be accepted as such by those making the claim), just as something universally-accepted as marriage *is* automatically marriage. Treating knowledge as having a nature which may turn out to be very different from what a given culture takes knowledge to be is the hallmark of epistemological scepticism. The importance of the principle of the Relativity of Incorrigibility is that it under-cuts the attempt to discover this nature by casting doubt on the first move which the sceptic makes—namely, to have found some case of knowledge which is a clearer case than others, and is thus a clue to the essence of what it is to be knowledge. It casts this by saying that the cases in which 'doubt plays no role' are cases in which *we* do not *let* doubt play a role, not cases in which we are in a different natural state.

To summarize the contrast between the Cartesian tradition and the Principle of the Relativity of Incorrigibility, the former thinks that the nature of knowledge is:

That about which no doubt is possible, or which can be inferred from propositions about which no doubt is possible (including both 'truths of reason' and truths about mental events),

whereas the latter takes knowledge to be simply 'justified true belief', where 'justified' is defined not by any reference to certainty but simply by enumeration—by pointing to actual procedures of justification which are used. To put the contrast still another way, the Cartesian tradition jumped on the fact that knowledge must be belief in what is true, and thought that by learning more about knowledge we could learn more about what is true. Thus we got *a priori* ontological conclusions deduced from sheer reflection on the nature of knowledge. The post-Cartesian tradition (exemplified by Wittgenstein, Austin, Sellars, Dewey, and Quine) rallies around the principle that empirical knowledge needs no foundation, emphasizes 'justified' rather than 'true', recognizes that 'justified' does not mean 'justified now and forever, beyond the possibility of revision', and consequently does not imagine that an exploration of how we know could lead us to conclusions which would clash with either common sense or science.

Yet another way of emphasizing the importance of this contrast is by noting different definitions of 'incorrigible' knowledge which would be put forward by the two traditions. The definition used by those who accept the Principle of the Relativity of Incorrigibility is:

To have incorrigible knowledge that p is to have a belief that p such that the question 'How do you know'—given a knowledge of the language and of your circumstances—is inappropriate, and such that there are no accepted procedures for resolving doubts about p, given the belief.

If this definition is accepted, then the Principle follows once it is granted that such procedures can come into acceptance and go out of acceptance. The definition offered by the Cartesian tradition is as follows:

To have incorrigible knowledge that p is to have a belief that p based on immediate awareness of the entities referred to by 'p'.

I cannot now try to give all the reasons I would like for holding that the notion of 'immediate awareness' is a mere philosopher's invention. I would merely suggest that such a definition is circular, in that no criterion for 'immediate awareness' can be offered save references to the incorrigible knowledge we have of the entities of which we are putatively immediately aware. We are immediately aware of what we can have no doubts about, and vice versa. So nothing is explained by such a definition. Its popularity, I believe, was due to picture-thinking—to thinking of the mind as an 'inner eye' which was capable of seeing only inner entities. But if we grant that nothing is gained by such a definition, then we are in a fair way to granting the principle of the Relativity of Incorrigibility. For the Principle says that our ability to have incorrigible knowledge about so-and-sos is not a function of a special relation in which we stand to so-and-sos. But 'immediate awareness' is just the name for that special relation. If it is seen that reference to this notion explains nothing, then the same arguments will work to show that no other name for this 'special relation' will explain anything either.

I have now said all I have time for about the importance of the Principle of the Relativity of Incorrigibility, but I have not yet given arguments for its truth. However, I do not know how to do this save by rebutting objections. Instead of dreaming up some objections and then knocking them down, I want to introduce a new topic into the discussion—one which provides an illustration of the way in which this Principle can be put to work in practice.

By offering such an illustration the strengths and the weaknesses (if any) of the Principle can be displayed. Further, this new topic—the present fate of materialism—will permit me to develop my claim that the tradition which accepts this Principle finds it hard to take seriously the traditional problems of ontology. I shall be arguing that an adoption of this Principle makes it uninteresting whether or not to materialism is true.

Until recently, debates about materialism have gone something like this:

Hylas: Since science seems to need to talk about nothing save atoms and the void in order to explain everything that happens, only atoms and the void are really real.

Philonous: But what is science save a scheme for ordering our experiences? Or, if it is more than this, how can it possibly deny that it rests upon experiences, and that these experiences are something different from either the atoms or the void?

H: What you call 'experience' is but another name for bounding atoms in the brain.

P: That is the sort of thing one would only say if one were defending a theory at all costs. What criterion of 'same' could one possibly use to show that two such different things were the same?

H: Two things are the same thing if talking about the one serves all the same purposes as talking about the other.

P: There you are. Talking about atoms and the void is never going to serve the purpose of describing what's immediately present to my consciousness—what I'm immediately aware of. No matter how much explanatory power such talk has, there will always remain the explananda.

H: But those things we are directly aware of are mere appearances.

P: Worse and worse. 'In the case of stabbing pains, it is not possible to hold that the micro-picture is the real picture, that perceptual appearances are only a coarse duplication, for in this case we are dealing with the perceptual appearances themselves, which cannot very well be a coarse duplicate of themselves.'[1]

For a long time, this rejoinder has seemed decisive. In recent years, however, Hylas has found a new move to make. He now replies:

---

[1] The quotation is from Richard Brandt, 'Doubts About the Identity Theory', in *Dimensions of Mind*, ed. Hook, New York, 1961, p. 70.

H: There are no such things as 'natural explananda'. What we are 'directly aware of' can be described in many different ways. One could train people to use the language of physiology to report on their inner states, simply by training them to use the name of the correlated physiological state whenever we now use 'stabbing pain', 'bitter taste', etc. I will, if you like, withdraw the term 'mere appearance', but I insist that there is no way of showing that it is *more* appropriate to report my reactions to stimuli in phenomenalistic language than in physicalistic language.

Hylas here invokes the Principle of the Relativity of Incorrigibility —the insight that what counts as an object of incorrigible awareness is a matter which is subject to revision in the course of empirical inquiry. If we did indeed train the next generation to abstain from phenomenalist language, then there would be no incorrigible knowledge of any statement of the sort usually classified as 'synthetic' (for introspective reports would now be corrigible by cerebroscopes). But no knowledge would have been lost, nor would any realm of being be lost to human sight, a given language-game would, for better or worse, no longer be played, but that is all that would have happened.[1]

Faced with this move, those who dislike materialism have moved a step backwards. They now focus on Hylas's claim that, roughly, two things are the same if the language used for describing the one serves all functions fulfilled by the language used for describing the other. This claim is hardly self-evident, as Brandt and Kim have noted in a recent article.[2] These authors rightly point out that the materialist can hardly accept a weaker criterion for the identity of events than the following: two events are the same, if all and only the same universals are truly applicable to them. But this means that those who hold that, e.g., thoughts and brain-states are identical have to say that the universals signified by a phenomenalistic language are the same universals as those signified by some part of a physicalistic language. Since, however, there are no rules for determining identity of universals (except the question-begging one that two universals are the same if they hold of all and only the same events), there is no reason to accept the identity of physical and phenomenal events save what Brandt and Kim call 'parsimony of a rather metaphysical sort'.

I think that there is indeed no other reason, and I think Brandt and Kim are right in saying that it is hard to imagine what importance the identity theory could have. But this is surprising, and needs explaining. In the recent past, materialism roused philosophical passion. In these latter days, its opponents no longer argue that it *can't* be true, they merely argue that there is no particular reason to think it true. Both friends and enemies of materialism tend to agree that the Identity Theory has (*pace* Smart) no explanatory power not possessed by a simply nomological correlation of the physical and the psychical. Both sides agree that the difference between mind-body Identity and mind-body parallelism is of no scientific interest—that what interest it has is purely philosophical. But instead of arguing in the good old ontological way, the controversy has shifted to quarrels about senses of the term 'identical'— quarrels whose upshot seems to be that there are various analogies and disanalogies between, e.g., the identification of chemical with physical universals and the identification of psychological with physiological universals, but no disanalogy so sharp as to make the latter identification outrageous and no analogy so close as to make it inescapable.[1] Nobody now argues that dire philosophical consequences will ensue if we do or do not accept materialism. Here is just the sort of historical shift which our account of the history of ontology as a discipline should be expected to clarify.

To explain the fact that philosophers used to feel that a great deal hung on materialism or its denial, and now don't, we must hark back to the genesis of the mind-body problem. It used to be

[1] This curt remark does not do justice to the careful and useful analyses of senses of 'identity', 'reduction', and related concepts found in, for example, May Brodbeck's 'Mental and Physical: Identity vs. Sameness', in *Mind, Matter, and Method*, ed. Feyerabend and Maxwell, University of Minnesota Press, 1966, pp. 40–58 and Routley's and Macrae's excellent article 'On the Identity of Sensations and Physiological Occurrences', *American Philosophical Quarterly*, III, pp. 87–110. I do not mean to suggest that these analyses and distinctions are unimportant, but simply that they do not issue in a decisive difference between the two identifications mentioned. Nor can I do justice here to two attempts to show that there *is* such a decisive difference—that offered by Putnam and Fodor (cf. Putnam, 'The Mental Life of Some Machines' in *Intentionality and the Mental*, ed. Casteneda, Detroit, 1967 and 'Robots: Machines or Artificially Created Life?' *Journal of Philosophy*, LXI; Fodor, 'Explanations in Psychology' in *Philosophy in America*, ed. Black, Ithaca, 1965) and that offered by Sellars, 'The Identity Approach to the Mind-Body Problem', in *Philosophical Perspectives*.

that parsimony was *not* the only motive for, if possible, getting rid of the mental. There were two other motives: if materialism were true, then (i) there would be no problem about how causal inter- action was possible between these different ontological realms. (ii) There would be no problem about whether and how sensations and ideas could be representations of reality, for the whole notion of 'representation' would be replaceable by a straightforward, if complex, account of knowledge in terms of appropriate responses to stimuli; an epistemic vocabulary would be replaceable by a causal one.

The first motive has gradually disappeared since Hume revised our notions of causality. These revisions have made it difficult to give an interesting sense to the question 'How can mind act on matter, and vice versa?', and the absence of empirical support for interactionism (as opposed to parallelism) has discouraged people from even trying. But, more important for our present interests, the first motive has been weakened by the fact that philosophers have increasing trouble making sense of the mental as a 'different ontological realm'. This latter notion depends upon the assump- tions that mental entities (*a*) are 'homogenous' with physical entities in that some of the same 'primitive' descriptive predicates apply to both, and (*b*) can be described independently of their relation to the person with whom they are associated. More specifi- cally, it depends upon the distinction between, e.g., a real dagger and an imagined dagger being a distinction between two *particulars*, both describable (in their 'essential' features) without reference to any other particular, rather than between one particular (a dagger) and *state* of another particular (a person). As long as we think in terms of two sorts of daggers—one simply located and conforming to one set of regularities, another not simply located and conforming to a different set of regularities (if to any)—the notion of 'distinct realms' makes sense.[1] The metaphor of 'realms' is founded on the image of subjects living divers laws in divers regions. It is des- troyed once the subjects that are supposed to be in different realms are no longer thought of as describable in the same terms. (This is

[1] The way in which the 'two sorts of daggers' way of thinking forms the foundation for traditional dualisms is beautifully illustrated by Lovejoy, *op. cit.*, pp. 12–32. In emphasizing the importance of the distinction between particulars and states, I am borrowing heavily from Sellars ('Empiricism and the Philosophy of Mind', in *Science, Perception, and Reality*). See also Smart, 'Sensations and Brain Processes', *Philosophical Review*, LXVIII, pp. 141–56, and Nagel, 'Physicalism', *ibid.*, LXXIV, pp. 339–56.

why Ryle's remark that 'imagined sights and sounds are not sights and sounds' has such poignancy.[1] It is not philosophically exciting to ask 'How can states of persons cause, and be caused by, daggers?' since this question naturally suggests a programme of research in physiology rather than a metaphysical or 'conceptual' perplexity.

Why did the philosophical tradition think of mental entities as particulars rather than states? The answer, I believe, is that they made the following assumptions:

(1) All our knowledge is either expressible in incorrigible statements or validly inferrable from such statements.

(2) We do not have incorrigible knowledge about anything except mental entities.

(3) No inference to propositions about the qualities of non-mental objects can be valid unless the incorrigible premises of these inferences themselves mention the *same* qualities of mental objects. (E.g. we can't know that tables are brown or that parallel lines never meet unless some mental entity is brown, or is parallel, or has some qualities which provide a *definiens* for 'brown' or 'parallel'.)

(4) Persons who do not have certain qualities (e.g. being brown, or parallel to something) can nevertheless know that other (non-mental) things have these qualities.

Accepting all this commits one to:

(5) Persons have immediate knowledge of mental entities characterizable by qualities which the persons themselves do not have.

It will then seem paradoxical to insist that mental entities, such as sensations and ideas, are states of persons. For how can I be aware of something brown which is a state of myself, but not a state of my body? To avoid this paradox, we imagine ourselves as

---

[1] *Concept of Mind*, pp. 250–1. This mention of Ryle should not be taken to mean that an adoption of logical behaviourism is required to overcome traditional psychophysical dualism. All that is required to overcome the epistemological dualism which begets psychophysical dualism is something much milder—the claim that the vocabulary for making statements about mental events can be introduced into language without antecedent awareness of such events serving as ostensive definienda for the terms of this vocabulary. As Sellars has shown, this claim is compatible with common-sense notions of sensations and thoughts as causes of behaviour rather than, so to speak, abbreviations for behaviour.

aware not of our own states, but of *particulars* (which we 'have' in some ill-defined way) which *are* brown, parallel, *et al*. Knowledge of these particulars will then stand in the same relation to knowledge of non-mental entities as knowledge of pictures to knowledge about the things pictured. Mental entities will be both particulars and representations.

As long as (1), (2) and (3) went unquestioned, the notion of mental particulars homogenous with (in the sense of sharing some 'basic' qualities with) physical particulars, as well as epistemological scepticism and the mind-body problem, were inevitable. As long as the problem of getting the Subject and the Object (and, *a fortiori*) the mind and the body, back together, there were motives for being a materialist. Once the notion of two sorts of daggers— or, more generally, the notion of 'homogenous' mental and physical entities—loses its hold, *both* traditional motives for being a materialist vanish, and are replaced by a purely aesthetic motive—'parsimony of a rather metaphysical sort'. It is because (1) – (3) are no longer accepted, much less taken for granted, that (in Taylor's phrase) mind-body identity has become a 'side-issue'.[1]

Summarizing, we may say that controversies about materialism have lost their interest because we no longer accept the traditional notion of mental particulars. But we can press the matter further. If the notion of mental particulars depended on accepting (1) – (3), which of these premises has now been dropped, and why? This question is too large for the present paper, but two points can be made fairly briefly. First, even if we accept (1) and (2), we shall still not be in a position to argue for the existence of mental particulars unless we accept (3). But (3) loses any plausibility if we follow common sense in holding that statements about persons' beliefs are sufficient grounds *all by themselves* for statements about utterly heterogenous things. (E.g. that the inference from 'we all think there is something red there' to 'Probably there is something red there' or the inference from 'None of us can imagine that

[1] Charles Taylor, 'Mind-Body Identity: a Side-Issue?' *Philosophical Review*, LXXVI, pp. 201–13. Taylor's own view is that everybody now grants that mind-body identity *might* be true and that the interesting question is whether it is, in fact, empirically true—which boils down to 'whether the most fruitful explanations are in psychological rather than physiological terms' (p. 211). I agree with most of what Taylor says in this paper, but I think it a bit misleading to suggest that philosophers should turn their attention to the empirical question he raises. Philosophers here can only wait and see, meanwhile appreciating the impact upon their own discipline of the fact that the only questions left to argue about in this area are empirical ones.

parallel lines could meet' to 'Parallel lines never meet' do not require additional non-empirical premises expressing 'transcendental' or 'conceptual' truths.) In other words, (3) loses its appeal if we cease to assume that in addition to the ordinary ways of justifying beliefs there must be a way of justifying this justification itself (specifically, a way of guaranteeing that the *received opinion* about colours, or geometry, is not just a good guess, but bound to be right).[1] This recent willingness to let common-sensical inferences stand on their own feet is not easily separable from the dissolution of epistemological scepticism which ensues upon the dissolution of mental particulars. But, as the example of Moore shows, it can be adopted even when traditional notions of mental particulars are retained. An adequate history of the twists and turns of recent philosophy would unravel this strand.

The second point is that the assault on 'givenness' common to so many recent philosophers is not (or should not be) an attack on (1) and (2). If one defines 'incorrigible' beliefs as beliefs which are (*a*) normally accepted simply by virtue of being held, and (*b*) are such that no generally accepted means for resolving doubts about these beliefs exist, then I think we can escape Austin's strictures[2] against incorrigibility. We can hold that certain sentences, used to make sincere statements by one who knows English (e.g. 'It now seems to me that I am seeing something red'; 'I cannot imagine parallel lines meeting') do indeed always express incorrigible beliefs. Nor need one deny (2)—for one could, given enough time and trouble, provide a justification for every other piece of knowledge one has in the form of an inference from such beliefs. (Though this is not to say that such an inference is in fact 'unconsciously' performed whenever one adopts a corrigible belief.) What is under attack, or should be, is the notion that if there were no such incorrigible beliefs (if, e.g., men had never noticed their inner states, or learned to talk the language of appearing), then we should be bereft of (i) knowledge about anything at all (even 'appearance') and, specifically (ii) awareness of the really real. This attack is a special case of a broader attack on the notion that there is an hierarchical *ordo cognoscendi*, which is not simply a matter of the

---

[1] The two dogmas which Quine has made notorious were the last gasps of the tradition which felt such guarantees to be needed. Both dogmas attempted to buttress commonsensical inferences by providing analyses of meanings which would 'explain' our confidence in these inferences.

[2] *Sense and Sensibilia*, Ch. 10.

structure of some given language at some given stage of the development of the race but is, instead, a reflection of (or at least a clue
to) some hierarchical *ordo essendi* which is capable of being grasped
by non-empirical methods. When the matter is put in these terms,
it becomes clearer why an attack on the Given is an attack on
ontology itself, as it existed during the Cartesian period. The
attack on 'naturally incorrigibly-knowable objects' and on 'mental
particulars' are part of a general revolt against the notion that
explanations and justifications of our talking, thinking, and valuing,
as we do can be given in terms other than the now familiar psychological, sociological, cultural, and historical ones. The development
of these new modes of explanation, as Comte and Dewey foresaw,
is having the same effect upon philosophy as a discipline and a
cultural form which earlier stages of scientific development had
upon religion. The particular philosophical issues concerning
mental particulars, incorrigibility, ideas as representations, and the
like which I have been examining can be discussed in their own
terms. But a full understanding of the changes which have made
the possibility of ontology so dubious would require a much
broader historical account of cultural change—an account on the
Hegelian scale. I do not wish to suggest that Western ontology is a
product of a few mistakes in the philosophy of language, or a few
mistaken epistemological or methodological premises. (That would
be like saying that Western religion is a result of a failure to understand that existence is not a predicate and that there can be no
atemporal causes.) But I do wish to say that *a priori* 'overcomings',
or defences, of ontology should be replaced by an attempt to go
through the traditional 'problems of ontology' one-by-one, examine
the premises which generate the problems, and see whether there
is any reason to believe these premises. The lasting value of the
linguistic turn in philosophy, as I have argued elsewhere, is that it
has begun such an attempt in a more systematic way[1] than has been
attempted in earlier epochs. Although the analytical jobs being done
by linguistic philosophers will certainly not be enough to let us
understand what happened in history, it is equally certain that they
are a necessary first step.

[1] Cf. *The Linguistic Turn: Recent Essays in Philosophical Method*, Chicago,
1967, pp. 32–3.

13

IN DEFENCE OF AMERICAN
PHILOSOPHY

RICHARD J. BERNSTEIN

Philosophers rarely hesitate to speak of 'American Philosophy', 'British Philosophy', 'German Philosophy', etc., yet the very notion of a philosophy characterized by a national or cultural group invites inquiry. What do we mean when we speak in this way? No matter how grandiose a philosopher's claims, or how minute his analysis, he certainly thinks that many of the statements that he utters and defends are true—even if he claims that there are no philosophic theses, or that metaphysics is akin to poetry, or that when we think we are arguing for profound theses, we are really shoring up our persuasive definitions. No matter what theory or analysis of truth we accept, the idea of an 'American' truth or a 'German' truth strikes us as absurd. So one may think that it is a muddle to characterize philosophies by a cultural matrix. A tough minded sceptic might concede that it is undoubtedly true that certain problems, methods, styles, etc. are favoured at different times and in different places, but while the historian or the sociologist may investigate the causes for these differences, they do not have much intrinsic interest for the pure philosopher.

Yet if we are honest with ourselves, we will be uneasy with this dismissal of the cultural identification of philosophic movements. One need not have much sympathy with the Hegelian notion of a *Zeitgeist* or the Marxist concept of ideology in order to recognize that there is a complex of shared attitudes, beliefs, problems, procedures and distinctions that enables us to characterize different philosophic communities and movements. Moreover this community (communities) of perspectives does make an essential difference to particular philosophic investigations. Like Hume's 'gentle force', this community of perspective exerts a regulative influence on the training of young philosophers and the direction of philosophic inquiry.

In this essay, I want to explore and defend some of the major theses that have been central to American philosophy. The discussion will focus on some of the pragmatic philosophers, although these themes are shared by other American philosophers. One must, of course, be cautious in making generalizations about American philosophy because a striking characteristic of the American philosophical scene, both past and present, has been its tolerance for a variety of different philosophic positions. We have our metaphysicians, existentialists, phenomenologists, logical empiricists, and analysts representing all shades of opinion. Nevertheless, I do think that there have been dominant emphases that give rise to a general orientation. The interrelated topics that I will be discussing are: inquiry, community, experience, and action.

INQUIRY

Despite the variety of philosophic movements that have developed in almost total isolation from each other during the past hundred years, there is a common motif that pervades many of them—anti-Cartesianism. Descartes elaborated a view of intuitive knowledge and of a reality grasped by intellectual intuition, a bifurcation of man into mind and body, and a 'solution' to the problem of error and sin that has been attacked over and over again. Far more than Descartes's individual mistakes have been criticized, for in so far as a Cartesian orientation supplied the framework for so much of modern philosophy, this general framework has been pounced upon by diverse critics. One of the most dramatic and effective critiques of the Cartesian orientation is found in a series of papers that Peirce wrote in 1868, in which many issues are delineated that were later explored by Peirce, the other pragmatic philosophers, and those influenced by the spirit of pragmatism.[1]

Peirce begins his critique by asking, 'Whether by the simple contemplation of a cognition, independently of any previous knowledge and without reasoning from signs, we are enabled rightly to judge whether that cognition has been determined by a previous cognition or whether it refers immediately to its object.'[2] Although the language is cumbersome, the point is clear. Peirce is questioning the notion of intuitive knowledge, whether it is conceived of as intellectual intuition or so-called knowledge by acquaintance, as

---

[1] Questions Concerning Certain Faculties Claimed for Man'; 'Some Consequences of Four Incapacities'; 'Grounds of Validity of the Laws of Logic'; Further Consequences of Four Incapacities'; reprinted in *Collected Papers of Charles Peirce*, Vol. 5, ed. Charles Hartshorne and Paul Weiss, Harvard University Press, 1934.

[2] *Collected Papers*, 5.213.

well as the philosophic motivation in making such an appeal to 'rock-bottom' knowledge. In the course of his arguments Peirce attacks 'the myth of the given', 'abstractionism', and the 'appeal to origins' which has conditioned so much of modern epistemology, including varieties of rationalism and empiricism.[1] The conviction that if we are properly to ground our knowledge, if we want to secure it and provide a basis for distinguishing knowledge from opinion, then we must discover the basic foundation on which all our legitimate knowledge rests, a foundation that is known by direct awareness—this motif runs throughout the history of philosophy. We must penetrate through the vagueness and confusion of what is manifest and get down to the solid building blocks of knowledge; we must reach the uninterpreted and unadulterated given and build upon it without error creeping in. Basic knowledge is intuitive knowledge or knowledge by acquaintance. It may turn out—and each of these possibilities have been explored—that the 'given' really consists of particulars, or universals, or essences, or sense data, or atomic facts, or synthetic *a priori* propositions, or even giveness itself.[2] And it has been thought that if we don't find such a foundation, we are condemned to vicious circularity, infinite regress, or a self-defeating scepticism.

Peirce's claim and strategy of argument is at once simple and devastating. He doesn't argue, as others have, that there may be such a foundation, but we do not or can not know it, but rather that the entire quest for such a foundation is misguided. Knowledge neither has nor needs a foundation. Indeed, knowledge would be *impossible* if we take the foundation metaphor seriously.[3] We never break out of our conceptual schemes, or more broadly, our systems of signs and have direct immediate *cognitive* contact with reality.[4]

[1] Each of these quoted expressions is taken from a contemporary philosopher who has criticized essentially the same set of doctrines that Peirce attacks in his critique of intuitionism. The arguments used to attack these doctrines and the alternative view of knowledge and concept formation developed bear a strong resemblance to Peirce's views. On the 'myth of the given', see Wilfrid Sellars, 'Empiricism and the Philosophy of Mind', reprinted in *Science, Perception and Reality*, New York, Humanities Press, 1963. On 'abstractionism', see Peter Geach, *Mental Acts*, New York, Humanities Press, 1957. On the 'appeal to origins', see Karl Popper, 'On the Sources of Knowledge and of Ignorance', reprinted in *Conjectures and Refutations*, New York, Basic Books, 1962.

[2] Cf. Sellars, 'Empiricism and the Philosophy of Mind', *loc. cit.*, p. 127.

[3] For a further discussion of this point, see my article, 'Peirce's Theory of Perception', in *Studies in the Philosophy of Charles Sanders Peirce*, University of Massachusetts Press, 1964, pp. 166 ff.

[4] Peirce does insist that we have brute compulsive encounters with 'reality,'

We do not encounter basic particulars, abstract ideas from these and thereby arrive at general concepts. We could never know anything unless we already brought concepts to bear on what we encounter. Nor do we first have concepts and then somehow put these together to arrive at propositions or judgments. Concepts and judgments are essentially interdependent. In a more contemporary idiom, Peirce's view about the pervasiveness of signification is echoed and illustrated in Wittgenstein's *Philosophical Investigations* where Wittgenstein exposes the metaphysical urge to transcend language and have direct immediate intuitive contact with that which is 'beyond' language. Wittgenstein shows, in multifarious ways, our failure to get beyond, above, or below the forms of life that permeate the complex webs of our language games.[1]

There are no ultimate epistemological building blocks and no ultimate ontological foundations in the sense of an unadulterated given upon which all knowledge rests. Knowledge is achieved and warranted through inquiry, and in the course of critical inquiry everything (although not everything at once) can be subject to critical review. The 'truth' ingredient in the foundation metaphor is that in any specific inquiry some premises, principles, and procedures are *taken* as fixed and given, but there is no intrinsic feature setting off a realm of immutable givens. Even in our perceptual judgments, there is already a hypothetical element. One of Peirce's most suggestive insights is that the logical structure of perceptual judgments is essentially the same as that of scientific hypotheses.[2]

When contemporary philosophers argue that all observation is 'theory laden', and that the line between observation and theory is not clear and distinct, but functional and changing, they are developing themes present in Peirce's attack on Cartesianism. To those who fear that this view of inquiry as a self-corrective process and of knowledge as warranted in inquiry means that we can never be sure that we ever really know anything, Peirce's answer is that they are looking in the wrong place for securing knowledge claims. It is not to be found in the search for origins, but in the evaluation of

but he carefully distinguishes such encounters from direct immediate knowledge. For a further discussion of this point see my article 'Peirce's Theory of Perception'. *loc. cit.*

[1] For an illuminating exploration of the similarities between Wittgenstein and Peirce, see Richard Rorty, 'Pragmatism, Categories and Language', *Philosophical Review*, 70, April 1961.
[2] See 'Abduction and Perceptual Judgments', *Collected Papers*, 5.182 ff.

consequences. Specifically, it is by satisfying the norms of the community of inquirers (norms which themselves can be rationally criticized and modified) that we find the basis for testing and evaluating knowledge claims. Peirce is not disturbed by the fact that any knowledge claim is subject to revision, for he argues that this is an essential characteristic of knowledge, viz. that it has consequences (whether logical or consequences affecting our conduct) that can be critically evaluated. Peirce's positive position is eloquently epitomized by Wilfrid Sellars's own criticism of the picture of knowledge suggested by the foundation metaphor when he writes:

'*Above all*, the picture is misleading because of its static character. One seems forced to choose between the picture of an elephant which rests on a tortoise (what supports the tortoise?) and the picture of a great Hegelian serpent with its tail in its mouth (Where does it begin?). Neither will do. For empirical knowledge, like its sophisticated extension, science, is rational, not because it has a *foundation* but because it is a self-correcting enterprise which can put *any* claim in jeopardy, though not *all* at once.'[1]

And the position that Karl Popper calls 'critical rationalism' shows a strong affinity with Peirce's own critical view of inquiry. In answer to the question, What are the sources of knowledge? Popper tells us that there are all kinds of sources of our knowledge, 'but none has authority'. 'All "sources" are liable to lead us into errors at times.' Instead of the traditional epistemological quest for sources, Popper recommends that we ask, 'How can we hope to detect and eliminate error?' The answer is, 'By criticising the theories or guesses of others and if we can train ourselves to do so—by criticizing our own theories or guesses.'[2] There is no single method for the perpetual task of criticism. All sorts of considerations may be relevant: observations, discoveries, experiments, arguments.

According to Peirce, it is not just the Cartesian appeal to foundations and intuitive knowledge that must be abandoned; we must root out the 'subjectivist turn' implicit in the Cartesian programme. Verification or validation is not a matter of a direct physical or mental 'seeing', or grasping something as clear and distinct. It is a matter of constant public criticism and testing. The only way of minimizing the types of human error that Descartes desperately

---

[1] 'Empiricism and the Philosophy of Mind', *loc. cit.*, p. 170
[2] 'On the Sources of Knowledge and of Ignorance', *loc. cit.*, p. 25.

wanted to avoid is through rigorous, open, mutual, public criticism. Validation is ultimately not a private affair, but is essentially social and intersubjective.

Peirce drove his philosophic wedge even deeper. He attacked the idea central to the Cartesian tradition, that we have 'intuitive self-consciousness'. He accepts the Cartesian dictum 'I know that I (not merely *the* I) exist'. The issue is how do we know this? Does this knowledge require us to postulate a special intuitive faculty? Peirce questions the evidence and arguments which support the notion of 'intuitive self-consciousness'. And he tells us that 'the only argument worth noticing for the existence of an intuitive self-consciousness is this. We are more certain of our own existence than of any other fact; a premiss cannot determine a conclusion to be more certain than it is itself; hence, our own existence cannot have been inferred from any other fact.'[1] Peirce admits the first premise, but the second premise 'is founded on an exploded theory of logic'. While a conclusion based on a single piece of evidence may not be more certain than this evidence, a conclusion based on a wide array of evidence can be more certain than any single fact that supports it. 'To the developed mind of man, his own existence is supported by *every other fact*, and is therefore, incomparably more certain than any one of these facts.'[2]

But if there is no 'intuitive self-consciousness', how do we become aware of ourselves and distinguish ourselves from other persons and things? Peirce's answer, which reflects a strain in Hegel's dialectic of self and other, is that it is by and through our brute encounters that we *achieve* an awareness of ourselves as distinct from other objects. 'We become aware of ourself by becoming aware of the not-self. The waking state is a consciousness of reaction; and as the consciousness *itself* is two-sided, so it has also two varieties; namely action, where our modification of other things is more prominent than their reaction on us, and perception, where their effect on us is overwhelmingly greater than our effect on them.'[3]

Although I have focused on some of the highlights of Peirce's analysis of the nature of inquiry, this general view of inquiry as a self-corrective process which neither has nor requires absolute beginnings or endings, and in which knowledge is an achievement warranted by the norms of inquiry and is subject to constant public criticism has been shared and developed by James and Dewey as

---

[1] *Collected Papers*, 5.237.   [2] *Ibid.*, 5.237.   [3] *Ibid.*, 1.324.

well as by many contemporary philosophers influenced by the pragmatic tradition.

Writing about the theory of inquiry near the end of his philosophic career, Dewey said, 'I tried the experiment of transferring the old well-known figures from the stage of ontology to the stage of inquiry. As a consequence of this transfer, the scene as it presented itself to me was not only more coherent, but indefinitely more instructive and humanly dramatic.'[1] There are many old problems that are thrown into a new perspective with this shift to the stage of inquiry, and there are new problems which make their entrance. The dialectic of philosophy during the past generation has followed a very similar route as that pioneered by Peirce, James, and Dewey. The recent criticism of the misguided epistemology ingredient in early logical positivism and atomism parallels the pragmatic criticism of epistemological atomism. The new emphasis on the role of context for understanding language and knowing, the suspicion of reductivist programmes, the breaking down of sharp dichotomies between observation and theory, analytic and synthetic, thought and action, and the developments of a new theory of concept formation to replace older abstractionist theories of 'concept empiricism', can be viewed as attempts to work out in detail a programme that stands at the centre of the pragmatic tradition.[2]

COMMUNITY

One of the cluster of issues that becomes dominant with the view of inquiry selected above concerns the role of the community. 'The community of inquirers' is central to the characterization of inquiry developed by Peirce. He went so far as to insist that 'the real, then is that which, sooner or later, information and reasoning would finally result in, and which is therefore independent of the vagaries of me and you. Thus, the very origin of the conception of reality shows that this conception essentially involves the notion of a *community*, without definite limits, and capable of a definite increase of knowledge.'[3] While it is frequently recognized that American thinkers have been concerned with the individual and individual-

[1] 'In Defence of the Theory of Inquiry', reprinted in *John Dewey On Experience Nature and Freedom*, ed. Richard J. Bernstein, New York, Liberal Arts Press, 1960, p. 148.

[2] The expression 'concept empiricism' is taken from Sellars. For his criticism of 'concept empiricism', see *Science, Perception and Reality*, pp. 307 ff.

[3] *Collected Papers*, 5.311.

ism, the importance of the 'community' and the 'social' as proper philosophic categories has not been sufficiently appreciated.

Traditionally, at least in philosophy since Descartes, these concepts have been treated in social and political philosophy. But as the above quotation from Peirce suggests, the notion of a community of inquirers is basic to his theory of knowledge, philosophy of mind, and metaphysics. It represents Peirce's alternative to the subjectivist turn that philosophy has taken since Descartes. Roughly speaking, it is the community of inquirers, or more specifically the norms shared by such a community that provides the authority for validating knowledge claims—an authority which others have sought to discover in sources or foundations. Peirce was aware of the danger of the tyranny of the community; consequently he speaks of an ideal community 'without definite limits'—a community committed to its own fallibilism and which shares the norm of constant self-corrective criticism. It is within such a community that the habits and dispositions required for developing the spirit of self-corrective inquiry are cultivated and founded.

The emphasis on a community of inquirers is closely allied with Peirce's theory of signs. Long before the current fascination with language, Peirce argued that signification (which includes more than language) is the core of philosophy, and he developed and continually revised an elaborate theory of signs. According to Peirce, all signification involves an irreducible triadic relation that cannot be built up from monadic or dyadic relations without loss or original significance. 'Now a sign has, as such, three references: first, it is a sign *to* some thought which interprets it; second, it is a sign *for* some object to which in that thought it is equivalent; third, it is a sign, *in* some respect or quality, which brings it into connection with its object.'[1] To appreciate what Peirce is up to, it is helpful first to see what he is opposing. According to the epistemologist who seeks to ground our thought in some 'given', there are basic terms (typically logically proper names) that refer directly to objects in the world. His picture of language is one in which we begin with these basic names and then combine them in determinate ways to arrive at statements or propositions. Naming here is conceived of as essentially a dyadic relation between the sign and its referent. But what this account leaves out (or at least leaves implicit) is that in order for a term to *function* as a name, it must be so *interpreted*. The mere association or conjunction of a term—

[1] *Ibid.*, 5.288.

whether spoken or written—with an object does not make the term a *name* of the object. Before we can know that a particular term is the name of something, we must already know what sort of thing a name is—or better what functions (and they can be diverse) names serve in a language. In Peircian terminology, every name and indeed every sign requires an interpretant; and, speaking of thought-signs, he writes 'there is no exception to the law that every thought-sign is translated or interpreted in a subsequent one'.[1] An excellent illustration of Peirce's point is found in the opening discussion of the *Philosophical Investigations*: Wittgenstein shows us that the view of naming suggested by the passage from Augustine is one in which we already understand a language game of naming objects.

For Peirce, every thought-sign requires a logical interpretant which is itself another thought-sign. If we take this claim seriously then we would seem to be involved in an infinite regress. Peirce is not only aware of this consequence, he insists upon it. But then it would seem that we never complete the process of interpretation, for every sign is open to further interpretation and determination. It is precisely this open or 'vague' character of signs that distinguishes thirds from the sorts of things that Peirce labels seconds and firsts. But while every sign is open to further determination, this does not mean that we must continually postpone our understanding of the meaning of a sign. It means rather that we never exhaust the meaning of a living sign. In *practice* we do come to terminal points, resting-places where there is no need to further interpret signs for the immediate purposes at hand. We can find both confirmation and development of this point in the *Philosophical Investigations*, for Wittgenstein shows us that while there is potentially a language game behind every language game, we *do* come to terminal points in our understanding of the meaning of signs. The point is concisely stated by Richard Rorty when he says that 'the permanent possibility of *practice* is what renders harmless the indefinite horizontal regress of interpretations', and when he notes that both Peirce and Wittgenstein are substituting *practice* in place of the traditional appeal to intuition.[2]

This brief glimpse of Peirce's theory of signs helps us to see that

---

[1] *Ibid.*, 5.284. When Peirce refined his theory of signs he distinguished three types of interpretant: the immediate interpretant, the dynamical interpretant, and the logical interpretant. See Peirce's letters to Lady Welby, reprinted in *Values in a Universe of Chance*, New York, Doubleday Anchor Books, 1958.

[2] 'Pragmatism, Categories and Language', pp. 219 ff.

all signification is essentially dialogic in character. For every sign requires an interpreter, or more technically, an interpretant which is itself a sign.[1] This process can be an internal one. But Peirce tells us that even a person 'is not absolutely an individual. His thoughts are what he is "saying to himself", that is, is saying to the other self that is just coming into life in the flow of time.'[2] There are revolutionary consequences of Peirce's insights when viewed against the background of modern philosophy—a revolution that has been carried out by philosophers working in the analytic and phenomenological traditions. For with the 'subjectivist turn' in modern philosophy there has been a tendency to emphasize the subjectivity and privacy of the individual in giving a philosophical account of thought and language. In the 'beginning' there is extensionless thought, and we are presumably directly aware of our own thoughts. Indeed, we are supposed to be more certain of our own thoughts than of anything else. Thoughts can be expressed in speech acts whereby something that is purely mental is mysteriously transformed into something having physical characteristics. Once we accept this sort of picture, all kinds of problems arise that have plagued modern philosophers. If we are directly aware of our own thoughts, but not the thoughts of others, how can we know other minds or even that there are other minds, and how can we know that there is anything else in addition to our own thoughts? How can we 'escape' from the privacy of ourselves and publicly communicate with others? Peirce's conception of signification and specifically thought-signs challenges this paradigm that lies behind so much of modern epistemology. Signification, we have noted, is essentially triadic, requiring an interpretant for every sign. It is only within a medium of social norms, rules, habits, and interpretation that language and thought can function. The privacy of our own thoughts is an *achievement*, not a *given*, that is logically dependent upon intersubjective communication. The issue is not one of denying privacy or the distinction between thought and overt linguistic performances whether spoken or written, but of properly understanding these concepts. According to Peirce the traditional picture is topsy-turvy, and it is only when we appreciate the essenti-

[1] For a discussion of why Peirce emphasizes the 'interpretant' rather than the 'interpreter', see W. B. Gallie, *Peirce and Pragmatism*, Penguin Books, 1952, pp. 118ff.
[2] *Collected Papers*, 5.421. For a further discussion of Peirce's claim that thought is a form of internal dialogue, see my article 'Action, Conduct, and Self-Control', in *Perspectivse Peirce, on* ed. Richard J. Bernstein, Yale University Press, 1965.

ally social nature of language and thought—a consequence that follows upon a close scrutiny of the signification—that we can escape the dead ends of the 'subjectivist turn' and open up the possibility of a correct understanding of language, thought and even privacy. For Peirce then, the social as a philosophic category does not stand at the periphery of our theory of knowledge and reality, but at its very centre.

In speaking of a community of inquirers or more generally a community of interpreters, it should be obvious that one doesn't simply mean an aggregate of individuals each engaged in his own investigations. It is precisely the shared attitudes, norms, experiences, and the mutual on-going criticism and co-operation that distinguishes such a community from a mere collection of individuals. It is in such a community that the individual can transcend his own private interests and biases and arrive at knowledge that is 'independent of the vagaries of me and you'. Such a notion of a community has important consequences for a variety of other philosophic problems; some of these have been explored by Royce, Mead, and Dewey. Royce sought to blend the notion of an ultimate community of interpreters with idealism in his reinterpretation of Christianity culminating in the beloved community. Mead focused on the dynamics of the social nature of communication. And Dewey sought to relate the idea of a community of inquirers to the practical problems of democracy and education. Dewey realized that the type of community required for, and fostered by, open free inquiry is not morally neutral. It at once presupposes and can cultivate a definite moral perspective. Such a community requires a respect for the reasoned opinions and hypotheses of others, a willingness to submit one's most cherished beliefs to the scrutiny of others, the courage to modify and give up if necessary one's belief in light of new evidence, discoveries, and arguments, a sensitivity to novel situations, and the creative imagination required to formulate new hypotheses and plans of actions.

The key to understanding Dewey's lifelong concern with education is found here. For he was constantly seeking the ways in which the attitudes, experiences, habits, and dispositions required for a free and open community of inquirers could be fostered in the schools. Moreover, it is this spirit of the critical community that is central to a democratic society. The danger that Dewey saw so clearly is that there are tendencies in contemporary technological society undermining this sense of community. So much of the present concern about alienation, impersonality, of treating persons as things was not unfamiliar to him. But he refused to despair. He took this condition as a challenge, for he believed that intelligence could guide action in the reconstruction of social institutions—especially the schools—in order to preserve and further develop a creative democratic society in a technological era. Since Dewey's time, the study of the nature and dynamics of forms of communal life have come into the foreground of the concerns of social scientists and have been almost totally neglected by philosophers. The latter claim must be qualified by recent trends in the study of ethics, where there has been a shift from the attempt to analyse ethical elements and concepts in isolation to the analysis of the social context of moral discourse. Nevertheless, philosophers have become so obsessed with the distinction of the descriptive and the prescriptive that it is commonly assumed that the philosopher's job is to describe the actual 'logic' of our moral discourse, not to prescribe or recommend new courses of action. While it is certainly true that many philosophers, past and present, have confused the description and analysis of moral discourse with normative ethics, Dewey believed that it is a mere dogma or prejudice that the philosopher ought to remain silent on the issue of what *ought* to be done. In this respect, he was arguing for the viability of an ancient ideal in philosophy. An understanding of the moral and social life of man is a necessary condition for any sound or reasonable recommendations, but the proper objective of ethics and social philosophy is *praxis*, i.e. in providing reasonable guidelines for moral and social action.[1]

EXPERIENCE

No topic has been treated more extensively by American philosophers than the complex one of experience. Much of what we have said about inquiry and community is intimately related to a theory of experience. Roughly speaking, the general temper of American philosophy has been empirical in its insistence on the vital role of

---

[1] Dewey's ethics have been misinterpreted by many of his critics because of their failure to appreciate his distinctive emphasis on the moral *agent* choosing and acting rather than on the technical difficulties of the moral critic and judge. For an illuminating characterization and exploration of Dewey's approach to ethics and its relation to other contemporary ethical theories, see Stanley Cavell and Alexander Sesonske, 'Logical Empiricism and Pragmatism', reprinted in *Pragmatic Philosophy*, ed. Amelie Rorty, New York, Doubleday Anchor Books, 1966.

experience in testing and warranting knowledge claims, in the suspicion of any philosophic appeal to a transcendent or transcendental
realm of principles or entities, in its commitment to a naturalistic
view of man and the universe. But at the same time there has been
an on-going attempt to provide a fresh theory of experience. Peirce,
James, and Dewey began with a critique of the variety of views on
experience inherited from traditional rationalism and empiricism.
The atomism, subjectivism, and reductionism ingredient in many
traditional and contemporary positions have been rooted out and
subjected to extensive criticism. The idea that experience 'really'
consists of disjointed bits, whether these are conceived of as sense
data, impressions or empirical intuitions, etc., has been attacked as
a radical distortion of experience.

Although the specific aspects of experience that have been explored by American philosophers display a great variety of concerns
and approaches, there have been common emphases. In the first
place, we find an attempt to correct the exclusively subjectivistic
interpretation of experience which takes experience to be something
essentially private. It is surprising that even philosophers who claim
allegiance to ordinary language still persist in speaking of 'experience' in this way. For the subjectivistic interpretation fails to cap-
ture the meanings of 'experience' when we speak of an 'experienced
craftsman', or of a 'terrifying experience'. The fact that most deeply
impressed American philosophers is that experience can be shared,
that it involves a total situation which does not consist exclusively
of mental events. When, for example, I speak of a terrifying experience, I am not merely referring to some internal events which
have been aroused by what is objectively neutral, but to a concrete
situation with all its complexities and ambiguities. To ask whether
experience is subjective or objective, or private or public is misleading, for these are distinctions that arise *within* experience or
concrete situations. Such distinctions are functional and call attention to changing aspects of experience, not to ontological or
epistemological dualisms. There is a strong affinity between the
conception of experience articulated by Peirce, James, Dewey, and
Whitehead and the notion of the 'phenomenological field' or man's
being as a 'being-in-situation' which is so prominent in continental
philosophy, although many American thinkers would be sceptical
of attempts to erect a new dualism that separates this 'realm' of
experience from the rest of the natural order. And there are also
affinities between this concept of experience developed by the

'classic' American philosophers and the growing sensitivity to the irreducible plurality of contexts, language games and life forms evidenced in recent analytic philosophy. Although logical empiricism and analytic philosophy have heavily influenced contemporary American philosophers, the modifications and criticisms that they have developed of an 'older' style logical positivism and atomism echo the criticisms of an even earlier generation of American philosophers.

A second characteristic of the investigation of experience has been the attempt to rid us of blinders imposed by an excessively epistemological concern with experience. The primary question concerning experience for much of modern philosophy has been what precisely is the role of experience in our knowledge of the world. But here, too, American philosophers have attempted to reveal how much more there is to experience than is indicated by narrow epistemological approaches. For Dewey, this 'discovery' was a major reason for his turning away from Hegel to a closer examination of new developments in biology and the social sciences. He, like James, felt that philosophers (especially Hegel) had exaggerated the role of knowledge in their examination of experience. Experience for Dewey is essentially a transaction of organism-environment; experience involves suffering or undergoing as well as manipulating and acting. There are precognitive or prereflective experiences or situations and inquiry or knowing arises in response to conflicts and felt difficulties within experience. The results of our inquiries can be founded in our experience; the ideal that Dewey advocated is one in which intelligence would constantly inform our experience, making it more coherent, meaningful, and satisfying.[1]

One of the ironies evident in the interpretation of American philosophers is the exaggeration and distortion of the 'practical' character of their philosophies. For what is most striking about the theories of experience developed is the central role of the aesthetic or qualitative dimension of experience. While critical of positions which attempted to isolate aesthetic experience as some special type of experience, they have argued that all experience—including intellectual and practical experience—has an aesthetic dimension which cannot be neglected in an adequate account of experience.

The 'new' understanding of experience that has been developed

[1] For a detailed discussion of the meaning and role of 'experience' in Dewey's philosophy, see my *John Dewey*, New York, Washington Square Press, 1966.

by American philosophers is one in which experience is a situation or context which is neither objective or subjective, mental or physical. James in his radical empiricism sought to develop a notion of pure or neutral experience which would undercut traditional dualisms that had infected the analysis and description of experience. Peirce argued that experience is best analysed in terms of his three categories; there is an immediate qualitative dimension, a brute dyadic compulsiveness, and an element of lawlikeness or generality ingredient in all experience. Dewey sought to apply insights gained from his understanding of biology, especially the concept of organic interaction or transaction, to an understanding of experience. But despite this diversity of approaches and claims, there is a common attempt to develop a less subjectivistic, atomistic, intellectualistic concept of experience which would serve as the basis for a 'new' empiricism.

ACTION

The concept of action and such related concepts as motives, intention, purpose and teleology has recently received a great deal of attention. The reasons for this concern are diverse, although we can single out some of the main currents. In part the analysis of this cluster of concepts has been stimulated by the recent interest in the philosophy of mind, due to an increased awareness of the inadequacies of traditional conceptions of mind and mental events. And it is here—in the analysis of human action—that traditional accounts are most deficient. In part too, the success (or lack of success) of the behavioural sciences has provoked an examination of what if anything is distinctive about human action, and the types of explanation needed to account for human action. There have been philosophers who have argued that a sensitive appreciation of the 'logic' of action concepts reveals that the models of scientific explanation—especially the 'covering law model'—are not applicable to explaining human action. In a spirit reminiscent of Kant, some philosophers have claimed that we need *at least* two different and irreducible perspectives or conceptual schemes for understanding and explaining man—one which approaches man as a natural or complex physical entity differing in complexity only from other physical entities; and one which captures the distinctive role of man as a rule-obeying creature capable of intentional action. But while the analysis of action concepts has been in the foreground of recent analytic philosophy, it has been no less prominent in continental philosophy, especially in phenomenological research. Here too, that emphasis has been on clarifying the distinctive nature of human action as a means for attempting to bracket what is considered to be the distinctive characteristic of men.

If one takes a broader view of the development of philosophy, we can see that the cluster of issues concerning action have dominated philosophic concern since the demise of Hegel. Marx, Kierkegaard, Nietzsche, and Peirce all agree that Hegel fails to do justice to what is distinctive about human action, and each in his own way sought to provide a more adequate account.

American philosophy, especially the pragmatic movement, has always been closely associated with the concept of action. But despite the vigorous protests of American philosophers, many still persist in thinking that pragmatism amounts to little more than the claim that all knowledge is for the sake of action, where action is understood as the achieving of some crude materialistic end. Or, it is claimed that pragmatism can be summed up in some simplistic slogan such as 'something is meaningful if it works', or 'something is true if it works'.

But what then are the essential contributions of the pragmatic movement to our understanding of action and its relation to human experience and knowledge? In the first place, we can see that the theory of inquiry helps to break down such traditional distinctions as theory and practice or knowledge and action. For inquiry is a form of directed, self-controlled activity involving manipulations and experimentation. Hypotheses that emerge in systematic inquiry are 'plans of action' ordering experience and directing us to further testing. Once the shift is made away from thinking of knowledge as some sort of contemplation to knowledge as the end-product of inquiry, then attention is shifted to those *practices* that are necessary for the discovery and validation of knowledge claims.[1]

A second major emphasis is reflected in Dewey's concern with the ideal of intelligent action. He tells us that 'genuine theoretic knowledge penetrates reality more deeply, not because it is opposed to practice, but because a practice that is genuinely free, social, and

[1] For a discussion of how the pragmatic shift of orientation affects the analysis of such basic issues as the distinction of analytic and synthetic statements and the concept of truth see Hilary Putnam, 'The Analytic and the Synthetic'; and Gertrude Ezorsky, 'Truth in Context'. Both of these essays are reprinted in Amelie Rorty's *Pragmatic Philosophy*. This anthology of selections is extremely helpful in *showing* one of the claims that we have been making, *viz.* that pragmatic themes pervade recent philosophic investigations.

intelligent touches things at a deeper level than a practice that is capricious, egoistically centred, sectarian, and bound down to routine.[1] Dewey argued that the separation of theory and practice has the most serious social consequences for us today. And he believed that the challenge to contemporary philosophers is to bridge the growing gap between theory and practice. He argued that the attitudes, methods, and openness of self-corrective scientific inquiry could be extended to the entire range of man's social and moral life. And his concern with education and social philosophy was directed toward the end of finding ways in which intelligent action could be cultivated and encouraged in a democratic society. In a passionate essay, 'The Need for a Recovery of Philosophy', he wrote:

'I believe that philosophy in America will be lost between chewing a historic cud long since reduced to a woody fibre, or an apologetics for lost causes (lost to natural science), or a scholastic, schematic formalism, unless it can somehow bring to consciousness America's own needs and its implicit principle of successful action.

'This need and principle, I am convinced, is the necessity of a deliberate control of policies by the method of intelligence, an intelligence which is not the faculty of intellect honoured in textbooks and neglected elsewhere, but which is the sum-total of impulses, habits, emotions, records, and discoveries which forecast what is desirable and undesirable in future possibilities, and which contrive ingeniously in behalf of imagined good.[2]

Both of the motifs mentioned above—the claim that inquiry itself is a form of directed activity and that the spirit of self-corrective inquiry could be extended to all modes of practice are based on and reflect more fundamental views concerning human action and conduct. According to Peirce, 'Thinking is a kind of action, and reasoning is a kind of deliberate action; and to call an argument illogical, or a proposition false, is a special kind of moral judgment.'[3]

In stressing the normative nature of reasoning Peirce claimed that in all reasoning one finds all the main elements of moral conduct—'the general standard mentally conceived beforehand, the

[1] John Dewey, 'Perception and Organic Action', reprinted in *Philosophy and Civilization*, New York, Minton, Balch & Co., 1931, p. 205.

[2] 'The Need for a Recovery of Philosophy', reprinted in *John Dewey: On Experience, Nature and Freedom*, New York, Liberal Arts Press, 1960, p. 68.

[3] *Collected Papers*, 8.191.

efficient agency in the inward nature, the act, the subsequent comparison of the act with the standard'.[1] One can also add that just as
in moral conduct one finds the criticism of accepted standards of
right conduct so, too, we can subject the norms and patterns of
right reasoning to further criticism. Reasoning itself is an activity
or a form of controlled conduct. And we find here one of the important consequences of Peirce's claim that thirdness is irreducible. For
when we appreciate the distinctive characteristics of reasoning,
especially the way in which it is normative and involves the use and
application of *rules* which are general, we realize the inadequacy of
atomistic or reductivist accounts of reasoning in terms of the regularity of discrete events.

In James and Dewey, too, the concept of action, especially
purposeful, intentional action, is the distinctive characteristic of
man. Dewey asserted that 'in just the degree in which action, behaviour, is made central, the traditional barriers between mind and
body break down and dissolve' and that 'when we take the standpoint of action we may still treat some functions as primarily
physical and others as primarily mental'.[2]

We find echoes of the pragmatic concern with the centrality of
action and activity in recent attempts to sketch the logic of our
action concepts. But I also think that the investigations of the
pragmatic philosophers provide a healthy antidote to some of the
excesses of recent discussions. The new dualism implicit in many
recent discussions of action presupposes a sharp contrast between
'actions' and 'motions', or between 'reasons' and 'causes', or
between the types of explanation employed to account for 'merely'
physical behaviour and human behaviour. But what the pragmatists
emphasized is that one can be sensitive to differences suggested by
these contrasts without introducing ontological or epistemological
dichotomies. And they sought to develop the proper categories by
which one could see human purposeful action as exhibiting distinctive characteristics yet continuous with the rest of nature.

It should be obvious that the four themes we have explored are not
only interconnected but exhibit and reflect a general orientation. In
the exploration of the nature of inquiry, American philosophers
have been responsive to the challenge of science and have sought to

[1] *Ibid.*
[2] John Dewey, 'Body and Mind', reprinted in *Philosophy and Civilization, loc.
cit.*, pp. 302–3.

understand what is distinctive about scientific inquiry and how it might be extended to other areas of inquiry. But they have been critical of any programme of reductive scientism. They have emphasized the 'social' and the 'communal' as philosophic categories which illuminate a whole range of philosophic issues, including the most central metaphysical and epistemological issues, and they have elaborated an alternative to the 'subjectivist turn' that has dominated so much of modern philosophy. They have explored new directions in the understanding of human experience, which are sensitive to the irreducible variety of experience and which contribute to an image of man who is continuous with the rest of nature, but who nevertheless exhibits distinctive characteristics most significantly manifested in purposeful action. And they have advocated an ideal of intelligent action in which man is thought of as neither a plaything of forces beyond his control nor a utopian manipulator of nature; but in which man can meet whatever conflicts, challenges and forms of alienation he encounters, imaginatively conceive of more desirable possibilities, and invent the instrumentalities needed to achieve them.

14

SIGNS, SELVES AND INTERPRETATION

JOHN E. SMITH

Towards the end of the last century and therefore some decades
before the 'linguistic revolution' in philosophy had taken place, C.
S. Peirce was developing his theory of signs and analysing the
process of interpretation through which signs are read or understood. At the same time Royce had taken note of Peirce's essentially
logical analyses of signs and their relations both to their objects and
interpretants, in the hope of extending Peirce's results to include a
theory of the human person and the communities to which he
belongs. There is much that is of relevance for contemporary philosophy in the proposals set forth by both thinkers. Therefore, I shall
develop, under the rubric of 'the theory of interpretation', two basic
themes; *first*, an account of the nature of sign functioning and the
process of interpretation along lines first suggested by Peirce, and
second, the application of the idea of interpretation to the problem
of self-knowledge and the nature of human community along lines
first marked out by Royce. Against this background, I shall further
develop the self-knowledge theme in my own way in the hope of
throwing some light on the important but elusive problem as to the
nature of the self.

I. SIGNS AND INTERPRETATION

Before proceeding to Peirce's theory, it is necessary to avoid a
certain confusion that invariably arises whenever the term 'interpretation' is used. This confusion is due to the fact that the term,
though it can and should be used in a technical sense, has a widely
known ordinary connotation according to which an 'interpretation'
is made to stand in contrast with a 'fact'. We are all familiar, for
example, with situations in which we say, 'We were not provided
with the "facts" of the case; all we received were "interpretations".'
Such a locution clearly implies an opposition between a recital or
description of what is the case—the facts—and some further determination or account of these facts which aims at 'interpreting' them
or saying what they 'mean'. The opposition implied in an ordinary

use of the term 'interpretation' is, to be sure, not without some foundation in experience. If we consider, for example, a witness testifying in a court of law to events at the scene of a crime, he might say, 'I saw the defendant *running* down the street, and I also saw that he was *very angry*.' It would normally be thought that testifying to the running is the report of a fact open to sense perception and we would not ordinarily claim that the witness was giving an 'interpretation' (unless, of course, *any* statement made by anyone is to be called an 'interpretation', in which case the term would have no differential meaning at all).

On the other hand, where the witness says he 'saw that' the defendant was 'very angry' we would normally say that he was interpreting in so far as being angry is not, like the phenomenon of running, something that can obviously be seen, but is rather to be apprehended by interpreting some sign such as a facial expression, a cry, or a gesture. From the standpoint of reciting the facts of the case, the running is just what it is; it is not a sign of something else (although it may be *taken to be* a sign for certain purposes), whereas the facial expression, the cry or the gesture are taken as signs revealing a certain emotion, state of mind or disposition. If the witness merely described the behaviour as he saw it, without 'interpreting', then the assertion about anger would not have been made and a report on the facial expression, the cry, the gesture would constitute exact parallels to the running. The point at this juncture is not to settle once and for all the question of the relation between 'fact' and 'interpretation', but rather to call attention to the confusion resulting from the uncritical contrast between the two implied in ordinary uses of 'interpretation'. Since 'fact' must be put down to objective states of affairs, to what is the case, to what is actually there to be encountered, 'interpretation', taken as the antithesis of fact, will be made to appear as no more than an accretion, a contribution of the mind, stemming from the interests and predilections of the one who interprets. Such a consequence is unfortunate on two counts; first, it identifies interpretation not as the unique cognitive act which it is, but rather as an opinion or conjecture about matter of fact, and second, to oppose interpretation to fact is to obscure the sense in which critical interpretation is based on and is responsive to the facts of the case.[1] In what follows the

---

[1] The foregoing paragraphs presuppose that the term 'interpretation' is *not* to be understood as referring to every activity involving thought, concepts and language, but only to the special activity of reading signs. For even if, as has been

meaning of 'interpretation' as a technical term will be made clear; at the outset, however, it is essential that connotations attached to the term in ordinary use be not allowed to cloud the issues.

In developing what he called 'a new list of categories' Peirce was struck by the peculiarity of a certain type of object which he called a *sign*. In addition to the immediate qualities and the abstract characteristics of things, and also to the network of actions and reactions in which the distinguishable items of the world participate, there is a class of items called signs; it is the peculiar feature of these items that they must be understood through a process to which Peirce gave the name of *interpretation*. Signs have the capacity of pointing beyond themselves—the sign is not its own object except in some special cases where a sign is part of another sign—to something else, but this pointing beyond is only actualized when the sign is read or interpreted by a mind or a sign-using animal. In the realm of signs, *to be* is identical with *to be interpreted*; unless a sign is taken as such and interpreted, it is only potentially a sign.

Peirce offered many characterizations of what it is to be a sign: let us consider several of them. In an article on 'Sign' in Baldwin's *Dictionary*,[1] Peirce defined a sign as 'anything which determines something else (its *interpretant*) to refer to an object to which itself refers (its *object*) in the same way, the interpretant becoming in turn a sign, and so on *ad infinitum*'. We may supplement this rather formal definition with some other passages in which Peirce elucidates the meaning of signs. In a paper on 'Meaning' written in 1910, Peirce writes:

'But in order that anything should be a sign, it must 'represent', as we say, something else, called its *Object*. . . . The sign can only represent the object and tell about it. It cannot furnish acquaintance with or recognition of that object; for that is what is meant in this volume by the object of a sign; namely that with which it presupposes an acquaintance in order to convey some further information concerning it.'

---

maintained, there is an element of 'interpretation' in the most evident cases of perception, we, nevertheless, must not overlook the difference between perceiving and interpreting as represented respectively by the running and the anger in the previous illustration. The running was just seen; there was no reading of signs. The anger, on the other hand, was not seen; the gestures, etc., were seen and taken as signs which were then interpreted as expressions of anger.

[1] Baldwin, James M., ed. *Dictionary of Philosophy and Psychology*, New York, Macmillan, 1901–5; revised edn, 1928, Vol. 2.

The following statement is from an undated manuscript; the passage is important because it brings out the 'realistic' strain in Peirce's theory in its stress on the sign being determined by its object. Peirce writes:

'A sign is a cognizable that, on the one hand, is so determined (i.e. specialized, *bestimmt*) by something *other than itself*, called its object, while on the other hand, it so determines some actual or potential mind, the determination whereof I term the Interpretant created by the sign, that the Interpreting Mind is therein determined mediately by the object.'[1]

From these passages we can derive an understanding of the main features of signs and the situation in which they function. Five features are noteworthy. First, the situation in which signs function always involves a triadic relation with three distinct terms related in a definite way. There is the sign itself, its object and the interpretant (i.e. the reading or interpretation) of the sign which refers to the object in the same way as the original sign. When we consider an actual process of interpretation and not merely the logical structure exhibited in interpretation as such, a fourth term is introduced—the interpreter or the sign-reading agent who performs the task. The interpret*er* or the one who grasps signs as such and attempts to read them, must not be confused with the interpret*ant* which is the interpretation given by the interpreter to the original sign. Some philosophers, operating on behaviourist assumptions, have often silently omitted the interpreter, substituting instead the interpretant which the interpreter proposes as the interpretation of the sign he seeks to read. The fact is, however, that no signs are self-interpreting and the triadic structure of interpretation always presupposes the interpreter in the form of the one to whom the interpretant 'occurs' or by whom the interpretant is proposed.

Second, a sign is always representative in character because it refers to an object other than itself. As representative, the sign does not furnish acquaintance with its object but rather presupposes that the interpreter is already acquainted, if not with the singular object of the sign in question, at least with the type or kind of object involved. If, for example, we say, 'Caesar is dead', the interpreter

---

[1] *Collected Papers of C. S. Peirce*, ed. Charles Hartshorne and Paul Weiss, Vols. I–VI, Cambridge, Harvard University Press, 1931, Vols. VII–VIII, ed. Arthur Burks, 1958, 8.177.

of the sign 'dead' must be able to think this predicate as characterizing an individual person who lived in the past and whose existence
is otherwise known to the interpreter. The sign 'dead' by itself does
not furnish this knowledge. The past experience of the interpreter
and the extent of his acquaintance with things therefore come into
play in every interpretative process.

Third, to be representative, a sign must be determined by its
object, otherwise the referents of signs would exercise no control
whatever over the realm of interpretation. On the other hand, if any
given sign is to receive an interpretant some mind or other must be
determined by that sign to think a certain content about the object
to which the sign refers. The object, therefore, determines the
thought of the interpreter in mediate fashion, and thus exercises
some constraint on the interpreting process. This point is of special
importance for the theory of interpretation because it helps us to
avoid the quite mistaken notion that an interpretation is a mere
superaddition laid over or placed on a set of data as an externally
related meaning content. While no interpretation is a 'copy' of
presented data, it does not follow that these data will play no part
in determining what their correct interpretation should be.

Fourth, implicit in the previous passages is the view that no
theory of interpretation can afford to dispense with an interpreter
or mind. Since it belongs essentially to signs to find interpretants,
an actual or possible interpreter is always required. No sign is its
own interpretant and every sign is addressed to a potential interpreter. Though natural processes may be, so to speak, self-propel-
ling, the process of interpretation considered apart from the interpreter is not. As will become clear, the fact that interpretation
issues in a dialogic process makes it peculiarly apt for throwing
light on self-knowledge and the nature of the self. No sign interprets
itself, but is always addressed to an actual or potential interpreter
capable not only of taking the sign *as* a sign, but also of providing
a possible interpretant. Some relation between interpretation and
a dialogic process now becomes evident. This fact brings us to the
fifth noteworthy feature of Peirce's analysis, namely, the future
orientation of interpretation and its procedure *ad infinitum*.

The interpretant of every sign is itself a sign addressed to an
actual or potential interpreter—the interpreter may be other than
the one who furnishes a given interpretant or it may be the same
interpreter at a subsequent time—and thus the process is, in principle, without a terminus. Of course, the context or purpose deter-

mining any particular process of interpretation may bring that process to an end as, for example, when a course of deliberation ends in a decision followed by an action, or when it is decided that 'for practical purposes' a given analysis can be terminated because it has reached a point of clarity and precision sufficient for those purposes even if, given other purposes, the process would have to continue. The open-ended character of interpretation mirrors, in this feature, the character of conversation between two selves. Such conversation is essentially a reciprocal interpreting of signs; it is also an inner dialogue which everyone of us carries on whenever we are deliberating, working out a critical theory by considering possible objections, proposing modifications and developing arguments, or when we are seeking some understanding of our own selves, our motives, purposes and intentions.

Before attempting to illustrate more fully the five features of signs and their interpretation contained in the passages cited from Peirce, let us summarize the features themselves. They are:

(1) Sign-reading through interpretation always involves triadic relations (and if we consider the interpreter, we introduce a fourth term).

(2) The sign represents its object, but requires that the interpreter be otherwise acquainted with (or have knowledge of) the object.

(3) The sign is determined by its object as is also the interpreter when he supplies the interpretant.

(4) Interpretation presupposes an actual or potential mind.

(5) The process of interpretation is, in principle, without terminus, since every interpretant is a sign addressed to an interpreter.

We may take as a basic illustration of sign functioning and the process of interpretation the situation in which an archaeologist uncovers an inscription which he desires to read. The case is, of course, special but only to the extent that signs in a natural language are involved and the question of 'natural' signs such as smoke, thunder, etc., is not considered. The archaeologist, through his knowledge of ancient languages, is able to identify the inscription as written in hieroglyphics. He now wishes to make the text of this inscription available to someone who reads, say, the English language, but who is unable to read or decipher hieroglyphics. To accomplish his purpose, the archaeologist becomes an interpreter by offering a *translation* of the original inscription in the form of a second set of signs, in this case, the second set will be expressions in English. The second set purports to interpret or to express in English what was expressed in the original inscription cast in hieroglyphics. With regard to (1) the triadic relation exhibited is evident; if the object represented by the signs constituting the Egyptian text was, let us say, the Nile delta, then the interpretants of these signs or the resulting English text would stand related to the Nile delta in exactly the same way as the hieroglyphic signs originally stood to that object. The three terms, sign, object and interpretant, are so related that what the first expresses about the second is identical with what the third expresses about the second.

As soon as the translator discovers the object of the signs before him—the Nile delta—he is able to interpret them accurately only in so far as he is otherwise acquainted with or knows the object in question. Peirce's point here is that the sign does not 'present' but 'represents' its object and in order for the sign to convey information about its object, the interpreter of the sign must be able to apprehend that object as something already known (2). The interpreter does not merely apprehend the sign and produce the interpretant, but he directs his thought to the object and understands it as characterized according to the meaning expressed in the sign that represents it. If the sign is to afford valid representation, it must be determined by its object and the interpreter must be determined in turn by the object when he seeks the proper interpretant. If the element of constraint exercised by the object is omitted, we are led to think of the world as exhausted by sign vehicles and their dictionary equivalents; the objective world disappears. A linguistic idealism results, and it comes to be believed that the interpreter is merely substituting an interpretant for a sign instead of actually thinking the *object* which the original sign represents.

The claim that interpretation presupposes an actual or potential mind raises issues that go far beyond present purposes. It is clear, however, at least in the case of artificial signs as represented by our Egyptian text, that when our archaeologist identifies the text as written in the sacred characters of an ancient civilization, he at once assumes not only that the characters of the text represent the Nile delta, but that the text itself as a set of signs represents an ancient mind or community of minds intending to express a meaning about that delta which he is trying to decipher. He places these signs in a category different from those 'signs' that might have been made by the claws or hoofs of some ancient bird or beast walking over a soft clay surface which later hardened and was preserved. It is not that an interpreter is prevented from seeking the 'meaning' of these latter signs, but he could do no more than search for their *cause*, since the relation of bird or animal to the surface is dyadic in character, a case, in Peirce's terms, of action and reaction, an essentially causal connection. From the reaction or result we infer the action or the cause; the characteristic triad is missing since the signs in question had no *intended* object. There is a claw and the clay surface with its imprint; nothing more. The triad appears, to be sure, when a later interpreter comes upon the scene and seeks to read the sign, but in that case the intended object is *his* intended object, *not* the intended object of the sign. In the case of the hieroglyphic text, however, we ask for the 'meaning' of the signs, referring to the expressions intended by an ancient mind or sign *using* animal.

The need for a mind is even more obvious if we attend to the fact that it belongs to the nature of a sign to be read or interpreted. It is only through interpretation that the being of a sign is realized. This process can be initiated only by someone capable of taking a sign as a sign and of being aware that it requires interpretation. The 'taking as' is an operation characteristic of a mind or sign-using animal. Our archaeologist had first to recognize his text as in fact a set of signs expressing meanings about intended objects; only then could he envisage his task as a translator.

The process of interpretation continues only as long as any sign addressed to an interpreter is actually read and hence is cast into the form of another sign. Unlike perception which terminates in its object, interpretation proceeds *ad infinitum*, since every sign interpreted is a succeeding sign which in turn requires the recursive operation.

As a prelude to considering the bearing of the foregoing account on the nature of the self and of self-knowledge, let us look more closely at the functioning of the interpreter.[1] An interpreter of the sort illustrated above, is essentially a mediator who brings two

---

[1] As previously indicated, the interpreter is the one who interprets; the interpretants are his interpretations. If we attend only to the latter, however, on the ground that 'logical' considerations require no more, we are likely to overlook some of the functions performed by the interpreter as an individual related to other individuals in a concrete situation.

distinct minds into relation. One who interprets is like a person with coins the value of which he knows in the realm where they are legal tender, but who is trying to discover what value, if any, these same coins have in another domain where other coins are legal tender. Each of us must understand those to whom we are related in terms primarily of our own experience. The question is, what of the experience of the other, what is that like as had by the other and how shall I be understood by him in those terms and how shall he be understood by me in my terms? The point is that I do not start out by knowing either the significance of his experience when interpreted through my own or the significance of my own experience when interpreted through his. The point is that a gulf must be crossed which is the gulf of individuation. It is the contention of this paper that that gulf is bridged by the process of interpretation in which we gradually and with effort come to see what the other means in his own terms and also to what extent our own experience is valid in terms of his experience. I am seeking to discover you not merely as I experience you, but as you experience yourself and vice versa, but each of us is forced to discover the other in terms of his own experience.

To return to our illustration, the mind expressed in the signs of the ancient text has now been interpreted or translated into equivalent signs in the English language to be read by an English reader. The interpreter says implicitly to the English reader concerning his translation, 'What I say to you is what the text said to me', and in this way he brings a contemporary mind into a unity of understanding with a mind long passed away. In performing his task the interpreter does much more than correlate or match terms one-to-one. He must find in the language *into which* he translates the appropriate way of expressing what he takes the signs of the language *from which* he translates to mean.[1] He must, that is to say, interpret or put a construction on the original signs and then discover how to express *that* interpretant in the other language. The familiar claim that the translator always offers an 'interpretation'

---

[1] Examples of idiomatic speech bring out the point very nicely. In his *Anthropologie* Kant, discussing the differences in human capacities from person to person uses the idiomatic expression, 'Er hat das Schiesspulver nicht erfunden'. A supposedly literal translation would have to be 'He did not invent gunpowder'. But if we want to know how we would express in English the meaning that is expressed in the German sentence (with, of course, help from the context) we would have to translate, 'He is no genius' or, more colloquially, 'He is no great shakes'. The latter says accurately in the language *into which* we translate, what had been said in the language *from which* we translate.

should be taken to mean that passing from the signs of one language to those of a second is not a process that can be entirely subject to rule; instead it always involves the ingenuity of the interpreter since he has to grasp the meaning of the original signs.

The mediating function of the interpreter lends itself to wide application; interpreters are at work in such diverse contexts as law, diplomacy, political institutions, education, religion and indeed throughout the entire fabric of cultural life. The lawyer represents a plantiff and interprets his case to the court; a diplomat represents a country and interprets its actions and aims to the representatives of other countries; the priest or pastor represents his religious tradition and interprets its meaning to the members of the community. The underlying motive of all interpreting is the creation of communities of understanding in which diverse persons are brought into some form of unity and conflicting claims are made less explosive by being contained within a framework of shared meanings and intelligent discussion.

If interpretation creates communities of understanding between distinct persons, it must be intimately connected not only with interpersonal relations embracing distinct individuals but also with the relations between a person and himself at different times. In short, interpretation is essential for a community of distinct individuals as well as for that peculiar community of relations with ourselves which each one of us represents. Royce was the first one to see this remarkably concrete bearing of Peirce's theory of interpretation. Let us now consider the light which it throws on the nature of the self and self-knowledge.

II. INTERPRETATION, THE SELF AND SELF-KNOWLEDGE

Royce proposed to extend Peirce's theory of interpretation at two basic points. The one is actually a prelude to the other. First, he argued that interpretation is a distinct and irreducible activity not to be confused with either perceiving or conceiving taken as distinguishable modes of apprehension. Second, Royce held that interpretation is especially suited for understanding certain objects which cannot be identified with either of the objects generally thought to be apprehended respectively by perceiving and conceiving. What Royce had in mind is obvious enough; the individual person and a community of persons represent 'objects' neither of which can be uniquely identified as singular matters of fact, such as particular instances of qualities like 'blue' or 'long' which can be perceived or, again, as objects of conceptual thought such as 'prime number' or 'frictionless system' which are never the object of any perception. Royce's insight may be recast as follows: where two distinct persons confront or encounter each other, neither person is for the other an object of the same sort as a particular instance of a perceptible quality or as something to be apprehended by conceptual thought alone. A person does not fit into either of these categories nor does a community of persons, because both are time-spanning or enduring organic unities peculiar in that they are unified by a *centre of intention* expressing itself through what can be perceived and conceived, without either unity being identical in type with the characteristic objects of either form of apprehension. Royce, therefore, proposed the novel idea that both individual persons and communities of persons are the appropriate objects of *interpretation* which, though dependent upon both perceiving and conceiving, is identical with neither because, through the medium of signs, interpretation reaches back into the centre of intention which is the core of both persons and communities.

The uniqueness of interpretation *vis-à-vis* other activities characteristic of a rational being is best seen in the singular fact that a person confronted by a sign can both perceive it as an object or thing in the world, and also describe it in terms of well-defined recurrent characters without being able to read or interpret it. To take a simple illustration—more complex and subtle examples occur in the domain of human speech, gestures and actions—a person may encounter a metal weather vane on the roof of a barn, he may perceive it through direct encounter and note the position of the arrow in relation to certain metal figures shaped to represent letters of the English alphabet, he may also set out to describe the geometric shape and content of the object before him, all without taking the object as a *sign* and therefore without reading its meaning. Nor will either increasing the accuracy of his perception with instruments or introducing more precise concepts for description alter the situation; a sign is not merely an object among other objects, but rather a representative device whose meaning must be interpreted.[1] The process of interpreting is not identical with that of

---

[1] If it is said that the sign vehicle can be perceived as an object among other objects, the point may be admitted, but then the sign cannot function as a sign until it is *taken as* a sign and interpreted. If I cannot read Arabic, being con-

correlating concepts with percepts in accordance with procedures of empirical verification in which the sensible fact is said to be the 'cash value' of the concept. The point can be illustrated with clarity in a familiar human situation. Consider a person who, like the Biblical Job, has been the victim of an almost uninterrupted series of disasters. His wife has died, his sons have been killed in battle, and he discovers that he himself has a dread disease. In despair, he cries, 'Life is not worth living!' Such an utterance is not a description of his situation nor is the utterance deducible from a description, since another person facing the same tragedies might give them an opposite interpretation. Still less is it an explanation of how the disastrous facts came to be. The exclamation is instead an *interpretation* aimed at reading the meaning of these facts. The victim sees the events as signs to which a meaning can be assigned. This meaning is intended as the import of the facts, but is neither a description nor an explanation of them.

To return to Royce's analysis, we must make clear the main purpose behind his having made a special point of distinguishing interpretation from both conception and perception. In his efforts to arrive at a theory of the self and of self-knowledge, Royce was led to reject the two antithetical approaches to the problem which seem to have been taken for granted since the period of Enlightenment. The empiricists, on the one hand, sought, like Hume, to apprehend the self through some form of perception, while rationalists like Descartes or Leibniz on the other, appealed to intellectual intuition. Royce's claim is that neither in my own case, nor in that of my neighbour can it be true that the self is identical with a singular perceptual datum or with some abstract character such as that of individuality or personality. He was proposing to abandon both the rationalists' thinking substance and the empiricists' series of passing states possessing the tenuous unity of memory in favour of a new alternative. Suppose the self were the sort of reality to be known and experienced as the appropriate object of interpretation —each person confronts another as a *centre of intention* expressing him or herself through the medium of signs, among which are included not only words, exclamations and gestures, but also actions and abstentions, and even the body itself. In every encounter, every

---

fronted with a page from the *Koran* printed in the original language, I can perceive a series of characters written in straight lines across the page, but for me they will *not* function as signs, since I cannot read them, even if I am able to recognize the characters as belonging to the Arabic alphabet.

conversation, the participant selves are *directly* present to each other, but no one of us knows the centre of intention of the other in an *immediate* way, i.e. without the reading of signs. Each of us is directly presented in the signs through which we express ourselves, but we are not identical with these signs, since they point beyond themselves back to the core self which is the centre of intention. So convinced was Royce of the necessity for interpretation in all self-knowledge and understanding that he was even prepared to identify the self *as* an interpretation; for him the enduring identity of the self in time is the success with which the present self interprets the past self to the future self.[1] Here I part company with Royce and shall develop the theme of selfhood and interpretation in my own way. I find much that Royce wrote on the topic illuminating and I agree both with his doctrine that the self as such is no simple datum among others, and with his equally emphatic rejection of all attempts (for example, that of William James) to understand the self solely in terms of relations holding between passing thoughts. But I do not believe, as Royce did, that we can legitimately regard the self as identical with an interpretation because the self as centre of interpretation is required as the interpret*er*. In my view, the self is experienced and known through interpretation, but it is not itself an interpretation. Such an identification would be at once too idealistic and rationalistic in its import. The self is, as I shall suggest, more than a mind; it is a dynamic, organic system of habits, feelings, desires, tendencies and thoughts, unified through plans and purposes framed and projected by what I call a centre of intention. This centre expresses itself through the instrumentality of the body where it is localized for the other person. When another seeks to understand or interpret me, it is my centre which is his target.

Let us consider more closely what happens when two persons engage in discussion, have an interview or hold a dialogue of some sort. We may omit for the present, the philosophers' problem of the existence of other minds—the argument from analogy and all that, in order to look at the situation as we find it. You and I confront each other primarily as living bodies in and through which meanings purposes, intentions, are being expressed. Each of us, therefore, is

---

[1] A clear, but simple, model of the process is found in the fulfilling of a promise. A promise made belongs necessarily to the past self; when the time of fulfilment approaches, the then present self recalls the commitment and inter-prets that past to the future self who is to realize the deed specified in the initial promise.

for the other as a series of signs, words, gestures, facial expressions and, over extended periods of time, deeds and actions, which need to be interpreted. These signs, however, do not appear either as isolated phenomena or as self-sufficient in their own right. As soon, for example, as you say something to me—ask a critical question, contradict what I have just said, propose an alternative view—I find myself supposing that that particular sign or set of signs is expressive of or proceeds from some more complex and fundamental intention. I think of you as 'aiming' or 'driving at' some goal of thought which is not fully expressed in any single expression. I think of you, moreover, not only as having a purposive centre of intention which is not exhausted in the signs you express on any one occasion, but also as a being capable of projecting a purpose or plan which extends to the unity of an entire life. I *presuppose* this unity of aim in your expressions and I attempt to apprehend it through these expressions themselves. It is, in fact, precisely because I presuppose this unity of aim on your part that I take your expressions as signs to be interpreted. I do not begin the other way around, starting with these expressions as *evidence for* the existence of yourself and your mind. In that case, I would be attempting to *explain* your being as an object or phenomenon rather than to *understand* you as a person. Without presupposing the unity of your aim—whether well or ill expressed—I would never have taken your expressions as signs to be interpreted in the first place. In personal encounter, each of us endeavors to apprehend the centre of intention presupposed in the other. The only access we have to that centre is through signs (this is true as well of the internal dialogues we carry on with ourselves in order to clarify our ideas, discover our interests, form plans, etc.), but the signs express that centre; they are not identical with it.

The process of interpreting in which we jointly engage represents an endeavour to bring about a community of understanding, not in the sense that the participants agree at every point in their opinions, evaluations, etc., but rather in the aim of coming to a common understanding of what each of us is saying. Notice, again, that interpretation differs from some related rational processes in which we also engage. When, for example, I seek to interpret what you say and to grasp what you are trying to express in actual conversation and encounter, I am neither *describing* your person, nor *explaining* your behaviour. Were I describing you as a person, I would be considering you not as a subject communicating yourself but rather as an object or the referent of sets of descriptive predicates. I might under such circumstances, record your words and depict your gestures, but I would not be engaged primarily in interpreting both words and gestures in order to penetrate your aim and centre of intention. On the other hand, were I attempting to explain your present state, I would once again be viewing you as an object and seeking to give a causal account of how you came to be what you are, your present constitution, physical, psychological, social, moral, etc. Again, in confronting you with this purpose in view, I would not be seeking to interpret what you say to me as an individual, autonomous subject; on the contrary, I would be viewing you as a 'case', a patient, an instance of a set of general laws said to exercise control over all human behaviour. But in interpreting, where I take your signs as expressive of a more or less clearly focused aim, I am meeting you as a subject, a person, I am seeking to discover what you mean to say and to penetrate your centre of intention. We encounter each other as two subjects seeking to create between us a community of understanding.

Consider as an instructive example, the following concrete encounter between two persons well known in imaginative literature. Hamlet[1] says to Ophelia, 'I never loved you', and Ophelia, both stunned and puzzled, says, 'But, my Lord, you made me believe so.' We have here a complex encounter and one that is by no means confined to the immediate occasion of the conversation. Each party has in mind a series of past deeds and encounters, gestures, conversations and indeed past interpretations. Each puts an interpretation on that past, an interpretation which is an attempt to sum up or express a unity of purpose and intention defining a single self. Hamlet is now prepared to interpret his past behaviour and to claim that whatever that behaviour appeared to express when it was manifest and whatever interpretation Ophelia put on it, he never was in love with her. Hamlet here assumes the role of interpreter with respect to his own signs; he seeks to say what his past behaviour meant from the standpoint of his present centre of intention. Ophelia, on the other hand, places a different construction on what was, at least in principle, the same set of signs. She not only interpreted Hamlet's behaviour—words and deeds—as meaning that he loved her but also hints at a specific intention on his part to lead her to make the very interpretation at which she did in fact arrive. Ophelia views Hamlet's behaviour, and Hamlet views his own behaviour as

[1] I am paraphrasing in order to simplify the situation.

the expression of an enduring centre of intention; the problem for both is to discover the proper interpretation of the signs through which that centre expresses itself or is made manifest. Ophelia does not confront Hamlet's behaviour merely as a collection of disparate acts, but rather as having the unity of import and purpose characteristic of an enduring self. This unity is neither a substance to be apprehended in intellectual intuition nor Hume's celebrated bundle of perceptions, nor again is it a series of passing thoughts somehow associated with a body. The self is an organic unity enduring in time; it is a togetherness of a *one*—the centre of intention—and a *many* in the form of the multitude of acts, thoughts, events which mark out the unique temporal history or career which for ever identifies not only the Hamlets and Ophelias of the world, but every human person.

The curious fact is that we often understand the many or the detail of the self more clearly than the unity or centre of intention, and yet that detail does not introduce us to the unique individual when it is taken apart from the centre of intention which it expresses. The contents of our lives, the places we visit, the persons we encounter, the music we listen to, the triumphs we enjoy and the tragedies we endure, are events with repeatable structures and when viewed as objective happenings they may be described and explained in generic terms as if they belonged to or expressed either nobody or 'anybody', which is the same. But just as the self is not a bare unity or centre of intention apart from the events in and through which it expresses itself, it is also not a mere collection of detail. The detail as the expression of my centre is what gives individuality and uniqueness to my history. The events of my life may be taken objectively as instances of general kinds, but my centre of intention is individual and unique, not to be taken as an instance.

The self in its concreteness, however, is not to be identified either with the one or the many, but with the togetherness of the two. Since the self is a living creature, that togetherness cannot be understood as a static affair; instead it must be a *unifying* which means a constant re-creating of identity in the course of change and development.

What sort of reality can this unifying be and how is it to be understood? Royce's suggestion of a *purpose* is right to the point. The dominant purpose that guides us fulfils the conditions for unifying. What makes us one person in the course or history of our lives is the overarching purpose through which we organize and harmonize the lesser desires, purposes and drives that constitute our life. When we grasp that purpose we grasp what enables us to endure as a unity. And when we seek to understand another, that purpose is our target; we must interpret all the signs expressive of the person in relation to that purpose in so far as we are able to apprehend it.

Interpreting and understanding each other is a difficult affair, not least because of our failures in interpreting ourselves. Contrary to widespread belief, it is not true that we are all in possession of clear interpretations of our own selves and suffer only from lack of insight into the selves of our neighbours. More often than not the situation is precisely the opposite. The measure of distance and objectivity we enjoy in interpreting the signs or behaviour of our neighbour cannot exist in our own case, because the interpreter and the one to be interpreted are one and the same. Hamlet's interpretation of himself has the marks of an *ad hoc* reading of the signs, a reading designed to suit present purposes, whereas Ophelia's interpretation is meant to be based on a slowly and steadily built insight into a fairly stable intention manifesting itself over a period of time.

In the end the great difficulty we encounter in attaining understanding both of ourselves and of others must lead to an acknowledgement that interpreting is as much an art as a science. For interpretation is always a creative and therefore risky enterprise. We must pass beyond ourselves and the problematics of our own experience to the interiority of another. Such an effort will involve us in a greater possibility of error than we are likely to encounter when we deal with another self in terms of description and explanation. And yet interpretation is the only instrument we have for moving from the signs we do encounter to the centre of intention which we never encounter as we encounter the signs that express it. And yet without grasping that centre we are not in communication or community with the other. Every venture in human understanding is an adventure whether we move outwards to apprehend the other or inwards to understand ourselves. Patience, tolerance and love—virtues often in short supply—are required for success, and no doubt this is why finding a truly understanding person is as precious as it is rare.

15

IS THE REAL RATIONAL?

ERROL E. HARRIS

I

In the climate of philosophical thought that has until recently
prevailed, to raise a question reminiscent of Hegel has been more or
less automatically to raise eyebrows—but it is not my intention, in
in this paper, to discuss Hegel's famous dictum: 'The real is the
rational and the rational is the real', though what I have to say may
have some bearing upon its proper interpretation. My concern is to
consider a question much more topical and much more closely
involved in contemporary scientific theory and empiricist philosophy. Not only the Hegelian overtones of the question, however,
but the very language in which it is couched is liable to upset some
modern philosophers: for what on earth can one mean by asking
whether the real is rational? 'The real' is a phrase that smacks of
hypostatization. 'Real' is a word useful and understandable enough
as an adjective, but can its use as a noun be anything other than
misuse at worst, and honorific at best? One might escape this criticism by saying that one means only 'everything that is'—the
universe at large; but would that improve matters materially? In
what sense can the universe be called rational or the reverse? It is
difficult enough to say what one means by rationality as attributed
to man, but when attributed to the universe the term smacks of
intolerable anthropomorphism and seems to entail some notion of a
world-soul such as the Ancients believed in. That is hardly a
plausible hypothesis in this day and age.

I shall not, however, enter into any lengthy semantical discussion; I shall simply use the short way with scruples of this kind by
giving more or less stipulative definitions of my terms. By 'the real'
I shall mean, as suggested, whatever there is—the sum-total of
things—and by 'rational' I shall understand whatever is systematic and orderly, coherent, and unified. As applied to man this
will mean that his thinking and action is orderly and systematic,
self-consistent and comformable to a unified plan (or, if you will, to
rules which are mutually compatible and coherent). As applied to
inanimate things it will mean they are structured and mutually

related according to principles which make them intelligible by such systematic thought.

The question now, I think, becomes tolerably clear. It asks if the world, the universe as a whole, all things that are, constitute a structured system such as is intelligible by orderly, coherent and self-consistent thinking, or if it is not.

II

I have maintained elsewhere[1] that science in general and physics in particular give evidence of the essential and intimate connection of diverse facts. In support of this contention I have quoted Sir Arthur Eddington's claim to 'make vivid the wide interrelatedness of things'. One of my critics has complained that I rely too much on Eddington's interpretation of physical theory, saying that other physicists believe that the empirical evidence is consistent with a universe of disconnected and random occurrences, which appear orderly and connected to us only because we impose upon them our own structural framework. If he is right, though man and his science may be rational, the real need not be; so the question I shall ultimately discuss is whether this position can consistently be maintained, or if we can reasonably consider our science as discovering the way things actually are.

That Eddington's position is not peculiar among modern physicists of note is apparent from the facts that Einstein, Lemaître, Gamow and E. A. Milne, along with some others, adduce strong evidence in support of the unity of the universe. And D. W. Sciama has written a most illuminating little book with that title arguing from a view of the physical world very different from Eddington's to essentially the same conclusion. Now, unity may seem a fairly harmless character to attribute to the universe; for, being the sum-total of all there is, there could hardly be two of the same ilk; but more is intended. Its alleged unity is not just its uniqueness, but its wholeness or the thorough-going interdependence of its parts and processes. What is being alleged is an integrated structure—a comprehensive systematic interrelatedness of things. If we find this to be the general character of the world we may, on the definition suggested, regard it as rational, so that this is the central point at issue.

Let me briefly review the evidence for this kind of over-all unity

[1] *The Foundations of Metaphysics in Science*, Allen & Unwin, London, 1965.

as given by the scientists mentioned. Eddington, by mathematical calculations based on a minimum of empirical assumptions, showed that the curvature of space determined the number of particles in the universe, that there was an essential connection between the forces acting within the atomic nucleus and that which governed the recession of the galaxies, and that the cosmic number is mathematically related to the masses of, and attractive forces between, the proton and the electrons in the atom. But Eddington was not alone in demonstrating this kind of unity. E. A. Milne similarly deduced, more or less *a priori*, that laws of motion, both Newton's and Einstein's, were deducible from the conditions of observation necessary to make then invariant for all observers, and that consequently the movements of all bodies were dependent ultimately on the total influence upon them of the rest of the universe. (For these laws of motion are equally dependent on the distribution and disposition of matter.) From these facts, again, he deduced Maxwell's equations as well as the velocity of light.

Nor were these theorists the first to think on these lines. Ernst Mach propounded the view (known as Mach's Principle) that inertial and Coriolis forces are the result of gravitational attraction upon terrestrial bodies of the fixed stars, or more generally, to interaction with all the matter in the universe. The theory has more recently been taken up by Sciama, who envisages the aim of cosmology as the production of a theory which is able to account in detail for the contents of the universe. To do this completely, he says, 'it should imply that the universe contains no accidental features whatsoever'. The unity of the universe, he contends, is the consequence of 'appreciable forces' acting between widely separated bodies. 'We can hope to understand any part of the universe . . . only by taking account of the whole universe.' The most important manifestation of this influence of the universe as a whole is the inertia of matter, which he holds to be 'a direct influence of the gravitational forces exerted by the fixed stars'. Another example of widespread interdependence is that the amount of light detectable in the night sky in conjunction with the gravitational constant gives a measure of the average density of matter in the universe.

But these examples, telling as they are, are relatively superficial evidences of the interrelatedness of things. The Special and General Theories of Relativity have knit the physical facts of the world into a single continuous whole. Measurements of space and of time have become inseparable; space-time is regarded as a single continuum constituting what physicists call the metrical field. Its geometrical characteristics (or curvature) are determined by, or more strictly are manifestations of, the presence of gravitational and electrical fields, of energy and of matter, all of which are mutually interdependent, matter and energy being mathematically linked by Einstein's famous equation $e = mc^2$. According to the Quantum Theory matter and energy overlap in other ways as well. Both behave sometimes as wave motions, sometimes as particles, each of which can be interpreted in terms of the other—electromagnetic waves as photons, particles as wave packets, and standing-waves as electronic orbits. Ultimately, the whole four-dimensional manifold curves round upon itself to form a single, unbroken, expanding hypersphere which is the physical universe, a closed and unitary system.

The great consensus of contemporary physical theory, therefore, seems to point to the coherence and systematic character of the universe, even if there are some physicists who interpret matters otherwise. To possible contrary views I shall return later, but at this stage we can justifiably maintain that the bulk of contemporary physical theory seems to support the idea that the real is rational in the sense suggested.[1]

But there is another way even more important for my thesis in which modern science seems to testify to the unity and interdependence of things. The physical world of which I have been speaking is only the basis of a continuous series of developing complexes which goes far beyond physics. Waves of radiant energy are, as we have noted, continuous with matter and wave packets constitute particles which combine in special ways to form the atoms of the various chemical elements. The composition of the atomic nucleus determines the nature of the electronic shells that surround it. These again determine the chemical properties of the atom and the structure of the molecules in which it becomes a constituent. The structure of molecules is the determining factor in the lattice, or 'leptocosm' of crystalline forms and crystals of highly complicated organic molecules are the constituents of living matter. Biologists have pointed out that some special sorts of crystalline (or paracrystalline) forms, known as 'smectic' and 'nematic' liquid crystals have characteristics very similar to protoplasm and that some of the

---

[1] It should be obvious from the examples cited that the sense suggested does not imply the possibility of deducing every detail *a priori* from one (or a few) self-evident axioms, but only a systematic coherence of parts and elements.

constituents of living matter are such liquid crystals. Furthermore viruses are thought to be crystalline in structure, though of a highly complex kind, and genes, the units of more complex living systems, are said to be like them. Beyond these again, Schrödinger has suggested that the chromosome is an aperiodic crystal, one whose pattern is not repetitive but is related to a periodic crystal as a tapestry is related to a conventionally designed wallpaper. There is thus a continuous series of material forms, each a more complexly organized structure than its predecessor, yet dependent on its predecessors for its structure and complexity, ranging all the way from radiant energy to living matter.

In all these examples the structural features appear prima facie to be static or spatial merely, but in actual fact they are throughout dynamic and spatio-temporal. At the level of life this becomes its dominant character. The living cell is a system of constantly active chemical cycles, and the organisms which develop from it are each of them immensely complex dynamic systems. They evolve and develop from the single cell to compound and integrated organisms of vast elaboration.

However irregular, indirect and vaccillating the process of evolution may have been there is no disagreement among biologists that it has been continuous. Whatever its 'mechanism', it has led from the emergence of life from non-living matter up to the eventual appearance of mammals and human beings upon the earth's surface. Somewhere, at some stage, in the course of this development, the organism has reached a degree of complexity and intensity of integration at which its activity has become a felt or experienced process and at this point something has occurred which goes beyond physics and perhaps even biology. Mere activity or reaction (in the chemical sense) is transformed into behaviour. That implies sentience and sentience is the starting-point of mental development which, as it proceeds, issues in perception, imagination, memory and intelligence.

The point I wish to stress is the *continuity* of this scale of development from the physical to the biological and psychological. It is a single continuum. No breaks are evident in it. No modern scientist would wish to postulate any act of special creation to account for any level or phase. Once again, in this continuity we find evidence of unity, and a unity regulated and ordered throughout, both in the internal structure of its parts and phases and in the temporal relation of successive stages. There is far more that could be said (and has been said elsewhere) to reinforce and to elaborate this insistent fact about our world, the unity of which is the progressive discovery, as well the constant quest of the scientific endeavour.

Professor Gerald Feinberg, in a highly illuminating article in the *Journal of Philosophy*,[1] has emphasized that the search for unity has been persistent among physicists (at least) throughout the history of science and may well end in the discovery that the world is so organized and regulated that only one set of laws and only one distribution of matter is possible—those of the world in which we live. Whether this be so or not, it seems safe to say that science at the present day offers a mass of evidence favouring the unity, organization and systematic coherence of the universe at large. If it is right, the real may justifiably be described as rational.

III

But now the crucial question must be raised: How far can we assume that what science tells us is indeed evidence of the actual nature of things? Doubts have been raised both by scientists and philosophers which cannot be ignored. Some scientists are apt to say that our theories are only models by which we try to understand the phenomena and they are models of our own making. They may not at all correspond to the reality despite the best we can do. They are the products of our thinking and may well be more determined by the nature of our minds than by the subject-matter that they seek to make intelligible. Science, therefore, may be only the kind of structure we impose on our experience in our effort to rationalize it and may, in Kant's language, have no legitimate application to things in themselves.

Other scientists will offer similar objections based on less speculative considerations. Modern Physics, they will say, reveals an ultimate indeterminacy and incomprehensibleness in things. The ultimate causal laws that determine the motions of elementary particles are in principle undiscoverable—in fact, it would be more correct to say that there are no such laws. All that we can do is calculate the probability of the behaviour of these ultimate entities and all our knowledge is but statistical. This probabilistic character of quantum physics infects, through physics, the whole of science. The fundamental reality so far as we have any indication of its nature seems to be wholly random and unaccountable in its acti-

[1] 'Physics and the Thales Problem', *J. of Phil.*, LXIII, 1, Jan. 1966.

vity—witness the behaviour of an atom in a radio-active substance. You may say with confidence that at some time within a calculable period it will disintegrate, but just when, or why, why this atom and not the next, what special cause or stimulus will set it off—these questions are simply—and in principle—unanswerable. Though there is thus in the final analysis no rational character in the behaviour of the fundamental micro-entities of the world, the vast numbers of random movements involved allow of an averaging and an appearance of uniformity and regularity in macro-events, which enable us to formulate general laws and make predictions reliable for all practical purposes. But these are at best approximations and are useful to us in the conduct of our lives, giving us a measure of control over our environment; but they are not evidence of any ultimate or intrinsic rationality in the nature of things.

On grounds such as these, some contemporary philosophers of science return to a position reminiscent of, but not identical with, that of Kant. They tend to say that the real is a disordered, disconnected, congeries of unpredictable atomic events, involving a vast number of unrelated atomic entities. But that in our endeavour to understand what is going on around us, we impose upon our experience of these events, an orderly structure, a linguistic or logical framework, which reflects not their character, but that of our own minds. Our theories are constructed to satisfy our own intellectual demands and do not reflect the nature of the reality they claim to render intelligible.

IV

E. M. MacKinnon has attributed this kind of theory to a group of modern philosophers who develop a late position of Carnap's and represent one form of the contemporary return from positivism to metaphysics.[1] The original positivistic doctrine was that the only legitimate, sensible statements about the world were those made in an object language the bound variables of which stood for particulars directly sensed or ostensively defined. Syntactical metalanguages could then be constructed in hierarchy and used to analyse the object language and one another. This meta-linguistic study was the province of philosophy and any statements about the world were relegated to the natural sciences extrinsic to philosophy. Latterly this position was modified to weaken the demand for verifiability of statements in the object-language, replacing it by one for confirmability, and to shift the application of the definition of meaning from propositions to systems of propositions. The phenomenalism of the earlier positivism was replaced by physicalism, but the question whether the 'physical thing' was the basic real was regarded as a question external to the semantic and syntactic inquiry and was relegated to natural science.

There followed Quine's attack on the dogmas of empiricism and his assertion that what is regarded as ultimately real depends upon the ontological commitments of the language used; and this again depends largely on pragmatic considerations, as the function of the language is that of synthesizing and organizing the manifold of direct experience. A strong preference is retained for nominalism and the admission of only atomic particulars as ultimately real, but some tolerance is shown for the existence of abstract entities and classes, so far as this proves useful and convenient for the development of methematics.

Everything, so far, has been made to depend on the range of the variables in existentially quantified propositions, which Quine takes to be the canonical norm. Wilfrid Sellars, however, has argued that no ontological commitment is involved in existentially quantified formulae: 'there is no *general* correspondence', he writes, 'between *existentially quantified formulae* and *existence statements*'.[1] The upshot of his argument appears to be, in MacKinnon's words, that 'Within a given system the provisional existential commitments are contained in statements of the form (Ex) (Nx) where "N" is a common noun and the bound variable ranges over the names of objects that are instances of this common noun'; and only common nouns stand for categories of entities.

Ordinary language, taken as a system of this sort is then regarded as a kind of naïve realistic theory of the world, what corresponds to, or in Sellar's view is, what he calls the 'manifest image' of man-in-the-world. But in this common-sense 'theory' there is nothing given as an irreducible datum—there are no ostensive propositions. All the predicates attached to the names of entities taken as real derive their meanings from the rules of the language and are not given by the entities through sensation nor derived from them by abstraction. All epistemological reductionism is barred. It involves what Sellars calls 'the myth of the given'.

The older positivism regarded ostensively defined entities as

[1] *Science, Perception and Reality*, Ch. 8, p. 225.

basic and the theoretical entities of scientific theories as logical constructs. But in the newer theories the scientific language is alternative to ordinary language. It is simply a different language game. Each functions as a theory of the world, one giving the 'manifest' image, the other the scientific. And they can be related hierarchically as different explanatory levels. The common-sense view is methodologically prior, but not necessarily prior in any other way. So that if science is accepted as the explanation of common sense, its postulated entities, or the ontological commitments of the scientific language, may be accepted. Consequently, Sellars is prepared to say, 'as a philosopher', that the manifest view of the world is only appearance and that common-sense objects do not really exist.

What, then, does really exist? According to Bernstein,[1] Sellars merely denies that one is irrevocably committed to belief in the existence of entities implied by the structure of any one language. Correspondence rules can be formulated which make the substitution of one linguistic system (e.g. the scientific) for another (e.g. common sense) feasible. Therefore, if we have good reason for adopting any system we have equally good reason for accepting its ontological commitments.

Now, this could be interpreted in either of two ways: (1) sceptically, to mean that there is no better reason to accept one language system than to accept any other. In which case our knowledge would be simply a conceptual scheme imposed somehow on raw experience and its relation to reality would be unspecifiable. The real would be an unattainable *Ding-an-sich*, about which we could say nothing as to its structure or lack of it. Language would be the measure of all things, of that which is that it is and of that which is not that it is not. But Bernstein tells us that Sellars rejects conceptual relativism of this kind. (2) The second way of interpreting the statement is that there is eminently good reason for preferring the scientific account to the common-sensical, though it is not the final account, nor that which, as science advances, may be given in future.

With this position I am strongly in sympathy. But what is the eminently good reason for preferring the scientific picture? If it is that it is the most complete and coherent account of man-in-the-universe that we can attain (i.e. the best possible explanation of our

[1] 'Sellars' Vision of Man-in-the-Universe', *Review of Metaphysics*, Vol. XX, 1 and 2, 1966–7, p. 289.

experience), well and good; but then it should follow, as I shall try to show hereafter, that the scientific view of the world, as a unitary structured system, is true of the real—the real would be rational. But if it is because scientific theory leads us back to a reality of atomic and unrelated facts (a random chaos of events rendered orderly in appearance only by the statistical techniques of a calculus of probabilities) the situation is quite different. While Sellars sometimes appears to favour the former position, there are isolated passages in his writings which suggest to the latter.[1] And the latter is a reversion to positivism on the one hand with its physicalistic associations, and, on the other hand, the quasi-Kantian view that, whatever the real world may be, or may be like, is inaccessible to our knowledge, that our experience consists ultimately of a string of particular sense deliverances which we reduce to order by imposing upon it a conceptual scheme, a language system, or a hierarchy of such schemes each functioning as 'explanatory' of the one immediately prior in the hierarchy.

V

Views of this latter type are appealing, and are formidable opponents to the belief that the real is rational, but are they in the last resort self-consistent? Can they be maintained without self-refutation? What is being maintained, in effect, is that everything we may properly be said to know about the world—everything that is intelligible and systematically explicable—is a product of the conceptualizing (or linguistic) activity of the mind, but the world itself is or may be intrinsically unintelligible, or utterly chaotic and irrational. It is thus a kind of idealistic theory, though oddly enough it is held by philosophers who profess empiricism, scientific realism and even materialism. Perhaps it appeals to them because it can accommodate both logical atomism and a view of science as systematic theorizing. The atomic facts, however, are not strictly part of our knowledge, but lie on (or beyond) its periphery, either as its ultimate source or as what it asymptotically points to.

[1] Cf. op. cit., p. 281: '. . . how much remains to be done before a nominalistic position is secure.' And p. 297: 'The identity of qualia with these classes of their instances provides a basis for the analysis of the relations of universals and classes at the level of complex particulars. For every statement about the properties of complex particulars or the classes to which they belong, is, in principle, translatable into sentences mentioning only basic particulars and the qualia and simple relations they exemplify. Indeed, it provides a basis for a completely extensional formulation of logical and semantical concepts.'

If such a view is to be taken seriously, it must plainly concede that at least the activity of the human mind in its scientific pursuits is orderly and rational. This is its central tenet—that scientific theory gives a picture or model of a systematic world because it is the imposition upon the primary data of a conceptual system. Though reality may not be rational, on this view, man must be. But this forces upon us a dilemma. Either we must hold that man's mind is something apart from, and foreign to, the world which it makes its object in science—we must maintain a rigid dualism between mind and matter (and this will include man's body). Or, if we align the human mind with the rest of nature, we must somehow explain how an eminently well-ordered and systematic rational activity can arise out of a chaos of purely random movements or a series of disconnected, atomic events.

If the world is sheer confusion, then the mind does not belong to it, for it cannot be part of it and at the same time, by its activity, frame scientific models of a systematic universe, or impose a rational framework of concepts upon the confused data of common experience. What does this must itself be orderly and systematic. In that case the mind must be some separate and different 'substance' —some *res cogitans* viewing the material world from the outside. Apart from all the difficulties of such a dualistic position for metaphysics and psychology,[1] it would be fatal to epistemology. For our knowledge, dependent as it is alleged to be solely upon the rational thinking of our own minds, would be *false* and so no knowledge. It presents us with an orderly and, at least in large measure, an intelligible world of which we take ourselves to be members. But if in reality the world were an irrational chaos from which our minds (though not our bodies) were separated by an impassable gulf, the scientific world picture would be sheer fantasy.

On the other hand, if our minds are intimately related to and dependent upon our bodies, and if both are a part and a product of the natural world, which science studies, then there must be some characteristic in the world of nature which would make it possible for such an ordered and rational activity as science itself to develop within it. The account of the world which the sciences actually do give makes this credible, for they offer us a world picture which is evolutionary, in which physical activity is structured from the beginning and develops in continuous stages into more complex and

[1] For an admirable discussion of these, see Hans Jonas, *The Phenomenon of Life*, New York, 1966.

highly integrated structures the activity of which steadily approximates to the rational activity of human beings. If this view of things is true, then the participation of the mind and its knowledge in nature is consistent with it. The fact that the existence of a mind, emergent from natural processes yet capable of knowing those processes scientifically, is consistent with such a theory is at least some presumptive evidence of the theory's truth.

Nevertheless, might it not still be argued that there is a possibility of an ordered structure and a systematic activity occurring amidst an otherwise disordered chaos? Where nothing is determinate, anything conceivable is possible; so in the random shuffling of atomic events an ordered series of any length or complexity may occur simply by chance, given sufficient time. This is an old familiar argument—we are all acquainted with the strange case of the monkey and the typewriter.

But it will not do. First, the atomic events must be distinct and identifiable to be shufflable, and physics can discover no such ultimate, distinct, identifiable events. This is because of the Heisenberg Uncertainty Principle, according to which precise determination beyond a lower limit is impossible; and of Pauli's Principle of Exclusion, which asserts that no two particles of like kind can have the same quantum numbers (or state of motion). As a consequence of these two principles, it is not possible physically to distinguish between two particles of the same elementary type, although their duality is a characteristic of the energy system to which they belong. In short, individuality and distinguishable particularity are dependent upon membership of an ordered system and not *vice versa*. But, if prior to some form of ordered structure, there can be no distinct, determinable or identifiable particles there can be no random movements or events—there would be nothing to shuffle, and order could not result, whether by chance or in any other way, from random activity. Shuffling a pack of faceless cards produces neither order nor disorder, and if order is a prior condition of distinguishing the shufflable units, it cannot at the same time be posterior to their random movement.

Further, the second law of thermodynamics lays down that the tendency of every closed physical system is towards disorder, and no purely physical process can derive a more orderly series or structure from a less orderly activity. As the universe is the sum total of things, it cannot be physically in contact or relation with anything outside of itself and cannot exchange matter or energy with any 'environment'. It must, therefore, be regarded physically as a closed system. The alternative is to regard it as infinite in space and time, a conception which modern physics has found untenable and unmeaning. The chance occurrence of an ordered series in a random chaos would therefore be contrary to thermodynamic law. Moreover, the laws of probability require for such chance occurrence of any long and elaborate ordered series a time scale so vast that it would exceed by far every currently accepted estimate of the age of the universe itself.

Now, all these arguments may be considered vulnerable because they depend for their cogency on the acceptance of scientific theory, whereas the validity of such theory and its applicability to the real world are in question. But, this refuge is not open to those who appeal to laws of chance and probability, because these laws themselves are deduced on mathematical principles from assumed empirical conditions, all of which are elements in our scientific thinking. You may not appeal to rational methods of deduction in order to prove the universe to be such that rational thinking cannot reveal its nature. It is, after all, reflection upon scientific theory, the quantum theory in particular, that leads some philosophers to argue for the random character of the primordial physical activity. I do not myself believe that that is a natural conclusion to draw from its findings, but those who do draw it are still appealing to science for their evidence. It is then plainly inconsistent to argue from this belief to the view that science is simply the imposition of a conceptual scheme by the human mind upon its raw experience and can tell us nothing about the actual world. If that were the case, it could give us no grounds for believing that the primordial physical activity is sheerly random, or that the real could not be rational.

On the other hand, if no appeal is made to science for evidence that the world is in itself devoid of order, and if this is merely assumed or postulated, the question must be faced how our ordered experience, as it is systematized in scientific knowledge, can be the experience of beings who are themselves members of a world assumed to be so utterly disorderly. Our minds could not then be either a part of the world or the product of any (*ex hypothesi* random) world process, and we should have to postulate a radical dualism. We might then presume some sort of (inexplicable) interaction between mind and matter. Perhaps we could say that the effect of the activity of mind on matter was to introduce order into its chaos, and the resistance of matter to mind would introduce

disorder into its experience. So we might explain the organic character of our bodies as a product of mind organizing erstwhile
random physical processes. This would be a form of vitalism highly
suspect in modern scientific circles and disruptive of any consistent
physical or biological theory. But, again, our view of scientific
theory would have to be that it is systematization of our sensory
experience, which, as a product of mind's interaction with the
chaotic world, could plausibly be viewed as confused and bewildering. Science, then, would not be 'true of the world', but simply our
imposition upon our experiences of ordering concepts. How we
could know all this to be the case or how it could enable us to act
physically with our bodies either on the actual world or on the
dream world we had created would then present new and intract-
able problems for the philosopher.

Alternatively, we might maintain a dualism without postulating
any interaction between the mind and the chaos of physical nature.
The world would then be a pure *Ding an sich*, unknown and unknowable. But then our 'knowledge' as an ordered system of experience would be knowledge of nothing real—a *mere* dream world
in which our very bodies would be part of the illusion. To know
(or even assume) that this were so, however, we should need some
evidence that the world *in se* was irrational and that our ordered
experience was not typical or true of it; and that *ex hypothesi* could
not be part of our rational (scientific) experience. If we had, somehow, two experiences of the world, one orderly and scientific, and
the other of a random unintelligible chaos, the former would be
incredible and the latter useless. Nor would it be clear on what
grounds we could claim that either version was 'true of the world'.

In despair we might opt for complete solipsism. Then if we
claimed that our own experience (now identical with all there is)
was rational, the real and the rational would coincide. But complete
solipsism must be incoherent for the rational world it professes to
present is a world in which the knowing subject is but one item
among innumerable others both like it and unlike. The ostensible
world would then contradict the solipsistic hypothesis and this
incompatibility would brand the real, both experienced and
hypothesized, as irrational. But on the basis of complete solipsism
even the allegation that experience as a whole is irrational could not
be made and would be worthless, for it could have no rational
foundation and we should be caught up in the unravellable toils of
utter scepticism.

We seem, then, to be left with one and only one self-consistent and self-supporting view: that if science is a rational activity and if our minds in thinking scientifically are rational, and if moreover our thinking is organically related to our bodies as members of the material world of nature, the real must in some way be rational in order for this to be so.

NAME INDEX

Acton, Lord, 145
Adams, E. M., 37
Adler, Felix, 56, 57, 67
Adrian, E. D., 35, 36
Aiken, H., 168
Alexander, S., 62, 230
Amiel, H. F., 211
Anaximander, 276
Andrews, Donald, 134, 135
Anselm, 219
Aquinas, St Thomas, 74, 89, 152, 159, 160, 166, 273
Aristotle, 35, 46, 54, 60–1, 62, 63, 65, 67, 69, 71, 72, 74, 75, 76, 80, 81, 88, 89, 112, 120, 126, 127, 128, 133, 144, 153, 159, 172, 175, 273, 274, 277
Arnold, Matthew, 211
Augustine, 211
Austin, J. L., 83, 218, 273, 278, 283, 291
Austin, John, 110, 114, 140, 145
Aveling, F., 212
Avenarius, 117
Ayer, A. J., 28, 110, 218

Babbitt, Milton, 130
Bach, J. S., 130, 134, 135
Bacon, Francis, 116, 143, 146, 148
Baier, Kurt, 97, 98, 99
Bakewell, Charles, 124
Baldwin, James M., 314
Barrow, Issac, 143
Barth, Karl, 186
Barzun, J., 21
Bateson, G., 109
Beard, Charles, 64
Becker, O., 227
Beethoven, van Ludwig, 46
Benedict, Ruth, 110
Bentham, Jeremy, 110, 140, 156, 157, 163
Bentley, Arthur, 66
Berdyaev, N., 227
Berg, A., 130
Bergmann, Gustav, 22
Bergson, Henri, 80, 87, 214, 218, 222, 230
Berkeley, George, 113, 117, 118, 122, 125, 211, 225, 248, 277, 279, 280
Bernstein, R., 337
Bidney, David, 110

Black, Max, 287
Blackstone, Sir William, 148
Blanshard, B., 34, 111
Boas, Franz, 80
Bodenheimer, Edgar, 111
Bohannan, Paul, 109
Bohr, Nils, 52
Bosanquet, B., 29, 215
Boswell, James, 28
Bowers, D. G., 112
Bowne, Borden, P., 248
Bracton, Henry, 138, 144, 148
Bradley, F. H., 62, 70, 80, 89, 90, 113, 124, 168, 214, 218
Brain, Lord, 35
Braitenberg, Valentino, 123
Braithwaite, R. B., 110, 116
Brentano, Franz, 123, 158, 159, 214
Bridgman, P. B., 119, 120
Brightman, Edgar, S., 248, 250, 255, 267
Broad, C. D., 45
Brodbeck, May, 22, 287
Brunschvicg, L., 70
Buddha, 129, 177, 178
Burks, Arthur, 315
Burtt, Edwin A., 250
Bush, Wendell, T., 56, 60
Bush, Douglas, 21
Butler, Bishop, 255

Caesar, Julius, 315
Caird, Edward, 29
Caird, John, 29
Campbell, C. A., 40
Carlyle, Thomas, 25
Carnap, R., 116, 218, 243, 277, 280, 335
Cassirer, Ernst, 64, 70, 77
Castell, Alburey, 121
Casteneda, H., 287
Castro, F., 183
Cavell, Stanley, 304
Charles I, 144
Chaudhuri, Joyotpaul, 145
Chisholm, Roderick, 101
Cho, Khin Maung Win, 112
Chomsky, N., 112
Chrysippus, 127, 148
Chubb, J. N., 221, 223
Cobb, John, 218

SUBJECT INDEX

GEORGE ALLEN & UNWIN LTD

Head Office
40 Museum Street, London, W.C.1
Telephone: 01-405 8577

Sales, Distribution and Accounts Departments
Park Lane, Hemel Hempstead, Herts.
Telephone: 0442 3244

Athens: 7 Stadiou Street, Athens 125
Auckland: P.O. Box 36013, Auckland 9
Barbados: P.O. Box 222, Bridgetown
Bombay: 103/5 Fort Street, Bombay 1
Calcutta: 285J Bepin Behari Ganguli Street, Calcutta 12
Dacca: Alico Building, 18 Motijheel, Dacca 2
Hong Kong: 105 Wing on Mansion, 26 Hankow Road, Kowloon
Ibadan: P.O. Box 62
Johannesburg: P.O. Box 23134, Joubert Park
Karachi: Karachi Chambers, McLeod Road, Karachi 2
Lahore: 22 Falettis' Hotel, Egerton Road
Madras: 2/18 Mount Road, Madras 2
Manila: P.O. Box 157, Quezon City, D-502
Mexico: Serapio Rendon 125, Mexico 4, D.F.
Nairobi: P.O. Box 30583
New Delhi: 1/18B Asaf Ali Road, New Delhi 1
Rio de Janeiro: Caixa Postal 2537-ZC-00
Singapore: 36c Prinsep Street, Singapore 7
Sydney N.S.W. 2000: Bradbury House, 55 York Street
Tokyo: C.P.O. Box 1728, Tokyo 100-91
Toronto: 145 Adelaide Street West, Toronto 1